The Economics of
Workers' Management

The Economics of
Workers' Management

A Yugoslav Case Study

JAN VANEK

London
GEORGE ALLEN & UNWIN LTD
RUSKIN HOUSE   MUSEUM STREET

First published in 1972

© George Allen & Unwin Ltd., 1972

ISBN 0 04 338053 0

Printed in Great Britain
in 10 pt. Times Roman type
by The Aldine Press, Letchworth

117070

FOREWORD

This volume contains major excerpts from a study undertaken in 1968–9 within the framework of the Programme on Comparative Economic Development of Cornell University (Ithaca, New York State). In view of his earlier contacts with and publications on the Yugoslav system, the author was approached by the Directors of the Programme with a view to preparing a monograph on the theory and practice of the economic system of Yugoslavia based on the worker-managed enterprise. Since an understanding of the behaviour of such self-governing producer firms operating within a competitive market is an essential prerequisite for any more general study of the economics of the system, it was agreed that the behaviour and performance of the worker-managed enterprise should provide the central theme of the investigation. Beyond these brief initial contacts, however, the author received no further technical advice, directive or help from the Directors of the Programme. The planning and implementation of the study, as well as the views and conclusions expressed therein, are entirely his own, as indeed is the responsibility for all possible errors, omissions or misinterpretations of fact and opinion.

Most major items of the background literature frequently referred to in the preparation of the study are listed in the bibliography.

In Yugoslavia, the author met with a remarkable amount of goodwill and co-operation on the part of various institutions, organizations and individuals too numerous to mention. Special thanks are due to all those who, particularly in the difficult circumstances of the spring and summer of 1968, generously gave their time and energies to provide information and guidance and to discuss the obscure and abstruse points arising in the initial stages of a complex model-building exercise. The Yugoslav Federal Council of Labour was of particular assistance, being instrumental in the implementation of the author's programme of visits to individual enterprises.

The bulk of the information and documentation used in preparing the study was collected directly by the author according to his own plan of work. The views based thereon are entirely his own and have not been discussed with or approved by any Yugoslav authority or organization.

The first draft of the manuscript presented here was completed between November 1968 and May 1969. Even though it does not fully cover all the various aspects of the behaviour and performance of the worker-managed enterprise, it is hoped that the study as it stands will be of help to the growing number of those who, throughout the world, are seriously attempting to understand the economic implications of a decentralized market economy based on public or worker-managed enterprise, and may welcome an introduction to the theory and practice of the Yugoslav form thereof.

It would be presumptuous to address a similar wish to the Yugoslav readers, who have their fill of both as part of everyday life and work. It is they, however, and indeed all the Yugoslavs, young and old, learned and illiterate, who were foremost in the author's mind when at his desk, and who were in a sense responsible for his accepting the real ordeal of an all too hurried attempt to compress, in a few abstract and inadequate formulae, their infinitely richer and real experience of man's uneasy progress in mastering his conditions and his future. This modest contribution to the understanding of human destiny must rightfully be dedicated to them all.

J.V.

CONTENTS

TABLES

Introduction

LABOUR IS NOT A COMMODITY—this revolutionary claim made in protest against early capitalism, and first spelled out in the 1848 Communist Manifesto, is nowadays widely accepted in social theory and would hardly give rise to much doctrinal controversy. It has even achieved official status within the world community as the introductory statement to the 1944 Philadelphia Declaration, preamble to the constitution of one of the United Nations' agencies, the International Labour Organization.

There is little doubt that in the course of the last hundred years, through a succession of changes, gradual as well as revolutionary, the status of labour in modern industry has been greatly enhanced in the actual practice of many countries, and the work relationship can only exceptionally be conceived of as a mere exchange of labour power against cash payment. Social security, legal or conventional minimum wages and other protective clauses, job security arrangements and various schemes for workers' participation all tend, to a varying degree, to transform the status of the workers in the enterprise. Indeed, there is a growing number of national systems or other instances where, through the cumulative effect of these various clauses and arrangements, the worker is made, albeit to a limited extent, a member of the enterprise or work organization.

These developments are clearly irreversible, for they correspond not only to basic requirements of justice and progress in the social and political fields, but above all to structural changes affecting the modern economy. On the whole such developments have been closely watched by specialists in most social sciences including, more particularly, labour sociology and law, political science and management. However, so far, they have received only scant attention from the various schools of political economy, East and West, even though they are most probably at the roots of some of the new problems facing economic policy makers which cannot be accounted for by classical theory. To a large extent these remarks are also applicable to Yugoslavia, despite the fact that since 1950 it has centred all its policy on the development of an economic system tending to give effect, in very specific and concrete terms, to the watchword referred to in the opening sentence.

It is understandable that the political implications of the transfer of factories to the workers, its impact on management techniques and social relationships, and even the impressive legal and institutional build-up of the Yugoslav workers' council system should have been the first thing to catch the attention of the hasty observer or commentator. Nor is it easy to reshape or even to replace the venerable tools of economic analysis inherited by the various economic schools from their classic forerunners. However, this must be done if the new system is to be appraised, in as much as it has attained its main objective in emancipating labour from the passive role of commodity, of a mere factor of production, and in making the working man bear the prime responsibility for, and reap the benefits of, all the economic activity.

All basic concepts of economic thought and policy call for re-adjustment in the light of this fundamental hypothesis.

It is the aim of the present study to contribute, in a modest manner, to the understanding of the economic system based on workers' management, with particular reference to Yugoslav theory and practice. It is not intended, however, to explore the system in its entirety but to concentrate in the main on the economic behaviour of the worker-managed enterprise and its performance, leaving aside problems of general economic policy arising out of its operation, such as national and regional planning, or financial and fiscal policy. It would be impossible to present such a full picture of the system in a single monograph. But the main justification for such a choice lies in the fact that the behaviour of the worker-managed enterprise as a subject of economic decision-making has hardly ever been explored in a systematic manner, even though this is obviously an essential prerequisite for the development of rational economic policy and planning in an economy based on workers' management. Such an approach may also be of greater interest to those who practise or intend to introduce more limited systems of workers' participation.

The limitation of the scope of our investigation is more open to criticism in so far as it excludes the social and political implications of the system. The worker-managed enterprise is not a mere collection of productive assets administered by or for an outside capitalist owner or owners, or a mere technical administrative unit of a centralized system of planning and managing of the economy; it is essentially a specific type of association of people (the workers or producers) grouped primarily for production purposes, but who while at work cannot set aside their social aspirations and preferences, and who necessarily must play a major part within the political system. In other words, while the two major economic systems which at present divide the world are compatible with a wide variety of socio-political or constitutional systems and can therefore be studied in relative isolation, the worker-managed enterprise is an inseparable part of the wider social and political system and constantly interacts with the latter. In this, it shares certain common features with the system of local self-government (communes) as it exists in most countries of the European continent, and with the self-governing craft corporation of the medieval city states—neither of which could be examined in isolation, but only as part of a wider socio-political framework.

Practical considerations also make it impossible to give a full account of the social and political theory, or of the Yugoslav practice, which derive from the operation of the worker-managed enterprise. But in examining the latter every effort will be made to bring to light the various possible or necessary interactions with the wider socio-political system and their effect on the behaviour and performance of the enterprise.

Finally, a full understanding of the self-management system as practised in Yugoslavia would require a separate treatment of its historical background and development. Here too, the limitations of space and time rule out such a systematic approach to our subject, but wherever relevant the historical dimension of the system will be briefly covered.

The Specific Object of the Study

The object of this study, more specifically defined, consists in developing, against the background of Yugoslav theory and practice, a general theory of the behaviour of economic productive units (the enterprises), managed by those who work therein (the workers or producers) whose reward for work is their share in the group's net income. The choice of the Yugoslav background is imposed by the fact that this is the only country where there is a consistent body of doctrine and practical experience relating to the operation of such an enterprise. This in a sense is a rather severe limitation, for clearly in other circumstances different patterns of behaviour may be expected to develop. Yet, as will be seen, the Yugoslav experience of nearly twenty years' standing is sufficiently complex and diversified to provide enough material for a full-scale encyclopedia, and a full exploration of most of the individual topics we propose to deal with would warrant a major treatise. Where possible, we shall nevertheless introduce relevant elements of non-Yugoslav thought and practice.

The model of the 'worker-managed enterprise' or 'Yugoslav firm'—as we may sometimes designate it for the sake of brevity—may be briefly stated as follows:

'Workers associate freely to form productive or other business enterprises which they manage either directly or through representative bodies. The workers' collectivity includes professional administrators, technicians, clerical and other personnel who all enjoy equal rights within the decision-making process, each performing the tasks assigned to him in accordance with his qualifications and aptitude. New members are recruited by the collectivities when required or desired, and existing members may leave if they wish; they cannot be expelled except for a clear reason, and then only in accordance with statutory procedures.

Each enterprise collectivity is fully independent in formulating its plans and policies and in the day-to-day operation of the business. It may associate with others, operate mergers, set up new enterprises or divide itself if so desired by a section of its membership. It can adopt any form of internal organization it sees fit and, more particularly, can constitute such autonomous self-governing work groups or sections as may suit its operations. It has to conform to the laws of the land but the latter must not discriminate in favour of or against any enterprise in particular.

Initially the work collectivity is given such assets as are necessary for the normal operation of the firm. The initial value of these assets must be maintained through adequate depreciation provisions and may be subject to interest up to a maximum fixed by law. Further investments may be financed either from the collectivity's own current income or through outside loans (normally subject to interest and repayable).

The results of the firm's economic activity are disposed of freely through the market. The difference between the cost of production and the market price, if any, constitutes the firm's income which the workers' collectivity may share out among its members, directly or in the form of common services, or retain for further expansion of the business, or in the form of a reserve fund. If the firm runs into deficit and cannot secure a loan it will be wound up or reorganized and the workers' collectivity as such will cease to exist.'

The enterprise thus defined is a highly abstract model reflecting only the most essential features of the 'Yugoslav firm'. The general economic system within which it operates has hardly been touched upon. Nor has the actual purpose of the firm's operation been fully revealed.

However, the indications given so far make it clear that such a firm has very little in common with the usual model of private or public enterprise. The main difference rests in the fact that it is managed *from within*, by those who are actually working members of the collectivity and who also bear the risk of, and appropriate the results of, their work and management activity. No such rights attach to the ownership of capital. Hence, the very concept of capital or investment is radically transformed. Similarly, labour vanishes as an abstract economic category procurable at a set level of wages, and is replaced by human beings who regulate their own activity and share out the results thereof. Where no wage is payable even the category of production costs loses its familiar features. Finally, no abstract criteria of economic rationality, such as profit maximization or a high rate of growth, can be imposed by outside owners. Hence the entire edifice of economic doctrine is likely to break down in the face of the unpredictable and possibly 'irrational' behaviour of the 'associated producers'.

These few remarks suggest the two main directions of the investigation. It seems essential to consider whether the worker-managed enterprise can behave in an economically rational manner, and if so what are the criteria and conditions of such rationality. The first step is to define the essential characteristics of the general behavioural model of the worker-managed enterprise and a second stage is to analyse in greater detail the position within such a general model of some of the basic categories common to all economic systems, such as capital, investment, labour and employment, production, prices and incomes, always in the light of the behaviour of the worker-managed enterprise. A number of related general issues, which are particularly relevant for the understanding of the behaviour of the Yugoslav firms, will also be examined within this framework; they include the setting up, liquidation and other changes in the firm's status, the methods of internal decentralization and work group autonomy, problems related to professional management, initiative, responsibility and a number of others.

At this stage, it must be made clear, however, that this investigation is not pursued, as it were, in the dark, without a working hypothesis based on practice. The autonomous worker-managed enterprises undoubtedly exist in Yugoslavia; they accomplish a wide variety of functions in the economic, social and political sphere. They do not pursue one single economic objective imposed from the outside, but aim at multiple targets determined from within, which vary in time and space according to local conditions and preferences. Yet they have shown a quite remarkable capacity to produce and to develop,

xvi

to react swiftly to changing conditions and policies. All these are well-known facts of everyday experience which can be briefly recalled but do not require demonstration.

In a sense, therefore, this study deals not with an abstraction, but with a very concrete type of autonomous work organization, the worker-managed enterprise as it exists in Yugoslavia, which represents a definite interest aggregate of real people living in a given time and space. Within this specific framework will be investigated and examined their real behaviour in different concrete sets of circumstances and an attempt made to apprehend their actual motivation, the causes which prompt them to act or react in one way or another, to make their choice among the numerous alternatives they are facing at any one moment of their existence.

This dual approach, aimed at ensuring a constant confrontation of practice and theory, seems indeed absolutely indispensable in this case. This study deals with an entirely new and unprecedented system of economic organization, an economic system in its own right, pursuing its own distinct aims and objectives, having its own institutions and norms of behaviour, its own distinctive features of concrete existence. A purely theoretical approach is fraught with serious dangers. Consciously or not, objectives, values and norms of behaviour belonging to other systems are assumed by foreign observers, and often even by Yugoslav authors, to apply to the behaviour or performance of the Yugoslav firm, so that the latter are inevitably found wanting, anarchical or self-contradictory. In reality such a firm or its workers are simply in no position to conform to norms which are entirely alien to them—no more than self-employed peasants or craftsmen could act as private capitalists or as parts of a central planning system, for were they to do so, they would rule themselves out of existence.

It therefore seems axiomatic that the worker-managed enterprise can only be usefully studied within its own frame of reference and against the background of its own objectives, values or norms, which in turn cannot be derived from pure theory alone, but must be constantly confronted with actual practice. Conversely, a purely practical or pragmatic approach, as is often encountered in monographs or case studies dealing with individual enterprises, offers no general explanation of the observed phenomena and faces the twin pitfalls of systematic eulogy or condemnation according to the subjective disposition of the author.

The dual approach that follows corresponds to the very essence of the Yugoslav self-management system, for it is the constant confrontation, or even conflict, between general theory (including corresponding policies) and enterprise practice which confers on the system its very specific and quite exceptional dynamism and adaptability. Indeed, the reality of workers' management can truly be grasped only through the constant change and diversification of all its features.

Change and diversity (provided they derive from the conscious activity of the working people) constitute the very essence of socialism as it is understood in Yugoslavia. Hence, any approach based on the concept of static equilibria or economic balance is fundamentally alien to, and incompatible

xvii

with, both the theory and practice of Yugoslav workers' management.

A last word of caution. Like any other system, the Yugoslav experiment is first defined by its general goals, which it shares with all other sections of the labour movement based on Marxist socialism, but which command a very distinct set of subordinate objectives and operative principles. These give particular prominence to the concept of the withering away of the State, including the system of central planning, and to the right of the freely associated workers (the enterprises) to regulate themselves and their relationships, both through the market and through co-operative arrangements (so-called self-organization of the economy). Hence the enterprises themselves are active participants in the very process of target setting.

The position is similar with regard to the second distinct, although closely related, order of reality, which we may call the legal-institutional system, whereby the general objectives and principles are translated into norms of collective behaviour. Here again, each enterprise or firm forms its own normative system which, far from being merely informal, is explicitly recognized as an autonomous legal-institutional structure and cannot be entirely apprehended merely as a part of the general constitutional system.

At a third level, that of actual policy and practice, relatively autonomous patterns of real behaviour must also be distinguished. (As will be seen later, the distinction between the 'enterprise' and the 'others' is particularly deficient here as the 'others' include a variety of primary subjects of economic activity.) Hence no abstraction can satisfactorily account for all the real or possible patterns of economic behaviour.

Moreover, there is necessarily a disharmony, and even conflict, both within and among each of these three levels or orders of reality, once it is taken for granted that they are not the product of some outside forces, whether natural law or the invisible hand of Adam Smith, the laws of the market or the so-called 'laws of socialism' as codified in earlier Soviet manuals. They are derived by contrast from the conscious activity of men both at work and in their search for a deeper understanding of reality. This premise, which corresponds to a forceful philosophical message of pluralistic and man-oriented socialism, is therefore not merely an abstract doctrine professed by a given society, but forms a necessary part of the system as practised in Yugoslavia, and also of any other system which aims at a real workers' or producers' self-government in the economy. A 'participative' system based on a fixed set of values, institutions and modes of behaviour, imposed from without and alien to those supposed to participate, is obviously inconsistent in theory and doomed to fail in practice.

This very basic premise is often overlooked even by some Yugoslav theorists and observers, not to mention foreign critics, who tend to forget that in the context of the self-management system the workers and their enterprise collectivities alone are in a position to determine their behaviour and evaluate their performance. The Greek maxim according to which 'man is the sole measure of all things' comes readily to mind in considering the Yugoslav enterprise. In a sense, therefore, as rightly observed by a well-known Yugoslav economist, 'the worker-managed enterprise cannot err;

actually,' he adds, 'if it makes a mistake, takes a wrong decision, it is in fact reacting correctly but is prompted by *wrong* stimuli of the wider system.'[1]

This may seem surprising, revolutionary perhaps, even to some Yugoslav readers. Yet it does not mean at all—as it did not for the Man of the Greek philosopher—that the worker-managed enterprise can adopt any behaviour whatsoever. It is obviously subject to innumerable constraints to which it must conform, albeit to a varying degree. To behave rationally, it must at least take them into consideration. Yet, as no one else determines its objectives and policies, the enterprise remains free (while at the same time being obliged) to make its own decisions, to choose its policy in the light of its own circumstances. In this sense, it certainly could err but only if it chose solutions contrary to the objectives it seeks to attain. In other words, in any given set of circumstances there is only one decision the enterprise may take if it is to behave rationally. But as the criteria of rationality are its own, other enterprises would be equally justified in choosing different courses of action. Nor can these be weighed against any general criteria of rationality applicable throughout the system.

It will have become apparent by now why the prime object of this enquiry is the worker-managed enterprise or its workers' collectivity, rather than the workers themselves. Such an enterprise or collectivity may take, as we shall see, most diverse shapes and forms but it cannot be defined as a mere collection or sum of the workers who belong to it. No doubt they also are, each one individually, economic subjects in their own right; they form a constraint and a motivational background from the point of view of their own enterprise, but the latter alone has a full and distinct economic existence.

To establish a clear distinction between the micro-economic level of the individual worker-producer, and simple groups thereof, a Yugoslav author has recently coined the new term 'mezzo-economy' to designate the enterprise as a specific category of economic analysis. He writes:

'The enterprise is a structure *sui generis*, an intermediary structure defined by its own specific intermediary concepts and parameters and which embraces microeconomic elements in their rudimentary form as well as embryonic elements of the macroeconomic system; thus, the concept of mezzoeconomy with its specific colouring offers a peg for the integration of plurally structured economies into the global economic system. . . . The economy of the enterprise conceived in this manner represents a concrete economic category which as an object of scientific investigation may be termed "mezzoeconomy"—for it represents one of many sub-systems of the national economy while at the same time it constitutes a complex economic system comprising numerous microeconomies (the economies of the members of the workers' collectivity).'[2]

This definition is particularly relevant with respect to the newer forms of Yugoslav enterprises which are increasingly taking the shape of federations

---

[1] Cf. B. Horvat, cited in *Gledišta* (Zagreb), No. 10, October 1968, p. 1405.
[2] Cf. Dr Z. K. Kostić, *Osnovi Teorije Mezoekonomije*, Zagreb, 1968, p.(v).

or looser confederacies, with several levels of autonomous and self-governing sub-systems, while at the same time forming variedly shaped alliances and functional consortia with others. The new term thus merely explicits a Proteic type of intermediary structure, found in every system but particularly stressed and formally recognized within the Yugoslav system in so far as it postulates self-government at all levels of decision and policy making.

Hence, it is the behaviour of the enterprise, and not of the individual worker, which actually shapes the whole worker-managed economy. The usual type of opinion survey among workers or managers may be relevant for some limited purposes and we may use it on occasion. Yet such surveys have no direct relevance for the behaviour of the worker-managed enterprise which has its own motivational framework, its own economic logic. To obtain some insight into the latter is the central purpose of this investigation.

Method, Sources and Scope

The above approaches to a definition of the worker-managed enterprise and the wider system it postulates clearly raise serious methodological problems for an objective study of the system, as they rule out all the usual fixed or predetermined criteria of rationality. Clearly, also, we have to penetrate a relativist man-centred universe which has so far hardly been explored by the social sciences generally, and scarcely ever been touched upon by economists, who tend strictly to adhere to the basic tenets of their respective schools of thought. This fundamental dogmatism and ethnocentrism of comparative economic science is particularly striking where the authors belong to the leading world powers. It leaves us with extremely limited tools of analysis for the purpose of this study.

Conversely, works of Yugoslav economic theory are much too outward oriented, and too involved in the day-to-day struggle to clarify and improve on individual features of the system, to provide a fully developed analytical model. We will nevertheless make a point of using to the full the results attained by the various Yugoslav schools and institutes in their endeavour to develop global or partial models of enterprise behaviour. Actually, the lack of a widely recognized economic theory of the Yugoslav system is largely compensated for by an impressive wealth of empirical studies on various specific aspects of the system which will be referred to below in greater detail.

Despite the lack of readily available theoretical background, several avenues of investigation are open. Clearly, any theory of the Yugoslav firm must rest on the analysis of the possible interest-spectrum of the workers' collectivity, economic and non-economic, real as well as virtual or hypothetic, present or future. As it owes its existence to Marxist ideology, the tools of Marxian economics come first to mind; they have the real advantage of being widely understood in Yugoslavia and of actually forming the conceptual background of the system. Marxist economic theory was, of course, developed as a tool for the analysis of a very specific economic system and was never meant to, or could, apply to different pre-capitalist systems such as the feudal order or natural peasant economy, or indeed to the great

Eastern empires. So in our worker-managed economy, granted that 'Labour is not a commodity', we may indeed ask what is the position of capital, of profits, interests and rent. Whither the labour theory of value and the surplus value it brings to light? All these do correspond to definite categories of the worker-managed system but in it their meaning is not merely modified but basically altered. As will be seen, we differ in this from some Yugoslav economists who, while acknowledging real modifications in the conceptual content, apply Marx's formulae directly to the worker-managed system as if it were symmetrical to capitalism (labour taking the place of capital and vice versa). Some symmetry of this kind is self-evident, but it does not hold in every respect and such an approach tends therefore in our view only to blur the picture. However ambitious it may seem, the first aim of this study is to clarify the conceptual framework against the background—as suggested earlier—of the complex interests of the workers' collectivity.

The position would be the same if the investigation was based on the conceptual framework of one or other among the non-Marxian schools of economics. The usual textbook notions, to which we may occasionally refer, call quite obviously for new definitions. This, however, does not imply an encyclopedia or catalogue of formal definitions. Such an attempt would not only be quite unreadable and of little use, but practically impossible to implement in the changing world of the worker-managed economy; despite strong attempts, the Yugoslav theorists have not succeeded in defining (and seem to have abandoned their efforts) even such basic concepts as the enterprise itself or the work relationship of its members. Indeed, Marx's monumental *Capital* is essentially a definition of 'commodity' under capitalism. Had we had time, patience and skill we could have attempted such a full-scale entry under the heading 'labour'. Lacking all three, we must leave most things to the reader's own creative imagination. As required by the subject and the state of our knowledge, the only possible approach is to remain at a very high level of generality, merely marking the limits of the areas corresponding to any given concept, and its relative elasticity, while at the same time attempting through concrete examples to show some of its real dimensions.

As for the Yugoslav practice, its central place in our analysis has just been pointed out. It may be approached at various levels of abstraction, several of which have been closely considered: these approaches fall under the following headings:

(i) *Enterprise case studies*, attempting to assemble for a number of selected typical firms all relevant data in order to bring to light the motivational background of key decisions in selected areas of policy. The idea of undertaking such a task singlehanded, or in co-operation with others, had to be discarded in view of the short period at the author's disposal. However, a considerable volume of such monographic material is available in Yugoslavia and reference will occasionally be made to it. While the existing works vary too widely in method, object and quality to supply a firm basis for comparative analysis, this approach, if made in a systematic manner, would seem to offer the only solid basis for a more general theory of the system;

only one of the major Yugoslav research institutes could undertake such a task, however.

This line of reasoning seems to have the full support of the Yugoslav enterprises. As early as 1957, in preparation for the first Congress of the workers' councils, most larger enterprises engaged actively in the preparation of reports on their own experience, often forming special study and drafting committees. Some of these extremely interesting reports were even printed in the local press but there is no evidence of their being subjected to systematic analysis. This self-assessment activity is far from extinct and, in any event, the yearly reports and accounts of the workers' councils provide an excellent basis for a systematic study of enterprise behaviour.

(ii) *Interviews* with leading members of the workers' management bodies and professional managements aimed at eliciting their understanding of the motivation and criteria for decision-making in their enterprises. Brief— mostly one-day—discussions of this kind were undertaken in twelve major enterprises selected by the author in three of the six constituent Republics of Yugoslavia and one of the two autonomous Provinces; they covered all the major types of economic decision-making recalled earlier, and were on the whole quite conclusive. Their message will be consistently reflected in the substantive parts of the study. A closely related source was casual or prepared interviews with individual members of enterprise managements, local authorities, and economic and trade union organizations.

(iii) *Systematic analysis of the enterprise summary accounts* and balance sheet which, in Yugoslavia, are available since 1958—although not accessible to the public since 1962—for all enterprises under workers' management, in a uniform presentation covering over one hundred items. They are documented by the Service of Social Audit of the National Bank of Yugoslavia, which took over the duties of the former financial inspectorates, and is responsible for the official audit of accounts of all enterprises and institutions. The annual volumes of the accounts, and balance sheets summaries have grown over the years in detail and coverage; in size they may be compared to the London or New York telephone directories. There is, to our knowledge, no equivalent in any other country in the world; it offers unlimited possibilities for correlat- ing the economic behaviour (e.g. investment or level of social services), employment and performance (increase in value added) of individual enter- prises or related groups thereof, as well as such basic data which define them as economic units (level and intensity of capital and labour input, location, etc.). A limited but rather ambitious programme for such an investigation has been drawn up, but shortage of time and lack of major institutional support made it impossible to get beyond a very tentative preliminary stage of investigation in this area. Documentation of this kind cannot be fully analysed without the help of a computer service, and requires a team of specialists. Despite their obvious interest and readiness to help, the Direc- torates of the S.D.K. and the Federal Office of Statistics were unable to commit their resources at a very short notice, particularly considering the confidential nature of the data to be studied. Several partial attempts by others were brought to the author's attention and reference will occasionally be made to them also.

The preceding paragraphs account for some of the sources. However, the author could not have undertaken in good faith the present project had he not followed developments in Yugoslavia for well over twenty years in a professional capacity, and as a major subject of interest for most of that period, during which he extensively visited the country, including its enterprises.

A few additional comments seem called for concerning the scope of this investigation. There is one important area which could not be covered, that of the non-economic activities such as health, culture, the education system, research, administration and social services generally. In all these, a form of workers' management has been introduced since 1963 and operates under variously adapted rules and procedures. The arrangement stresses the economic side (costs, etc.) of all these services, the need for their efficient operation, yet it does not transform them into factories or businesses. It may indeed give rise to conflict with the major social objectives, particularly in this early transitional period. The particular problems of the economics of social services, and their behaviour when made into self-managing work organizations, are obviously of a very special nature, and should be dealt with separately.

Yet it is important to note that the self-management principle is now universally applied in Yugoslavia, and that workers' councils or similar self-management bodies are found in work organizations outside the economic sector, be they hospitals, schools, courts of law, research institutes or cultural establishments. Their staff are not wage or salary earners but members of a work collectivity, sharing out the net income of their organization or institution.

Hence, when entering into economic relationships with these institutions, particularly as their suppliers, the enterprises of the economic sector will not have to deal with the usual centralized government procurement services, but with decentralized self-management bodies not unlike their own, which act and react against the background of similar interest patterns. While going very far in the direction of institutional and local self-government in line with the 'all peoples' defence' strategy, the Yugoslav People's Army as an economic entity seems at present to be the only major institutional customer, and the last remnant of the 'public sector' in the traditional sense of the term.

Another question which needs clarification is the time span covered. This is a dynamic synthesis of the present, extending back to 1964–5, coupled with occasional excursions into earlier periods which will be duly brought to notice, and not one particular moment or an in-depth study of one particular system.

General Presentation and Plan of the Study

The present study grew out of what was originally planned as a substantial monograph concentrating on the abstract models of economic behaviour of the Yugoslav worker-managed enterprise, and covering also their actual behaviour and performance in respect of the main areas of their economic activity. However, it soon became apparent that the subject could not be properly dealt with in such a summary manner.

First, it appeared impossible to present to non-Yugoslav readers a purely formal economic model or models of the worker-managed enterprise without a minimum of background information on the country where it operates, on its aims, objectives and institutions, including the worker-managed enterprise itself, its institutional structure and the rules and procedures governing its internal decision-making and operations generally. Although limited to a bare skeleton, such an introductory overview therefore now forms the first part of the study comprising five separate chapters. These do not purport, by any means, to give a full account of the various background items: they merely present a selection of such key data as seemed absolutely essential for the understanding of the behaviour of the worker-managed enterprise in Yugoslavia. Institutions of basic importance—such as the workers' councils or the commune—as well as other aspects of the system which would by right require separate monographic investigation, have been dealt with in a few sentences or paragraphs. It is hoped nevertheless that this expanded introduction will help in overcoming some of the difficulties encountered in most of the non-Yugoslav and economic literature on Yugoslavia and on workers' management. The latter are typically seen against an assumed background of objectives and institutions totally alien to them, little or no regard being paid to their specifically Yugoslav human institutional, and physical environment.

The central theme of the study is approached in Part II. The formal models of economic behaviour of the worker-managed enterprise are discussed in Chapters VI to IX, which give a brief account and evaluation of some of the major foreign and domestic models proposed by others in recent years and present the author's own conclusions for an alternative framework of interpretation of the behaviour of the Yugoslav firm.

Owing to the unexpected wealth of accumulated material, and in view of the pluralistic and multi-functional nature of the worker-managed enterprise, these five chapters alone represent the material originally contemplated for the whole study. Although they do not offer a full review of all possible models and do not adequately reflect any one of them, this—to the author's knowledge—first attempt at a comparative approach to the study of the economics of a producers' self-governing enterprise may be of some help to the growing number of these who, in Yugoslavia and elsewhere, devote their energies to paving the way to scientific understanding of an economic system based on democratic principles and respect for human values.

While the call for participation—at work and in all other areas of men's activity—the claim for workers' control and economic democracy, for justice and equal opportunity for all men and women is heard with ever increasing strength throughout the world, the economic consequences of the corresponding reforms or evolutionary changes together with the conditions of feasibility and efficiency of an economy based on the full participation of all, have so far remained largely unexplored. They are thus most likely to constitute the weakest link and, often, the main stumbling block in any practical experiment. While based on one national system and a single experience, and thus by no means directly applicable elsewhere, our exercise in abstract model building can no doubt help others to understand the choices they are facing and to choose with due regard to their particular circumstances.

To construct abstract models is, however, an empty, meaningless exercise unless such models are shown to reflect the real world and prove of use in interpreting real observable phenomena. While the model proposed in Chapter IX is derived from study of the real behaviour of Yugoslav enterprises, in the following chapters an attempt is made to use it in interpreting the observed behaviour of Yugoslav firms in their actual operation. Particular attention is given to growth, capital assets and investment (Chapter X) and to amortization, interest and loan-financing (Chapter XI).

Equally thorough application of the model would need to be made in other areas of enterprise operation if a full understanding of the behaviour of the worker-managed firm were sought. This massive task could not be accomplished in a single volume, however, and only summary attention is given to some of these other areas in the final chapter, which summarizes the findings of the previous two chapters before considering questions of employment, business management and remuneration, and touching on a few further aspects. All these subjects are however covered extensively—albeit not systematically—in the main text of this volume.

The object of Chapters X, XI and XII is much wider, however, than building a mere verification of an abstract model. They aim at pointing out the main traits of behaviour shown so far by Yugoslav firms in these various areas of their activity, and at relating this behaviour to their various objectives and specific circumstances. A complex cause-effect analysis is thus attempted for the various functional areas of the worker-managed enterprise quite independently of any abstract model.

Part II covers the various areas commonly considered in formal economics, but the issues dealt with do not exhaust the full range of problems which are specific to the worker-managed enterprise and economy. Some of these wider problems (covered briefly in Chapter XII), which call for a further study in order to ensure orderly operation, are related to the internal characteristics of the worker-managed enterprise: problems of entry and exit of firms (i.e. setting up, amalgamation, liquidation, etc.), their co-operation and integration, as well as internal decentralization and work group autonomy; and problems of economic initiative and responsibility, professional management and the like. Others relate to more external considerations, such as to planning and economic policy, and particularly the fiscal, monetary and financial policy instruments which form an integral part of the worker-managed economy.

Part One

Workers' Management in Yugoslavia: An Overview

The behaviour of worker-managed enterprises cannot be examined in a purely abstract setting as is commonly done in modern economics when dealing with private capitalist enterprise: actually no economic system except capitalism in its purest form can be properly analysed as a purely rational abstraction.[1]

In a system based on workers' management the real environmental factors (physical, institutional, psychological and sociological) are of paramount importance, for participation in the decision-making process postulates real physical presence and full-time participation in the production process. The decision makers and their environment are inseparably merged into a single whole. Moreover, in view of the requirements of modern technology, the worker-manager—unlike the self-employed craftsman or peasant —is typically associated with others in numerically important work collectivities. Hence, the actual shaping of the rules and procedures which define the collectivities' internal structure—the decision-making and income distribution process—is also essential for an understanding of the behaviour of enterprises or work collectivities.

A general survey of the most essential data which appear directly relevant to the system of workers' management as practised in Yugoslavia will be found in the first part of the study. They are grouped under five main headings: the Yugoslav setting; the aims and objectives of the system; the constitutional framework and economic policy; the worker-managed enterprise; and the enterprise planning and income distribution process. In the absence of any general study on modern Yugoslavia, this information, although not comprehensive, is designed to give a general background to the Yugoslav worker-managed enterprise.

---

[1] In all other systems, the peasant or monastic-religious economy, the mediaeval city corporation, the feudal or imperial bureaucratic order or the 'managerial corporation' within the New Industrial State of Galbraith, real men in real settings are in one way or another personally involved in the decision-making process. Consequently, their concrete situations and possibilities, their philosophy or ideology, their preferences and dislikes, necessarily affect the substance of their decisions, generally to a much greater extent than purely 'rational' considerations of profitability. In other words, only an absentee capitalist can be represented—at least for the purposes of economic manuals—as a faceless being, with any degree of plausibility.

CHAPTER I

The Yugoslav Setting: Geography, Population, Social and Economic Background

The interdependence of geography, social history and economic development is brought to light with particular clarity when considering the extreme regional differences within Yugoslavia. These are hardly less, and in many respects possibly stronger, than similar differences found elsewhere in considering a whole continent, such as, for instance, the whole of Latin America. Yet there are also powerful socio-political forces which make the country a meaningful whole, the very concept of self-management at all levels, including workers' management of enterprises, being one of the major unifying factors.

The largest single country of the Balkan peninsula, Yugoslavia's territory covers less than 100,000 square miles (255,000 km), an area comparable to that of Great Britain or Italy. Up to 60 per cent of this territory consists of relatively high mountainous areas (mostly over 3,000 feet) which, with the exception of the Alps in Slovenia, render communications exceptionally difficult. The 20 to 25 per cent of fertile lowland along major rivers also consists of several quite distinct geographical regions, none of which have direct access to the narrow coastal area on the Adriatic sea facing Italy.

The mountain areas are divided between forests and an arid stony sierra, both quite unsuitable for modern agriculture. Because of their size, they constitute Europe's second biggest reservoir of hydraulic energy (after Norway); they also contain some of Europe's major deposits of non-ferrous metals such as copper, zinc, lead, mercury and bauxite, as well as considerable but rather low quality reserves of coal and iron ore, both rather unimportant by world standards. Along with the more developed coastal area they also represent a vast but as yet largely untapped natural reserve for the development of European tourism and for intensive fruit and vegetable production. The fertile lowlands provided in the past—in conditions of very limited domestic consumption—the bulk of the then predominantly agricultural exports and, despite the small area they cover, can still produce well in excess of the rapidly growing demand of the non-agricultural section of the population.

The total population of the country reached the figure of 20 million early in 1968, as compared with 17·4 million in 1961 and 15·6 million in 1939, despite very heavy losses during the war period (1·7 million). The rate of

29

birth and of natural increase of the population remain among the highest in Europe although rapidly declining in recent years (19·5 and 10·8 per thousand in 1967 as compared with 28·6 and 17·7 in 1954, the latter being the highest recorded figures).

The composition of the population presents an extraordinary complexity, combining all kinds of overlapping historical, political, religious, linguistic and cultural criteria of ethnic identity. The Slav people, who settled most of the present Yugoslav territory after the fall of the Roman Empire, although forming a number of distinct State entities at various periods of their earlier history, never succeeded in unifying the country prior to 1918. This was mainly due to their very exposed position on the military boundaries separating Europe from the Eastern Byzantine and Turkish Ottoman Empires. The influence of the major neighbouring powers (Austria and Hungary in the north, Venice in the coastal regions, and the Ottoman Empire in the southern and eastern parts of the country) was dominant, particularly in the last three or four centuries. Their military enterprises and the constant resistance of the local population inhibited normal social and economic advancement during that period.

The one-time northern boundary of the Ottoman Empire still constitutes a major dividing line between the more developed—or 'westernized'—northern regions of Slovenia, Croatia and northern Serbia (Voivodina), and the peoples of the less developed southern and eastern parts of the country. This is somewhat paralleled by the religious division between the Eastern Orthodox populations and the Catholic influence in the north and west, an historic division which corresponds to the major distinction between the linguistically very close peoples of Serbia and Croatia, each accordingly using their own alphabet, the Cyrillic and Latin respectively. A particular mixture of population is found in the central mountainous areas of Bosnia and Herzegovina where Serbian and Croatian populations are intermingled with nearly as many Yugoslavs of Muslim origin, sometimes classified as ethnically indetermined. The decision is now pending to recognize these people, who speak Serbo-Croatian, as being of 'Muslim' nationality. There are numerous other peculiarities of religious background, still relevant for the present, which cannot be dealt with here. A noticeable feature, however, is the total absence of Protestant influence which may be seen, at least by those accepting Max Weber's theory of development, as a contributory cause of the striking deficiency of private entrepreneurial motivation among the Yugoslav populations throughout the last century and particularly during the inter-war period of national independence. The people of Montenegro derive their specific nationality from the uninterrupted tradition of independence of their mountain principality, while they do not differ significantly from the Serbian people in other regards. Thus, among the five Yugoslav peoples, the Serbo-Croatian linguistic group is numerically predominant (approximately 80 per cent of the population), while two of them possess their separate languages, the Slovenes in the extreme north-west, and the Macedonians in the south-east.

There are moreover some ten recognized minority ethnic groups, the two

Table I

Social and Economic Characteristics of Yugoslav Peoples according to Principal Territorial Divisions

Republics and Autonomous Regions of Serbia[1]	Bosnia and Herzegovina	Montenegro	Croatia	Macedonia	Slovenia	Serbia Total	Serbia Proper	Voivodina	Kosovo	Yugoslavia (total or average)
1. Population 1967 (in thousands)	3,735	727	4,340	1,551	1,679	8,117	5,046	1,920	1,151	19,949
2. Rate of Births										
(a) 1950–4 average	38·2	32·1	23·2	38·4	22·8	27·4	26·1	23·3	43·5	28·8
(b) 1967	24·5	21·5	15·8	26·1	18·1	18·1	15·1	14·0	37·9	19·5
3. Death rate										
(a) 1950–4 average	13·9	10·0	11·7	14·5	10·9	12·4	11·3	12·4	18·0	12·4
(b) 1967	6·8	6·2	9·7	8·0	10·0	9·1	8·7	9·6	9·6	8·7
4. Illiteracy 1961[2]										
(a) Percentage of all population over the age of 10	32·5	21·7	12·1	24·5	1·8	21·9	23·0	10·6	41·1	19·7[3]
(b) Age group 20–34	24·7	10·3	5·01	16·5	0·8	13·7	12·4	6·5	36·2	13·0
5. National income (1966)										
(a) In 1,000 million dinars	11·1	1·5	24·0	4·8	13·5	36·8	24·3	10·7	1·8	91·8
(b) Per capita (in thousands)	3·0	2·1	5·5	3·1	8·1	4·5	4·8	5·6	1·5	4·8
6. Employed population 1967										
(a) in thousands	485	71	913	233	504	1,355	865	399	91	3,561[4]
(b) as percentage of total population	13	10	21	15	30	17	16	26	8	18
7. Average monthly personal incomes of those employed, in Dinars (1966)	677	675	748	620	849	717	720	727	641	730
8. Private saving deposits (December 1967)										
(a) in millions dinars	592	125	1,753	856	1,382	2,841	—	—	—	7,549
(b) as percentage of national income	5·3	8·3	7·3	17·8	10·2	7·7	—	—	—	8·2

[1] In the usual order of Yugoslav statistics (Serbo-Croatian in Latin alphabet).
[2] Persons able to read but unable to write counted as illiterate.
[3] Compares with 1953 illiteracy rate of 25·4 per cent (14·1 for men and 35·8 women).
[4] Including those in private employment (99·4 thousands in 1967); apprentices excluded.

most important of which form a major section of the population in two separate plurilingual regions of Serbia (Albanians or Sqiptars in Kosovo, Hungarians in Voivodina). The other recognized ethnic minorities (which have their own school systems, publications in national languages, etc., including the right to use their national flag) are the following: Bulgarian, Czech, Italian, Romanian, Ruthenian, Slovak and Turkish. The 1939–45 war and the German occupation caused the disappearance as ethnic groups, through physical elimination, of the Jewish (mostly Sephardi, Spanish speaking) and Gypsy populations; expulsion of the members of the German minority followed the Liberation in 1945. Individual members of these groups still form a more or less important part of the present Yugoslav society.

All these separate ethnic groups present very distinct social characteristics which are only partly related to the widely varying levels of their economic development. This background of wide socio-economic differentiation in turn gives an understanding of the wide differences in the economic behaviour of individuals, their social preferences and attitudes although the explanations derived from it are far from sufficient or complete. Nor are the differences in the socio-economic characteristics of any one population at a given point in time directly correlated with the rate of change or of progress in other areas. As no general or economic sociology of the peoples of Yugoslavia is available, Table I shows a few key indices covering the major social characteristics and levels of economic development of the various populations.

The table requires a few brief comments. The differences between the populations of the more developed and less developed regions are sufficiently important to speak for themselves. Yet at the same time, there is no real homogeneity within the two groups; Slovenia being consistently well ahead on all counts in the first group while in the second group the autonomous region of Kosovo is markedly behind the three southern republics. The central position of Serbia proper, close to the Yugoslav averages, is also clearly apparent. While Slovenia is on the whole close to the general standards of Western Europe, the region of Kosovo and other portions of the south of the country are merely emerging from the state of primitive non-monetary economy. Until recently their national income was usually estimated at levels comparable to those of the least developed areas of the world (fifty US dollars per capita for Kosovo in the post-war period). It should be added that the data included in the table are mere random samples from a wealth of other indicators such as the composition of the population according to age groups or to sectors of economic activity, size of households, divorce rates, income of the self-employed peasants, etc. They all bring to light very considerable differences in the customs and attitudes of the various populations while at the same time showing significant differentiation even within the developed and the less advanced areas.

Particularly significant for the purposes of this study are the striking differences in the comparative rates of private savings (line 8 of the table). The two numerically weak linguistic groups are well ahead of the general

32

population, while the less well-off among the two (Macedonia) has by far the highest saving ratio. Similar extreme behavioural differences may be noted regarding numbers of students at university level (not included in the table) where Macedonia is again one of the leaders, ahead of Slovenia even as regards absolute numbers. This contrasts with the progress of literacy (line 4 of the table) where Macedonia seems to be behind most others. Generally, however, the rates of change in the indices show clearly the widely differing dynamics—reflecting the attitudes and preferences, perhaps even the varied aptitudes—of the different peoples.

Yet these data are mere statistical averages. Within each region or population, similar or even greater differentiations may be observed. The latter are probably even increasing due to advancing urbanization and industrialization in a great number of centres while more or less extensive pockets of the archaic way of life are still preserved in the remoter rural areas. Their persistence is shown by the most recent surveys. These differences constitute the major background factor of all social and economic policy, for it is only at the sub-regional level that a relative homogeneity of population and of socio-economic conditions may offer a concrete basis for action—despite the necessary mediation of the region based mainly on the common ethnic-historical background. The duality of ethnic nationality and micro-regional origin remains of the greatest relevance for most Yugoslav citizens.

Yet there are a number of major features which are largely common to all Yugoslav peoples. The rural origin of the vast majority is the most striking, historical circumstances of the past having prevented—or arrested at an early stage—the development of a feudal or town-based class society in the past, while modern industry remained virtually non-existent until the second world war. Under foreign military rule and in the absence of major social differentiation based on property, the largely egalitarian horizontal relationship of the smallholding peasantry as well as their practice of direct and informal self-government in local matters survived in some areas until quite recently and can still be traced in the prevailing patterns of social behaviour of the present time.[1]

The fact of belonging to the same wider linguistic group and forming a contiguous geographical area was of course the main rallying front of the Yugoslav populations in the nineteenth and early twentieth centuries. However, the centralized state created after the first world war around the former Serbian kingdom showed little internal cohesion and stability. Its utter collapse in the face of the German invasion was only an outward sign of social disintegration from within. In a sense, therefore, a true sentiment of national unity was acquired only through the experience of the second world war, through the common struggle and resistance of all the peoples against foreign military occupation as well as against various narrowly nationalistic movements in some areas. The struggle of the Partisan movement, with

---

[1] Writings by the Yugoslav Nobel Prizewinner in literature, Ivo Andrić, now widely accessible in English, provide, in the absence of specialized works in comparative anthropology and sociology, the best clue to some of the major background factors of the complex communities of Yugoslavia.

predominantly rural support and under Communist leadership, rested on the full recognition of the separate identity of the various peoples of Yugoslavia, including their right to full independence.[1] At the same time, the cruel memories of the internecine divisions and strife made it absolutely imperative to overcome the underlying socio-economic differences while ruling out all possible causes of intolerance based on ethnic, religious or racial origin or similar grounds. A deep consciousness of the need for respect and equality of all groups as a condition of overcoming such divisive forces has thus become a basic factor of social relationships within present-day Yugoslavia.

The velocity of socio-economic changes experienced since 1945 by all the groups, despite wide variations in the rate of these changes between sectors, is another striking feature common to all the various peoples and most local or sub-regional communities. In view of the absence of domestic capital resources, technical knowledge and entrepreneurship, the pre-war governments could only envisage a limited and mostly foreign-sponsored industrial development. Actually, their policy aimed at preserving the agrarian character of the country as part of the national heritage. The economic crisis of the thirties caused deep paralysis of the economy and made the country an easy prey to economic penetration by Nazi Germany: a well-known schoolbook case.[2] Where there had been wide acceptance of immobility, or at most limited progress, the wartime resistance and post-war reconstruction originated a common will to develop and to modernize as rapidly as possible while relying essentially on the peoples' own resources and capabilities which only came fully to light when they were facing incomparably better equipped and organized invading armies. Political misunderstandings and economic conflict with the outside world have tended to strengthen attitudes based on self-reliance and solidarity during the post-war period. The real and visible results which were achieved in all regions, despite various setbacks, helped to strengthen and to spread among the various peoples a climate of self-confidence and trust in their future. As a result uncommonly high rates of progress are taken by all not only as a possibility but as a basic norm of social and economic policy.

It is generally believed in Yugoslavia that the country has overcome the earlier conditions of severe social and economic underdevelopment which prevailed a generation ago and has been recently approaching in most areas the levels of countries near the middle of a hypothetical scale of development. In many fields progress is most impressive. Where yesterday there were no schools for most children, full education is now open to practically all, and in their native language. Universities have sprung up with such speed that the numbers of students already exceed several countries of Western Europe. Similarly rapid progress has been achieved in the field of public health and other socio-cultural services, some of which were developed beyond all comparison (particularly the so-called Workers' and Popular Universities).

---

[1] First expressed in September 1942 in an article by the leader of the Partisans and present President of the Republic, Josif Broz Tito, this principle remains a key provision of the Yugoslav Constitution.

[2] Cf. *inter alia*, C. P. Kindleberger, *International Economics*, pp. 284–5.

Pre-war industry, quite insignificant by European standards (200,000 workers, employed mostly in extensive production)[1] and over 50 per cent foreign owned (including most key sectors and larger enterprises) has increased about sevenfold as regards employment and production and is now placed entirely under domestic control. Entirely new lines of industrial production have been introduced to cover all major sections of industrial activity, particularly for investment goods, mechanical and chemical industries, electrical engineering, shipbuilding, etc. Even agriculture, rather neglected in the early years, has made very rapid progress since 1956, with the small public sector reaching top levels in productivity and modernization, but not without making significant impact on the remaining mass of private smallholders. Similarly, the rather important but formerly archaic crafts sector has been preserved and largely modernized with a mostly self-employed working force of nearly 400,000. Where an outmoded (largely narrow gauge) railway system provided the only mechnical means of transport (there were no more than 3,000 automobiles in 1939) an up-to-date bus transport system now links up even the most remote areas. Nearly all sub-regional and local urban centres, formerly for the most part rural and trading communities, have acquired some industry and modern building development which hold out the promise of better living to the wider surrounding rural areas. The latter are increasingly joining the towns as major customers for durable household equipment and building services. Holiday facilities have also been developing at a rapid pace and have become widely accessible, at least to the urban population.

Much still remains to be done to bring the socio-economic conditions of living of all the population up to the levels corresponding to modern standards of development. While in less than ten years it was possible to double the number of classrooms, many are still used for two or even three shifts of children, and school development will have to continue at a high rate to keep pace with the rapidly growing population. The road system, generally very primitive in the past and practically non-existent over vast areas, is only beginning to receive the attention it deserves in the face of the massive development of public and private road transport. Even today, there are a number of communes in Croatia with no road whatsoever (even the so-called modern village roads). The situation is much worse in less developed areas. Railways and communications generally, as well as the provision of modern housing, will also require unusually high levels of investment for many years to come.

The most serious and urgent population problem facing the country today is the attainment of a satisfactory level of employment in the non-agricultural sectors of the economy. Post-war development successfully arrested the

[1] As rightly observed by Bobrowski, such a level of industrialization would appear at first sight similar to that of Russia in 1914. Yet the similarity is only an apparent one as Tsarist Russia at that time already had a solid kernel of concentrated heavy industry, of which there was hardly a trace in pre-war Yugoslavia. Most of pre-war Yugoslav industry resembled fairly big craft workshops, while the larger firms were nearly all engaged in extensive mining operations. The only major sector commanding some modern technology and great numbers of skilled workers was the State Railways system.

growth in numbers of the agricultural population and by 1961 its share in the total had already fallen to less than 50 per cent (as compared with 80 per cent in the pre-war period), yet the surplus of under-employed rural inhabitants is high by the standards of any modern economy. Estimates vary from one to four million according to the criteria used by different authors. An agricultural population of over 9 million, out of a total of 20 million, must quite obviously release 'several million' people in the process of modernization. In view of the increasing speed of technical progress in agriculture and the largely unfavourable geographical conditions, redeployment of the rural population in modern agriculture in significant numbers is out of the question. Yet the rate at which they are leaving the land is on the increase, particularly in the mountainous areas. Moreover, the rate of natural increase of the active population is exceptionally high and continues to grow, causing corresponding additional pressure on employment outside agriculture. Due to widespread higher education and vocational training, this pressure is no longer felt only at the unskilled level, but in nearly all occupations and levels of skill. While emigration of several hundred thousand workers provided a temporary relief in recent years, the population pressure on the employment market has become a commanding factor at present.

The very high rate of social change and economic conditions of the last twenty years brought the formerly undifferentiated rural societies face to face with new problems arising out of the uneven levels and rates of development of the various groups or individuals. Those at the top of the scale complained at being held back in their progress in comparison with more advanced countries, while those in less favourable circumstances feared that their hopes of attaining real equality might be for ever thwarted. This new debate gathers much strength from the fact that all the evidence is being constantly recorded and analysed in great detail by a hierarchy of statistical offices at national, regional and local levels and kept there before the eyes of the public by all the information media. This is a major reason which caused the author to omit as a matter of principle specific references to support individual statements. In fact, it seems quite improper to avoid responsibility by extracting from a major study one figure or one statement which may be disproved elsewhere by the same author or by others. A short list of Yugoslav and other sources is appended. In a sense the whole society of Yugoslavia may be seen as a living and debating social and economic inventory to a degree which seems without parallel. The positive value of this phenomena, as well as its dangers, need no comment.

The content of this debate must, however, be briefly referred to as it casts light on one major sociological characteristic of the people involved. Despite the fact that the social and economic differentiation is comparatively limited within the country as a whole, and particularly within its various regions, by any standard of international comparison, opinion surveys show the prevalence of egalitarian preferences among all occupational categories and in all areas, though they may vary to some extent in degree, the higher categories and better off regions being slightly more ready to tolerate greater social differentiation. Workers invariably prefer to avoid lay-offs and to create new jobs even if they have to bear most of the costs themselves. Nor is there, generally speaking, an actual claim for higher differentials by management staff or technicians, contrary opinion by most 'management experts' notwithstanding. Most significantly, not only did recent surveys among university students show massive support for the reduction of the existing differences (i.e. by the very people who were to benefit from greater income differentials), but the same claim was at the root of their movement of public protest in the spring of 1968, which resulted in major changes in general economic policy. While exceptional reward for a tangible achievement may be accepted as rightful, possibly not without reluctance, yet any real or apparent privilege meets with radical criticism. Under such public pressure, for instance, strict legal limits had been set in 1968 on the size and equipment of secondary country or seaside residences (so-called 'weekend' houses), although they are an increasingly common item of the family budgets. The socially acceptable margin between the exclusively moral and egalitarian motivations for progress and development, and the requirement for personal and collective reward for achievement, is still very narrow.

A major public debate at the end of 1967 centred on a special reward due to a specialist who managed to put afloat in one year a major agricultural concern and had reserved under contract a special share in the resulting surplus. The amount involved was quite considerable by Yugoslav standards, although not uncommon elsewhere (approximately twelve times the average worker's income). Although finally solved in accordance with the provisions of the contract, the case no doubt marks the extreme limit of possible tolerance in such matters. As noted with a measure of bemused self-criticism by a contributor to the weekly journal of the League of Communists, Yugoslav society remains so far predominantly moralistic (rather than materialistically or economically motivated).

A last point should be made. As the reader has probably already noted, we have paid little attention to national income comparisons and related indices. This does not mean that we lack confidence in Yugoslav statistics. Indeed, the introduction of proper statistical services is one of the major achievements of post-war Yugoslavia; the local (communal) statistics as well as the monumental series of special surveys are largely without parallel. There are two related sets of difficulties in this connection, however: first, we lack any set monetary standard for international comparison; and second, even within Yugoslavia, the real value of the national currency (the dinar) differs quite considerably. A brief explanation may however be useful for the understanding of any later reference to values in Yugoslav currency.

Since the monetary reform of July 1965, the exchange rate of the new Yugoslav dinar has been set at 12·5 for one US dollar[1] (as against the former official rate of three to one, with a wide spectrum of varying special rates for tourists and various other special import and export markets). Aimed at insuring international convertibility, this rate is obviously excessive for

[1] A further devaluation of the dinar took place in January 1971, creating a new exchange rate of 15 dinars for one U.S. dollar.

evaluating the domestic value of the currency. In our experience, most of the consumer prices in dinars oscillate around those prevailing in France (in French francs) and a rate of one dollar to five dinars would not seem out of place for the conversion of domestic prices. West German tourist agencies found that their clients save in Yugoslavia, at the official exchange rate, up to 50 per cent as compared with domestic prices. However, Yugoslav citizens would benefit even more as the tourist does not share in various free or low-priced services including health, education and housing, and their consumers' basket is presumably less import-oriented. In other words, the present level of per capita income can be situated anywhere between 400 and 1,000 US dollars, the usual Yugoslav estimates corresponding approximately to the arithmetic average of these two figures. However, in real terms, a conversion based on any fixed rate is simply not meaningful. A striking example is a teacher or professor who certainly performs to standards at least equal to those in any other country and whose income enters into the national accounts for anything between 500 and 2,000 dollars at the official rate. A theatre ticket in a regional capital may cost as little as 0·08 US dollars and a bus fare half that amount. Export or tourist oriented goods and services may on the contrary reach much higher price levels.

A similar situation obtains on the domestic markets due to regional price differentials, which are known to vary considerably for major items such as rents, meat, fruit and vegetables—frequently exceeding 100 per cent—in the urban centres for which such data are available. Differences of much greater magnitude would undoubtedly become apparent if similar data were available for prices in rural areas. If inter-regional differences in subjective needs and habits as well as objective possibilities of spending were also taken into consideration, it would be apparent that a given level of income corresponds to exceedingly diverse levels of consumption and subjective satisfaction. Incidentally, this differentiation tends to alleviate—and often even reverses—the regional differences in levels of per capita income referred to earlier. It also means that any comparison in money terms must be approached with the greatest caution.

CHAPTER II

Self-Government of the Working People and Workers' Management: Objectives and Means of Implementation

The preceding chapter presented the reader with a minimum digest of basic data on the geographic, social and economic environment within which the Yugoslav system of workers' management originated and developed throughout the years. Yet, however dynamic they appear, these background data are in themselves meaningless abstractions as long as they are not viewed as concrete parameters which make it possible to grasp the real content and limits of the objectives of the system, and of the policies aimed at their implementation.

The behaviour, economic or otherwise, of the basic economic units of a system, or their performance, could only be meaningfully interpreted in the light of its general goals and its specific action-oriented objectives. A brief survey of the latter will be found below.

The Yugoslav system has been known abroad since 1950 as 'Workers' Management', a term which remains important and refers more particularly to the theme of this study, i.e. the management of economic enterprises by all those employed therein. Through the years, however, this narrower concept of self-government at production level has generated its own participative environment both in the non-productive sectors and at higher levels of the economy and of government, usually referred to as 'Self-Government of the Working People'. The two concepts are obviously closely related, the latter being wider and including the former as one of the various forms through which it is being implemented. Both are in a sense objectives in their own right, for their implementation requires specific re-ordering of all social institutions and relationships (dealt with in the following three chapters).

Both 'workers' management' and 'self-government of the working people' are, however, complex terms which elude any simple and exhaustive definition. They resemble certain other very general concepts such as 'humanism', 'democracy', 'planning', 'private enterprise', 'dictatorship of the proletariat' (or of any other class for that matter), which affect all social disciplines and indeed cannot normally be examined save in relation to some definite object. Significantly, therefore, very few Yugoslav writers have analysed either of the two concepts *per se* and, where they have done so, it was against the background of one particular area or branch of science.[1] In our view, both concepts can best be understood as general principles (or imperatives) which aim at re-ordering all social reality but which (like 'democracy', etc.) can only be apprehended in relation to specific situations in time and space. They are by no means neutral, yet they are neither a full system nor a definite set of objectives.

If we concentrate on the Yugoslav setting, we find some more definite, yet not fully satisfactory, answers. No short comprehensive definition is available, nor is one sought or deemed to be necessary. A few partial approaches to a definition, mostly assembled by Professor Pusič[2] may be of interest.

'The sociopolitical basis of socialist democracy in Yugoslavia is constituted by workers' management, in the shape of the workers' councils and other self-management bodies of the producers, by the self-government of the working people within the basic cells of the social order (i.e. the communes), and by the most varied forms of social self-government through bodies wherein the citizens and the organizations concerned are called upon to participate.' (Programme of the League of Communists 1958, p. 342.)

'. . . self-management is a system of (social) relations, a social institution and part of social structure; as a political form of organization of the working class it tends to achieve economic emancipation of labour, to eliminate economic coercion over the producers.' (Social Sciences Institute, Belgrade, 1963.)

'. . . workers' self-management, a key institution of our society, (is) a relatively permanent, structured whole (comprising) those socially recognized and protected tasks and relations through which citizens satisfy their needs in the fields of production, reproduction and distribution of goods, as well as their needs for corresponding services, on the basis of social ownership of means of production.' (J. Goričar, 1965.)

'. . . workers' management tends to transform State ownership of those means (of production) into social ownership over same . . .' (J. Goričar, 1957.)

'. . . workers' management is a new social relationship which is opposed even to social ownership of means of production . . .' (J. Djordjević, 1967.)

'. . . The socialization of means of production may take various forms in its progress from State or (state) mediated ownership—which characterizes the early stages of development of socialism—towards as direct as possible social ownership placed as directly as possible under the management of the emancipated and associated working people . . .' (Programme, 1958, p. 308.)

'Thanks to the workers' councils, the working class not only emancipates itself from the capitalists, but through its own activity, both conscious and spontaneous, it actually becomes independent from the State administrative

---

[1] We know of only one work dealing with self-government (or self-management) as its sole subject. Yet even there it is presented by the author against the exclusive background of the theories of management and government. (cf. Dr E. Pusić, *Samoupravljanje*, Zagreb, 1968, 295 pp.) There is no corresponding work covering the economics of the system.

[2] *Op. cit.*, pp. 51–5.

40

apparatus and indeed in a full sense transforms the latter into its own instrument.' (Kardelj, 1957.)

There are, however, at least two authoritative documents to which we can refer: the Programme of the Legaue of Communists of Yugoslavia, adopted in 1958; and the Federal Constitution of 1963. Both have been the subject of wide public discussion, are widely known and often referred to, and the general principles they enunciate remain fully operative. The two documents are consistently built around the concepts of workers' management and the self-government of the working people, set in a wide perspective of economic and social objectives of the system.

The Programme is a fully fledged statement of objectives and means of implementation which, due to its size and loosely detailed presentation, cannot be reduced to a brief summary. Yet this document contains the most comprehensive and systematic exposition of the system which has so far been produced in Yugoslavia, and we will occasionally refer to it in the more detailed analysis of enterprise behaviour. The Constitution of 1963 is more suitable for our purpose here, particularly as it gives in its preamble a cogent presentation of the aims and objectives of the system, and the principal means of its implementation. The concluding section (VIII) of the preamble is particularly relevant.

It reads as follows:

'The socio-political relations and forms (of organizations) provided under this Constitution aim at widening the conditions for the further development of socialist society, for the overcoming of its contradictions and for such social progress as would, on the basis of a complex development of the productive forces, high labour productivity, abundance of goods, and of a full development of man as a free personality, permit the implementation of the basic principles of Communism: "From each according to his abilities—to each according to his needs." To this end, all State bodies, bodies of social self-government, organizations and citizens are called upon, through all their activities, to widen and to strengthen the material foundations of society and of the life of individuals by means of constant development of the productive forces, increased labour productivity and constant promotion of socialist social relations; to create conditions under which socio-economic differences between intellectual and physical work will be overcome and where man's labour will become a still fuller expression of his creativity and personality; to enlarge and to develop all forms of social self-government and of socialist democracy, particularly in the areas where the functions of political power still predominate, to limit coercion and to create conditions for its elimination, and to promote relations between people which are based on the conscience of common interest and free activity of man; to contribute to giving effect to human freedoms and rights, to humanization of the social environment and of man's personality, to the promotion of solidarity and humanity among people and to the respect of human dignity; to develop all forms of co-operation and *rapprochement* with all nations in line with the progressive

41

tendencies of mankind, in order to consitute a free community of all nations of the world.'

The Yugoslav system shares with all others sections of the Marxist movement the ultimate goals explicitly stated in this section of the Constitution, i.e. the attainment of a society where all goods are freely available, and the full emancipation of man. The two goals are clearly complementary, as one would be meaningless without the other. They are also unattainable at present, or in the foreseeable future. Each commands a hierarchy of intermediary objectives which are not necessarily in harmony: the requirements of economic growth and efficiency on the one hand, and those of human progress and development on the other.

The particular characterization of the Yugoslav system is that it requires an equal pace of progress towards both sets of objectives, indeed with possible priority to the second as it is up to the men directly concerned to determine their own pace of economic progress. Hence, as in any multi-target system, the target setting cannot aim at maximum solutions at any one level but involves a complex search for widely acceptable social and economic optima. The underlying optimistic hypothesis is that such balanced optimum solutions may in the long run prove at least as efficient as a search for absolute maxima in any one single direction.

Economic Objectives and Policy Instruments
The articulation of the various objectives in the economic sphere is comparatively simple. The major features of the economic system and policy were clearly laid down during the post-war years under central planning: transfer to State ownership of all means of production above a minimum size (leaving out small workshops and family holdings in agriculture), high priority for industrialization, particularly the creation of new mostly heavy industries, a high rate of investment and of employment expansion, development of essential social services, and priority development of the less advanced regions. Much more than these fundamental policy choices, it was the *methods* of central planning which were found wanting and which were in fact to be replaced, first in the enterprises by workers' self-management, and subsequently in the wider socio-economic context by the various forms of self-government of the working people.

At the start, when it was a case of setting up a limited number of major production units, planners were certainly best able to mobilize and allocate capital and labour efficiently for these high priority projects. But, as the economy grew and diversified, with growing claims for resources from all areas and sectors, only local initiative could provide sufficient criteria of both economic efficiency and social priority. As regards production planning, the targets set by the plans were necessarily quantitative, their fulfilment being no guarantee of satisfaction of real needs, and they offered little scope for adaptation to changing conditions. Again, only local decision-making centres could cope with the infinity of problems arising in a rapidly diversifying economy.

The work collectivity of each enterprise, partly in conjunction with the local commune, was thus entrusted with a growing number of entrepreneurial functions, and may now be said to perform them all, while at the same time accomplishing ordinary work or management duties. It also bears the corresponding responsibilities.

Clearly, in view of their different position *vis-à-vis* the enterprise, the worker-managers can do more in some areas, and perhaps less in others, than a private entrepreneur or central planner, and their decisions will necessarily rest on different criteria. (To look more closely into this will be one of our main preoccupations in Part II of the study.) Yet the main specific objective of the system in the economic field is the introduction of entrepreneurial initiative and responsibility into the public sector of the economy. Aimed at stimulating both growth and quality, the entrepreneurial responsibility covers all areas of the enterprise's economic existence, such as regulation of current production and sales, introduction of new products and new technology, allocation of income, new investment and replacement of capital stock, employment, selection of technical and managerial personnel, saving, borrowing, etc. The economic motivations of the entrepreneurial work collectivity are twofold: on the one hand, it provides for each of its members remunerated employment, the stability of which is dependent on the existence—expansion or decline—of the enterprise itself; on the other hand, the level of the present and future income of each member is also dependent on the results of the enterprise during the corresponding period of time.

In both cases, the results of the actual work, physical or intellectual, and those of the entrepreneurial decisions are merged into one amount—the 'income of the enterprise'. The enterprise collectivity allocates this income to investment, to social services and to remuneration of its members. It does this in accordance with prescribed procedures, but determines freely the size of each allocation, the shares of its members being proportionate to their work as defined under general standards.

This procedure of 'income distribution' will be briefly described in Chapter V. It is of necessity exceedingly complex as it forms a meeting point for all production and distributional decisions within a given period, a sort of national accounts in miniature coupled with concrete decisions on each item (and innumerable sub-items). It provides a sort of *tableau économique*, reduced in size but made very much alive, which may be considered the key instrument of the entire system of workers' management.

The income distribution procedure tends at the same time to give effect to two related major objectives of the Yugoslav system: the appropriation of the results of their work by the producers themselves, and their distribution according to work. These objectives derive from the concept of labour as the only source of all values (labour theory of value). Yet it is not an abstract average labour that receives equal and average reward. The real workers in a given enterprise share out the concrete results of their work and entrepreneurial initiative. Where past work has been transformed into capital, investment is also a factor. In other words, where productivity (in the widest sense) is high, where goods are produced that best meet the needs of the

43

consumer, where costs are lowest, the reward per unit of work will reach a much higher level than in the average or marginal enterprises. Nevertheless, the system largely preserves an egalitarian character, for those entitled to a share in the income (i.e. the workers) are numerous, hence their individual shares will necessarily remain small. Obviously for this very reason the income distributed to workers cannot be compared to that of a capitalist enterprise, not only because of its size but by reason of its economic destination: it will normally be utilized *in toto* for current consumption. On the other hand, the incentive value of even minor differentials at the level of the average workers' income may often be stronger than that of the corresponding amount of capitalist profit.

Workers' management clearly postulates full economic autonomy for the enterprise. The latter cannot accept orders or specific directions from a planning office or any other administrative agency, as this would not be compatible with the entrepreneurial initiative of its work collectivity, nor with income distribution according to work. The only way in which its success or failure can properly be evaluated is through the free exchange, in competition on an equal footing with other producers, of the goods and services they have to offer. The exchange value of the goods and services provides the only objective standard of performance.

A competitive market is therefore an essential element for the practical operation of the system, even though it is by no means one of its objectives. Great attention was given in Yugoslavia, particularly in the early years, to the establishment of necessary conditions for a truly free exchange of goods and services, as this was the most important departure from established practice under central planning. The autonomy and equality of status of all enterprises were particularly stressed in relation to market requirements, and legal and economic instruments were introduced to prevent restrictive practices, monopolistic behaviour, etc. The market should obviously extend not only to current sales and purchases, but to all aspects of the enterprise's operation, including medium and long-term investment and financing. Clearly, however, there can be no 'labour market', as enterprises are not in a position to offer any fixed wage to new recruits, nor can job seekers offer their services at a given price. Specially devised instruments are therefore required to ensure proper deployment of the available workers.

The free market is not, of course, incompatible with the fixing of minimum standards, nor with general guidance of the economy through monetary and fiscal policies, provided that both are general in character, non-discriminatory and equitably applied, and that they do not affect too directly the autonomous decision-making process within the enterprise. The need to limit the process of economic government essentially to rule-making—as distinct from direct administrative intervention—is a necessary consequence of this requirement. It also explains the importance attached to replacing traditional state bodies and administrations by methods of direct self-government, derived from the enterprise, at all the higher levels of economic policy-making and government.

Nor can the market be the sole criterion of efficient decision-making within the system. It clearly offers some guidance as to the best possible solutions, even though in most cases a number of equivalent or nearly equivalent alternatives will be left open, even after the most thorough economic analysis. Whatever the case may be, however, the work collectivity of any one enterprise cannot be construed as an automaton blindly accepting the ruling of the market. Like any other self-employed producer, it will attach at least equal importance to its own subjective preferences, likes and dislikes, feelings of solidarity, etc., its readiness to accept risk, its own time horizon (or subjective rate of interest), etc. It is only within this subjective framework of internal preferences, which vary necessarily from case to case, that the market can be seen as an indicator of rational decision making. Yet, even given such limitations, the market clearly presents the enterprise collectivity with definite criteria—unavailable under central planning— which rule out decisions or policies which would lead to negative results, the reward for which would not reach the minimum level acceptable to the collectivity (again a variable, subjective criterion). In a more subtle way, it allows the work collectivity, at any level of performance, to strike its own balance between economic efficiency—including the various competing economic objectives—and subjective welfare criteria.

Socio-political and Welfare Objectives
The immediate economic objectives of the self-management system un-doubtedly received most attention during the early stages. Yet both the theory and the internal logic of the system rapidly brought to light an even wider variety of increasingly ambitious objectives of a socio-political and welfare character. Some of these were indeed directly built into the economics of the system's early watchword 'Factories to the Workers'; the liberation of the worker from the constraints of the traditional employment (master and servant) relationship was one of them. The consequent disappearance of labour as an element of cost, as a mere factor of production, was another.

The hierarchy of socio-political and welfare objectives which derive from the ultimate goal of emancipation of man (a man for whom work is the main and necessary attribute) is exceedingly complex. It extends to all areas of man's activity, but is primarily concerned with his work status and condi-tions. In some areas these objectives are in conformity with the economic ends of the enterprise, while in others they may be in apparent contradiction. They are built on the confidence—which may appear Utopian to many ob-servers yet not unlike the findings of modern physics—that devious ways may often prove shorter and faster than those apparently more direct, provided one respects the real centres of gravity and of resistance. In the main, it is again the enterprise collectivity that has to solve the resulting contradictions, against the background of its own interest and performance.

The setting-up of a true work collectivity in the enterprise is the obvious first objective. No such collectivity could be composed of mere hirelings, wage earners or salaried employees, nor could any casual assembly of abstract 'labourers' or even 'managers' be entrusted with rational and responsible decision making. Only a permanent—or at least relatively permanent—status

45

of membership of the worker within such a collectivity appears compatible with the self-management system. Nor can anyone else but the collectivity itself have formal control over the acceptance and exclusion of its members, as well as over all matters concerning relations within the work collectivity. Sufficient guarantees must at the same time be given to individual members against all possible violation of their rights, even by the majority of the membership.

This objective thus corresponds to a basic internal requirement of the system. At the same time, it is almost identical to the more fundamental claim for workers' emancipation from the unequal contractual relationship where labour's status is that of a commodity. In a narrow legal sense, its implementation presents no major problem. Appropriate legislation, along with more specific rules and procedures within each enterprise, coupled with external judiciary appeals or arbitration, can be devised quite easily, although the final result must necessarily be infinitely more complex than a piece of legislation governing a contract of employment. The elimination of fixed wages, replaced by shares in the enterprise's income according to work, provides the required economic content of the new form of work relationship.

Yet more is required to make the collectivity and its enterprise operational. A coherent decision-making structure must be organized, efficient but open to the entire membership, and the required capital resources must be secured in one form or another.

The specific features of the decision-making process adopted in Yugoslav enterprises will be briefly explained in Chapter IV. The general objective is direct, active and personal involvement in the actual decision-making process of all those who care, for they all participate in, and bear the responsibility for, the results of the operation of the enterprise. It is a basic tenet of the workers' management system as understood in Yugoslavia that these are two inseparable elements, two sides of one coin. Participation in decision making is meaningless unless backed by corresponding responsibility and reward. If the motivation is purely moral (as indeed is possible under very special circumstances such as war or other types of national emergency) the 'participants' have no objective criteria to arrive at a decision, most of them will soon become disinterested and their actual powers will be wielded by some outside bureaucratic forces. In other words, such a system would lack institutional stability. Similarly, while it is possible for a time to interest workers through a complex system of income or profit sharing, the logic of such a system will require sooner or later that workers be actively associated in the shaping of the scheme itself, including decisions on wider policy issues; should this not happen, the whole system must fall into disuse—or explode from internal conflict—for it is impossible to share in responsibilities for decisions in which one has not been actively involved.

Direct participation—or direct democracy—is therefore favoured above all other forms. Decisions by referendum, through discussions at general meetings of all workers, or at least the consultation of all prior to any major decision, are clearly preferred to any other more restrictive process of representative government. Wide publicity for all draft proposals is an essential prerequisite. Internal decentralization of the enterprise becomes in itself a positive value as it enables workers to decide directly on as many points as possible. Actually, through its stress on self-government, the system makes it difficult to implement decisions which would be actively opposed by those concerned. The effect on the enterprise's income and the workers' earnings provide a rational limitation to such an opposition.

In a modern enterprise it is, however, impossible to do without a formal representative system when dealing with current business and preparing decisions. Here again, the objective is to spread participation as widely as possible, through decentralization of the worker-management bodies, rotation of their membership, wide use of specialized committees, and the possibility for non-members to participate in discussion. To avoid open contest among groups, no separate lists of candidates are allowed. In larger enterprises, representatives are normally designated within smaller constituencies (departments, workshops) to ensure that they be personally known to, and keep in touch with, the membership. Of late, there is a distinct trend throughout the system to replace 'representatives' by 'delegates' with a specific mandate, directly answerable to those who chose them.

Is such a system compatible with efficient management? This question, which is often asked by outside observers, has little meaning within our present context, as we are merely attempting to bring to light the hierarchy of non-economic objectives of workers' management. It certainly is in conflict with the traditional concept of management, the 'management prerogatives' dear to the Anglo-American management theory, or the principle of 'one single (responsible) manager' which until lately was the key of the Soviet industrial system. In our perspective, the particular set of objectives just outlined derives directly from the main goals of the system and is therefore a necessary part thereof. They are an essential condition of good workers' management. They may seem costly in terms of formal efficiency, but if freer men work better and more sensibly than those under constant supervision, the results should normally be positive.

One point is certain: the system requires another type of management, and in most cases other managers as well. We should add that Yugoslav legal theory tends to reserve a separate sphere of competence to executive management, but encounters serious difficulties in the practical implementation of this principle. In any event, the economic and social policy choices which are our main concern in this study are clearly within the primary competence of workers' management itself, and there is little need to elaborate on this subtle distinction.

Another major objective of the system, which at the same time corresponds to its institutional requirements, is the transfer of ownership to the enterprise property (its funds) of the means of production it needs in order to operate normally. (It may be useful to make it clear that the Yugoslav Constitution guarantees private ownership of all personal property, savings, etc., which are not designed for productive purposes.) As workers' management had been introduced in 1950 exclusively in the public sector, i.e. in enterprises nationalized earlier, or developed by the State or other public

47

bodies, the transition did not raise any major problem at the time. Yet, it soon became apparent that if the principle of State ownership were to be preserved, the work collectivities could not feel secure enough in the long run to manage and develop the enterprise to the best of their abilities, as indeed they were expected to do. They would at all times face the risk of being deprived of their assets—as indeed had occurred in the early days due to various emergency measures—by virtue of decisions taken by outside bodies claiming to represent the State as public authority or founder of the enterprise. At the same time, both as a matter of principle and of practical policy, the possibility of making the workers—individually or collectively—the owners of such assets could not be seriously considered within the framework of a system based on workers' management.

Private ownership of the means of production (other than personal tools) is not only contrary to the basic tenets of socialism but would also constitute a particularly vicious violation of simple justice at the level of development reached by Yugoslavia. All productive assets in existence had been safeguarded and developed thanks to an uncommon measure of sacrifice by the entire population, and not merely by any particular group of workers employed in a given enterprise. Granting a right of ownership of assets to such a group, at a stage where conditions of equal development were far from attained, would mean despoliating the rest of the population of an equal chance of future development. A system of workers' management combined with private—albeit workers'—ownership of assets would be quite inoperative as shown by the experience of most of the producers' co-operatives so constituted, unless the right of decision making were tied to the ownership of capital, thereby creating new class differences between the workers themselves.

Although the impossibility, both in theory and in practice, of private ownership of capital assets by the workers employed in the worker-managed enterprise is one of its most strongly stressed characteristics, the Yugoslav system is frequently interpreted precisely in terms of workers' ownership of the firm by foreign observers, who find therein a facile argument to hail the return of private enterprise or to prove the betrayal of socialism. The question of so-called 'workers' shares' or other forms of participation in ownership of assets did actually give rise in Yugoslavia to a short-lived debate of purely academic origin in 1967 and early 1968, but the idea met with no wider public support. The problems raised by the capital assets in a worker-managed economy will be reviewed in some detail in Chapter X.

It was gradually determined that assets should be considered as a permanent grant to the enterprise as a legal person (not to any group of workers in particular), a grant corresponding to a real and inalienable right to such assets but to which certain obligations attached, including that of proper and considerate management, the maintenance of at least the initial value of the assets and the payment of a legal interest to a general investment fund. This means that enterprise assets cannot be expropriated (except against equitable indemnification and under general legal procedures), that they cannot be used up by, or shared out among, the work collectivity, and that

48

they cannot be distracted from their economic purpose. For lack of a better term, this very specific right of usage is referred to in Yugoslavia as 'social ownership', the intention being to stress the absence of any owner in the sense of contemporary civil law (as based on Roman tradition). The same rules, which exclude the right to misuse or consume such assets, also apply to any additional assets created by the work collectivity and re-invested in the enterprise.

Technical difficulties have caused some relaxation of the rigid principle of maintenance of the original value of the assets, particularly where it impeded downward price flexibility, or the continued operation of enterprises in declining sectors of industry. A more far-reaching trend seems to be emerging of late which aims at suppressing all limitations in the management of assets, including the payment of interest, so as to make the assets appear in their true form, not as capital, but as mere material support of human activity. This school of thought is ready to rely fully on the free conscience of the producers as sole guarantee of the best use of enterprise assets. If, as is possible, this view should prevail, the emancipation of capital would be complete and there would be nothing left but 'things' as objects of man's economic activity.

While the gradual implementation of the concept of social ownership in all fields of activity has on the whole been achieved, various related problems have been frequently appearing in recent years, some of which remain open. Suggestions by some authors that workers, or even the public, could acquire shares (not voting but with the right to dividends) in certain enterprises received no significant support in enterprises themselves or by the general public. They actually aroused strong opposition in most quarters and were largely forgotten. Yet similar participative schemes were legally authorized and can be freely negotiated by the enterprises in order to secure co-operation of foreign companies. The issue of interest-bearing bonds to workers and the domestic public has also been authorized in certain special cases. As in most other areas, the Yugoslav practice remains open to experiment, even in regard to this central objective of the system. It may be expected that theoretical discussions and practical experiments will continue in this area in the years to come, with a view particularly to defining the limits and content of the rights pertaining to productive assets. A major breakthrough towards a more radical elimination of capital as a factor of production—which indeed is closely linked with the emancipation of the workers themselves—is not entirely impossible, although the technical difficulties remain tremendous.

While the various non-economic objectives considered so far are a necessary corollary of the institutional build-up of the system of workers' management, there are two other sets of related objectives. One is aimed towards the welfare and social activities of the members of the work collectivity, and the other towards their participation in shaping general policies at all levels of government.

Welfare and social activities within the enterprises were already a major function of the enterprise under the system of central planning. During the post-war period, due to prevailing scarcity of all goods, and particularly

49

food, priority given to industrial development entailed priority supplies to workers through their enterprises, for no one else but the enterprise could adequately organize their distribution; works canteens became a key feature in all factories. The economic aim of this policy, common to all countries at that period, was to preserve the lowest possible levels of prices and wages in the interest of reconstruction and development. Yet much more was aimed at, particularly in Yugoslavia. Although not called upon to participate in management, the worker was to enjoy absolute priority in what could be termed socio-cultural rehabilitation. Literacy training had absolute priority, along with elementary induction to work and workers' education generally. Holiday homes or workers' hostels were the priority area in the field of leisure. All this, combined with a very high rate of political activity, was aimed at preserving the dynamism of the resistance era well into peacetime reconstruction and development.

When installed in their new functions, the worker-managers had thus much to get on with. Much more was still to be added. They had to take in hand all their own training, including professional examinations and grading, and soon became the major sponsors of more advanced schemes such as on-the-job training abroad for specialists and university level studies. Initiatives to provide for the most urgent needs in housing were also taken. They became self-insurers (in addition to the general system of social security) in some areas of social security such as short-term sickness benefits; they were mainly their own masters in safety and hygiene; and they formed a basic unit of the commune-based military strategy of the 'All peoples' defence'. Although the workers' management system laid an unprecedented emphasis on their economic activity and functions, they remained a basic centre of the socio-cultural and political life of the non-agricultural community.

This is clearly related to one major element of the general goal of emancipation to which all these objectives were geared, i.e. the disappearance of the working class as a class distinct from and opposed to general society. Stated in positive terms, it means a possibility given to the workers to promote themselves to human existence and dignity by their own effort, to create their own human destiny. The socio-cultural activities within the enterprise are, of course, only one of many steps along this path; yet their importance at an early stage of development is more than obvious, for there was no other framework within which they could be adequately located.

Under the workers' management system, this welfare objective is, of course, optional, the corresponding activities voluntary and free. Yet, however big the challenge, they also correspond to an objective necessity. For the system itself postulates that no one else will undertake any of these activities for or in the name of the workers; they may get help and suggestions from the outside, and farm out or even discard some of these activities, or set up special institutions for the purpose. As an extreme case, they may choose to do nothing or, on the contrary, concentrate all their resources on this area; whatever will be done will be their own responsibility. Yet practice shows that the negative choice is an impossible one; hence this objective is not merely derived from abstract theory, but corresponds to a fundamental necessity. These welfare and socio-cultural activities have obvious economic implications as they are part of the enterprise costs. They have a direct impact, both in theory and practice, on the behaviour and performance of the enterprise.

The second key non-economic objective of enterprise self-management is entirely outward-oriented. As an essential agent of economic decentralization, the self-governing enterprise is also a basic unit of a fully decentralized, hence pluralistic, political structure. This involves two different levels: one, more down to earth, is merely an extension of the concept of economic democracy to all levels, a major objective in itself. If the enterprises are to be truly self-governing, they must also themselves make all decisions or policies as may be required at higher levels. The second aim is much more ambitious. It is rooted in the great expectation of Marxist doctrine of the withering away of the State, and all related forms of social and economic coercion. It is also a response to an obvious practical need of a society which wants to grow out of coercive patterns imposed by a national struggle for survival coupled with a deep social revolution. It may be, and often is, interpreted in terms of a struggle against all forms of bureaucracy, of alienated government.

In both cases, the similarity of the argument with those of the early advocates of parliamentary democracy based on citizens' sovereignty is obvious. Yet the citizens of the time were modelled on the landowners and industrialists who alone took part in the 'vestry assembly' of their parish communities and who could hardly see their equals in the common labourer or other members of the 'lower classes'. The self-governing enterprise is one of a few possible forms which fulfils the requirements of full citizenship. It has the means to command the public media, it can obtain a hearing in all public assemblies and it has wide experience and relationships at its disposal in a wider territory, possibly even abroad. The average individual worker or citizen remains wrapped, not only in Yugoslavia, in multiple sectional cocoons and cannot form considered opinions on wider issues. Experience has demonstrated beyond reasonable doubt that he inevitably abdicates his right in favour of professionals, political or military. Yet, through a modern enterprise, if democratically instituted, he may make his weight felt on real issues.

The means through which these objectives can be implemented are many. To define them in concrete terms is the main object of the following chapter. Ideally, the enterprises and their work collectivities may form associations at all levels as they see fit, and govern themselves by means of a delegate congress. This overall concept of generalized self-government seems to underly all the various approaches made so far: the setting up of occupational or business associations of enterprises, of statutory representative organizations (chambers), and of parliamentary assemblies composed of enterprise representatives, the reshaping of the existing trade union structure to make it an integral part of the workers' management system, the limitation and gradual suppression of centres of bureaucratic power and coercion at all levels of the State and of political and social organization, and their replacement by elected and responsible bodies. Significant progress has been made along these lines. Yet, perhaps more so than in any other area, major difficulties of a

51

technical nature and passive resistance by individuals and groups who felt their positions endangered, were encountered. The lack of precedent as well as the need to preserve some measure of institutional similarity with foreign countries have contributed to slowing down developments in this area, but these are still very actively pursued.

Before concluding this chapter, a few general points should be made.

First, as the reader may have noticed, the various objectives we have just outlined are those of the Yugoslav system as a whole, and cannot be attributed to any enterprise in particular, nor to an abstract or 'average' enterprise. In all the areas covered, a line is clearly to be drawn between the general objectives of the system and those which the enterprise sets out for itself. With regard both to its economic and social activities, each enterprise is not only empowered to adopt, but actually has to specify, its particular policy targets, formally through its Articles of Association (by-laws) and its various planning documents, and informally through all its other decisions and activity. Its policy may be substantially at variance with the outside system (which in itself has a very considerable flexibility), as long as such variations do not entail a permanent retrogression in the light of a major objective. Hence, no model based on a dogmatically interpreted set of the system's general objectives could properly be used for evaluating the actual behaviour and performance of worker-managed enterprises, without taking account of their specific and differentiated objectives at any given point of time. Nor could a study of the system be based on such a dogmatic assumption, for it would go against a key feature of the system itself, i.e. the right of self-determination of the enterprise and its work collectivity, which would be meaningless if limited to mere current decision making, and so must encompass the definition of its own particular objectives.

A second point must be made. Our design to make explicit the objectives proper to the enterprise has caused us to neglect the individual worker, the individual citizen, although it hardly needs to be stressed that he is the only real subject of all self-management activity, as well as the only object of same. Nor does the mediation of the enterprise, necessary as it may be in most respects within the Yugoslav setting and in the light of the requirements of modern technology, eliminate or even submerge his individual personality, be it in the works or outside. All the instruments of the system take the utmost care to define and protect the right of the individual member of the work collectivity, often perhaps overstretching their preference for justice as against efficiency. This again is not only derived from theory, but seems to have the active support of most enterprises. They only rarely tend towards a summary collectivist discipline, but mostly go to great lengths to deal with individual cases.

An example among many others: the possibility of transferring a worker to another job without his consent is surrounded by so many legal guarantees that it became a practical impossibility and a moot point of legal theory. The complexity of the appeal procedures open to the worker within the enterprise is certainly without parallel anywhere; even final decisions are open to extraordinary appeals and revision, etc. All these guarantees and procedures are widely availed of in practice, thereby contributing to the actual shaping of the system. It should not be forgotten, however, that the economic interest of the parties—which would be absent in a purely bureaucratic structure—impress a good deal of common sense in the search for agreed solutions.

A further, if extreme example is a recent special delegate conference of all railway enterprises of Yugoslavia convened to rule an appeal on an individual case of indiscipline. This was criticized as the cost amounted to tens of thousands of man-hours, yet it may have avoided losing millions. In any event, the decision belonged to and the costs were borne by the work collectivities concerned.

It should also be recalled in this connection that besides the worker-managed enterprises which dominate the modern sector of the economy, the Yugoslav community comprises millions of individual producers, mostly self-employed peasants, and some two hundred thousand independent craftsmen or traders whose economic existence is fully protected.

Moreover, parallel to the development of the self-management system, close attention was given to the development of an adequate system of civil rights and corresponding guarantees for their implementation. These indeed are seen as an essential prerequisite of workers' management and social self-government generally. True, the existing political system—which may be defined as that of one Party tending to none—enjoys constitutional protection, as do the principles and objectives of workers' management. Public expressions of ethnic, religious or similar intolerance, or organizations based on corresponding attitudes, cannot claim any similar privilege. Within these limits, including the whole area of economic and social policy and behaviour we are concerned with, any opinion can legally be held. One could hardly find elsewhere a wider range of differing points of view as are hotly debated in public. Indeed, even regarding the reserved areas we have just mentioned, rather than an excessive vigour it is a relative tolerance or even slackness in their enforcement, which in our view would strike an independent observer, and which would seem to cause more concern to the general public.

Particular attention has been paid to the so-called economic and social rights of the citizens, such as their right to education, to social security and health protection, to work and to freedom of work and, above all, to equality of rights and opportunity. All the more traditional personal rights and privileges of citizens have also been constitutionally guaranteed and put into effect. Special mention should be made of the widest judicial guarantees—which extend also to the enterprises and work collectivities—aimed at guaranteeing to all citizens or organizations full access to the ordinary or constitutional courts, not only with respect to any alleged violation of their rights, but for any action or lack of action within the prescribed period by any State body or other organ of authority. Yugoslavia is thus one of very few countries, if not the only one, which allows to all its citizens—and its enterprises—a full right of appeal in all administrative matters. A complex judiciary system has been developed for the purpose and is being widely availed of.

53

The economic and social objectives of the Yugoslav system of workers' management thus escape any formal definition. Nor can the existing statements of objectives, such as the Programme of the League of Communists and the Constitution of 1963, be readily summarized, in view of the multiplicity and complexity of the intermediary objectives and instruments for their implementation. Such a formal definition or summary would moreover contradict the basic premise of the system under which the formulation of objectives and policies is a fundamental prerogative of the work and producers' collectivities at all levels, including more particularly the worker-managed enterprise.

The overall twin goal of the system, i.e. the full satisfaction of the economic needs of men and their full emancipation as producers and citizens, can thus be pursued through a variety of intermediary objectives and a diversity of policies, corresponding to concrete situations in space and time but not necessarily reduceable to a common denominator. A number of major objectives exist, however, which provide more specific guide posts to the understanding of the behaviour of the Yugoslav firm. They are all linked by the fundamental postulate of a gradual approach towards true equality for all, individuals or collectivities: equality of rights, of opportunity, of access to social resources and services. The imperative of progress towards equality provides without doubt the main operative principle of the whole system in the pursuit of the various intermediary objectives.

CHAPTER III

Institutional Background and General Economic Policy

Territorial Self-government and the Federation

The major post-war constitutional development was the recognition of the political and administrative autonomy of the major ethnic groups (or complexes) by the formation of six autonomous republics, and two autonomous provinces within the Republic of Serbia. For several of these, such as Macedonia and Slovenia, this meant the formation of their first national governments in history. Lower administrative units inherited from the past, the communes and districts, were preserved but transformed—through a system of local and district people's councils—into an instrument of political self-government. Yet in the area of economic and social policy the country remained highly centralized, under an all-embracing system of central planning and administrative management of the economy, with all essential powers concentrated in the hands of the federal government.

As a consequence of the introduction in 1950 of workers' management within the enterprises, and also as a result of independent parallel forces pressing for greater decentralization and local autonomy within the political system, major changes became imperative. Initiated by a communal reform in 1953, the resulting developments have transformed the whole government structure; major reforms were still under consideration in 1968. Only the general guide-lines of these reforms, as well as a minimum nomenclature of the system, can be referred to here.

In its most general feature, the reform process may be said to aim at the setting up of the two main relatively independent levels of territorial self-government, each relatively sovereign within its own sphere, i.e. the communes and the republic. The autonomous provinces share in most of the prerogatives of the republic and indeed tend and aspire to a similar constitutional status. The prerogatives of the Federation are limited as far as possible to specific functions delegated by the constituent republics. At all levels, self-government powers are entrusted to a dual system of assemblies, one elected directly by the people, while one or several others represent the enterprises and other work collectivities. Executive functions are entrusted to councils or specialized committees elected by the assemblies, with administrative services being conceived as mere technical support to the elective bodies. The only exception seems to be at the federal level, where a few more traditionally shaped departments have been preserved, particularly Foreign

Affairs and National Defence, the heads of which are appointed by the Federal Executive Council.

The *communes* are basic political and socio-economic organizations of people in a given area. Their number has been considerably reduced in the course of the years—to approximately 500 (as against some 10,000 under earlier systems). Each forms a small district with an average population of 40,000, and should be able to provide all the essential services to the population and to cope with the corresponding self-administrative functions. All matters relating to public administration, economic, social and cultural questions (unless specifically reserved to the republic) are within its terms of reference. The communes have general regulatory and planning powers, levy local taxes, and generally seek to promote local economic and social conditions. In relation to the enterprises they appear on the one hand as a form of local union or federation, since one of the communal assemblies—the economic council—is composed of representatives of the enterprise work communities. On the other hand they are a primary level of supervision over the operation of the enterprises, and may even co-operate in certain major decisions or step in if major emergencies arise. Moreover, the communes are economic organizations in their own right, not only by reason of the various communal service organizations they supervise more directly, but also because of the quite considerable funds at their disposal for economic intervention and development. They are largely dependent on the enterprise as a source of these funds, only a limited amount of subsidy being available to the least developed among them. A commune at average or above average level of development may be deemed financially autonomous and unable to reckon with outside funds in case of a setback. The problem of economic development of the economically weakest communes is not within the scope of this report; yet in such a case it is still the commune that will have to act as the main promoter of local development.

Local enterprises are thus responsible for their own supervision and help in promoting the local economy. Local problems and local prosperity are of essential importance to the enterprises and their work collectivities, not only as taxpayers and the main beneficiaries of local services (education, health, transport, etc.), but also as regards local employment opportunities and levels of employment.

Enterprise representation within the commune is kept in check by the communal council, designated directly by the population (usually within local communities or sub-divisions of the commune corresponding to former villages or sections of urban settlements). Yet, on the whole, the enterprise representatives forming the economic council of the commune seem better equipped to deal with matters of social and economic policy than members of the communal council with their more political background. The representation of a larger enterprise within the communal assembly may indeed often carry the day, thanks both to its numerical strength and to the economic weight of the interest it represents. The financial needs of any commune being practically unlimited, many of them are known to have engaged in fierce competition in order to get in even minor taxpayers, including private

56

craftsmen. There is also a good deal of competition among the communes in setting up road transport enterprises and similar more mobile industries. All of them may be thought of as welcoming any new enterprise or venture that may contribute to local development and alleviate the burden of local taxes. They are thus definitely part of the market structure.

An average commune may thus be thought of as a small but quite powerful republic, with its own 'president', a dual assembly, its official gazette, and a full set of committees and technical services dealing with all government matters.[1] Political party competition is lacking, yet each commune is the focal point of many varied interests, expressed not only by some amorphous 'people' or 'working class', but actually organized into a multiplicity of definite interest groups. The enterprises are among the most powerful and certainly the best organized among them.

The communes have now entirely supplanted the earlier districts, which survived for many years in some of the larger republics as an intermediary co-ordinating structure. At present, the communes may merely agree to establish joint services in certain areas such as health or education. However, in major cities, comprising several communes, a partial transfer of the communal authority to the municipality is allowed for. Similarly, within each commune, the enterprises may transfer to the latter such services as they normally provide themselves to their members (e.g. transport or catering). On the whole, care is taken not to make the communal boundary into too strict a division between the neighbouring populations. As in the enterprises, referenda are frequently used at the communal level, particularly in fiscal matters or for major joint ventures.

The Republic, neither superior to the commune nor a federation of communes, is an expression of another type of sovereignty: that of an ethnically (or otherwise) defined people. Its government structure resembles that of the commune, with an Executive Council replacing the President, and several specialized assemblies or Councils of the working people (economic, health and culture, public administration) instead of a single economic council. Of late, its competence has been widening even in such areas as national defence and foreign relations, as well as taxation and public financing. It has rather limited co-ordinating and supervisory powers with respect to the communes, except where less developed areas are concerned. Special funds are provided for their development. Within the general principles defined by federal laws, they have full legislative and executive authority. The whole territory of the Federation remains a single area from the point of view of the economic system and policy, including trade, finance, etc. Limited fiscal differentiations do, however, exist and even the possibility of internal excise duties has recently been mentioned.

The Federation was, and remains, the object of great reform activity. The massive administrative machinery for managing the economy under central

---

[1] The internal structure, procedures and powers are regulated by the Constitution (Statut) adopted by each commune. English translation of some of these documents is available (Communes of Kranj and Pozarevac).

planning had been abandoned by 1953. For a number of years (up to 1960 or so) the Federation remained through a system of indirect planning, resting mainly on wide use of fiscal and financial policy instruments (taxes, customs, interest rates, sectoral and regional allocation of investment capital, etc.). It also engaged directly in major development projects. In the sixties, the general trend was to stabilize the levels and neutralize the impact of taxes and other fiscal instruments, to transfer the capital market to autonomous, self-governing banking agencies and to eliminate all direct development activity by the Federation. A 1967 Amendment (No. III) to the Federal Constitution expressly prohibited all federal investments unless specifically authorized by a federal law. No such law has been adopted or proposed since. By the spring of 1968, the Federation had been stripped of all powers of direct intervention in the economy, and hardly any use was made of any limited powers remaining.

No room was left for active planning at the national level. The two major remaining active instruments in 1968 were destined to extinction. Five or six major investment projects of the Federation (one railway line, one big hydro-electric scheme undertaken jointly with a neighbouring country, and several big power generation stations in the south of the country) were due for completion and not expected to be replaced. Funds due as interest payment on enterprise basic capital were still collected at the federal level to finance regional development, but this scheme was also to be gradually discontinued (although financial help to the less developed regions is expected to continue in some other form, perhaps as interest free loans). The transition to the system of workers' management deprived the central government of the control over all the State monopolies or other public enterprises (railways, post and telegraphs, alcohol, salt and tobacco, state mines, agricultural estates, etc.). Even the government printing works have become autonomous non-budgetary worker-managed enterprises.

Under the 1963 Constitution, the only two areas of primary responsibility of the Federation are those of national defence and foreign relations.

The Federation guarantees the unity of the socio-economic system, of the system of income distribution, including the monetary and credit system, and of the political system, including the self-government and other rights of workers and citizens. Its power to act is limited to issuing legislation on the general principles governing these matters. Executive powers are exceptional: control of currency, levels of minimum bank deposits and foreign currency reserves, maximum rates of interest, etc. Special powers may of course be granted in case of emergency, as for instance the urgent anti-dumping measures taken in 1968. Generally speaking, however, even foreign trade and connected operations (loans, etc.) are outside the scope of direct government control.

The main stress is thus on the activities of the Legislative Assemblies. Among these the Economic Council, the members of which are designated by the corresponding communal assemblies, undoubtedly has a major weight in economic and social matters. It certainly had an impact on the institutions

58

and policy in the areas falling within its terms of reference, an impact which could in a sense be termed negative (as it resulted in the elimination of all active economic policy and planning), were it not in line with the internal logic of the system of workers' management. It was felt that an institutional and policy vacuum was necessary to open the door for the truly self-governing initiative of the enterprises and other basic organizations.

The administrative services of the federal government (the Federal Executive Council) and of the various specialized councils or committees replacing the former government departments were correspondingly reduced to a minimum, particularly in such areas as the economy, finance and labour. They were hardly able to keep abreast of general developments and prepare draft legislative proposals, let alone to interfere in individual cases. Significantly, the technical committees of the National Assembly had to create their own small secretariats to deal with matters on their agenda.

There is no formal binding plan which would in any manner affect the enterprises. Instead, it has become customary for the National Assembly to discuss and adopt, along with the yearly Budget, a Resolution on the economic and social perspectives for the coming year containing very general guidelines for executive action. Despite its generality the preparation and detailed wording of this document is usually the cause of heated controversy and can often only be completed after innumerable amendments. While there is little doubt that direct enterprise representation at National Assembly level has asserted itself fully, particularly as a brake on the Executive, and that it will remain a permanent feature of the system, it is now widely agreed that in its present form the Assembly is not the best forum for the elaboration of positive policies. The need for more definite planned perspectives, which is urgently felt by most enterprises, particularly at the level of certain major sectors, such as transport and energy, or even textiles and agriculture, makes it probable that a more direct link with industry and its main branches will be sought.

Mention should also be made here of some technical aspects of the single economic system extending to the whole of Yugoslav territory. The most important of these is the Service of Social Audit, which checks the accounts of enterprises and other decentralized bodies or organizations, not only from a formal accounting point of view but also on the substantive propriety of any expenditure, write-off, depreciation practice, etc. It may report any abuse for prosecution and take protective measures. Its task is made easier by two procedural rules: (i) all enterprises must follow a federally prescribed, unified decimal system of accounting and periodical balances; and (ii) all their intakes and expenditure must be run through a single current account, such accounts forming a unified national system. While not normally accessible to third parties, these uniform data systems make it possible for the inspection services to obtain rapidly an insight into the operation of an enterprise or, for that matter, of the economy at any level. Their existence makes it possible to operate effectively a complex system of income sharing (dealt with in Chapter V).

Political and Social Organizations

The introduction of the workers' self-government system required similar changes in the structure and activity of political and social organizations. Among these, particular importance attaches to the Party and the Trade Unions, as their activities are more directly connected with the enterprise.

The *Communist Party* emerged at the end of the war at the head of nearly one million armed partisans, having liberated the country after four years of merciless struggle against foreign invaders and domestic collaborators. It represented the sole political force capable of governing the country as it alone was able to command support in all groups of the population, and in all parts of the country, and had an articulated programme of development for a new Yugoslavia. This would have been impossible for a numerically small and illegal organization as it was before the war,[1] were it not for the wide support of the population, including particularly the mountainous rural areas which had been subjected to fierce persecutions by foreign forces and their local allies. Peasants then formed the majority of the Party's membership. Non-members were more loosely organized, according to varying local patterns, into a National Front, later renamed the 'Socialist Alliance of the Working People'.

As it set about realizing its design for a one-Party state pressing for highest rates of development under a system of centralized planning, the Communist Party could not disregard its specific background and war experience. Although it largely followed the then only available development model, that of the Soviet Union, an open and violent conflict with all other ruling Communist Parties of Eastern Europe (the Cominform) developed in 1948. This opened the way to the autonomous development of both theory and practice and it aimed at replacing Party rule and discipline by the self-government of the working people.

The formal changes were rather similar to those operated in the State bodies. These were wide decentralization, publicity of all discussions and accounts, abstention from any form of command over or within public or economic bodies, wider membership and reduced power of the executive bodies and reliance mainly on the decisions of general meetings or congresses. The Party, having changed its name to the 'League of Communists' in 1958, considered itself the guardian of a moral heritage and of a dynamically interpreted ideology. It set its own limits to its authority which ruled out direct intervention in the running of any enterprise or State body, as well as the cumulation of offices in the three sets of organizations by the same persons; regular rotation of office holders was introduced as a general principle.

Although there were many changes, one single fact is more likely to clarify

---

[1] In the period following the first world war, however, the Yugoslav population showed widespread support for the Communist Party (even though perhaps less massively than in the neighbouring but defeated Hungary and Bulgaria). After carrying the first post-war election in several major towns, including the capital, and rural districts, the Party was declared illegal; following the bankruptcy of the parliamentary system, all parties were later dissolved and a royal dictatorship installed.

the changed position of the self-managing enterprise within the system. This is the absence of any central directive planning, endorsed or approved by a Party, for the implementation of which the latter would bear a direct responsibility. Should it intend to intervene, no party organization, within or without the enterprise, has any binding framework against which it could assess and/or attempt to rectify the behaviour or policy of the enterprise. Growth, efficiency, better services and incomes, more employment and productivity as well as many other targets spelled out in general terms but impossible to quantify provide no firm yardstick for such intervention.

Nevertheless, the League of Communists remains the key political factor. Its basic organizations are found in all but the smallest enterprises and in all communes. Yet they have hardly ever prevented them from following the natural course of their policy but, to the contrary, can mostly be found among the protagonists of enterprise or communal autonomy. The moral-ideological issues are the League's major area of apparent concern. Yet some key appointments, although publicly advertised and selected on merit, are filled in the majority of cases by League members. The position of the enterprise director, as distinct from other members of top management, is one which until recently was hardly ever sought by candidates who were not members of the League.

The League's active influence is more strongly felt at higher levels, in the Republics and the Federation in particular. The major outlines of the system were clearly inspired and laid down by the League, its Congresses and other national bodies as well as key individuals. The League's own internal reform programme clearly conditions parallel developments within all other organizations, and its Congresses or major pronouncements have marked the successive milestones of the country's post-war history. Similarly, the personal authority of the League's Chairman and Federal President, Josip Broz-Tito, and the wide allegiance he commands in all regions and classes of the population, form a basic unifying factor. The League also has a great number of highly articulate theoreticians and specialists in the socio-economic disciplines which contributed to the implementation of the basic objectives of self-government. Each region or group has their spokesmen who can make a real contribution to the discussions and developments in the various areas.

The withdrawal of the League from what may be called 'active politics' has brought to the fore the *Socialist Alliance of the Working People*, an organization open to all adult citizens and to which most are affiliated. Its meetings and congresses discuss all matters of general interest, particularly those relating to local or regional development, but their specific role is to organize, with the widest possible participation of all citizens, the selection of candidates for all public offices, and the accountability of the elected representatives. While in all elections for public office candidates are presented on a non-Party basis by the electors themselves at open meetings, the actual organization of this process is in the hands of the Socialist Alliance which also presents a final balanced list in order to allow for adequate representation of the various groups. The Alliance also reduces the list to manageable size when the meetings of electors have put forward too many candidatures.

61

Plurality of candidates is usually standard practice, particularly at local levels.

The *Trade Unions* have also seen their role radically modified by the new socio-economic system, and have experienced particular difficulty in finding their place within the self-management system. Without any significant traditions to build upon,[1] a trade union movement was formed in 1945 with a view essentially to serving as an organizational link between the Party and the State (the economic planning machinery) and the mass of workers grouped in the individual enterprises and industries. Two tasks were then of major importance: to ensure minimum conditions of living and of welfare, particularly in helping to organize priority supplies and certain services, such as holiday homes; and to develop a massive workers' education and training system. At the same time the unions served as the principal channel of information and communication with the workers in general drive for reconstruction and development.

Most of these tasks became rapidly anachronistic and disappeared following the introduction of workers' management, particularly those related to planning, for the enterprises themselves and their workers' management bodies were able to deal with them directly and more effectively. This in turn made it possible for the trade unions to liberate themselves from the enormous bureaucratic establishment which had been necessary to deal with these administrative tasks. They were left with the general function of the representation of workers' interests at industrial and national levels (as distinct from those of the individual work collectivities), including continued participation in workers' educational activities and certain aspects of welfare. Additionally, they tended to exercise, for lack of any other competent authority, some measure of co-ordination of the worker-management bodies of the country; they convened the first national congress of the Workers' Councils in 1957 and do occasionally, and with growing frequency, convene similar meetings at regional or branch levels. The Central Council of Trade Unions convened a second National Congress of the Self-Governing Producers for 1967, which was postponed until May 1970. They are also one of several channels for the workers' individual grievances in addition to the workers' management system which, *inter alia*, is the major channel for the processing of grievances, the Labour Inspectorate, the Courts, the League of Communists and various state bodies, including the Office of the President of the Republic. Trade Unions are also entitled, as are the various communal, State or other bodies, to ask the workers' self-management bodies to reconsider one or other of their policies or decisions which may entail an infringement of some moral or legal principle.

The trade unions are among the active organizers of numerous research activities and consultations on matters connected with workers' management. In 1967, for example, the Central Council of Trade Unions assembled a large

---

[1] The predominantly rural character of pre-war Yugoslavia and lack of concentration of industry offered little scope for the development of workers' unions and such unions as had been formed were mostly illegal. Statutory bodies known as Chambers of Labour (similar to those still existing in Austria) offered some material support for informal activity and liaison among workers in pre-war Yugoslavia.

volume of documentation on the strike activity of the workers. Some 1,500 work stoppages were reported since 1957, yet only tacitly acknowledged and hardly explained in the context of the system. As a result of the consultations which followed, such work stoppages received a more definite status within the self-management system.

Stoppages usually take place in protest against some particular situation or decision within or, less frequently, outside the enterprise, which has deeply antagonized a group or the whole work collectivity, and where there is little hope of redress by other means. Their main aim is to attract outside attention and intervention (possibly the eviction of those held responsible, e.g. the enterprise director). The specific causes of these work stoppages are lack of work, low prices, dissatisfaction with the share in income, lack of cash and consequent delay in payment for work, particularly where no advance notification had been given (but also to put pressure on a debtor of the enterprise. They hardly ever reflect a direct claim for higher incomes as there is no one against whom such claim could be directed.

Trade Union Congresses take an active stand on major issues: in 1963, for instance, the Fifth National Congress stressed two major claims at variance with the prevailing policy of the enterprises: to drastically reduce the rate of investment with a parallel increase in workers' personal incomes; and more shift work to achieve better use of available capacity. The Sixth Congress (1968) formulated in the strongest possible terms the immediate objective of lowering the pensionable age by five years for all workers (i.e. fifty-five for men and fifty for women).

The option was never taken to transform the unions into a higher level of workers' self-government, even though a close analysis of the records of their more recent Congresses would show a distinct development in this direction. Indeed, the delegates tend mostly to concentrate on reporting on the state and problems of their enterprise or industry and on claiming policy changes which would help to expand (or to arrest a decline, etc.). Investment, taxation, credit policy, exports and other economic issues receive attention at least equal to that given to working conditions and welfare, as they are identical in their object. Even the claim of the Sixth Congress to lower the pensionable age, for which most delegates held imperative mandates from their constituents, was mainly motivated by the need to solve urgent employment problems. A full account of the government's economic policy was demanded by the same Congress and obtained from the Federal Executive Council. While a suggestion to keep the Congress in permanent session was not accepted, the Congress did convene a national conference to review the implementation of its decisions within a period of six months. Definite progress towards a kind of permanent industrial congress seems possible. A more radical solution has subsequently been adopted by the League of Communists in a further effort to reduce the powers of executive bodies. This solution, which may serve as a precedent to other organizations, consists in setting up a permanent conference which meets at appointed times during the year or at any other moment if so required.

The unions' basic organizations remain in existence inside each enterprise

63

as a separate body. It is at this level that it proves most difficult to find a specific and important role for an organization with practically the same constituents as the workers' council yet without definite powers.

In addition to these organizations enjoying some official status, there are a considerable number of *other associations or societies* which are allowed under the general legislation on the right of association. National associations have been formed by several of the traditional industrial craft groups, such as railway machinists and foundry workers, as well as by various technical professions, accountants, economists, etc. Although they do not bargain (collectively or otherwise) with the enterprises, they hold some sort of watching brief on behalf of their members, while maintaining common standards within the profession at the inter-enterprise level.

The two major Christian denominations, Orthodox and Catholic, are quite specific organizations, governed by special legislation, which may through their ideology and social activities influence a section of the public. There are no separate non-religious unofficial groups with a wider impact on the public, although there is a distinct tendency for trends or schools of thought to form around various periodicals, institutes and similar informal patterns of association.

Economic Organizations and Social Research

The worker-managed enterprises are in themselves a form of social organization but with dominant economic objectives. While the members of their work collectivity may affiliate as individuals to the various public and social organizations described above, the enterprises as such may form a variety of organizations of their own. Moreover, they are both engaging in, and are the subject of, a variety of activities which may be loosely defined as 'social research' and which in themselves provide additional organizational links within the economy.

The system of central planning—at least in the form developed in the post-war years—provided all this exclusively through its own administrative structures. The economic ministries and their industrial directorates were the sole spokesmen, the sole mode of organization and the sole framework for applied research for all enterprises within the economy. Their disappearance left an important institutional vacuum which had to be filled.

As regards *organizations of the enterprises*, in the early years the main intention seemed to be to break the existing enterprises down into basic production units, so as to ensure the best possible conditions for a competitive market. Strict rules prohibiting any price agreements or market limitations were introduced and strictly applied by the new economic tribunals. Yet the newly independent enterprises were in great need of joint forums or consultative meetings on foreign trade problems, allocation of scarce currencies and similar matters, and some informal liaisons were initiated shortly after the suppression of the corresponding State bodies. They were the starting point for a great number of voluntary branch organizations to which most enterprises tended to affiliate. Their field of activity expanded rapidly to a wide range of problems of enterprise management and economics, but

64

with varying degrees of intensity and integration in different sectors of the economy. They also provided an important meeting point for management and workers' councils representatives (usually the chairmen) at the industry level. These so-called *occupational associations of enterprises* received full legal status in 1957 and played a growing part in the economic life of the enterprises up to the early sixties, when they were integrated—as special branch councils—into the parallel system of statutory organizations, the Economic Chambers. The most active among them continue in existence despite their lack of formal legal background.

The *Economic Chambers* were set up by legislation in 1957 as an official system of representation of enterprises at regional and national levels, at first separately for the major branches of the economy: industry, commerce, transport, foreign trade, crafts, etc. With obligatory membership and contributions they mustered very considerable resources and developed a variety of joint activities. They participated, along with the trade unions, in all consultative arrangements in the field of planning, social legislation, etc., drew up some of the key documents shaping the behaviour of the enterprises in important policy matters, and developed an important research and publication activity of their own. Later reforms amalgamated these various specialized Chambers into one single organization comprising a hierarchy of regional, republican and federal Economic Chambers. This measure has considerably weakened their direct ties with the membership as well as their practical service activities. The obligatory contributions (membership fees) are often criticized by the enterprises as yet another fiscal measure for which no adequate service is forthcoming in return. The 1968 Annual Conference of the Federal Economic Chamber even refused to examine the draft proposals of its programme and constitutional amendments presented by the Chamber's Executive. The Chambers remain nonetheless one of the principal organized bodies within the State, forming a counterpart to the trade unions, and appear as major initiators of activities, advising on policy and preserving standards of conduct within the economy.

Since 1960 stress was laid on a third, entirely novel, mode of economic organization, first known as integration or co-operation of enterprises, the '*self-organization of the economy*'. This corresponds to the right of the enterprise to enter any kind of economically or socially beneficial combination. No precise definition is possible, for such a combination may serve practically any lawful purpose and take any shape or form: long-term technical co-operation, horizontal or vertical integration arrangements, specialization, group agreements on standards of output or income, joint financing of new ventures, joint entry into foreign markets, solving training or employment problems, integration of university departments or Institutes with groups of enterprises, as well as hundreds of other possibilities. The arrangements may be purely contractual, or take the form of a joint institution, an arbitration tribunal, a delegate conference, etc. The new centre of responsibility—and of income sharing—may be endowed with legal personality and other bodies may join (for instance, the communes or their specialized funds or institutions, the banks, etc.). It is hoped that, through these forms of association, the enterprises will overcome their own narrow definition as separate institutional units and forge ahead in search of new tasks.

In legal theory a new, more general concept tends to supplant that of the enterprise or work organization: the 'organization of associated labour', a term which is also applied to similar looser groupings within the enterprise (the autonomous workshops, etc.). This policy thus aims at loosely-knit constellations or confederacies of work groups, held together not by a complete unity of interest (as in the case of amalgamated enterprises), but through practical but mostly complex communities of purpose. Some of the confederal units' 'workers' parliaments' may even be able to deal with republican governments on an equal footing, and their voice is reported and listened to throughout the country. The early concept of pure market competition is partly lost in the process—but not the market as such.

Autonomous state or regional *banking institutions* appeared in Yugoslavia in the early 'fifties as a necessary element of the system of workers' management. They dealt mainly with the current financial operations of the enterprise, including short-term credit. The overall allocation of long-term investment funds to industries or branches of the economy remained for many years a major instrument of economic planning. For their allocation to individual projects, a system of competitive bidding was experimented with in the early years, but proved impossible to administer. Since 1954 a system of Social Investment Funds has been developed at all levels of government, allocating investment credits according to general criteria set out by the plan. The allocation process remained competitive in that fixed terms were set for various classes of investment projects, but the rate of interest was only one of several allocational criteria, which also included such items as the length of repayment period, participation of the investor, priority to investment projects nearing completion, etc. Representatives of the economy participated with experts in the process of allocating investment funds. The General Investment Fund at the level of the Federation was more important than similar funds at the communal and republican levels. This system met growing criticism, even on technical grounds, in a rapidly expanding and increasingly complex economy. It was, however, particularly resented for political reasons as the last major element of administrative intervention in the economy, particularly unsuited to dealing with the specific needs of regions. The investment Funds were therefore abolished in 1965 and their resources and activities handed over to a reformed system of *business banks*. A limited amount of the General Investment Funds resources were, however, reserved for a new Federal fund for the less developed regions. This fund draws its resources from the interest paid on their basic capital by all enterprises.

Under the new system, all enterprises or other economic organizations (communes, co-operatives, etc.) may freely associate with others in order to found banks, provided that certain minimum conditions are met regarding the number of the founding members (twenty-five or more), and the amount of funds they contribute to the bank's basic capital. Within general limits set by the central monetary authority for maximum and minimum rates of interest, liquidity ratio, etc., the founders freely determine the general policy of their bank. The actual decision making is entrusted to a credit committee and to the director, who is appointed according to the general procedure governing all enterprises. All matters concerning the organization and procedures of the bank are regulated by the constitution of the bank, drawn up by the founders. Voting rights are proportionate to contributions to the bank's capital, up to a maximum of ten per cent of the total votes. The staff also participate in the bank's assembly within the same limits, and share the bank's net income with the founders.

The bank thus represents a specific type of business organization of the associated work communities and its own employees. Several hundred business banks have been created under these provisions but their number has rapidly decreased to less than a hundred. Each is entitled to operate all over Yugoslavia. If dissatisfied, the founding members may affiliate to another bank. Nor are they prevented from doing business with banks other than the one they have founded. A distinct climate of inter-bank competition has thereby been achieved. As indicated earlier, each enterprise must have one main current account, through which all movements of funds must be cleared.

In addition to the National Bank of Yugoslavia, which has overall control of credit and currency, three specialized banks have been set up under federal legislation: the Investment Bank, the Bank for Foreign Trade, and the Agricultural Bank. These too are open to relevant major enterprises, to which they channel major policy measures, either directly or through the business banks.

The new scheme brought about wide decentralization and differentiation in the area of credit and financial policy generally. It brought a new dimension to the activities and interests of each enterprise or organization, while creating an entirely new class of business organization. It is too recent and not yet stabilized enough to allow for any general evaluation or comment. As business concerns, the banks were certainly successful in the first three years of operation, to the point where strong criticism was voiced against the rapidly rising incomes of their employees. Along with some other branches where personal incomes rose out of reasonable proportions (such as foreign trade, lotteries, economic chambers, electricity generating), a temporary ceiling on personal incomes in banking was imposed by the Federation in the autumn of 1967; the lifting of this restriction being made conditional on the enterprises concerned finding themselves more suitable criteria for income distribution in line with the general objectives of the system of workers' management. For banks, the possibility of relating the cash incomes of employees to those of the work collectivities they service has been among the suggested solutions. In December 1968, all but thirteen of the existing business banks entered into such a 'self-regulating' agreement on income distribution which has been approved by the Federal Executive Council.

A more fundamental criticism is that the banks continue to administer a sizeable proportion of national income which, although created by the enterprises, is not directly at their disposal. While it is difficult to imagine a system where each enterprise would be its own exclusive banker, it would seem that the multi-enterprise schemes of self-organization, referred to earlier, tend to centre increasingly on joint and reciprocal financial arrangements, which by-pass the banking system and remain under the direct control of the participating enterprises.

On the whole, it would seem that the banking and credit system has not yet found its final shape and it certainly remains a major problem. It nevertheless allows circulation of funds and is not mentioned as a major cause of difficulties.

There is a constant complaint, however, by the spokesmen of the less developed regions that the banks have not ensured sufficient flow of capital to finance development projects even under comparatively more attractive conditions of profitability. While a certain regionalization of capital allocation has certainly been the result (and partly the objective) of the new banking system, particularly in the first years of its existence when both experience and capital resources were limited, the banking system cannot by itself solve the problems of the underdeveloped areas which require other sources of financing. The contribution of the Federal Fund for development is an essential one, but its resources were not fully used during the initial period, and are probably not sufficient to meet all urgent requirements.

Research in general, including social sciences, economics and technology, provides yet another link between enterprises. With the minor exception of the State Academies, all applied research was formerly provided for within the planning system. The disappearance of this administrative planning structure led to the formation of many research institutes. At first their main purpose was to assist the various State bodies, now deprived of the support of the massive officialdom. To help the isolated enterprises in their struggle for institutional development, and progress in technology and management practices, was their second major objective. Consequently, during the earlier period, the State budget was their main source of finance.

Major institutes were formed in nearly all possible fields of enquiry we are concerned with: economic and social sciences generally, management training and productivity, industrial economics, investment, foreign trade, mining, market research, industrial and urban development, as well as a wide range of specific techniques or branches of the economy. Until quite recently, however, labour and employment problems were largely neglected, and only two minor institutes dealt specifically with problems of workers' and local self-government.

In recent years these institutes came under public criticism as one more remnant of an administrative system. Limitation or suppression of budgetary financing was generally agreed to be the sole means of helping the researchers to establish true co-operation with the real world and to respond to the concrete needs of the economy and of society as a whole. In other words the various research institutes or other centres were to earn their own keep through co-operating with the enterprises and other bodies. This development is now fairly advanced, the enterprises providing over three-quarters of all their funds.

Their influence on general policy is quite considerable. So far, however, the content of their activities does not seem fully adapted to the special characteristics and needs of the self-management system, particularly in the social sciences. As they had to develop their activity on their own, against the background of little or no domestic tradition, with few if any specialized staff, some have tended to remain in the more secure waters of abstract theory or legalistic argument and commentary within their narrowly defined disciplines. Others, certainly the majority, opened wide the doors to foreign experience, taking advantage of any help that offered itself in terms of available methodology, scientific exchanges, scholarships, etc. This predominantly Western influence—partly a by-product of indispensable economic assistance—led to over-specialization, mostly in mechnical techniques largely irrelevant or ill-adapted to the self-management system. Gallup poll techniques, with very little testing, were largely identified with sociology. Far-fetched mathematical formulae were frequently introduced into all social sciences, including economics, without any test of the applicability of the underlying hypotheses to the special world of workers' self-government. Empirical investigation of the real world at home in all its complexity has hardly begun, and a really creative contribution has not yet emerged in the work of most of the Institutes. This also partly applies to the technological institutes which have, in most cases deliberately, concentrated on applied research. Hence, despite individual exceptions, the difficulty of communication with enterprises remains quite considerable, and the 'mechanical introduction' of foreign methods and experiences is often deeply resented.

Economic Policy and Planning, 1950–68
Within the context of the self-management system, the basic purpose of the various organizations and institutions referred to so far consists of co-operating with the enterprises in shaping general policies above the level of the enterprise. In as much as such policies are co-ordinated with a view to attaining definite social and economic objectives and include corresponding implementation provisions, they may be referred to as economic and social planning.

The institutional framework of the policy or plan formulation is the complex range of organizations and institutions briefly reviewed in the first part of this chapter. However, the actual behaviour of the enterprises could not be understood and evaluated unless at least the most essential data are provided concerning the concrete content of the policies and planning instruments introduced since 1950 in order to adapt the economic system to the objectives of workers' management.

As already suggested, the general trend throughout this period was to move away from all forms, or even residual elements, of centralized administrative planning and direct State intervention in the economy, while developing a complex set of financial and fiscal instruments which would respect the basic autonomy and equality of each individual enterprise, but which would none the less make them all, as an aggregate, adopt policies or patterns of behaviour in line with social objectives outlined by the plan or other general policy statements. In recent years even this method of indirect planning has been left at rest, as a growing number of such instruments were made inoperative, or stabilized.

This progression took place by leaps, by major transformations of policies and instruments, usually geared to the same date as the beginning of a new stage or, as it is usually termed in Yugoslavia, an economic reform or a new socio-economic model. Six or seven such stages or models may be distinguished in the period 1950–68.

(i) *The central planning model* was preserved until the end of 1951, while far-reaching administrative reorganizations and simplifications were paving the way for the suppression of all State bodies and offices entrusted with direct management of the economy (*inter alia* some two hundred ministries and other industrial directorates). This was a period of trial run and experiment for the newly formed workers' councils. They bore no real economic responsibility since, whatever their income or losses, the financial results of the enterprises were cleared through the State budget. The workers continued to receive a fixed wage (whether by time worked or according to output) as provided for under appropriate plan-based regulations. Except for an irrational system of output norms and bonuses (for there were no objective criteria for their determination, nor was anyone materially interested in seeing them objectively determined), the system allowed for no direct material interest of the workers or managers in the efficient operation of the enterprise but rested essentially on their moral commitment. The corresponding merits of central planning have already been referred to. It made it possible to make rapidly at the centre the basic choices regarding the overall direction and rates of development, to set a first basis for further industrialization and to mobilize national resources for the implementation of the planned objectives. Its one lasting feature was the categorization of all jobs according to qualification and skill.

(ii) *The system of Accumulation and Funds,* as it was commonly called, operated in 1952 and 1953; it represented the most radical change in the history of the Yugoslav enterprise (and perhaps of public enterprise generally) for it freed the latter from all major administrative controls in order to make it work and manage its business as best it could on its own. The only planned instruments were the rate of capacity utilization and a progressive levy (partly designed for purposes of self-financing) on the enterprise income.

The rate of levy was highly differentiated from industry to industry (according to its earning capacity, the planners' preferences and the expected level of market price equilibrium), but identical for all enterprises of the same industry.

The differentiation of the rates was quite unprecedented in fiscal history, reflecting the conditions of extreme penury prevailing at the time. It ranged from 40 per cent (shipbuilding) to 2,782 per cent (copper sheet and wire drawing). A tax free minimum of 9,000 dinars per worker (later differentiated into four separate minima according to qualifications) was soon introduced with a new progression in the rates of the levy.[1]

Tax rates were mostly very high, yet the basic principle was there: whatever the enterprise earned (after tax) was its own, to be disposed of as its workers and their councils saw fit. In other words, the collective wage fund of each enterprise was defined in relation to its net income of pre-set criteria without any fixed rate or limit either on the volume of employment or on any particular worker's wage. The workers' councils set their own rates for sharing out the wage fund among members of the work collectivity. The wage fund of each enterprise was formed according to the following simple formula:

$$\text{W.F.} = \frac{\text{Net Income}}{1 + R \text{ (rate of levy} - \text{accumulation and funds)}}$$

This was also a time of real price revolution: prices were seeking their market levels. Some of the basic commodities kept cheap by the planners' choice (such as coal), rocketed to tenfold their earlier price levels, while on average they tended to pass the 300 per cent mark. The self-managing enterprise was for the first time, and for a short period, allowed to show its aptitude for rational behaviour in adapting its policies to real requirements in other areas such as production, remuneration systems and, particularly, employment, involving changes of a similar magnitude. The difficulties arising out of such a buoyant transformation of all established habits and relationships were somewhat alleviated by the scarcity of nearly all goods and the corresponding possibilities of rapidly redeploying both capital resources and staff, including those liberated by the State administrations, trade unions and other similar bodies.

However, the single progressive levy actually imposed on labour, or rather on the surplus income per worker, showed major deficiencies, causing severe inequalities among the enterprises. In 1953 its rate had to be fixed individually for each enterprise which meant a clear departure from the principle of fiscal equality of enterprises. Nevertheless, this period brought to light, more clearly than anyone had expected, that the works collectivities were well able and indeed eager to manage their own business and could do so with efficiency provided that they were able to work within an adequate fiscal and financial environment.

(iii) *The Period of Transition* from 1954 to 1956 showed further elaboration of the system, through a continuous succession of reforms and the introduction of more complex instruments. Because of the main feature of its remuneration system, it is usually called the period of *accounting wages and profit-sharing*. Each enterprise retained for its workers a basic (accounting) wage fund proportionate to their numbers and qualification levels (valued uniformity for all at 6,000, 7,000, 8,800 and 12,000 respectively for non-qualified, semi-qualified, qualified and highly qualified workers). This basic

---

[1] For a more detailed account, and some examples of the corresponding fiscal tables, cf. *Industry and Labour*, I.L.O., Geneva, 15 September 1952, pp. 281–4.

wage fund was part of the enterprise costs. It also retained a fixed proportion (e.g. 50 per cent) of any surplus or profit, but the use of the latter for wage payment was strictly limited and subject to a fixed ceiling. The enterprise remained largely free to distribute the available monies according to its own rules. Nevertheless, the system clearly implied a retrogression compared with the earlier, in principle unlimited—although heavily taxed—income distribution model. The 'surplus' distributed to workers averaged 10 to 20 per cent, a comparatively minor incentive, while the actual interest of the enterprise lay mostly (as under the planning system) in inflating the basic accounting wage costs (*inter alia* through excess employment), and implementing of low standards for individual norms of output and over-generous bonus schemes. The capacity of the enterprise to react promptly to any change in fiscal policy (including all loopholes left open) may be accepted as an established fact since that period. Negative as it may appear in a given context, it also points to its ability to react to even minor changes in its general business environment.

During this same period, major instruments of indirect planning or fiscal guidance were taking shape. The interest payment on both the basic and the circulating capital of each enterprise was more uniformly regulated, as were the rates and procedures governing depreciation, inventories and so on. The turnover (or purchase) tax—widely differentiated—was more actively used for production guidance and containment of excess demand. After a negative experiment with the allocation of investment capital by way of open auctions, a mixed system of investment financing was gradually perfected in which self-financing became a permanent feature, but was complemented by additional loans or grants from public investment funds. On the whole this was a period of comparatively slow growth, where a mass of new and mostly unprecedented concepts and practices was gradually introduced and 'digested' throughout the economy, at what amounts to a breathtaking pace of adaptation and change. During these years a great number of major development projects were also being completed which were to bear fruit during the following years.

(iv) *The first period of relatively free income distribution* (1957–60). As the complex fiscal and financial instruments of indirect planning acquired more definite shape, with a relative stability implying their active use for current policy guidance, the enterprises regained wide autonomy concerning their right to dispose of and to share out their income. Following a year of transition (1957) no definite limit was imposed on the amount which, out of its earned net income, the enterprise could distribute as remuneration or allocate to other purposes (welfare, investment, etc.) provided it followed certain complex procedures involving the active participation of the commune. The concept of a 'surplus' income (or profit) was partly preserved, since the earlier 'accounting wage rates' were retained as minimum tax free incomes, while any surplus was subject to a new progressive income tax, the rates of which were uniform throughout the economy. The rates of the tax progressed rapidly according to a sliding scale but reached a definite maximum at

70 per cent (for distributed incomes over and above twice the minimum) with significant rebates for increased volume of production. Even at the highest levels of income, the enterprise could reckon on a share of no less than 30 per cent of its additional net income (plus possible tax rebates).

The reaction of the enterprises and of the economy was positive. Production, employment and productivity progressed at a rapid pace, regularly well ahead of planned targets. The progressive tax on surplus income had the great virtue of making expansion, both of employment and of capital assets, less costly for the more efficient enterprises, thereby providing automatic guidance for development and growth which enhanced general productivity. The enterprises did not fail to grasp the opportunity. They proved the system's ability to attain unexpectedly high rates of growth—well over 10 per cent annually—during a prolonged period and in conditions of relative price stability.

During this period the enterprises also used their new economic freedom to engage in wider experiments in internal distribution of incomes. Numerous innovations were introduced aimed at achieving a more direct link between the enterprise income and the individual worker; a systematic job evaluation was completed in many enterprises. The most important and lasting among such initiatives was the effort of a small but growing number of enterprises which aimed at decentralizing the income distribution process, so that income would be formed and shared out within smaller groups. The so-called 'economic units' (workshops, departments, etc.) were accordingly endowed with a measure of self-management autonomy.

Despite continuing rapid rates of progress in all areas, this early income distribution system raised growing criticism on a variety of counts. It contained major 'administrative' features inherited from the earlier period both in its procedures (particularly the assent of the commune to income distribution rules) and its content (the minimum *wages* as the basis of personal income). These had an inhibiting effect on the enterprises' independent experimentation with their own system building and decision making generally. The progressive tax on enterprise income was criticized for imposing too great a burden on the more developed areas where most of the enterprises with high per capita incomes were located; for inhibiting the initiative and growth of the most profitable enterprises (subject to the highest rates of taxation); and for encouraging extensive growth of production and employment rather than productivity and quality of product. The rapid growth during that period also generated various imbalances in foreign trade and required ever widening administrative intervention in this area. Full income autonomy of the enterprises was therefore attempted in 1961, through a complex of changes, now called the 'small reform'.

(v) *A fully autonomous income distribution system* was introduced on 1 January 1961 and opened a new transitional period of rapid change which was to last until mid-1965. The most striking change was the replacement of the progressive tax on excess (or surplus) income by a tax levied on the whole income at a single flat rate (15 per cent initially). At the same time, the enterprise was granted full independence in establishing its internal rules for income distribution and taking corresponding decisions. No trace was left of the earlier duality of basic wage (or income) and the 'surplus', the enterprise having a single bulk sum at its disposal—the net income after tax—to share out as remuneration for work or for other purposes.

The new system led to the desired changes in two main areas: the redistribution of income in favour of the more advanced regions and profitable enterprises was automatic; and the reaction of the enterprises in increasing productivity was as rapid as could be expected. Yet several major difficulties arose in consequence: the rate of growth was substantially reduced, as was the rate of increase of employment; and the already widening differentiation of income levels between the more and the less profitable enterprises was reaching insufferable, although not entirely unexpected, proportions.

It appeared that the reduction of the tax burden did not provide the expected incentive to the high income enterprises, for it actually meant a windfall gain for most of them, which they were unable to share out among their workers who already enjoyed above average income. Where such distribution was attempted, it was widely criticized as socially unjustifiable and brought to a halt by administrative intervention. The natural tendency of the leading enterprises was therefore to work the additional monies into their costs as far as possible, while proceeding with the greatest caution in liberalizing their distribution policies.

On the other side of the spectrum, in the marginal enterprises, the new linear tax imposed an additional financial burden which often acted as a brake on production. But, contrary to the expectations of there form 'economists', it proved impossible to liquidate *en masse* such marginal firms, not only for obvious political and social reasons, but for economic and technical considerations as well. The State bodies and the banks were obliged to yield to the mounting pressure for tax exemptions, subsidies and/or short-term credit, and found themselves rapidly involved in a general rescue and growth promotion operation which brought utter confusion to the streamlined objectivity of the system. The operation was successful in so far as it brought about the highest ever rates of growth (16 per cent at constant prices for industry both in 1963 and 1964), but it also caused unprecedented inflationary pressures (including on producers' prices for the first time), and a serious set-back in the balance of foreign trade. This in turn generated a rapidly growing propensity to invest in most enterprises which also appeared to be out of control. A national campaign by the trade unions and other bodies to reduce investment—and to channel funds into personal incomes and consumption—significantly elicited no response from the workers' councils at this time.

Yet, this period is deeply imprinted on the memory of the enterprises as a very significant experience. They showed once again, but at an incomparably higher level of development and sophistication than in 1953, their ability to cope with unforeseeable changes of the greatest magnitude, not only without serious damage to themselves, but also achieving a true leap forward in production, employment and productivity. In the three years 1962–5 industrial production alone rose by 45 per cent (at constant prices), employment and productivity increases contributing in approximately equal shares to this result. Growth rates of much greater magnitude were attained by individual enterprises.

While largely lost from public sight and supervision behind the bouncing screen of the general economic situation, the developing of internal mechanisms of decentralized income distribution was actively pursued in the enterprises. They were not responsible for the general débâcle of financial and monetary policy but it cast a new discredit on all administrative intervention in the economy. Neither was any systematic planning or even indirect guidance of the economy able to survive these events. Remedies were sought and applied with great urgency and boldness, mainly in the area of financial and monetary policy, forming part of a much more ambitious complex of measures called the 'Economic and Social Reform'.

(vi) *The Reform of 1965* (operative date 1st July) had as its immediate economic objective the stabilization of the economy and bringing about of such qualitative changes as to permit the full inclusion of Yugoslavia in world markets. While the enterprise already enjoyed full economic autonomy from a formal or legal viewpoint, it was resolved to make it the only dominant force in the economy too, through the volume of funds at its direct command. This objective was partly covered by the changes in the investment and banking systems referred to earlier.

The measures taken were many and manifold, yet they all aimed at creating a stable economic environment for the enterprise rather than inducing it to adopt any definite policy. Their global impact was manifestly one of a rigorous deflationary and restrictive policy in financial and monetary matters. The Federation and, for the most part, the Republics and communes were stripped not only of legal powers but also of most of the means or funds which were at their disposal for purposes of economic intervention and development generally.

The major short-term measures included:

(i) A severe devaluation of the currency and the introduction of a single exchange rate of the new dinar (replacing one hundred former units).

(ii) A review of all former price levels with a view to improving the position of formerly handicapped sectors, particularly where price controls prevailed, and an adaption to world prices; a considerable leap in all the price indices resulted. The usually stable producers' prices in industry—already under inflationary pressure in 1963 and 1964—rose by 15 per cent in 1963 and an additional 10 per cent in 1966 before acquiring a new stability. Retail prices as well as the cost of living indices showed considerably greater increases during the same period (well over 50 per cent) as did the personal incomes of workers in money terms (over 100 per cent). On the whole, a completely new set of prices and income relationships was created in all areas of economic activity.

    (iii) A severe reduction of import duites, the tariff protection of domestic producers being brought down below the levels applied in most other countries, accompanied by a full liberalization of foreign trade generally.

    (iv) Suppression, or at least significant reduction, of all other indirect subsidies or preferential clauses, with a view to insuring the greatest possible equality of all enterprises in relation not only to domestic but also to international markets.

    (v) The basis for direct taxation was no longer the total net income of the enterprise but only the portion thereof which the enterprise distributed in the form of personal incomes to its workers. A flat rate—in the region of 25 to 30 per cent—remained applicable. In other words, it is the remuneration for labour that bears a major portion of all fiscal levies; if social security and similar contributions are added, the total charges on the net workers' income amount to over 60 per cent. All temporary restrictions or controls over the free distribution of incomes by the enterprises were lifted.

The overall financial and monetary objectives of the Reform were on the whole attained. The exchange rate of the new dinar was largely stabilized and conditions for free international trade became operative.[1] The pressure on the enterprises in the area of quality, presentation, technical progress and commercial adaptability brought visible results. The part of newly created income left at the free disposal of the enterprises (as opposed to that administered by the State and other outside bodies) increased significantly and the comparative position of some essential sectors which had lagged behind in the past (agriculture and raw materials in particular) improved considerably.

In principle, all tariffs were brought down below the maximum of 20 per cent (automobiles were the only major exception) to make an average of approximately 10 per cent. As compared with earlier highly protective tariffs (and highly differentiated exchange rates to promote exports), the new system placed the enterprises on a nearly equal footing in external trade relations while widely opening the economy to international competition (as well as to dumping practices in view of the relative inflexibility of the new tariffs). The impact of such a major and sudden change was truly shattering for most industries.

However, the economic costs of the Reform were considerable, and increased with time. The differentiation in income between sectors and individual enterprises widened strikingly, some of the key industries (such as the metal trade, and particularly machine tools) experienced great difficulties, while windfall benefits accrued to others, often in the non-productive sector. Investment demand fell drastically under the impact of credit restriction and reduced consumers' demand. The general rate of growth consequently

---

[1] The new dinar is often regarded as a hard or convertible currency, particularly by the Comecon countries; there is however no free transfer of capital (as distinct from payments for trade purposes), and Yugoslav tourists are entitled only to a limited amount of foreign exchange under a strict yearly quota.

reached the lowest recorded figures and because of a continuing rise in productivity, a net fall in employment was recorded for the first time in 1967. This brought about a phenomenal increase in private savings by those employed, enjoying higher incomes but less employment security, and a more restrictive credit policy by the newly decentralized banks. The enterprises found it difficult to define their policy in the face of drastic and sudden changes in most areas, and in the absence of even an indicative plan for guidance. The lack of flexibility of financial and fiscal policy instruments—which could not be modified except by legislation—caused considerable delays where urgent measures were required. (Lack of protection against the growing practice of the dumping of foreign goods, and of sufficient credits for export industries to compete abroad on an equal footing were two of the long-standing major grievances of the economy.) Both the sub-marginal and the most profitable enterprises could only display apparently irrational patterns of behaviour, facing the determined withdrawal of the State from active economic policy and intervention, with no alternative self-governing framework ready to take its place. Contrary to the expectations of some economists, it again proved nearly impossible to liquidate the sub-marginal enterprises, while some of those enjoying boom conditions displayed an inordinate lack of self-discipline in income distribution. The resulting income differences gave rise to increasing public protest.

Yet, although the self-managing enterprises had so far proved able to cope adequately by themselves with employment problems—absorbing and training not only the additional labour force but also some of the rural surplus—it was in this area that the deflationary stabilization policy met with massive problems which proved insoluble in the short run. There were no previous methods or rules available by which to regulate levels of employment, training and retraining, or the entry into employment of newly trained apprentices, students or of young untrained workers. Although several hundred thousand workers were able to emigrate, mostly to Western Europe, while the number of new job seekers reached a post-war low,[1] the 'spectre' of an estimated army of one million unemployed in the early seventies began to overshadow all other results of the Reform by the end of 1967 and early 1968.

Possible anticyclical measures to revive economic activity began to be envisaged during the spring of 1968, both within the federal legislature and executive bodies, as well as at academic meetings—although with little reference so far to employment—and some moves were made to fill major loopholes, as in the case of dumping or export credits. Nevertheless the economy, composed of self-managing enterprises, was unable to put its case

---

[1] 99 thousand in 1966 compared with 186 thousand in 1969 and a predicted 235 thousand in 1975. This is one more example of the most drastic changes linked to historical or material conditions which loom behind each corner of economic policy making in Yugoslavia, are impossible to cope with by means of current policy and yet are not even perceived in advance by central planning bodies. These figures are based on an 'outsider's' voluntary contribution to a symposium on employment organized by the Society of Serbian Economists, dealing with 'investment as a possible means to reduce employment', a theme for which no 'competent expert' was available in early 1968 (cf. *Ekonomska Misao*, No. 2, June 1968, p. 303).

forcefully enough to change the built-in inflexibility of what may be termed an 'ultra-liberal' or 'pre-Keynesian' set of policies.

We were personally able to witness the desperate efforts of some to state their case and the self-imposed silence of most spokesmen of enterprises when they were losing all hope of convincing the representatives of central State agencies and of 'economic science' whom they faced at various national meetings and conferences. In the prevailing climate of the time, the latter were certain to carry the day. Even the word 'Keynesian' was used as name-calling by protagonists of 'pure' liberal economics. This was largely due to the wide acceptance of the Reform thoughout the country in view both of its liberalizing character in the political sphere and the numerous economic advances it promised and effectively brought about in terms of standard of living, and the quality of goods and services, including the wide availability of imported consumer goods. Wide sections of the public were ready to cope with temporary problems for the sake of more long-term advances on a wider front; many indeed benefited directly in material terms. While those who faced the greatest difficulties obviously lacked the time and means to state their case adequately, it would be wrong to infer from this that their point of view was not always reflected through various communication media, sometimes with a most forceful urgency.

This time, contrary to all precedents, the change came unplanned, overnight, as a result of student protest, particularly in the Federal capital. Although derived from a minor incident, the students' grievances which, characteristically, were addressed mainly to the 'Party' and to its Chairman and President of the Republic, brought to light the major weaknesses of the economic policies being pursued. The absence of open support by the workers and their enterprises was noted by many observers, yet the official reaction which amounted to a full change of economic policy points clearly to wide and popular demands extending well beyond the student body. It is true, however, that the situation could not be felt as deeply in a great number of enterprises where incomes were reaching record levels. Both the League of Communists and President Tito reacted promptly to the events and the resulting Directives of the League's Presidium became a charter of a new growth and employment-oriented general policy. These were also largely taken up by the sixth Trade Union Congress meeting at that time.

Although no new economic 'model' was contemplated, and the general objectives of the Reform remained operative, the Directives deeply transformed the economic climate and the approach to economic problems. In essence, they were an appeal to all public bodies to make a more active use of their constitutional powers to ensure a more balanced and rapid implementation of the major economic goals of the system: economic growth, full employment, and equality of opportunity. Practical experience has shown that these cannot be attained merely by rigidly relying on a set of immutable instruments, conceived as non-discriminatory because of their linear shaping, yet for that very reason severely discriminatory, as well as inhibiting development. The need for solidarity and closer co-operation and understanding as well as economic criteria was widely recognized as forming an essential part, not only of political stability but of the economic performance of the system as well. It is important to realize that this conclusion was derived not from abstract model building but from concrete practice.

The measures taken until the end of 1968 remained formally well within the existing 'model', but included major quantitative changes in financial policy, such as a wide relaxation of consumers' credit, export credit facilities and financial coverage for major long-term modernization projects in essential public services such as the railways and telephone systems. Unexpected and very large public expenditures due to military tension in the area further helped to give new swing to the economy by the end of 1968. Additional resources were also deployed for the purpose of retraining and manpower development. 'System-wise', however, only one major step was in this area, obliging the enterprises to review their needs for and to adopt rules governing the recruitment of highly-qualified school-leavers and university students as trainees.

In a medium and long-term perspective, the return to sustained higher rates of growth would seem to depend, in the view of the enterprises in most sectors, on the elaboration of consistent development perspectives or programmes, either through the existing constitutional bodies or through arrangements devised by the enterprises themselves through their efforts at 'self-organization' and 'self-contracting' referred to earlier. The energy, transport and building industries, together with sectors such as the metal trades or textiles, are all in dire need of this perspective policy. Just as urgent is the call for a global solution of the employment problem.

It is impossible to predict whether 15 June 1968 or 1 January 1969 will appear as operative dates of a new socio-economic model. Nor is it possible to anticipate possible solutions for the problems which appear most urgent. Future analysts may show that while all eyes were glued to the dangers of bureaucracy, the self-management system was actually escaping at that time another, perhaps more lethal menace, that of the reign of a scientific intelligentsia, of a hierarchy of real or pretended scientists and scholars, once termed the most despotic, arrogant and contemptuous of all possible ruling elites. *Quién sabe?* Undoubtedly, however, a fresh influence was brought to bear by the young generation, brought up on the humanistic ideals of self-government and striving to see them implemented.

To sum up, during their eighteen years of existence the Yugoslav firm and its workers' councils have accomplished a long tour through a labyrinth of economic models and policies of all kinds, which has taught them many lessons. They certainly proved able to leap or lie quiet as required by circumstances, yet not always as they were told or expected to. No one could pretend to sit in judgment over their performance at any particular time, in view of the inextricable complexity of their particular history and material circumstances, combined with a constant change of policy, environment, and their own subjective aims and preferences. They have certainly failed so far to take their full share in the modelling of their environmental policies and programmes for they first had to look after and nurture their own internal growth and development as social institutions and as economic agents and

79

Table II

Aggregate Behaviour of the Yugoslav Economy 1952–68: Production and Employment by Major Sectors; Employment Prices and Incomes

A. NUMERICAL INDICES

	1952	1957	1959	1960	1961	1962	1963	1964	1965	1966	1967	1968
1. Production indices												
(outside agriculture)	—	—	61	70	74	77	87	100	105	107	106	112
Industry	24	47	56	65	70	75	86	100	108	113	112	119
Construction	—	—	64	75	81	82	91	100	89	85	90	—
Transport	32	—	66	79	82	86	93	100	108	113	117	123
Retail trade	24	—	59	66	74	78	88	100	105	111	119	127
Agriculture	43	—	95	86	83	86	95	100	91	106	105	101
2. Employment												
(a) Total (in millions)	1·7	2·4	2·7	3·0	3·2	3·3	3·4	3·6	3·7	3·6	3·6	3·6
(b) Enterprises (all)	1·4	2·0	2·3	2·5	2·7	2·8	2·8	3·0	3·0	3·0	3·0	3·0
Industry	0·6	0·9	0·9	1·0	1·1	1·1	1·2	1·2	1·3	1·4	1·3	1·4
3. Prices indices												
(a) Producers—Industry	86	89	89	91	94	95	95	100	115	128	131	131
—Agriculture	—	—	53	57	66	73	81	100	143	166	161	154
—Construction	—	—	55	63	78	81	86	100	121	150	161	—
(b) Retail—Industrial goods	80	82	81	83	87	92	94	100	125	153	165	171
—Agricultural	37	50	53	59	66	77	85	100	144	176	180	183
—Services	29	—	53	74	82	87	91	100	130	164	186	206
4. Incomes (1,000 million dinars)												
(a) National income total,												
—in current prices	8·51	18·3	22·7	26·9	31·1	34·7	42·0	55·9	73·6	91·8	—	—
—in constant prices (1960)	—	21·0	25·3	26·8	28·3	29·5	33·1	37·3	38·5	41·8	—	—
Industry	—	8·2	10·2	11·6	12·4	13·3	15·4	17·9	19·3	20·6	—	—
(b) Personal incomes indices (monthly averages)												
—nominal earning	25	—	49	56	61	67	79	100	138	191	217	238
—real earnings	52	—	75	79	79	79	88	100	102	116	123	128

Table II

(a) Total Production, Industry, Construction[1]
(Chain Indices)

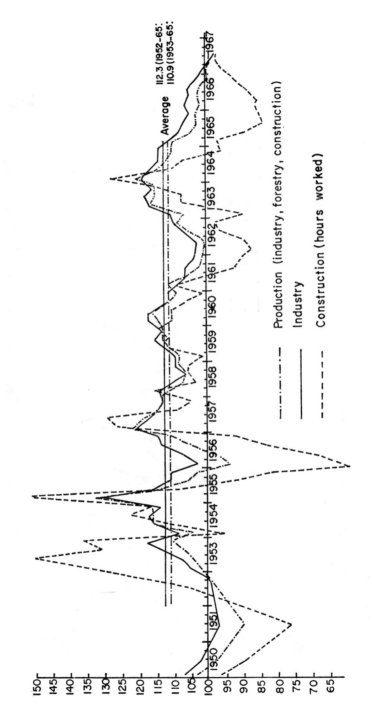

Production (industry, forestry, construction)

Industry

Construction (hours worked)

[1] See footnote overleaf.

Table II B. (*Continued*)

(b) *Industrial Production, Employment and Labour Productivity*[1]
(*Chain Indices*)

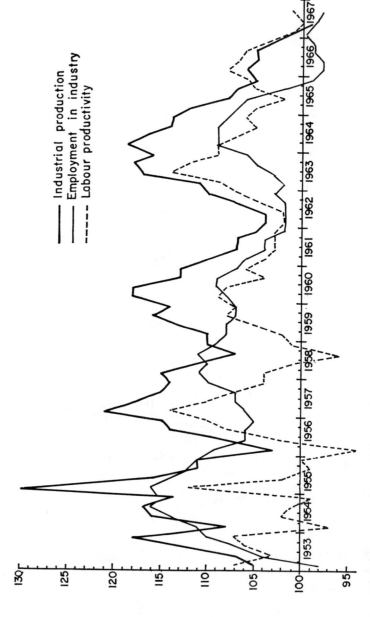

Industrial production
Employment in industry
Labour productivity

[1] According to B. Horvat, *op. cit.*, pp. 9 and 11. Original titles: Table (a) 'Economic Cycles in Yugoslavia'; (b) 'Cycles of Industrial Production, Employment and Productivity'.

self-contained centres of productive activity. Their particular failure may be considered as serious, indeed menacing, in the long run, yet it is not irredeemable, for they certainly managed to assert fully their individual existence and at this level performed on the whole beyond all reasonable expectation. One can hardly think of another form of enterprise which would be able to face up to a kaleidoscopic succession of drastic changes, only partly recorded in this section, to adapt to it and to still continue to produce and to develop. While no summary review can be given of the plan and policy instruments in force over the years, the resulting aggregate behaviour and performance of the enterprises are partly summed up in Tables II A and B.

To avoid misunderstanding, a complementary remark concerning *economic planning* is required. Clearly, the economic model developed in the sixties left very little room for even the most indirect and indicative forms of planning. Indeed, all formal planning activity was for a time abandoned after the 1965 Reform (taking planning to include instruments for implementation of targets, as well as research and forecasting). Rather than an outright rejection of the very principle of planning, this development reflected the failure of a particular method and institutional set-up at a particular time.

This failure may be briefly explained as follows: rapid and steady growth in the late fifties brought the economy to a new level of development and complexity, where earlier simple methods of forecasting and indirect planning were no more applicable. The changes resulting from the 1961 reform made the behaviour of the economy even more unpredictable and a series of wrong forecasts (gross under- and over-estimates of the rate of growth, etc.) brought existing methods into discredit; the five-year plan then in operation (1961–5) was officially abandoned. The inordinately high rates of growth in 1963 and 1964 made consumers' as well as investors' behaviour totally unpredictable in view of drastic changes in demand patterns (sometimes skipping a whole stage in the 'normal' progress of technology). The 1965 Reform was followed by the adoption of a development plan for 1966–70 which was essentially no more than a forecast, offering no real guidance to the economy. It also proved largely erroneous. On the whole it is the lack of knowledge of the possible reactions of the economy (in other words of the behaviour of enterprises and of consumers when faced with changing policies or conditions), and the absence of an adequate institutional relationship between the enterprises and the planning bodies at higher levels, which seem to have been the main causes of past difficulties.

Planned guidance of the economy remains one of the key principles of the Yugoslav Constitution, and the necessity of finding an adequate methodology is felt with growing urgency.

CHAPTER IV

The Worker-Managed Enterprise as an Institution

In the present chapter the enterprise will be presented from an institutional angle while its *modus operandi,* and particularly the planning and income distribution process, will be dealt with in the following chapter.

The Yugoslav worker-managed enterprise has only very little in common with the concept of private or public enterprise of the Western countries or with that developed under Soviet central planning, although it clearly developed from the latter. Its two main distinctive features are that it is a public corporate body and that it finds within itself both the motivation for action and the corresponding decision-making structure. It is not a mere technical unit under the command of outside owners or authority. A combination of self-governing commune and producers' co-operative would seem to provide the closest analogy. It certainly represents a phenomenon of extraordinary complexity.

For our purposes, it is essential to recall here at least two major aspects of the Yugoslav firm:

(i) its legal status and internal structure, and
(ii) the actual concrete dimensions of its existence, such as size, specialization, rate of change.

The self-governing enterprise is the basic agent of all economic activity and the only complete form through which such activity may be performed in Yugoslavia. The communes, banks, self-employed craftsmen or peasants are also—each in their own area—basic economic agents, yet their business or entrepreneurial activity is limited in various ways as compared with that of the enterprise. Like most Yugoslav institutions, enterprises are too complex to allow for a formal, even legal definition. The 1965 basic law on enterprises only suggests certain major elements of such a definition in its first article, which reads:

'By freely combining their work on the basis of social assets and self-management, the working people in an enterprise organize and constantly expand production, trade or other economic activities, so as to satisfy their individual and collective interests and the general interests of society.'

Free combination of workers, a self-governing decision-making structure, availability of the necessary productive assets and their social ownership, freedom to engage in productive or other lawful economic activities, the development imperative and the plurality of purpose appear as the major characteristics of the enterprise. The Basic Law contains 298 other articles, and there are several other major pieces of legislation (particularly those governing employment relations, the election of the workers' councils and other management bodies and the management of enterprise assets) which all add new, and often essential, elements to such a definition. The main points may be summed up as follows.

The *work collectivity* comprises all those (and only those) working in the enterprise: manual workers, technicians and managers alike, all enjoying equal rights as members. Within the limits of the law, the collectivity adopts rules and plans, defines the internal structure of the enterprise, elects collective management bodies and appoints individual managers. Wherever possible, the collectivity decides directly on all major issues in a general assembly, by way of referendum or in any other manner as may be provided by the enterprise's own by-laws (statutes).

Except in smaller enterprises (less than seventy workers) a permanent representative body, the *workers' council*, is elected to deal with all policy issues and other items reserved to it by law, the enterprise by-laws or other rules, including appeals against all other decisions. The workers' council comprises at least fifteen but often well up to a hundred members; half of these are elected each year, exclusively from the members of the work collectivity (other than the director of the enterprise). No immediate re-election for a second term is permitted.

Each year the Council elects its executive, the *Management Board*, which deals with current issues of a general nature, as well as specialized boards or committees required by law or the by-laws of the enterprise. Employment, discipline, grievances and suggestions, investment, social services, housing, etc., are commonly reserved to such specialized committees (with a varying degree of decision-making autonomy).

The Workers' Council and the Management Board also appoint all members of higher management. There is a single executive Director (or General Director) of the enterprise, appointed by the workers' council for a four-year term, who may be re-appointed, according to a special statutory procedure. In brief, the selection process is regulated as follows: the conditions to be fulfilled by a candidate are defined by the enterprise by-laws; the vacancy is declared and advertised by the workers' councils; and the applications are examined by a panel, appointed half by the workers' council, half by the commune, which presents to the workers' council the name of one or several candidates. Should the council reject their recommendation, the whole procedure is repeated. The Director directs all current business and implements the decisions of the collective management bodies. He is also legally responsible for the observance of statutory provisions. Accountable to the council, he may be dismissed within his term for bad management or gross incompetence. In principle, the recall of the Director is subject to a procedure similar to that governing his appointment. In practice, however, once a resolution to recall the Director has been approved by the workers' council, it automatically stands as final. In most cases of major conflict, the resignation of the Director would precede (and thereby avoid) the formal vote of no confidence. In the case of a vacancy, the workers' council appoints the interim director.

In enterprises of a certain size, similar self-management bodies are also formed at the level of the various production and administrative units, and the process of decentralization may be repeated again within larger firms. Three tier, and even four tier self-management structures are by no means uncommon. The directors of the lower units are similarly appointed or elected by the work collectivity, or its self-management bodies, without any outside intervention. In a very large firm, several dozen self-management bodies of all kinds and levels, including specialized committees, may operate simultaneously and co-operate in the shaping of production and business activities. Hundreds of people may be directly associated with these activities within a single enterprise. There is a distinct tendency to pass down to the workshops, for direct decision by the workers themselves, as many issues as possible. (In one enterprise, for instance, the monthly share of income reached each workshop in a bulk sum to be shared out or retained as reserve according to the decision of the workers' assemblies.) The general management services (accounting, commercial, etc.) are themselves frequently endowed with self-management bodies and considered as autonomous service activities with their own funds and current income. As far as is compatible with the enterprise's own plans and operations, any such autonomous section may accept outside contracts or commissions and develop its own business and investment policies. Indeed, under a new basic law on enterprise income, which came into force on 1 January 1969, such arrangements, formerly purely internal, and resting on the enterprise by-laws alone, received a full statutory basis as a typical form of work organization. They may be endowed with full legal personality comparable to that of the enterprise itself, and deal independently in their own name with customers and other outside persons and bodies, as well as with other similar units within the enterprise or elsewhere. Moreover, as we have already mentioned, the existing enterprises may themselves combine in similarly larger self-governing units. The earlier model of a single enterprise is thus deeply eroded and gives way to an infinitely more flexible concept of 'autonomous organization of associated labour'.

According to a special enquiry of the Federal Office of Statistics, in 1966 out of 516 enterprises employing 1,000 workers or more, 408 had a two-tier, 69 a three-tier and 5 a four-tier self-management structure, while no decentralized self-management bodies were found in 34 enterprises. The central workers' councils and management boards had 4,228 and 700 permanent committees respectively; workers' councils were elected in a total of 5,480 units, while 1,692 others practised direct decision making by members of the work units. The total membership of these bodies (not counting the direct decision makers at workshop level) amounted to over 120 thousand (with possible overlapping where one person may hold two or more posts).

Detailed breakdowns by region and sectors, as well as information on the skill, formal training, age, etc., of members of such bodies, their chairmen, the enterprise directors, were also made available.[1]

All this amounts to an immensely complex decision-making process for which it is difficult to find an analogy or a precedent. According to most accepted management theories, it should paralyse all decisions, all action. Yet this conclusion is obviously incompatible with Yugoslav experience. There have certainly been cases where internal conflicts led to delays or inefficiency but, on the whole, there are few examples of actual paralysis of decision making within an enterprise. On the contrary, there are very few examples of collectivities as active and action minded as the average Yugoslav firm. There seems no need to prompt the self-management bodies into activity: they meet more often than is legally required, and their agendas are mostly full to bursting. New projects, big or small, are actively pursued in all areas, especially investment, training and social development. Directors often acquire extraordinary authority, others are sacked or not reappointed and internal reorganizations and external co-operative arrangements are continuously under active consideration. The often nearly paranoiac rate of growth (rates of 30 or 50 per cent per annum are not uncommon for an enterprise or sector) would indeed be quite incompatible with inactive or unbusinesslike management. The particular success of foreign trade enterprises and export services generally seem to point in the same direction. Indeed, even the most outspoken critics of other institutional aspects of the Yugoslav system have hardly ever found the self-management bodies in the enterprises dormant or intrinsically inefficient. The extremely prompt reaction of the Yugoslav firm to even minor changes in fiscal or financial policy may be recalled as additional evidence. In nearly all cases the enterprises tend to 'over-react' as compared with what was expected by the law and policy makers.

Some explanations of this apparent 'activism' seem essential for an understanding of the operation of the self-management institutions. First, things appear infinitely less complex when seen from within a particular enterprise, for it does not operate scores of alternative institutional models but only one, its own, which has not been parachuted there by some outside benefactor, but represents the result of years of discussions and experiment, progress and setbacks. Its concrete features are thus largely familiar to the participants and carry very definite names and specific meaning. Written rules and informal models of institutional behaviour have formed with the passage of time and become known in very concrete terms to the members of the work collectivity.

Second, the self-management bodies actually *must* act. The 'must' rests not on some legal obligation to hold meetings at regular intervals, but on the fact that the enterprise cannot make a single move without the proper deliberation or decision of one of its collective management bodies. First of

[1] Cf. Federal Office of Statistics, *Bulletin* No. 492, October 1967. Corresponding but less detailed data are also available for all Yugoslav enterprises in each issue of the Statistical Yearbook.

all, no action is possible unless there are properly approved rules and regulations governing the matter. We have already mentioned the enterprise by-laws, which may be likened to a works' constitution, but an enterprise would normally have a dozen or more other specific rules and regulations (on employment, income sharing, personal incomes, output norms and bonuses, safety and hygiene, and many others including the rules of procedure of its councils and other bodies). Each requires from time to time to be amended, revised or completed. To deal with any new phenomenon, a general ruling by the workers' council is usually required, failing which an action may be void of legal effect and cause considerable financial damage or outlays.

An example at hand—among scores of others—is disciplinary discharge for a cause not specifically provided for under the enterprise works and regulations, where full damage for loss of earnings are always awarded by the courts. The latter tend also closely to review the process of adoption of such rules, particularly their publicity (the awareness by those concerned of their existence). In consequence, in larger enterprises both the draft rules and the final text to be published and distributed in printed form to all members of the work collectivity, sometimes formally promulgated in the enterprise Official Gazette. All enterprise by-laws and rules are also subject to review by the constitutional courts (similarly to all other legislative instruments), either at the request of anyone concerned or under *ex officio* proceedings initiated by the Public Attorney. Price lists, where prescribed by the by-laws, rates of travel allowance, the granting of power of attorney and similar items must be covered by similar rulings. Moreover, no capital spending, investment, borrowing, changes in inventory, or any other unusual expenditure (publicity, individual grants, etc.), not to speak of a reduction or increase in employment, can take place unless properly authorized and agreed to by the works council or any other body as determined by the by-laws. Extracts, minutes or certified copies of relevant decisions form an essential part of documentation. Any request for an *ex post* validation of any unauthorized spending on other 'oversight' can be a most painful exercise for a director or executive. The advance approval of such varied items (as indeed the consideration of mission reports by the workers' councils) may be time consuming, yet there is no adequate alternative (save the setting up of an *ad hoc* committee). Indeed, we have noted even in most monotonous litanies of disparate objects a sudden upsurge of interest resulting in a change or a suggestion for future action.

The wide practice of such reserved powers, which cover scores of items not mentioned here provides perhaps the strongest motive force for the constant activity of the workers' management bodies. Another major factor is what may be termed 'outside changes' in legislative or financial and fiscal policy, in the market conditions, etc. It is in everyone's interest to follow them very closely, anticipating them as far as possible, for they may very soon affect the enterprise income, or else delay may cause a loss of possible advantage or additional income. If left unattended, a situation of this kind must finally affect the personal income of every member and is likely to lead to particularly lively reactions followed by an upsurge of activity. A particular contribution can be made by junior technicians or managers, as well as by qualified workers of some seniority for, whatever system of reporting is adopted, they often know well beforehand and can by-pass ordinary management channels.

This leads to another point which should be stressed. The unity of space, direct personal contact, local availability of means of implementation and relevant information considerably shorten the decision-making process. The advantage of not having to seek the approval of, nor to receive directives from, boards sitting in faraway capitals or anonymous services of a central ministry were often strongly emphasized by those who had shared in management responsibility under earlier systems. The concomitant risk of the workers' councils being too easily led into over-ambitious innovations by enthusiastic technicians or managers was, of course, quite considerable, particularly during the earlier period and offers an additional explanation of the relative instability and over-reactiveness of the entire economy.

The last point to be recalled is that the self-management bodies are not alone within the enterprise. They may be asked to act on the suggestion of other organizations within the enterprise, or even by outside public bodies or individuals. Although rather infrequently availed of, it is the accepted practice that they would consider issues suggested by the League of Communists, the trade unions or the youth organizations. As public or social bodies they are bound to consider—although again by no means to adopt or to implement—recommendations of the local commune, or of any other higher State body or economic organization. They may have to consider reports of various public inspectorates (finance, labour, etc.), and may be approached by similar bodies in other enterprises or by individual firms within or outside their own enterprise.

Unlike other self-governing bodies, particularly above the local level, where such multiplicity and complexity of decision-making institutions may more easily lead to relative paralysis or inefficiency, the enterprise self-management bodies live with and work under constant pressure of economic, social and personal issues which require urgent solution. Delay or error may not only be costly in general terms (as, for instance, in the case of an oversight of a central bank, a customs authority or a social security agency), but the cost must also be borne by the decision makers themselves and their workmates. Complex decentralization thus appears necessary to expedite the decision-making process, placing it under direct pressure from those who bear the risk of, or stand to benefit from, the consequences of any particular decision.

There is an obvious possibility of *conflict* within such a highly decentralized, non-hierarchical structure of management. In many cases specific solutions are provided, as in the case already mentioned of appeals by individual workers. Where divergencies occur between a wider body (the workers' collectivity or council) and the executive (management board, director), the former's view would normally prevail both in law and in practice, except where the latter is backed by a specific statutory provision (or opposes an illegal decision, etc.). Where conflict arises between two equivalent bodies

89

(e.g. workers' councils), voluntary arbitration may be resorted to. Where no agreement is forthcoming, the question usually remains open, both parties having to face the economic consequences of their non-co-operative attitude. Such conflicts are comparatively rare—as compared, for instance, with conflicts with other enterprises or outside bodies—and recourse to internal arbitration is quite exceptional. The economic pressure to settle fast is indeed extremely forceful. Contrary to the views of some foreign observers, the work collectivity is not a stock market operator dealing with paper certificates and able to withhold them for an unlimited period, but a body of producers for whom any delay means not only loss of current income but also a much greater piling of indirect costs and other real or potential losses.

The work collectivity, in other words 'labour', is thus in command of the entire decision-making process within the enterprise. It is not entirely isolated from the outside world, yet forms a much more self-contained, self-regulating, self-directing and self-perpetuating microcosm than any other form of enterprise, private or public, which depends not only on the will or whim but also on the personal fortunes and philosophy of its owner, the responsible ministry, or another outside decision maker. It is as if it were its own causation, alone bearing the responsibility of its success or failure.

The assets, or capital, or means of production are in most cases (but not all) an essential part of the enterprise, but only as a sleeping partner, with no active rights or duties. The legal concept of social property, equivalent to absence of ownership, had already been developed in the fifties and raises no major practical problems. The analogy with a foundation or endowment offers a quite satisfactory approximation of the legal position of assets.

At the start, each enterprise (its work collectivity) has the right to receive such assets, in terms both of basic capital or fixed assets (physical means of production, buildings, etc.), and of circulating capital for current production, as are necessary in order to develop its normal activity. In the case of existing enterprises, this meant that such means or funds which were actually at their disposal were entrusted for management to the work collectivity at various times. As regards new enterprises, the assets are supplied by the founder, normally as a repayable grant under contract. They are formally taken over by the newly elected workers' council when the enterprise is ready to start productive operation. Should they appear insufficient, the work collectivity has a claim against the founder to cover the difference. Similarly, additional funds are normally set aside to cover possible losses arising from the early experimental phase of the enterprise operation. An inventory and balance sheet are established stating the original capital endowment of the enterprise subject to the assent of the workers' council.

From this point onwards the enterprise has no claim to acquire additional assets from others, nor can anyone deprive it of any part of its endowment capital. The latter must always be preserved at least at its original value (but not necessarily in its physical form). The work collectivity can use the assets in any manner compatible with the object of the enterprise, provided it observes the principles of sound business management. It is expected to create new productive assets through its productive activity (self-financing) and may also secure further funds through credit borrowed from the banks or other sources.

Assets which were part of the original endowment are subject to interest at a rate fixed by law (recently 4·5 per cent annually, with lower rates applicable in a number of instances). Similar payments are due in respect of assets or funds created by self-financing, while interest on borrowed capital is based on free agreement with the lender, subject to the maximum rates fixed by the National Bank (8 to 10 per cent annually in 1968). All fixed assets are subject to depreciation at the minimum legal rates (varying from 0 to 12 per cent), or by the enterprise itself (e.g. for patents and licences). Higher rates, and even differentiated rates for identical items in various departments, may be introduced by each enterprise if it desires. Finally, because the enterprise is obliged to maintain the original value of its capital, it must replace from its current income the book value of any scrapped items of inventory or other losses on stock or inventory.

The enterprise may, of course, sell any items of its inventory provided it replaces them by others of the same or greater value. If it holds superfluous or unused capital assets, it may also escape the obligations relating thereto by transferring them free of charge to another enterprise or other social organizations which would accept the corresponding interest and depreciation costs. Such a transfer amounts to a reduction of capital in the former, and a corresponding increase in the latter enterprise, the global value of social assets held by the self-management sector remaining unchanged.

All decisions concerning the enterprise assets are within the terms of reference of the workers' council. Failure to comply with the legal provisions may entail the dissolution of the council and penal liability of the enterprise and the responsible members of management. If unable to meet the financial liabilities arising from the assets at its disposal, the enterprise is placed under a public receiver and, unless new credit or subvention are forthcoming, has to be wound up or reorganized.

The main purpose of all these provisions—which constitute a mere skeleton summary of the actual regulations governing the management of assets[1]—is to ensure sound and rational management of the assets by the work collectivity and to equalize conditions between enterprises according to the volume of funds and assets at their disposal. The need for capital varies very considerably from industry to industry and from enterprise to enterprise. Some may work successfully with very little funds, or indeed none, while others may require and dispose of very considerable funds per head of worker. Similarly, one enterprise may operate departments or sections with widely differing levels of capital intensity. In both cases, the charges made against the available capital assets aim at making the work collectivity watchful over expenses attaching to the assets placed at their disposal, and at limiting their demands for additional investment to projects whose profitability is well in excess of the corresponding charges and risks.

---

[1] Additional factual explanations of the working of the system are given as necessary in Part II.

The capital assets are nothing more than the result of past accumulated labour and the corresponding charges can be thought of as constituting a form of remuneration to those who in the past abstained from direct consumption as well as an assurance that their past sacrifice will not be cast away by the present generation. The level of charges corresponds to the relative scarcity of such accumulated assets. As already mentioned, the interest payments on the endowment capital are presently credited to the Fund for regional development. In other circumstances, they could as properly constitute a major resource of pension schemes and workers' compensation generally, while current development could properly be financed from current taxation and/or credit. The hardship suffered by the post-war generation now in their fifties—who have borne the full burden of the struggle for independence as well as of post-war reconstruction and early development—has been put forward as one of the arguments for reducing in their favour the age of retirement.

The *economic object of the enterprise* is of particular importance. Legally, each enterprise has a definite principal activity which is registered in court at the time of its formal constitution and spelled out in more detail in its by-laws. For statistical and related purposes, it is classified as belonging to the corresponding sector and branch of industry, and it affiliates to organizations and elects representatives along with other enterprises of the same branch and/or sector. The law provides that, in addition to various social or service activities, the enterprise may also engage in subsidiary economic activity other than that for which it is registered. It may also register other principal activities it may engage in at various times. Industrial enterprises always include transport and marketing of their products, including retail activities, among possible secondary operations. Moreover, any department or section of an enterprise, including its central services (e.g. research, management organization, accounting) may engage in direct business or service relations with others, and such side-line operations may with time develop considerably. Formally, there is no obstacle to an enterprise moving rapidly from one type of activity to another according to its best interest and using any comparative advantage it may have. Financially, the possibility of freely allocating both the depreciation funds and self-financed capital make such rapid transfers perfectly feasible. (Depreciation and self-financing at the rate of 30 per cent per annum—quite modest by Yugoslav standards—makes it possible to develop entirely different operations of similar magnitude in less than three years.)

Very few enterprises, and certainly no branches or sectors, in Yugoslavia are therefore purely specialized in manufacturing, transport, or commercial, etc. This applies to the 'confederate' or other agglomerated enterprises already mentioned, such as the agricultural-industrial combinates, and to most enterprises of a certain size and 'age' which have had time to meet with the need to diversify or transform their economic activity. There are numerous examples of such major changes prompted by various circumstances, including the transfer of secondary activities to more specialized enterprises, and changes in the geographical location of firms, to which there is no legal obstacle in Yugoslavia.

Although initially developed from the breakdown of 'clean' sectors, typical of central planning, the Yugoslav firm is now an aggregate of different activities; each is a competitor or potential competitor to others in its own, as well as in other, sectors or branches. If it is referred to as an 'industrial' 'transport', or 'commercial' enterprise, it is a figure of speech similar (although more precise) to calling a town an industrial or commercial or agricultural centre. Each enterprise has at any given time a clearly defined economic object or objects, but could not be compared to any other merely because it is classified in the same branch or sector for purposes of national statistics of accounting. Limited data on 'clean' sectors and branches are available but their very 'cleanness' makes them inapplicable to real enterprises.

The economic object of the Yugoslav firm is not subject to any major statutory limitation and may encompass wide areas which are not normally classed as 'economic activity', such as various types of consultancy (management, accounting, etc.) and similar intangible service activities. It may normally include any activity which is not contrary to law and public order and the cost of which may be covered through sales or any other exchange based on synallagmatic contract.

It is not possible to analyse here in more detail the characteristics of the enterprises according to the main object of their economic activity, nor to explore the specific characteristics of the various branches or sectors of the Yugoslav economy. Some of their main features will be found in Table III, which also presents the usual classification of firms according to the principal sectors and branches. More detailed classification exists according to some two hundred narrower sectors, or groups of enterprises, but this data is not normally made public as data concerning individual enterprises are considered confidential. However, the data referred to here are only an infinitesimal part of the documentation publicly available. The full documentation is normally available to the Yugoslav Institutes and researchers and can also be obtained by individual enterprises (usually with the names of individual enterprises removed) which are in a position to compare their own behaviour and performance to those of others in their own or in related sectors. To operate such comparisons is a—sometimes forgotten—statutory duty of each enterprise.

The Yugoslav firm is similarly solely responsible for the development of *technology and skill*, which in a wide interpretation corresponds to what some authors refer to as the 'residual' or 'unknown' factor. These are obviously not open to any comprehensive statutory regulations nor can they be meaningfully expressed by any statistical or accounting data. Rules can obviously be set, and indeed exist, covering hundreds of specific items coming under this heading, and many corresponding statistical indices can be assembled and are available. No common denominator can however be found to cover all the extremely diversified possibilities and conditions.

Yet it is precisely in this area that the self-governing character of the Yugoslav firm may prove of particular value. For technology is only rarely a problem of finance or investment alone, but rather of the will to learn and

Table III

Major Characteristics of the existing Worker-Managed Enterprises in Yugoslavia: Workers Employed, Value of Assets, Volume of Production (1966)

A. NUMERICAL INDICES

| | Total | | | | Number of Enterprises Employing . . . Workers | | | | | | |
	Total	Up to 6	7–15	16–29	30–60	61–125	126–250	251–500	501–1,000	1,001–2,000	Over 2,000
Total (all enterprises)	14,237	1,674	1,744	1,701	2,384	2,439	1,841	1,243	654	365	201
1. *Industry and mining*	2,467	28	44	63	181	391	544	533	343	205	135
Electricity	80	2	—	—	8	10	15	20	17	6	2
Coal and coke	68	1	—	1	3	7	9	14	14	5	15
Petroleum	4	—	—	—	—	1	—	—	—	1	2
Metal trades	347	—	2	3	8	43	82	87	56	33	33
Shipbuilding	19	—	—	—	—	1	7	4	3	1	3
Chemical	145	1	2	4	16	33	32	25	11	14	7
Building material	244	1	3	4	29	73	67	48	14	4	1
Wool processing	268	—	—	1	5	33	81	58	49	34	7
Paper	38	—	—	—	1	3	7	7	10	8	2
Textiles	328	—	—	1	9	26	67	101	71	33	20
Food	201	1	5	3	16	43	43	47	19	17	7
Printing	305	22	30	33	60	62	47	29	19	2	1
Mining exploration	16	—	1	—	3	2	4	1	4	—	1
2. *Agriculture and fisheries*	2,742	354	439	466	566	418	244	143	61	35	16
Agric.–ind. combinates	268	1	6	4	13	40	52	61	42	34	15
Fisheries	60	8	14	16	8	4	6	4	—	—	—
Water management	99	4	6	16	15	19	24	11	3	—	1
3. *Forestry*	148	2	6	16	23	15	14	15	31	22	4

Table III (Continued)

				Number of Enterprises Employing ... Workers							
	Total	Up to 6	7–15	16–29	30–60	61–125	126–250	251–500	501–1,000	1,001–2,000	Over 2,000
4. Construction	706	7	89	94	58	75	118	115	69	53	28
Planning and designing	258	7	83	82	42	30	10	3	1	—	—
Building	359	—	—	4	9	35	92	91	53	47	28
5. Transport and communications	397	6	14	13	42	82	64	81	51	28	16
Road transport and haulage	206	1	3	5	28	45	39	50	25	8	2
6. Commerce, catering and tourism	3,319	570	385	326	597	639	450	253	79	18	2
Foreign trade	149	—	3	3	24	33	37	31	15	3	—
Catering and hotels	1,195	309	153	142	228	188	106	59	7	3	—
Artisanate (Production)[1]	2,729	307	433	442	625	561	29	59	11	—	—

[1] The two 'sectors' not covered are 'Artisnate' (Personal Services) (364 enterprises) and 'Others' (1,365 enterprises).

	Enterprises According to Value of Fixed Assets (Number of) (in 000 dinars)										
	Up to 15	15–50	50–150	150–500	500–1,500	1,500–5,000	5,000–15,000	15,000–50,000	50,000–150,000	over 150,000	Total assets per worker (000 dinars) (average)
Total (all enterprises)	1,376	979	1,448	2,382	2,763	2,530	1,431	798	323	207	45·3
1. Industry and mining	24	22	40	106	352	666	585	377	180	115	48·1
Electricity	1	—	—	2	—	2	3	9	23	40	289·1
Coal and coke	—	—	—	—	7	12	17	12	9	11	32·0
Petroleum	—	—	—	—	—	—	—	—	—	3	114·5
Metal trades	1	1	2	5	29	106	92	71	31	9	39·8
Shipbuilding	—	—	—	—	2	4	5	3	2	3	53·1

Table III (Continued)

	Enterprises According to Value of Fixed Assets (Number of) (in 000 dinars)										Total assets per worker (000 dinars) (average)
	Up to 15	15–50	50–150	150–500	500–1,500	1,500–5,000	5,000–15,000	15,000–50,000	50,000–150,000	over 150,000	
Chemical	—	—	2	7	23	37	36	19	13	8	68·7
Building material	—	1	1	12	45	102	63	12	6	2	27·6
Wood processing	1	—	—	3	38	84	70	50	18	4	22·3
Paper	—	—	—	—	2	7	5	9	7	8	98·3
Textiles	—	—	1	12	54	82	89	63	23	4	29·0
Food	—	—	2	3	23	49	59	46	16	3	47·3
Printing	19	20	30	49	74	63	34	13	3	—	28·5
Mining exploration	—	—	1	2	3	3	4	2	1	—	20·3
2. Agriculture and fisheries	108	117	255	570	678	541	286	134	42	11	52·5
Agric.-ind. combinates	2	—	—	4	13	44	86	75	35	9	56·2
Fisheries	4	6	11	13	9	10	7	—	—	—	30·1
Water management	1	—	3	3	10	18	31	24	7	2	92·5
3. Forestry	1	1	5	10	17	21	16	27	28	22	22·9
4. Construction	14	57	78	100	149	163	88	38	19	—	12·1
Planning and designing	11	56	69	65	38	17	1	1	—	—	15·1
Building	3	—	1	22	92	117	71	34	19	—	11·7
5. Transport and communications	12	5	3	13	25	78	90	84	30	57	71·5
Road transport and haulage	1	—	1	4	10	56	55	40	6	33	135·9
6. Commerce, catering and tourism	492	213	286	542	733	673	262	106	12	—	52·5
Foreign trade	1	1	3	11	21	57	439	15	1	—	137·0
Catering and hotels	252	84	90	188	230	209	98	41	3	—	25·4
7. Artisanate (production)	413	299	507	714	555	210	29	2	—	—	12·2

Table III (Continued)

Enterprises According to Value of Net Product [Value Added] (Number of)
(in 000 dinars)

	Up to 15	15–50	50–150	150–500	500–1,500	1,500–5,000	5,000–15,000	15,000–50,000	50,000–150,000	Over 150,000	Product per Worker
Total (all enterprises)	170	510	1,277	2,692	3,493	3,272	1,798	823	176	26	27·0
1. Industry and mining	14	8	15	95	345	795	666	405	109	15	26·2
Electricity	1	1	—	—	2	9	21	38	8	—	69·6
Coal and coke	—	—	—	—	9	17	22	11	8	1	20·6
Petroleum	—	—	—	—	—	1	—	—	2	1	104·0
Metal trades	—	1	1	6	31	102	109	68	28	1	22·7
Shipbuilding	—	—	—	—	1	6	6	3	2	1	29·6
Chemical	—	—	—	—	12	46	45	26	8	1	36·9
Building material	1	—	—	7	73	112	36	7	2	—	23·6
Wood processing	2	—	—	13	34	114	79	34	2	—	15·9
Paper	2	—	—	3	3	11	7	13	2	—	23·9
Textiles	1	—	—	—	19	103	116	75	9	1	18·3
Food	1	—	2	4	23	66	54	41	5	—	26·5
Printing	5	6	9	41	86	71	55	21	1	—	34·7
Mining exploration	—	—	—	3	3	3	5	1	1	—	26·8
2. Agriculture and fisheries	24	70	338	727	807	520	179	61	12	4	22·5
Agric.-ind. combinates	—	1	1	11	30	79	78	53	11	4	22·1
Fisheries	4	3	13	17	11	7	5	—	—	—	18·5
Water management	1	1	2	16	21	41	14	2	1	—	29·9
3. Forestry	—	1	3	23	31	25	37	28	—	—	20·9
4. Construction	—	—	10	104	144	226	123	79	20	—	22·9
Planning and designing	—	—	9	89	96	48	14	2	—	—	43·2
Building	—	—	—	6	37	151	83	63	19	—	21·5

Table III (*Continued*)

	Enterprises According to Value of Net Product [Value Added] (Number of) (in 000 dinars)										Product per Worker
	Up to 15	15–50	50–150	150–500	500–15,00	1,500–5,000	5,000–15,000	15,000–50,000	50,000–150,000	Over 150,000	
5. Transport and communications	—	1	14	15	62	117	113	55	15	5	27·2
Road transport and haulage	—	—	2	3	36	74	67	23	1	—	29·5
6. Commerce, catering and tourism	63	209	284	500	663	833	565	182	18	2	38·4
Foreign trade	—	1	1	2	1	28	66	46	4	—	67·3
Catering and hotels	28	148	163	256	329	296	58	7	—	—	23·0
7. Artisanate (production)	36	135	318	714	946	512	64	4	—	—	19·7

Table III

B: EXAMPLES OF TYPICAL DISTRIBUTION OF THE ENTERPRISE POPULATION IN YUGOSLAVIA (1961–2)

Table (1)*

Distribution of Industrial Enterprises according to Social Product (Productivity per Worker)

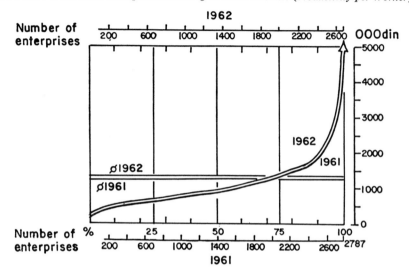

Table (2)*

Distribution of Industrial Enterprises according to the proportion of Personal Incomes in Total Income available for Distribution

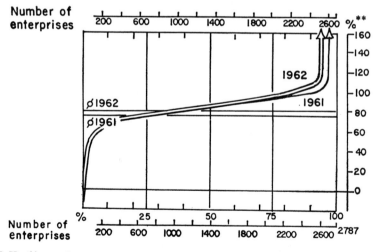

* V. Krstić, *op. cit.*
** Percentages of over 100 refer to enterprises with negative current results after distribution of incomes, covered by drawing on reserves (subsidies, etc.). The upward swing in this table thus corresponds to negative performance and vice versa.

to adapt. A minor investment can produce revolutionary progress, provided that it is backed by the will of all concerned to put it to full use. Failing such will, massive investments may prove of no avail. Often, indeed, no apparent costs are necessary in order to achieve significant results. Similarly, the importance of skill is obvious and widely recognized, yet it is not mainly a question of costs or aptitudes, but rather of will to progress—will to make full use of the available facilities and resources. A mass of quite imponderable elements enter into play and may have decisive impact: work and management organization, human relations and discipline, job security and satisfaction, career prospects, the active involvement of all concerned. With identical factor endowment, two enterprises—in Yugoslavia as anywhere else—may achieve quite different standards, both in quantity and quality of production and in terms of financial results, according to whether they have succeeded or not in solving satisfactorily problems arising in these various areas. As it alone is responsible for whatever ways and means it applies, the Yugoslav self-governing firms stands a good change of adapting, rapidly and efficiently and, with due regard to local customs and preferences, the required skills and techniques. At the same time, should major strains develop within the work collectivity, it faces the danger of being left on its own for periods of time much longer than under a system of central planning (possibly until the time it faces bankruptcy). In all this crucial area of entrepreneurial responsibility, its behaviour and performance will differ vastly from those of any other form of enterprise, in view of the different and quite specific 'interest spectrum' of the work collectivity. In its concrete forms, behaviour and performance in this area will of course vary widely from enterprise to enterprise, according to local circumstances and conditions.

Several lengthy chapters would be required in order to deal adequately with the wide variety of items we have referred to under the somewhat arbitrary heading of technology and skill. As they are neither directly measurable in quantitative terms, nor reducible to a common denominator, they are mostly neglected in purely economic analysis. Yet they correspond to the central economic purpose of the self-management system, as distinct from central planning based essentially on quantitative controls: i.e. qualitative improvement of the enterprise's economic behaviour and performance. Failure to recognize the importance of such qualitative factors would mean that the central economic object of the self-management system was being missed and a mere skeleton caricature presented. While it can avail itself of outside advice and assistance in a variety of shapes and forms, the Yugoslav firm is alone in command of all such 'residual' factors (as distinct from abstract capital and labour) which determine its real behaviour, quality of performance, and success or failure in the real world.

A brief comment is required concerning the institutional forms governing the *setting up and liquidation* of enterprises, as well as other cases of changes in their institutional status and identify (such as amalgamation or division). The *entry and exit of firms* is obviously of great importance for the behaviour of the system as a whole.

Institutional solutions were first introduced at the end of 1953 and, despite considerable subsequent changes in the relevant legislation, appear to be one of the most stable features of the system. Any public body, or institution, social organization, enterprise or group of citizens may appear as prospective founders of an enterprise, provided they find the necessary finance. This may vary from practically nothing in the case of a small workshop or consulting bureau, to hundreds of millions for a modern plant of considerable magnitude. Even productive enterprises of some size may be founded with insignificant financial endowment in view of the operation of the depreciation system, whereby written-off but still workable equipment can be acquired at little or no cost, e.g. by a rural commune in a remote area, and operated at the start at very low levels of remuneration (e.g. a rural quarry, brick works, small textile mill). Under the earlier system of public investment funds, the local and regional authorities, particularly the communes, played the role of principal initiators and sponsors of new enterprises. In principle, however, all prospective sponsors competed on equal terms for the allocation of the funds' credits. At present, this system is continued only for the benefit of the under-developed regions, while all other founders have to approach one or other of the business banks to secure such funds as may be necessary, this procedure being designed *inter alia* to give a better chance to projects sponsored by existing enterprises. Where no credits are required, the founder may proceed on his own (subject only to compliance with rules regarding technical standards, urban development, safety, etc.) and, provided complete documentation is submitted, is entitled to have the enterprise registered by the local court and put into operation. Where a longer period is necessary to develop the enterprise, provisional management is appointed and workers' representative bodies with consultative powers may be elected. When ready to start its operations, the enterprise is formally constituted and handed over to a newly elected workers' council, which then has to adopt the enterprise by-laws and rules and open a competitive examination for the appointment of the director. The founder may reserve the right to repayment of the invested capital, as well as legal interest. He may also reserve certain rights for a limited period (such as the exclusive purchase of production), but the new enterprise is entitled to re-negotiate these, or to have them reviewed by the courts, should they be contrary to normal business practice or equity. No right to interfere in the actual management of the new firm can be reserved to or exercised by the founder.

New enterprises may also be formed by voluntary division of an existing enterprise or, more frequently, by the separation of a self-contained department or service, where the work collectivity prefers to take full responsibility in its own hands. This is the right of any such collectivity, provided existing conditions permits its operation as an independent enterprise. If such separation is not granted by the workers' council, the collectivity in question may petition the courts. It has the right to its share in the assets of the enterprise and must accept corresponding liabilities. A similar right of secession may also be exercised by the work collectivity of a productive or service department of an institution or organization, able to operate as an economic enterprise. For instance, the former publishing house of the Central Council of Trade Unions obtained its establishment as an independent enterprise, the parent organization setting up a new editorial service of its own.

Two or more enterprises are free to merge if they see fit. They determine their future relationship themselves, which may result in the complete disappearance of the existing enterprises or take the form of looser federal or confederal arrangements. The holding of a general referendum on a proposed merger seems mandatory in recent practice. In fact, such mergers have been widely encouraged in recent years, great emphasis being given to the advantages of co-operation and integration in all branches of the economy.

There seems to be no provision for a voluntary winding-up of an existing enterprise. The members of the work collectivity having no stake in the social capital, and being free to part at any time, subject only to a period of notice, such provision would indeed seem meaningless.

The cessation of activity is envisaged only where the enterprise cannot cope with its financial obligations, such as taxes, repayment of credits and interest, or if it is insolvent in current operations, or has insufficient income to provide minimum remuneration for work. The appointment of a public receiver may be requested by a creditor of the enterprise or effected directly by a commune called upon to advance funds to cover the minimum remuneration due to members of the work collectivity. The appointment of a receiver, if and when effected, automatically entails the recall of the director and dissolution of all the workers' management bodies, the receiver exercising all management authority. Again, all those affected by such a measure, be they the dissolved council or a group of workers, can and frequently do fight their case in the courts. There is a voluminous body of case law and legal opinion concerning the status and powers of the public receiver, which are neither arbitrary nor all inclusive, particularly as there is no succession to the regulatory powers of the workers' council.

If an arrangement is made with the creditors, or additional credits are secured, or the commune is ready to bear the deficit for a time, or if business conditions improve, the receiver will retain his powers with a view to reorganizing the enterprise and handing it back to the work collectivity within a period of one year at the most. If no alternative is found, a liquidator will be appointed and the remaining assets of the enterprise disposed of in the best interests of the creditors.

In some cases, the appointment of a receiver has been requested by the workers' council or collectivity even prior to reaching insolvency (and also as a vote of no-confidence in the director, who is thereby automatically removed from office). The enterprise is legally obliged to inform the commune in advance if possible, where it is likely that it might not be able to meet its financial liabilities (and not merely when it has actually become insolvent). While voluntary winding-up is not provided for, a request to have a receiver appointed where conditions or relations rapidly deteriorate seems a most logical and rational step if the work collectivity does not feel up to solving their difficulties themselves. Others in similar circumstances may grant extraordinary powers to the director and/or take radical measures themselves to revise their plans and their *modus operandi*. The institution of receiver proved unexpectedly successful as it succeeded in nearly all cases in reorganizing the enterprise and putting it afloat again. A recent survey of some 160 enterprises placed under a public receiver showed that only in one case did the procedure result in final liquidation of the enterprise, while all others recovered. This would seem to point to the non-economic origin of most of the difficulties, where the removal of the director or other key people was conducive to swift improvement. In some cases, also, the influx of new credits, and more concentrated attention by various public or social bodies to the specific problems of the enterprise, have been of help. Nevertheless the receiver is sometimes resented as an alien element within the system and removal of the institution has been formally proposed by certain trade union bodies. It seems difficult however to find a viable alternative.

The liquidation of enterprises is exceptional and usually only occurs in the case of minor shops or workshops with little or no capital resources. Much more frequent is the disappearance of enterprises as a result of mergers, which account for most of the slow but continuous decline in the number of enterprises for a number of years past.

It is extremely difficult to obtain a precise idea of the extent to which the entry and exit of firms, as well as other changes in the firm's identity, occur in actual practice. They are registered with the local courts and brought to public notice through the official gazettes of the various republics and communes. The data normally published by the Statistical Office only show net changes in numbers, and it would be extremely difficult to evaluate the importance of such phenomena for lack of a common denominator. The statistical 'movement' of enterprises could be expressed in absolute numbers, in terms of workers employed, or in terms of capital, but none of these could truly reflect the importance of the changes in question. We are nevertheless obliged to the Federal Office of Statistics for having assembled such data as were at its disposal and which are reproduced in Table IV as an illustration. In general terms, it may be said that the entry and exit of firms play an important part in the practical operation of the self-management system, affecting on average some 10 to 15 per cent of firms annually (but certainly much less in terms of workers and capital). The public in general, and particularly the responsible members of the enterprise work collectivities, seem to be well aware of the changes—planned or in progress—as regards the setting up of new enterprises, possible mergers, or possible failure of others. Such factors are a major item in the factual background of enterprise planning and policy-making activity.

As already mentioned, most enterprises of some size are combinations of autonomous units which, to a varying degree, can be regarded as enterprises in their own right. For the whole economy, the number of such units recorded in 1966 was over 15,000. More significantly, in 516 enterprises employing more than 1,000 workers, 7,172 such autonomous self-governing units were found to exist in 1966 (283 factories, 1,660 departments and 5,221 other work units.[1]

[1] Cf. Federal Office of Statistics, *Statisticki Bibtten* No. 492, October 1967.

Table IV

Entry and Exit of Firms in 1960 and 1961

| | Number of firms at beginning of the period | Exit due to | | | Entry due to | | | | Number of firms at end of period | Number of autonomous departments[1] |
		Liquidations	Mergers	Statistical changes[2]	Setting-up of new firms	Mergers	Divisions or separations	Statistical changes[2]		
1960										
Total	25,015	1,071	2,309	184	1,501	51	21	194	23,218	16,288
Industry and mining	2,638	34	87	15	124	3	9	143	2,781	971
Agriculture	6,849	270	874	4	205	25	3	2	5,936	260
Forestry	375	3	79	1	10	—	1	—	303	330
Building	656	17	24	7	50	—	1	12	671	564
Transport and communications	409	17	22	31	29	1	—	5	374	5,105
Commerce, catering and tourism	8,125	355	907	13	429	13	4	5	7,301	8,553
Crafts	4,806	246	274	105	413	9	2	24	4,629	473
Communal services	1,157	129	42	8	241	—	1	3	1,223	32
1961										
Total	23,218	1,001	1,858	79	1,271	198	47	99	21,895	17,019
Industry and mining	2,781	41	96	15	91	17	4	47	2,788	993
Agriculture	5,936	271	866	2	135	103	8	3	5,046	236
Forestry	303	24	88	2	18	—	—	1	208	397
Building	671	15	13	4	68	—	6	10	723	615
Transport and communications	374	13	8	—	84	1	5	2	445	4,944
Commerce, catering and tourism	7,301	364	519	7	392	52	16	13	6,884	9,333
Crafts	4,629	190	236	40	290	17	8	15	4,493	465
Communal services	1,223	83	32	9	193	8	—	8	1,308	36

[1] Departments located on the territory of communes other than that of the parent enterprise (with separate reporting for statistical purposes).
[2] Changes in the nature (object of activity) of firms.

Little can usefully be added here concerning the actual shape and operation of the Yugoslav firm. The real dimensions of its existence are all recorded in great detail in massive volumes of statistical and accounting data, as well as innumerable special studies. Starting with the work collectivity, its composition by age, participation, income differentials; workers' councils and other self-management bodies, their elections and compositions, as well as that of their committees, number of meetings, their agendas, the holding of referenda, the appointment and recall of directors, their qualification and length of service; the composition of capital and distribution of income; growth of production and rate of investment; technical equipment, its age, or degree of amortization; hours worked or missed, rate of shift work, as well as innumerable other aspects of the enterprise existence and operation can be found duly recorded, often since the early fifties, and in minute detail for every region, branch and/or industry. The position is rather similar as regards analytical studies.

Yet the very wealth of data, and frequent differences in their interpretation, make it difficult to formulate general conclusions. If anything, they tend in the opposite direction, i.e. to show that most generalizations may be proved both right and wrong, or, in other words, that there is hardly anything impossible in the changing world of the Yugoslav firms.

All that can safely be stated is that the most varied institutional possibilities of the system are on the whole widely availed of, without there being any clear-cut regularities. In other words, the various key institutional features of the Yugoslav firm may be thought of as a set of signposts or guidelines, which may appear in widely differing shapes and forms in the concrete practice of any one enterprise.

The question of *size* may also provide a useful example. Table III provides data concerning the size of the Yugoslav firm according to number of workers employed, assets, etc. The range of sizes covered may be deemed infinite for all practical purposes, from less than six to over 2,000 workers employed, from less than 15,000 to over 150 million dinars of basic capital. Most enterprises tend to concentrate in the category of larger firms, those employing over 1,000 workers, and with 5 million dinars or more capital, accounting for most of the country's economic activity. This corresponds to a distinct trend in recent years towards the enlargement of existing enterprises, and the Yugoslav firm may be thought of as somewhat larger, at least in terms of employment, than its average Western counterpart (but distinctly smaller than enterprises in most Eastern countries). Yet again, thinking in terms of such average data may be quite misleading, if not meaningless, for purposes of economic analysis, for a combination of several plants, or mere extensive workshops, or a chain of retail shops, may appear considerably larger than a truly integrated industrial concern, a steelworks for example. Similarly, measurement in terms of net income (value added), which at first sight would seem to provide best synthetic indicators, would prove of little value in view of the tremendous differences between individual enterprises or narrower sectors.

Even greater difficulties would have to be overcome in order meaningfully

105

to assess the Yugoslav firm in terms of what we referred to as skill and technology. Like the whole Yugoslav economy, the average firm is of recent origin, and has a relatively young work force and new technology, rarely encumbered by traditional practices or old techniques, open to innovation and the integration of new skills. To an outside observer, this should appear particularly striking at the level of business activity and management organization, for practically everything had to be newly devised or invented in this area and the 'emancipated' managements showed little lack of initiative, frequently under pressure from junior technicians or specialists and from leading members of the workers' management bodies. Development and investment mentality was largely predominant, often fierce in the extreme, at least up to the 1965 Reform and the consequent slackening of activity. Similarly, the acquisition of new skills was actively pursued by workers at all levels of qualification and training. Not surprisingly, less has probably been achieved in increasing the rather leisurely work tempo and intensity of production inherited from the centrally planned State enterprise. Yet there is no lack of opposite examples, particularly in the areas of earlier development, where older industrial traditions are more likely to survive, with more resistance to change and innovation. In such areas managements are more hierarchically minded or dormant, with workers interested less in new skills than in reaching higher levels of actual performance.

Although their points of departure are extremely varied in all aspects of their existence (their labour force and its skill, their capital endowment and level of technology, their market position), all Yugoslav firms are nevertheless equal, not only in the purely formal institutional sense, but also in that they are free to take stock of, and use as best they can, all the human material resources at their disposal, with a considerable degree of flexibility in the methods and objects of their economic activity.

CHAPTER V

Enterprise Planning and Income Distribution Process

The *distribution of enterprise income* is the most central, the most vital and the most specific feature of the system of workers' management. It is the *central* clue to all management, activity, for the income of the enterprise for any given period—being the difference between all receipts and expenditure—is the sole means of expressing in quantitative terms the results of the enterprise operation during that period, while its allocation commands the enterprise's future. Any item of the accounts, however minute, reflects corresponding work and management activity, their success or failure, and suggests possibilities for future action. The income distribution process is the most *vital* part of workers' management for, if it were lacking, the whole institutional framework would become meaningless. Conversely, full autonomy in income distribution would satisfy the fundamental conditions of workers' management even in the absence of any formal institutional framework (as may indeed be the case in very small enterprises) or make the setting up of such a framework imperative should it for any reason be wanting. In other words, it is only to the extent that the enterprise controls its income, and can allocate it according to its best judgment, that it may truly be called autonomous and self-governing. It is only through the income distribution process that the work collectivity and each of its members can rationally appreciate their interests and define their best course of action. Finally, the income distribution process is the most *specific* feature of the system since, unlike its institutional framework, it has no direct analogy with any other form of enterprise, as the income is shared out by the workers within their enterprises and according to their work.

In its widest interpretation, the concept of income-sharing covers all aspects of income creation through work or production: the valuation of the product through the market, the allocation of part of the newly-created value for general social needs, and for economic and social development, as well as the actual sharing out of the residual income among the workers in accordance with their work. It therefore embraces in one single process the full spectrum of key areas of economic decision making which, in other systems, appear as distinct, mostly unrelated, stages or procedures of operation of the enterprise, company, bank, planning agency, etc. It is the one central modality which bends the multifarious work and management activities of the self-governing enterprise into a meaningful whole. In its general features it also represents the one specific requirement, not only of the Yugo-slav system, but of any system of workers' management, or advanced partici-pation, as its basic condition of rationality in economic decision making.

The income distribution process is no less closely tied to the social or humanistic objectives of the system. As observed by the Yugoslav President:

> 'To make every individual participate in the process of management and of decision making, to give to him the widest possibility of seeing for himself the results of his work, of valuing them and dealing them out, means turning him into a man who is free and independent both economically and socially, who draws his living from the results of his labour, who is emancipated from all forms of tutelage and from the last sequels of the wage-earning relationship.' [1]

The right to participate in sharing out the income, and in the income itself by virtue of his work, is also the most basic constitutional right of the member of the worker-managed enterprise. All his other rights and duties may be considered as derived therefrom.

The income distribution process is, correspondingly, at the very centre of attention of all public and social bodies and organizations, of social and economic research, and of the discussions in the public media and within the enterprises themselves. It is a subject of wide bibliographical coverage in Yugoslavia. Its development since 1952 is the commanding feature of the history of the self-management system as a whole. Its legislative coverage—including the body of legal opinion—is most extensive. It is also the focal point of all financial and fiscal policy. It also represents the centrepiece of the national accounting system and financial comptrol. Similarly, the income distribution process has a privileged position within the enterprise's own system of internal regulations, decision making and comptrol and is, as such, dealt with, with the most special care and attention.

Informally, the amount and growth of the enterprise's income, and the way it handles it, are part of its identity, of its social prestige and economic relevance. Despite strict formal equality of all firms, it is obvious that a progressive and prosperous enterprise will carry considerably more weight in its socio-economic environment as compared with one on the verge of bankruptcy or surviving thanks to subsidy. In proportion to its retained income, the enterprise will indeed be able to fashion its own social and eco-nomic environment; at a high level of thrift, it may largely emancipate itself from the realm of economic necessity and create its own welfare area, its own 'pole' of social and economic development.

A full definition of the complex process can hardly be attempted. From an economic point of view, it can be thought of as representing a conscious, self-governing creation and allocation of that portion of national income which is formed by and within the enterprise. It is both a continuous process and a periodic position statement, covering all necessary inputs and the resulting outputs of the enterprise. Its static, accounting representation for any given

---

[1] J. B. Tito, Report to the Fifth Congress of the Socialist Alliance, 1960.

period is the periodic combined balance sheet and account statement, to which we will refer later. Graphically it may be represented in terms of flows of the values created, through the production process, into the various funds corresponding to different categories and levels of consumption (including amortization, investment, etc.).

Even more important, although hardly allowing for any precise representation, is the dynamic role of the income-sharing process, whereby any decision or performance at any given time can be seen as shaping the enterprise's future (and vice versa). A *tableau économique* with a full time-dimension, covering the full circuit of economic activity, it offers the basic framework for rational, conscious work and decision-making activity by the work collectivity, by means of which the effects of any change or lack of change in any item of the accounts can be appreciated with respect to all others. This does not mean that all decisions and every type of work (or lack of same) can be adequately appreciated in quantitative or money terms. Yet they all have some quantitative or financial implication and can therefore be reflected (even if not always adequately) through the income-sharing process and discussed within its framework.

In other words, through the income sharing process, all the work and decision-making activity of the enterprise tends to become a conscious self-regulating and self-governing process. Outside controls which are indispensable in the case of a hired worker or manager cease to be required, since new criteria of economic rationality can be derived from within the enterprise itself through the income sharing process. This, then, is the essential condition of its emancipation, of its freedom of action.

As noted earlier, the position of the enterprise work collectivity in this respect is not without analogy to that of central planners, except that the latter merely decide in abstract terms on the activities of others, while the former must also implement in concrete terms, by its work, its own decisions. The freedom of the work collectivity is therefore in a sense much wider, for it does not impose its will on anyone but itself, and bears alone the consequences of its own decisions. By the same token, such freedom is much more limited—or less abstract—for the work collectivity cannot decide or undertake anything unless it is ready and able to implement it.

Considered from yet another angle, the work collectivity is fully free only in such areas as are solely its own concern. It may freely regulate its work or production, allocate the income already earned for investment purposes and social activity or share it out as remuneration. It may freely plan them for the future. Such freedom is obviously by no means absolute or infinite, and is subject to such roles of procedure as make its exercise 'conscious'. Full freedom (or full independence) within the context of the self-management enterprise may thus be defined as a conscious search for optimum allocation of resources in the light of a plurality of self-determined objectives. The collectivity may sometimes be faced with legal or institutional limits or criteria, or else it may have to adapt to objective conditions of the outside world, particularly when dealing or competing with others on and through the market. Yet, in nearly all cases, and indeed in all areas which are significant for its global performance, a number of alternative solutions will be open to it, particularly in a long-term perspective, safeguarding its freedom of choice and the concomitant full responsibility for success or failure. Were such alternatives not present, there would be no workers' self-government, in the sense at least in which it is understood in Yugoslavia. An apparent major exception is the direct tax on the enterprise income which in its present linear form is not discriminatory but does not provide for alternative choices either (such as where tax rates were related to certain criteria of performance, to levels of employment, etc.). Yet, as the enterprise fixed freely its rates of depreciation (above and beyond the legal minimum), it largely determines the volume of its income and thereby tax liability. In any event, in its economic activity and decision making, the worker-managed enterprise—contrary to the usual model of enterprise under other systems—cannot be regarded as dominated by externally set rules or laws derived from a planning system or from the market. It is much rather called upon to dominate such laws through its conscious work and management activity, and to make use of them for its best advantage in the light of its own habits, preferences and objectives. The income distribution process provides the enterprise with an essential instrument to this end.

The Role of Planning in the Yugoslav Firm

Before proceeding to survey this process in more concrete terms, a few explanations must be given concerning *enterprise planning* activity. While income distribution is common to all Yugoslav firms, the enterprise may or may not engage in planning its future activity. The need for planning, *inter alia* within the work organizations (enterprises), is referred to in the Preamble of the 1963 Yugoslav Constitution, but there is no binding legislation on the subject. The enterprises lay down themselves through their by-laws the principles and procedures (if any) governing their planning activities. Yet clearly, in an enterprise of some size, a work or management activity can only rationally be conducted within the framework of definite targets which define the activity of each unit for a period of time, and which correspond to the more general and more long-term objectives of the enterprise as a whole. Similarly, no rational income distribution can obtain in such an enterprise unless performance can be measured against planned targets. Consequently, most large enterprises and a good proportion of medium-sized firms engage in one way or another in formal planning of their future activity. In smaller firms with less complex operations the income distribution process can provide, by itself, an adequate basis for future action. Recent surveys have shown that less than half of the enterprises which were expected to plan their future activity actually engaged in formal planning exercises. Yet, the question is more one of semantics as it is hard to imagine a major firm without some elements—perhaps not entirely co-ordinated—of planning.

Enterprise planning is thus voluntary, but forms in most cases an essential complement to the income distribution process. It has at present little or no connection with national planning. It can rather be construed as a projection to a future date of the key items of income distribution: volume of production and sales, cost, other expenditures and personal incomes of members. Fully integrated plans are normally constructed for a twelve-month period, with trimestrial or even monthly sub-divisions. Medium and long-term (or perspective) development and investment programmes are also a current feature in enterprises of some size. They do not attempt, as a rule, a full integration of targets or forecasts—although their expected effect on future income obviously provides the principal criteria of rationality.

Actually the planning process appears to have been brought to a considerable degree of sophistication in most of the more advanced enterprises, the relative complexity of the process being compensated by over twenty years of practical experience and of adaptation to the specific requirements of the enterprise. It clearly is not something that could be introduced overnight—or according to a blueprint.

As an example, we may quote the list of preliminary elements for an annual plan as defined in the by-laws of a medium-sized enterprise (with above-average reputation in matters of organization and management). Appropriate dates were stipulated for each, so that a formal co-ordinated draft plan could be submitted to the Workers' Council by a set date. The following main items were listed:

Market analysis for the following year (to be completed as the first element of the planning process)
Investment maintenance programme
Draft plan of sales
Survey of production capacities
Draft production plan
Draft plan and documentation for technological changes
Draft proposals for purchase of basic materials
Proposals for utilization of production capacities
Proposals for purchase of materials for structural maintenance
Draft personnel plan
Draft purchase plan for materials
Draft plan for education and vocational training of workers
Draft production funds plan
Draft investment plan
The costs plan
The personal incomes plan
The financial plan.

Complementary programmes:
of the scientific research work
of social security, social activities, information service, safety, welfare and other benefits
programme of developments in managements organization and income sharing system
programme of market analysis and publicity.

Co-ordinated draft annual plan for reference back to the various departments for discussion and comments

Formal draft plan submitted to the Workers' Council.

The actual process of elaboration of the annual or long-term plans of the enterprise has been shown in the form of the following chart by Yugoslav authors.[1]

Table v

Elaboration and Adoption of Annual Plans Within the Enterprise

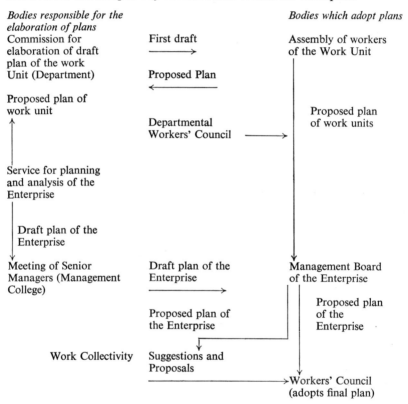

Bodies responsible for the elaboration of plans		*Bodies which adopt plans*
Commission for elaboration of draft plan of the work Unit (Department)	First draft $\longrightarrow$	Assembly of workers of the Work Unit
	Proposed Plan $\longleftarrow$	
Proposed plan of work unit $\uparrow$	Departmental Workers' Council $\longrightarrow$	Proposed plan of work units
Service for planning and analysis of the Enterprise		
Draft plan of the Enterprise		
Meeting of Senior Managers (Management College)	Draft plan of the Enterprise $\longrightarrow$	Management Board of the Enterprise
	Proposed plan of the Enterprise	Proposed plan of the Enterprise
Work Collectivity	Suggestions and Proposals	
		Workers' Council (adopts final plan)

The chart is largely self-explanatory. The only point which should be stressed is that there is no clear-cut division between the various bodies and stages of plan elaboration. The whole process is located within the walls of one single enterprise (although sometimes in a limited number of distinct

[1] Dr M. Novak and Professor V. Franc in *Planiranje u Radnim Organisacijama* (Planning in Work Organizations), Zagreb, 1968, p. 53.

locations) and concerns people who know each other and are in daily contact. Thus, neither the top management nor the workers' council are faced with a proposed plan of which they would know nothing in advance, as they have of necessity participated in its elaboration, within their own services or work units, since the very early stages. Similarly, in its true dimension, a plan for the forthcoming year is nothing but a continuation of current developments and policies well known to all, and cannot therefore come as a major surprise to the various participants. The whole exercise will much rather consist in detailed elaboration of current policies with particular attention to specific adjustments, improvements or economies in the enterprise operations.

To sum up, the plan of the enterprise will normally consist of a series of co-ordinated plans covering all aspects of its operation during the forthcoming period: sales, production, investment, supplies, employment and personal incomes, total and unit costs, vocational training, welfare and social services, distribution of the planned income, planned foreign exchange balances, and the planned indicators of success. Corresponding plans—as far as applicable—will be established for all the constituent autonomous units of the enterprise.

In an ideal world, where everything went according to plan, such detailed, all-embracing, fully decentralized enterprise planning would make all decision making—other than purely executive decisions—superfluous. More particularly, as all prices and elements of cost are covered, it would ensure an automatic flow and distribution of funds down to the basic work units or accounting centres; there would be no sharing-out decisions to take at the end of the planning period, and the workers' assembly would merely be called upon to approve the accounts. The position would not be much different if all went better than planned, with reasonable proportionality of the surplus incomes or the savings on costs.

Paradoxical as it may seem, these ideal conditions seem on the whole to apply to the bulk of the enterprise population despite the buoyant and unpredictable behaviour of the economy as a whole. Very often deviations from planned targets, such as for prices and costs, largely compensate each other, as do unforeseen developments affecting individual materials or final products in a typical multi-product firm. Most enterprise plans will also contain substantial explicit or hidden internal reserves which would allow for maintaining planned levels of operation, even against unforeseen setbacks of some magnitude.

Reserve funds—in excess of legal reserve—would normally be present not only at the enterprise level but also in the various work units. Moreover, both the enterprise and its constituent units would generally be able to draw on various other funds, such as those designed for amortization or welfare; in a sense, the bulk of personal incomes in excess of the guaranteed minimum forms an additional reserve. If the latter has to be drawn upon heavily, the decision-making process is likely to be brought into action. Most bigger enterprises visited in 1968 had a well-developed system of inter-departmental borrowing, some actually being in the process of transforming it into what they called an 'Internal Bank'. In two cases, the latter was about to start operation as an internal saving institution, open also to individual members of the work collectivity. A complex situation thus tended to obtain. In turn, unused reserves are a likely source of internal and 'invisible' investment, which may explain some behavioural peculiarity of the Yugoslav firm to be referred to later.

A major revision of the plan, or its full collapse, need only therefore occur when unfavourable developments of considerable magnitude are faced, particularly where there are no alternative production lines readily available (as for instance in a coal-mining enterprise). Alternatives in production would in any event be the first area to be explored. Decision-makers within the self-governing enterprise face an extremely elastic situation in most key areas, such as the working time, paid or unpaid leave, levels of remuneration, work intensity and may mobilize considerable reserves and other resources (e.g. through limiting welfare benefits). For instance, a major coal mine reported only eighteen working shifts per man in the early months of 1968 with production mostly for stock, but reached up to twenty-nine shifts later in the year as demand picked up. Production and incomes per shift varied as well. At the same time, attention was directed to various measures aimed at achieving greater regularity of demand (through consumers, family credit based on monthly payments, electricity generation, etc.) as well as diversifying production even in unexpected directions such as the shoe industry, and prefabricated parts for building.

No one's prior agreement is necessary—within legal limits—for all those concerned are part of the decision-making process. Often indeed, a single change of a planned indicator may solve the problem and save the plan. For instance, a large factory producing heavy mechanical equipment, following the investment slump resulting from the 1965 Reform, when faced with paralysis due to accumulation of stock, merely doubled the planned margin of its sales department (from 5 to 10 per cent) and succeeded thereby in bringing its accumulated inventory back to normal. This meant of course that all the other departments—particularly production—accepted a corresponding reduction of their planned incomes including the planned incomes of the workers. The latter may have nevertheless fared better than planned if they achieved savings on other costs, and certainly did so as compared with the possible stoppage of all production due to lack of demand. The same firm was successful in its parallel effort to develop entirely new lines of technically advanced consumer durables, which found a ready market.

Plan revision may also be required where performance is considerably in excess of planned targets, but such adaptations will clearly be infinitely less painful. In both cases, moreover, the plan itself may contain various adaptative devices (sliding scales, etc.) which would allow it to remain operational even in face of major changes. The various production departments may, for instance, only have to bear the full cost of increased prices of supplies below a certain limit, or only in a given proportion.

Where practised in its more advanced forms, this complex system of enterprise planning will—save in exceptional circumstances—strip the income-sharing process of its earlier lustre where the workers' council was seen as sitting on bags of accumulated income (or perhaps deep in the red) and dealing out the surplus value in a sovereign fashion. However, the planning process, as complex and precise as it may be, does not render the process of income distribution less meaningful. In fact, the whole plan can only be rationally constructed on the basis of a definite income distribution model. If the enterprise plan is in essence a delineation of the future behaviour of the enterprise, such behaviour can be neither forecast nor defined in a normative sense from within the enterprise by the work collectivity, unless the latter is aware of where it stands with respect to the results of its work, and can assess the benefits and risks involved in adopting alternative patterns patterns of behaviour. Obviously, the knowledge that some prices are subject to definite ceilings, while others are not or are guaranteed; that it is or is not subject to highly progressive taxation; that one or other item of expenditure is imputable to costs (hence tax free); that it may or may not obtain advantages or face penalties (through taxes, etc.) if it adopts such or such policy; knowledge of the tax liability of its welfare schemes, or of the incomes served in respect of work, as well as scores of other factors, may have a major impact on its behaviour. Hence, if it engages in planning, this will affect the content of its plans. In preparing their drafts or proposals, the enterprise planners must be constantly referring to an applicable model of income sharing when seeking the optimum solutions. Should they fail to do so, they would indeed engage in a meaningless, irrational exercise.

Even under a system of co-ordinated planning within the enterprise, the process of income distribution remains therefore the main key to understanding its behaviour and evaluating its performance. Indeed, the economics of the self-management enterprise can only be meaningfully approached through the medium of this particular procedure. It not only represents the central instrument of economic decision making within the Yugoslav firm, but also supplies the whole conceptual framework of the people who are actually making the decisions. Above all, satisfactory income distribution is an essential condition for the attainment of both the economic and the social ends of the system. As it has no direct equivalent elsewhere, the actual technique of income-sharing within the enterprise merits a somewhat closer analysis.

The Technique of Income Distribution
In the changing, adapting world of the worker-managed enterprises of Yugoslavia, the technique or form of income distribution represents one of the most stable and uniform features of the system. The combined periodic balance sheet and account forms introduced in the mid-fifties had hardly undergone a major alteration by 1968. Nor had the uniform decimal accounting system adopted in 1954 which is one of the major backbones of the system as a whole. A new partly modified and simplified system of decimal accountancy has been introduced as from 1 January 1969. The ten new classes of accounts contain only 140 analytical accounts which must be kept by all enterprises—as against over 800 of the earlier system. The main aim of the change, in addition to technical updating, is to grant the enterprises more

115

freedom to adapt their accountancy to their own requirements of accounting comptrol, costing and operational analysis.

At the same time, the formal requirements in the field of financial accountancy and income distribution are for all practical purposes identical for all enterprises in the country (as well as for such other forms of 'organizations of associated labour' as may exist within or outside the enterprise, including other forms of 'work organizations' such as banks, social institutions and even public authorities). The advantages of such a unified accountancy system, which is an inheritance of central planning, are obvious from the point of view of financial and fiscal comptrol and efficiency analysis. It also makes it possible to establish directly (and not by sampling or other random methods) the values corresponding to any one of the analytical accounts of the enterprise at all levels of the economy, the results being rapidly available to the authorities or institutions concerned. Data on such varied items as depreciation allowances, allocation to investment or welfare, personal incomes, cost of business travel (and scores of others) may be closely followed and analysed for all possible purposes at local, regional, industrial and national level.

The operation of each enterprise or of any group thereof can thus be constantly analysed and compared to others. Trends can be established, and if necessary acted upon by others, including financial or fiscal authorities as well as policy makers at all levels. This basic transparency of the economic operation of the enterprise, deriving from its 'social' character, must always be kept in mind, for it directly influences its behaviour in all matters.

The actual income sharing model of the Yugoslav firm clearly rests on the conceptual framework of Marx's theory of value, which it adapts to a system of producers' self-management, while solving the conflict of interest inherent in capitalist enterprise. It makes use of the distribution formula suggested by Marx for a socialist economy.

Briefly, the argument runs as follows: Labour is the source of all values. Through their work in the enterprise, the associated workers produce commodities, the value of which is socially acknowledged only if and when they meet real requirements of the society. Such social valuation of their work normally occurs through a series of market exchanges where the workers and their enterprises appear as customers. The socially acknowledged value of the commodities belongs to no one but those who produced it, and they are entitled to share it out among themselves according to their work. Before doing so, they must provide for the general needs of society: for the replacement of the fixed capital used in the process of production; for the expansion of future production by means of additional investment; and for their own common or welfare needs. The capital they use in the process of production being the result of accumulated past labour, placed at their disposal by society, they may owe to the latter a special contribution proportionate to its volume, and corresponding to its relative scarcity. Such contributions also tend to equalize the position of various groups of producers equally endowed with capital resources. The residual income includes both the basic value of their labour, as measured by the cost of its simple reproduction, and

116

any surplus due to their particular effort at work, skill or entrepreneurial ability. The two components, analogous but not indentical to wages and profits under capitalism, are inextricably merged in one whole: the income of the work collectivity. The latter is to be shared out freely by its members, on the basis of full equality and according to everyone's part in the production process. To evaluate the latter, objective criteria must be fixed in advance, and the principle of equal pay for equal work observed.

This distribution process leads of necessity to some inequalities of income between enterprises, according to the relative success of their operation as valued through the market. Within reasonable limits, such inequalities are justified in conditions of relative scarcity of goods, as they provide an essential criterion as to the value society attaches to various commodities in the light of its real needs at any given time. The associated producers are thereby guided to minimize their costs and to select lines of production, levels of quality, techniques, etc. commanding the highest income per unit of labour input. The ensuing reorientation of methods and lines of production tends automatically to reduce the existing income differentials. However, as long as techniques continue to progress, such differentials tend to widen again under the impact of each innovation. Moreover, the associated producers could continue to produce at different levels of income if they chose to work with less intensity, less skill, or were less willing to adapt to change, or indeed found their operational optimum at different levels. While ensuring a minimum income for work already performed, society would undertake no formal responsibility for work representing little or no value and would guarantee no income to those who are fit for work but choose to abstain.

Finally, the normal course of the process of equalization of rates of income (somewhat analogous to the decreasing rates of profit under capitalism) can be inhibited, or even reversed, where individual enterprises, for whatever reason, enjoy monopolistic positions on the market. In such cases, unless the producers themselves act in a responsible manner, society must intervene to protect its interests and to ensure more equitable conditions.

This ideal theoretical income-sharing model operates at three distinct stages or levels. (There would be four if the actual allocation of the total personal income of the work collectivity among individual workers were also included. This is normally not the case as the individual shares are determined in advance by appropriate rules and call for no separate decision when past income is allocated.)

The *first stage*, or primary distribution of the social product, corresponds to the business operation of the firm. Through sales (and possible internal consumption, particularly investment), the gross income of the enterprise is formed, reflecting the volume and quality of production and the assortment of products offered in response to demand requirements. Material costs (all non-labour costs) are deducted from the gross product reflecting, in a similar fashion, the work collectivity's ability to organize the production process efficiently. The various items falling within this first stage of income distribution cannot of course be regulated *ex post* by the work collectivity; it cannot decree a greater volume of sales or lesser costs than those actually shown in its accounts. Yet, if the income distribution is seen as a continuous and forward-looking (planned) process—with, say, monthly balancing—the enterprise has every possibility of modifying each and every item falling under this heading directly or indirectly to its best advantage.

Viewed from the outside, this primary income distribution is, of course, effected principally under the impact of market conditions which are objectively defined at any given time, although they are also to a great extent the result of conscious social activity. Protection by means of custom tariffs against dumping etc., comes first to mind, but there are many other items of major importance. The very existence of the enterprise is the result of such conscious activity in the past (including possible privileged investment, planners' errors, etc.), and the effective demand it meets reflects to a large extent the result of conscious development activity of other producers. This being generally acknowledged, and indeed made transparently obvious through the system of social accounting, the right of the work collectivity to appropriate the results of its work cannot by any means be equated to the dogmatic definition of private property under early capitalism. The work collectivity is expected to examine in a conscious manner the various factors which contributed to the formation of its income and to act in consequence in a responsible manner. Should it fail to do so, it obviously cannot claim absolute privilege based on ownership.

The *second stage*, the so-called secondary distribution, ensures the division of the net product, in other words the value added, between the general needs of society and the residual portion to be used by the work collectivity. The primary purpose is to provide for common needs of the workers which cannot be satisfied within the enterprise itself, such as national defence, education, and general administration. A portion of their income is thus alienated by way of taxation, which they have helped to shape through their representatives, but which nevertheless remains externally determined. Ideally, the work collectivities are expected to, and in practice increasingly do, provide the necessary means by way of voluntary contribution to, or participation in, such wider social activities.

A secondary purpose of taxation, which was a major factor up to the 1965 Economic Reform, was to provide additional guidance to enterprises in their policy making, and to limit excessive inequalities of income, particularly where due to monopolistic positions or other special circumstances. It was commonly believed, up to 1965, that enterprises shaped their policies in the light of such fiscal instruments, rather than being guided primarily by market considerations and, as indicated earlier, the active use of such instruments for planned policy guidance has, for this very reason, been largely discontinued. The efforts made in 1968 to overcome the resulting economic stagnation brought them to some extent back into active use. However, since under the legislation now in force the enterprise freely determines its rates of depreciation in excess of the legal minimum, it is actually determining the amount of its taxable income. Indeed, this is an outstanding example of how a change in the formal rules of the game (i.e. departure from the rule of

118

uniform binding rates for depreciation) can change the apparent behaviour of the enterprise for, under the new system, the enterprise has every interest in reducing the accounting value of new investment (after tax), and increasing correspondingly the provisions for amortization which are deducted from its taxable income, although the two are partly serving the same purpose.

The *third stage* of income distribution necessarily involves a formal decision of the work collectivity (the workers' council) although in fact, as explained earlier, the content of such a decision may have been largely pre-empted at the planning stage. Now, the collectivity is faced with its net income (after tax) to share out according to its best judgment. The only legal obligation it must comply with is to serve its members the guaranteed minimum income in proportion to the time spent at work. Under normal conditions, considerably higher incomes will already have been paid out to workers as an advance, by virtue of the enterprise rules and/or plans of operation. Should it be facing a deficit the enterprise may draw on its voluntary reserve or, in more serious cases, its legal reserves as well.

The meaning of 'deficit' in the self-management firm is extremely ambiguous. The enterprise may already show negative results in the first stage of distribution (before tax) which would mean that the value added is actually negative. If somewhat better off, it may still be unable to pay the full amount of taxes, and these may be correspondingly reduced as explained earlier (deficit after taxation); finally it may be unable to pay the minimum incomes for work. In all these cases it may draw on its legal reserves (if any) and, failing this, be placed under a receiver and liquidated. Yet again, the firm will be subjectively in deficit if it has paid out more in advances for work than it has earned or even if it did not earn enough to pay such incomes as it planned. In such cases, it would normally reduce other voluntary spendings or draw on its voluntary reserve funds. In fact, personal incomes must constantly be kept within the limits of net income. In other words, the income distribution process can be thought of as an all-embracing incomes policy at the enterprise level and, by extension, at all the higher levels of the economy.

In normal circumstances, however, the net income of the enterprise will be well in excess of the guaranteed minimum. The workers' management bodies must then consider the position, particularly regarding the influence of outside factors on the formation of their income, and act according to their best judgment in allocating the available income, in the light of their needs and preferences. As a matter of principle, they have a duty to consider the need for further expansion of activities, and allocate a fraction of their income to the corresponding investments. The importance of such self-financing cannot be determined from the outside, and will vary considerably with time and changing circumstances. In practice, values ranging from 0 to well over 100 per cent of personal incomes may be encountered.

In the past, various allocational formulae were devised to help the enterprise in finding objective criteria for this decision, and various forms of social pressure were applied to enterprises found loath to take their full share in the development process. Yet the campaign against 'investment inflation', launched since 1964, has stripped self-financing of much of its earlier aura, and the corresponding decisions are now largely made in a neutral environment. Many enterprises continue to use some of the earlier distribution models on a voluntary basis and have included in their rules or plans a provision fixing the proportion of their net income they expect to plough back in normal circumstances.

Seen in the context of its practical operation, the enterprise is never as free in this regard as it may appear in abstract legal or economic theory. It will usually have past investment credits to repay, and other investments in progress. Competition, as well as technical progress, will force it to expand or to modernize. Much of the available finance will thus be committed by decisions taken at other times and under the pressure of outside developments. All enterprises will be interested in building up their reserve funds in order to face up to temporary setbacks in the best possible conditions, and prevent any reduction of incomes. Reserve funds are simply self-financing in respect of current operations of circulating capital.

The position is rather similar, both in law and in management practice, regarding the provision to be made for the satisfaction of collective needs of the workers by drawing on the enterprise income. Again, such funds will be largely pre-empted by earlier decision (existing welfare schemes, housing under construction, etc.) of the work collectivity. It should be noted that nothing prevents the collectivity from providing for the needs of the wider social community, or joining forces with others, particularly the local commune, to meet such needs. The legal or economic freedom again very often have to yield to the imperatives of real life.

Formally speaking, the work collectivity has thus completed its task, having arrived through successive deductions at a residual amount which it intends to distribute among its members as their personal incomes. And so indeed it has. But the process is a circular one. A start can be made at any one point to bring all others into place and shape. More particularly, the work collectivity could start by determining the level of personal incomes it wishes to pay to its members, and allocate its income in consequence. Should it engage in a costly welfare scheme (e.g. housing) this would provide the convenient starting point. Similarly, where investment in progress, or the desired growth rate is the determining consideration. This is particularly true where income distribution is seen—as it should be—as a continuous process of adaptation and planning (with monthly or quarterly accounting) through which the close interdependence of all the items of the accounts chart can be clearly seen and acted upon in the light of the work collectivity's own preferences and of any outside changes or new stimuli. In other words, the income distribution process provides the necessary framework for rational decision making through which the effect of all changes, past or planned, internal or external, can be gauged and alternatives analysed. Since income distribution actually plays this role in the Yugoslav firm, it also provides an indispensable tool for assessing its behaviour and the operation of the self-management system as a whole.

The distribution process is also circular in a somewhat different sense as it

120

has cut across, between two arbitrary points of time, the necessarily continuous and self-contained production and business activity of the enterprise. All the inputs used up during that period reproduce themselves to the same extent and grow, or possibly shrink a little, and in this new form provide the starting point for the enterprise's operation during the following period. Yet this circular reasoning in terms of a short period is not entirely adequate. In purely material terms, the time horizon of the real workers will be much longer, considerably so in an average Yugoslav firm. It may perhaps be twenty years or more, as some would include their families. Many would be concerned not only with the simple growth of income, but also with their own advancement and the development of the firm (and indeed the community) as a whole. An entirely new dynamic background for decision making thus comes to light, for which no adequate verbal expression exists. Compared to the short term income-sharing period, the true economic time horizon may appear practically limitless. This by no means implies that the economic object of an individual's present needs to be of exceptional magnitude. The desire to move from a mud hut or slum dwelling to a 'two-room modern flat with central heating' may constitute sufficient motivation for a semi-skilled worker to press for phenomenal growth of the enterprise, such growth offering the only real possibility for the attainment of his particular personal objective.

From the moral angle, also, the accounting period appears too short to be fully relevant. No doubt the workers are not the same as when they started; they have learnt and changed in the process. They may have found new horizons for their activity, geographically, or in the command of the techniques or economics of their enterprise, they may have had to face severe setbacks, seen some of their hopes thwarted. More probably, however, no such single development could be properly situated within a short period. Major breakthroughs, crises or conflicts which basically alter the enterprise may occur once in a decade, but their preliminaries, as well as their impact on the moral climate of the enterprise, on its policy and performance, may last for a good many years. No full explanation can therefore be reasonably sought in any one particular set of accounts. A time series can tell a lot more about any one particular enterprise, but can hardly be compared to that of any other, for each is by definition under the command of its own internal developments, its own time horizon and moral climate.

As a visual help to understanding the income distribution process, the latter has often been graphically represented. In our view, these can hardly make things clearer than a simple summary of accounts shown by the concrete example of Table VI, which appeared in the annual report of one of the enterprises visited in 1968. As is customary, the table compares the results of 1967 with those of the previous year. (The plan for 1968 would contain an additional column for that year.) Although corresponding to real data, the figures given are purely illustrative. Each item would, of course, call for a separate explanation both as to its legal institutional background and its relation to the particular line of production and business of the enterprise. While this is clearly out of the question here, it should be noted that, in

Table VI

Summary of Annual Accounts Reflecting the Income Distribution Process
(*As reproduced in the Financial Report of the Workers' Council of Enterprise A*)

	Annual Accounts For:		Index
	1966	1967	
	(in 000 new dinars)		
I *Gross income*			
Total sales	334,957·95	401,448·04	119·85
Customers	26,131·77	39,761·39	152·16
Total receipts from sales	308,826·18	361,686·65	117·12
Other incomes[1]	2,563·56	2,167·51	84·55
II *Total income for distribution*	311,389·74	363,854·16	116·85
III *Determination of the net income*			
Cost of materials	151,221·41	167,052·87	110·47
Services	5,791·39	5,657·07	97·68
Rentals and hire	278·79	501·97	180·05
Costs of publicity, fairs and representation	261·43	427·73	163·61
Investment maintenance	3,891·39	3,796·76	97·57
Goods purchased from others for resale through retail network	23,293·65	39,198·55	168·28
Depreciation	12,176·69	21,400·58	175·75
Transport costs	4,716·24	5,787·70	122·72
Other costs	617·41	481·35	77·96
Extraordinary expenditures	1,800·58	1,923·00	106·80
IV *Total material expenses*	204,049·00	246,227·72	120·67
V *Net product*	107,340·74	117,626·43	109·58
Interest on bank credit	4,715·55	6,720·40	142·52
Interest on capital	2,075·21	2,758·62	132·93
Insurance premiums	3,950·40	4,999·36	126·56
Contributions and membership fees	199·30	322·71	161·92
Water tax	1,602·21	1,875·87	117·08
Turnover tax	806·82	1,167·95	144·76
Supplementary contribution to social security	1,045·97	1,038·27	99·26
Personal incomes charged to costs[2]	1,763·39	2,594·80	147·15
Other costs imputable to net product	499·70	232·28	46·48
VI *Total expenditure charged against gross income*	220,707·60	267,922·30	121·39
VII *Net income for distribution*	90,682·14	95,931·85	105·79
Reserve funds of enterprise	4,994·22	5,153·47	103·1
Contribution to common reserves	676·75	486·86	71·94
Gross personal incomes	70,335·97	75,468·15	107·30
Contribution to Skopje[3]	293·50	296·46	101·01
Allocation to capital funds	3,441·31	6,026·89	175·13
Allocation to the common consumption fund (welfare, etc.)	10,940·38	8,500·00	77·69

[1] Non-recurrent incomes, such as receipts from doubtful claims against customers written off in an earlier accounting period.

[2] Separation grants, travel allowances *per diem*, etc.

[3] Reconstruction of the capital of Macedonia after earthquake; in essence a supplementary tax on personal incomes.

122

addition to the summary balance sheet (not reproduced here), the financial report of the workers' council contained twenty pages of more detailed analysis of most of the important items of the accounts with verbal explanations of major changes or disbursements and recommendations for further action.

Moreover, in a more voluminous annual report (seventy-nine pages), the workers' council of the same enterprise reviewed in greater detail *inter alia* its own work, questions of employment and training, the problems encountered, the results achieved in terms of physical production of the central services, development of exports and the reports of the bank and financial inspectorate. From this very considerable wealth of facts and figures, it would seem of interest to note that out of the 4·9 thousand workers employed, 626 were members of the central or departmental councils and/or management boards, which held a total of 562 sessions during the year. While fluctuations and increases in employment were slight (12 and 4 per cent respectively in 1967), massive changes occurred in the composition of the work force, with an increase since 1965 as high as 160 per cent in the number of highly qualified workers (669 at the end of 1967), and 50 per cent for those with university training (217). There was a correspondingly rapid fall in the number of those without qualification (61 per cent fewer manual workers and 9 per cent fewer auxiliary office staff, down respectively to 432 and 238). The magnitude of the change, which cannot be directly accounted for in financial terms, was thus very considerable, and was mainly accomplished through the implementation of the enterprise's own personnel and training policies at its own costs.

The official forms used for annual balances and account statements are, of course, considerably more detailed and allow for a much closer analysis of the enterprise's operation and results, including particularly its output or income per unit of labour time (normally in hour units). In 1967, for instance, this official form contained 216 items altogether. In view of its size, it cannot be reproduced here, After being approved by the work collectivity (the workers' council) and the income allocated, the balance-cum-account-statement is submitted to the Service of Social Audit (already mentioned) for purposes of national accounting, financial check and economic analysis. Table VII is an extract of a survey of enterprise accounts (1959–60) for an industry, a sub-group of same, and an individual enterprise. Only forty-seven out of ninety-three items are reproduced here. The figures given are again real ones, but their only purpose here is to illustrate the type of data available for all enterprises, and the nature of possible differences in factor endowment, policy and performance.

The actual presentation of the accounts provides not only a formal basis for the whole decision making process, but also tends to shape underlying mental patterns and reasoning processes. Those who participate in any manner in the decision-making process will at all times consider the financial implications of their decision against this concrete background, not any other which may be used elsewhere or appeal to an outside observer. Although they may seem uncommon to most readers, the conceptual framework, the

123

nomenclature and the practical operation of the income-sharing process have for a long time been integrated into the current practice of the Yugoslav enterprises, and raise no problems at the level of elementary understanding. The voluminous specialized literature which continues to deal with the subject tends increasingly to get beyond the stages of the earlier elementary manuals, and to approach it at much higher levels of sophistication, both as regards theory and use in enterprise practice. The original contribution of the enterprises or local levels are becoming increasingly important in this particular area of management theory and practice.

The income distribution model is open to practically unlimited decentralization, down to each 'accounting centre' which may be a workshop, a department or any autonomous work unit. An autonomous work group or unit does not require a separate accounting service (nor would there be one in a typical case), the decentralized accountancy being kept by the central accounting services. All that is needed are proper records of production and costs, which should be available anyway in a properly organized firm. Such decentralization exists in practice in many enterprises, often in a suitably simplified manner, with such items as do not directly interest the work units (e.g. various taxes and contributions) remaining an exclusive part of the central distribution process. The autonomous units—accounting and distribution centres—may actually trade and do business among themselves, at conventional or real terms, and carry as costs, or pay directly for, the services provided by the central departments of management. The more autonomous accounting units there are, the greater is the apparent proportion of costs on their accounts and the smaller their net income, or value added, including the personal income of the workers. Consequently, in a highly decentralized accounting and self-management structure, it is savings on production costs that will be seen as the primary factor making for increased personal incomes, and vice versa.

As a very rough approximation, in an enterprise where the production process is strictly continuous, and total costs reach an average level of 60 per cent of the gross product, a decentralization into forty units would make the costs appear to reach 98 per cent, on average, in each unit. The sum of personal incomes would be reduced to less than 2 per cent in each individual unit. A saving of 2 per cent on costs would thus, in an average unit, allow for a doubling of personal incomes (or employing up to twice as many workers, or realizing significant internal investments, etc.) in that unit.

At whatever level it may be considered, workshop, department, enterprise or association of enterprises, the income distribution process makes it possible to obtain a clear view of the effects of all decisions with economic implications, including the economic effect of the enterprise's social policy or welfare schemes or cultural activities. This specific property of the system is of particular importance as regards remuneration for work which, in the shape of wages, largely—and indeed rightly—escape purely economic criteria in most modern economies. Although wages and labour continue to be treated as purely economic phenomena or factors of production in traditional liberal economics, particularly where abstract mathematical methods are

124

Table VII

Extract from Social Accountancy Survey of Enterprises

Annual Balances and Accounts, 1959–60 [*of an Industry, a Sub-Group of same, and of an Enterprise of the Sub-Group*]

(*in 000 millions old dinars*)

No.[1]	Definition of Item	Industry A			Sub-Group B			Enterprise C		
		1959	1960	Index	1959	1960	Index	1959	1960	Index
	(a) *Fixed assets*									
2	Buildings	82·38	88·19	107	14·36	14·83	103	1·33	1·59	119
	Means of production	151·06	164·14	108	26·27	27·36	104	2·85	3·56	124
	Fixed investments in progress	10·62	14·99	141	1·40	2·27	162	0·52	0·25	47
	Cash resources of investment fund	24·08	26·20	108	3·87	4·81	124	0·14	0·34	242
12	Total fixed assets (present value)[2]	166·16	183·16	112	26·36	28·66	145	2·82	3·52	124
	(b) *Special funds*									
13	Resources of collective consumption fund (welfare etc.)	34·38	40·92	118	3·71	4·56	123	0·83	0·96	108
16	Reserve fund and cash reserves of other funds	9·05	11·47	126	1·80	1·81	101	0·17	0·00	00
	(c) *Circulating capital*									
18	Cash resources	9·51	9·33	98	1·22	1·37	112	0·31	0·02	06
19	Customers	75·46	120·21	159	11·81	18·04	153	0·97	3·76	386
20	Suppliers	12·12	15·16	125	2·72	5·38	198	1·55	1·81	116
21	Stock of raw materials and sundry equipment	104·31	138·84	133	16·83	20·64	123	3·50	3·14	89
22	Production in progress	48·37	65·60	135	10·15	13·52	133	3·32	3·74	142
23	Stock of finished products and merchandise for resale	19·92	34·08	171	2·09	3·14	151	0·24	0·31	128
24	Other assets	26·09	37·32	143	3·99	4·68	117	0·66	0·89	73

[1] Current numbers of the original tables are given so as to indicate where items of minor importance have been omitted, as for instance No. 1 (Land). Where relevant, the definitions of the analytical items omitted will be given in footnote under the corresponding sub-total. Such sub-totals are underlined.

[2] Omitted items include: land, 'other fixed assets', and several 'corrections of value of assets' (amortization, etc.).

Table VII (Continued)

No.	Definition of Item	Industry A			Sub-Group B			Enterprise C		
		1959	1960	Index	1959	1960	Index	1959	1960	Index
25	Total circulating capital	295·81	420·22	142	48·87	66·78	142	10·78	14·42	133
26	Total assets (12 and 25)	461·96	603·37	130	75·24	95·44	130	13·60	17·95	131
27	Losses (deficit I)[1]	0·02	0·03	144	0·02	—	—	—	—	—
	(d) Origin of assets (i.e. debit side of balance sheet)					Omitted				
	(e) Labour									
40	Total of hours worked (in millions)	337·67	416·99	110	58·21	64·96	112	3·12	4·20	134
42	Minimum guaranteed personal incomes	35·83	39·07	108	5·32	6·01	113	0·29	0·38	132
43	Personal income actually paid out	55·19	68·16	123	8·53	10·40	122	0·54	0·71	130
	(f) Distribution of gross product									
44	Gross product (total receipts)	408·81	516·92	126	54·24	70·07	129	4·08	6·25	153
45	Cost of material	212·45	261·94	123	26·05	34·13	131	2·17	4·00	184
46	Cost of services	9·99	15·75	157	1·16	2·03	174	0·03	0·14	436
47	Cost of investment maintenance	6·14	7·58	123	1·13	1·43	132	0·14	0·17	126
49	Merchandise purchased for resale	16·97	22·74	135	2·02	2·24	111	0·11	0·20	190
50	Depreciation	10·11	10·65	105	1·79	1·84	103	0·16	0·13	117
51	Total costs[2]	260·61	324·98	120	32·60	42·10	129	2·61	4·68	179
52	Income (41 less 51)	148·28	192·17	129	21·65	27·99	129	1·47	1·57	106
63	Interests, taxes and fees[3]	30·19	34·96	116	3·23	3·60	111	0·33	0·40	120

[1] Losses here included are those (of the most serious kind) where the operation of the enterprise resulted in negative value added and consequent reduction of the capital assets.

[2] Item No. 48, 'Other costs', omitted.

[3] Includes the following items recorded separately: interest on investment credit; interest on fixed capital; interest on other credits (circulating capital); interest on circulating capital; land tax, vocational training tax; contributions and membership fees; federal and local turnover tax.

Table VII (*Continued*)

No.	Definition of Item	Industry A			Sub-Group B			Enterprise C		
		1959	1960	Index	1959	1960	Index	1959	1960	Index
69	*Other disbursements chargeable to gross income*[1]	3·66	4·86	133	0·48	0·64	132	0·02	0·02	117
78	*Net income for distribution*[2]	75·74	95·99	127	11·22	14·15	126	0·75	0·79	106
79	Personal incomes of workers	57·21	69·18	121	8·51	10·92	128	0·44	0·61	139
80	Reserve funds (legal and voluntary)	3·89	5·08	130	0·66	0·84	127	0·11	0·15	145
81	Allocated to investment	2·17	2·05	95	0·25	0·18	71	0·59	—	—
82	Allocated to circulating capital	0·69	0·70	101	0·05	0·15	268	—	—	—
83	Allocated for collective consumption	2·22	2·57	116	0·39	0·09	22	0·08	—	—
85	Non-allocated reserves	9·41	16·53	177	1·35	1·99	147	0·07	0·03	38
	(g) Summary									
86	Enterprise share in income	80·77	100·91	125	11·70	14·79	126	0·76	0·81	106
87	Total personal incomes	60·63	73·52	121	8·99	11·56	128	0·46	0·63	138
88	Share in income of the wider social collectivities (taxes etc.)	67·52	89·61	133	9·96	13·25	133	0·71	0·76	106
	(h) Indices									
89	Number of workers (thousands)	151·7	166·8	110	23·28	25·98	104	1·2	1·7	134
90	Total assets per worker[3]	3,046	3,620	119	3,231	3,673	114	10,889	10,687	98
91	Income per worker[3]	979	1,152	117	930	1,077	116	1,178	932	79
92	Personal income per worker[3]	401	441	110	386	445	115	365	375	102
93	Net income per worker[3]	497	572	115	481	543	113	596	471	79

[1] Includes more particularly 'personal incomes' chargeable to gross income (daily allowances, etc.) and supplementary contributions to social security (in respect of above average rate of industrial accidents, etc.).

[2] The intermediary items (Nos. 70–77) not shown here cover more particularly the tax on enterprise income, tax rebates and other minor adjustments. This tax was abolished in 1965 and the income tax is now levied only on that part of the net income which is distributed as personal income of the workers (item No. 79).

[3] In thousands of the old dinars.

practised, or in dogmatic Marxist analysis, it can hardly be questioned that notions such as the 'iron law of wages' or 'absolute pauperization of the working classes' have been emptied of content by the non-economic forces in the modern Welfare State, by the influence of trade unions and, in particular, by the policy of full employment. Yet, such non-economic forces obviously disrupt the 'normal' operation of the private enterprise economy for they eliminate the 'free' determination of levels of employment and of wages by the market and are hence the cause of permanent social strife and inflationary pressures.

As personal incomes in the Yugoslav firm, wages can be discussed and determined in rational terms. The work collectivity has an unlimited freedom to fix its 'rates' as high as it may, in millions perhaps, yet what it will be able to pay out is no more—and no less—than what it has actually earned. Pressure on wage rates becomes meaningless in the absence of any outside owner who would appropriate the enterprise profits, be it the State or a private entrepreneur. The enterprise may actually start by determining the volume of funds it intends to distribute as personal incomes, particularly at the planning stage of the process. It has then to find the means of accommodating them into a balanced set of accounts, actual or planned. The same applies to all other projects, of an economic as well as a social nature, which the enterprise is able to formulate, whether it intends to open a new workshop, buy more efficient machinery or develop its own holiday centre by the sea. It may, of course—and probably will at the start—overstretch its capacity, over-invest or over-plan its welfare schemes. It may burn its fingers in the process, but for many the lesson drawn from their neighbour's experience will suffice to keep within bounds the wilder flights of fancy. In any event, the annual accounts will have to be balanced at the end of the period—save for such outside credits as may have been secured during the year—and should the results prove contrary to expectations, the work collectivity has every possibility of taking corrective measures. Such moments of crisis appear to have played a decisive role in the development of business and personnel policy consciousness in a great number of enterprises. Where, on the contrary, unexpected surpluses appear, the work collectivity has the more pleasant, but also more risky task, of planning the collective and individual future of its members freely.

The personal income of the individual worker. The work collectivity has determined the amount set aside for distribution as personal incomes of its members, as remuneration for their work and management responsibility. For purposes of purely economic analysis, this could appear sufficient: the amount allocated directly to the workers as remuneration has been fixed and, the number of workers and working hours being known as well, the average income per head or per hour can easily be calculated. In a sense, indeed, the share of income allocated to every hour worked during the year reflects all the various stages of income formation and distribution within the enterprise. Each worker for every hour spent at work participates in every item of receipts and of expenditure which passed through the enterprise accounts during the year, and his direct share is finally determined by the allocations to the investment and welfare funds. If average hourly production doubled,

128

if savings on unit costs were considerable, *ceteris paribus*, his cash income will correspondingly increase, and vice versa. This would be directly applicable in a small enterprise, where all are paid strictly equal rates, or in the case of a worker who worked exactly the average number of hours carrying the average 'rate' of share in the enterprise income.

However, this fourth stage of the income-sharing process is not all that simple in practice, and the solutions may directly affect the overall behaviour of the enterprise. Two basic principles apply:

(i) the worker must be remunerated according to his work
(ii) no remuneration can be paid out unless there are specific governing rules set in advance.

As to the first principle, it is in the first two stages that the global value attaching to work performed within the enterprise has been determined; by society at large in an objective manner through the market and, more subjectively, through the various instruments of financial and fiscal policy. At the third stage, the work collectivity itself had an opportunity to value its own direct performance or merit, and has allocated a corresponding amount to remunerate its members directly. Their actual distribution is automatic, for the extent to which each individual member participates in the total amount has been fixed in advance, with respect to the job he holds, by the appropriate rules of the enterprise. No decision taking is necessary in this respect at the stage when the enterprise's accounts are approved and its income distributed. A mere accounting operation is involved.

The rules governing personal incomes are of a permanent nature, but may be amended by the appropriate self-management body (normally the workers' council). In an enterprise of some size, such rules would normally determine only the general principle, leaving the actual determination of rates to similar rules adopted within the individual departments or autonomous units which, as a rule form and share out their own income within the framework of the planning procedures referred to earlier.

The actual rates are fixed separately for each job or group of jobs, the work collectivity being free to choose criteria of job evaluation and introduce income differentials. Formal job evaluation procedures seem widespread, whereby the rate attaching to a job is expressed in points according to levels of skill, responsibility, conditions and physical strain at work, etc. Others may still define the value of each job in money terms, but even here the currency unit merely has an accounting value. Output norms and bonus schemes may be included, but are not exceedingly popular. It will be realized however, that the decentralized remuneration system can itself be seen as a combined collective output and bonus scheme, since the funds available to each 'accounting unit' vary both with the the volume of production and with savings on costs; moreover, if fewer hours are worked, each will draw a larger share. The trend towards decentralization of the income distribution process receives great attention both in theory and in enterprise practice; it allows each work group to have direct control over the income it creates, and its

129

distribution. Where provided for by the enterprise rules, members of such groups dispense with the formal valuation of their respective jobs and share out their collective incomes according to their own understanding of each others' past performance, merit or needs. A departure from the formal job evaluation system is noticeable in a growing number of enterprises on another point as well, i.e. that of formal 'skill' or training which is no longer taken into consideration where the same work is performed by workers belonging to different formal categories based on skill.

The possibility and, indeed, the growing practice of forming reserve and investment funds at these various levels of decentralized self-management units has already been referred to; the economic and social importance of this development, and the difficulties it raises from the point of view of statistical and financial comptrol are considerable. Among other things, the difference between the reserve funds of the enterprise and the reserves of the workers' private households may be obliterated to a large extent. Where a worker knows that large reserves are held by his work group, he may adapt his private consumption and saving behaviour in consequence and vice versa. Similarly, where workers have confidence in the future of their jobs, they may indeed be ready to draw on their private reserves while little or no income is forthcoming to their group, thereby indirectly supplying additional working capital to the enterprise. Seen against a rural background, this is much less surprising than in a purely urban working-class environment. (The difference between these two types of environment or background is in fact quite perceptible in Yugoslavia despite the predominantly rural character of most regions.)

Although no longer bound by any existing statute, most enterprises continue to classify all jobs into four basic categories according to the skill or training levels required for its performance: unskilled, semi-skilled, skilled and highly skilled for manual workers; and low, medium, higher and high level of training for the non-manuals, categories corresponding to the difference between an ordinary labourer or handyman and a fully-trained craftsman; and between primary school and university training to individual jobs being further differentiated within each category. The enterprise regulates all such differentials freely according to its needs and preferences. In principle, it could eliminate them altogether or introduce income differentials of exceptional magnitude, the rational criteria being, of course, the local availability of the various skills and the enterprise's own needs regarding manning. Where special skills are required in an unattractive location, particularly as regards top level managers and technicians, special arrangements may often be negotiated directly with the candidate, and may result in uncommonly high income differentials. Any worker has the right to have the valuation of his job reviewed at the time he is recruited, or subsequently under procedures provided for by the enterprise by-laws and other rules. There will normally be a job evaluation committee, and the possibility of appeal to the workers' council.

In fact, however, the differential as between the lowest and the highest category is quite small, perhaps 1 : 2 or 1 : 3 on average. It is significantly

130

less than the differentiation in per capita incomes between individual enter-prises. Yet it seems sufficient to provide individuals and groups with a real incentive to improve their qualifications, not only for the sake of contributing more to the overall results of the enterprise, but also for their personal advancement on the job. In fact, as it regulates the amount and quality of capital at its disposal, the enterprise fixes not only the volume of its employ-ment but also regulates the quality of its work force. Income differentials and training policy are the principal means to this end. They are closely inter-related, for the more is spent on training, and the better its quality (planning, etc.), the less is likely to be spent on attracting locally unavailable skills. If all skills could be made available in sufficient numbers under training schemes operated or financed by the enterprise itself, the corresponding income dif-ferentials could be considerably reduced or even disappear. Making higher skills available to candidates of local stock is highly desirable by itself in a multi-ethnic society, where domination by 'foreigners' is necessarily resented and may lead to serious friction. A well-developed training scheme and corresponding welfare expenditure are of even greater value for individual members of the work collectivity likely to benefit, for the higher classification attained through enterprise operated or financed schemes would also be recognized should they seek employment elsewhere. In their own enterprise, it gives them a right to corresponding promotion.

In another context, the whole income distribution process would indeed merit closer examination from the point of view of the individual and his interests, both material and moral. As his pay packet reflects the state of all the enterprise accounts, and varies a good deal in consequence both in time and in space, he is objectively interested in all that affects his enterprise's operations and finances. He can hardly be expected not to take notice at least of major developments which may affect his earnings. If a major order is received, or else a new technique introduced, or monies lost through fraud or carelessness, the consequent benefits or losses for everyone can be estab-lished with reasonable accuracy. Similarly, bad performance of some is borne by all others, and not likely to be condoned for ever. Any social, welfare or cultural activity can also be seen as part of the costs, even by the individual worker who may press to have them raised to meet real requirements. The underlying interest patterns will vary greatly from worker to worker. They may also vary according to age, level of education, seniority, training, income, sex and family responsibilities, regionally as well as according to ethnic origin and scores of other particular circumstances. There is hardly any aspect of the Yugoslav enterprise for which there is more empirical evidence.

Some sort of equilibrium of the individual and collective interest patterns is normally attained at various points of the enterprise existence, either as a result of open conflict (perhaps appearing merely as a split vote on a major issue) or through gradual adjustments. This equilibrium would not normally reflect an abstract cross-section of the interests of the entire collectivity, but will be largely under the influence of those 'who care', those who for any reason are ready and able to contribute to shaping enterprise policy. This may include sociologically unsound equilibria, where restricted and/or closed groups dominate in decision making, but even in such cases definite equilibrium must exist if the situation lasts despite latent opposition. The enterprise cannot avoid seeking its own optimum economic solutions even where wider social consensus is lacking. Whatever the underlying interest pattern, or distribution of effective power within a given enterprise, the resulting equilibrium policy cannot be presumed identical to that obtaining in any other firm, nor can it be seen as permanent in a long-term perspective. It is the result not of an abstract decision-making centre, which may be expected to act in a strictly uniform manner (a not entirely plausible hypothesis underlying most formal economic thinking), but reflects by definition widely differing customs, preferences and outlooks or real groups of working people. By no stretch of the imagination could they be assumed to pursue identical short- or long-term targets or seek the same range of satisfactions at identical levels. This is particularly striking in the Yugoslav setting in view of the exceptional differentiations of the country's populations, but would apply to other societies as well. It would seem that—contrary to widespread belief —such identity of outlook cannot be supposed or expected, even in the case of the directors or, more generally, top management of Yugoslav firms, nor even with respect to basic questions involving enterprise economics or their personal interests (e.g. level of investment and self-financing, income differentials). To a large degree, they have indeed been emancipated from any outside command and must be expected to act according to their personal preferences or scales of value. They certainly should not be thought of as always sitting 'on the other side of the fence', nor could one say in advance which line they would take with respect to any given problem, including choices the enterprise faces when planning its future activity or sharing out past income.

*　　*　　*

This introductory part provides only a few major signposts. No dogmatic conclusions should therefore be drawn from any sentence or paragraph since it may contain only a most inadequate summary of an extremely complex theory, institutional set-up or practical experience. A full volume would hardly suffice to place in proper perspective any one of the hundreds of items so far briefly mentioned or merely implied. An adequate commentary on any one of the key pieces of relevant legislation, or indeed on the relevant rules of any one enterprise, would require similar treatment. Nor is there any lack of adequate material available to make such full exploration of all the relevant issues possible. On the contrary, it is the very wealth of available information which renders a full coverage practically impossible and imposes arbitrary choices on the observer. On the subject of income-sharing alone, following the 1965 Reform, over 9,000 published items were reported in a recent bibliographical survey, this figure being obviously exclusive of the documentation available in individual enterprises or on a local level.

It should be made clear, however, that no similar difficulties are faced by the Yugoslav worker-manager who by definition is not similarly ubiquitous, but clearly aware of his particular time and space co-ordinates. For the accountant, no doubt, income-sharing may mean a few more sleepless nights, with some overtime to compensate; for those of the Social Accounting Service, the financial inspectors, they may reach Scheherazade's target figure. But no one seems seriously to complain, and no major breakdowns occur in the general administration of the scheme or in its implementation at the technical-accounting level.

The problems or difficulties to which the various aspects of the Yugoslav setting may give rise with respect to the operation, behaviour or performance of the self-governing enterprise, and the favourable impact it may have in other respects have not yet been discussed. No critical assessment was implied or attempted, but will be one of the main subjects of our enquiry in the following parts of the study.

Part Two

The Economic Behaviour of the Worker-Managed Enterprise

The Yugoslav setting and the Yugoslav firm have been reviewed in Part I in very *general* terms. Special emphasis must be laid on this last restrictive clause, for obviously the various characteristics of the Yugoslav system and its socio-economic background presented so far could by no means suffice to determine the real behaviour of any one firm, or of Yugoslav enterprises generally. More particularly, only very few precise data have been presented concerning the real dimensions of the various environmental factors, or even their relative importance, and their changing patterns in time and space.

A simplified account could provide more knowledge but would more likely, as often happens, cloud the issues. Yet it is clear that these environmental facts and circumstances are known to, and may be considered as given from, the point of view of any one concrete firm at any concrete point of time and space. The behaviour of the worker-managed enterprise will clearly respond not to an abstract environment, described in general terms for the country as a whole, but to very concrete circumstances, values and objectives perceived and interpreted—with a possible margin of error—by those who, in various ways, participate in the formal and informal decision-making process. Basically, therefore, as in the case of any other independent producer, the behaviour of the worker-managed enterprise will be as if subjectively determined, hence unique. In other words, each enterprise must be thought of as forming, and indeed as transforming or creating as time goes on, its own model of behaviour, both economic and social even though it operates within a common framework and under conditions of formal equality with others.

Despite these obvious limitations, due to the lack of precise definition of the enterprise environment and the impossibility of assuming uniform patterns of behaviour, our ambition in this part of the study is to explore, at levels of both general theory and common practice, the real behaviour of the Yugoslav firm with regard to questions of economic and business policy.

The central question of our enquiry may now be stated as follows: despite the uniqueness of each firm's circumstances and objectives, are there any reasons to expect in theory, or does practice show any definite trends towards, certain regular or probable patterns of behaviour by all, or most, worker-managed firms, or indeed by certain classes thereof, with respect to any definite area of their economic activity? Is there at least a possibility of defining the limits within which the worker-managed firm may be expected to operate? What are the factors or causes which enhance or inhibit such patterns of behaviour as may have been found prevalent or indeed desirable? Are they specific to Yugoslavia, or could they reasonably be expected to operate in other settings as well?

While some observers tend to adopt ready-made behavioural models, mostly drawn directly from capitalist economics or Marxist theory, paying little or no attention to their applicability to the Yugoslav economy, it seems proper, and indeed absolutely essential, to ask such basic questions at this stage in view of the unprecedented nature and of the very specific objectives of the system of workers' management. Unless the theory of the system is fully understood and made explicit, it would be totally unscientific to apply to it such tools of analysis that were developed to meet the requirements of capitalist or centrally planned economies; to impose on it entirely alien models of behaviour, as is often the case, appears utterly preposterous, a proof of most arrogant ethnocentric prejudice, or even worse.

Equal attention could obviously not be paid to all the innumerable facets of economic theory or economic activity of the enterprise in practice, and it seemed proper to limit the enquiry to a few major economic functions, as seen in the context of the Yugoslav firm.

The fact of dealing only with the economic functions of the worker-managed enterprises should not be taken as implying that lesser importance is attached to its role in social development, which indeed is absolutely essential. But this area of the enterprise activity would seem less controversial, as few would question the worker-managed enterprise's ability to adapt readily to local circumstances of behaviour in areas such as culture, welfare, training, leisure or sports, housing, etc. A vast area of social conflict in modern industry would thus seem likely to tend to locally acceptable solutions; the 'acculturation' of the rural workers to industry should be considerably facilitated; and egalitarian patterns of behaviour would be more likely to be promoted or preserved.

However, in order to bring fully to light its social development potential, the worker-managed enterprise must first show an adequate capacity to develop economically and to earn enough to satisfy the growing social and individual needs of its members.

A further reason for dealing mainly with the economics of the Yugoslav firm—in addition to the practical considerations mentioned earlier—is that it is precisely its capacity to adopt rational, development oriented economic policies, and to implement them effectively, that may appear as more controversial to some observers, particularly when seen against the background of Western rationalism and liberal economics. No definite proof is intended, however, nor would it appear possible at the present stage; all that is offered are a few major avenues leading to a better understanding of the specific rationality of the Yugoslav system, and particularly of the worker-managed enterprises, and some results of Yugoslav practice.

Before having a closer look into some of the key areas of the enterprise economic activity, it seems essential to review briefly the global models of economic behaviour of the Yugoslav firm which have been proposed by foreign or Yugoslav theorists or are actually applied in the enterprise practice.

Chapters VI to IX are devoted to such a survey of formal economic models, while Chapters X and XI review in detail the theory and practice of enterprise behaviour with regard to growth, capital, investment, amortization, interest, and loan-financing. The final chapter covers some other areas of long-term and current economic behaviour of enterprises, including employment, remuneration and business management, and briefly reviews some wider aspects.

CHAPTER VI

General Models of Economic Behaviour (1) The Illyrian Firm of Professor Ward

At the launching of the self-management system, in 1950, and for a number of years thereafter, no formal model of the expected economic behaviour of the new type of enterprise was proposed either in official statements or in economic doctrine. Naturally, there was a general expectation that workers' councils would ensure greater efficiency of their enterprises and, more particularly, be better able to steer them through the period of economic crisis following the complete disruption of all trade and other relations with the Cominform (or Comecon) countries—often referred to in Yugoslavia as economic blockade—when little or no economic relations were as yet established with the rest of the world. To adapt to a situation where central planning became meaningless was the first practical economic target.

The most important target was of a political nature, linked to the need for decentralized decision making in a 'multi-pluralistic' society where, in terms of a resolution of the Sixth Congress of the Communist League, full decentralization based on the self-governing autonomous enterprise appeared as 'the only workable way of treating the country's economy as one whole while combating regional particularism'. Early development was thus largely centred round an essentially political concept of workers' management as a means of full economic decentralization compatible with a single economic and political system.

The operation of the new enterprises as economic units was nevertheless clearly conceived in terms of Marxist economics, with its terminology and basic concepts adapted to the very opposite of the capitalist enterprise: a situation where the entrepreneurial responsibility is attached to (living) labour and where the latter appropriates the entire product. A full elaboration of a complete model on this basis was, however, not attempted until the early sixties.

In gradually introducing the self-management system, on an essentially pragmatic basis, its protagonists were obviously conscious of the numerous uncertainties and possible dangers they were facing in the absence of any experience or empirical evidence of economic behaviour the enterprises might actually adopt. Although optimistic expectations prevailed and were on the whole borne out (for were they not the system would clearly never have been launched or would have been halted at an early stage), particular caution was always exercised and precautions taken in a number of areas corresponding to two possible negative patterns of behaviour:

(i) the possibility of the enterprises reducing their production and seeking higher incomes through price increases, employment restriction and other forms of monopolistic behaviour; and

(ii) the possibility of the work collectivity using up all its income for personal or collective consumption, thereby not only failing to contribute to the necessary expansion of the economy as a whole, but actually consuming the available social capital and means of production.

Although never specifically spelled out, a negative model of possible deviant behaviour was clearly present in the minds of responsible legislators and politicians, It can be read out from the documents of the time, with their numerous warnings or legal safeguards against such deviations, diversely termed 'capitalist mentality', 'enterprise egoism', 'local particularism', 'primitivism', etc. When, in the later fifties, they felt able to proclaim that 'the working class has not "eaten up" its factories', the Yugoslav leaders seemed to experience no less relief than Columbus first reporting on the new continent.

No one has ever formally attempted to construct such a negative or deviant model of behaviour,[1] nor would it seem to serve a useful purpose here. Marx's critique of the capitalist enterprise, the lessons drawn both from past practical experiments and theoretical discussions within all sections of the workers' movement on the subject of workers' control or similar systems were certainly not lost on the Yugoslav leaders. Such awareness was certainly always present in Yugoslavia, particularly during the early period, and checks corresponding to possible deviant behaviour were always part of the system. Obviously, also, as in any other system, such deviant behaviour does not meet with social approval and may give rise to formal or informal social sanctions. Actually, the frequent and extreme violence of such social criticism is a major characteristic of most Yugoslav public and cultural media and, contrary to a superficial interpretation, would seem to witness the importance attached by all sections of society to the attainment of the most ambitious humanistic ideals built into the system, and the eradication of the corresponding deviant patterns of behaviour.

Historically, the merit of proposing a first formal model of economic behaviour for the Yugoslav firms belongs to an American author, Professor B. N. Ward (University of California). Applying directly the results of purely econometric analysis of the capitalist firm, the only modification being the search for unlimited increase in profit per head of 'labourer' (and not of the capitalist enterepreneur), Professor Ward's model is both extremely simple and utterly unrealistic. It corresponds—even if not in the author's intention—to a possible negative or deviant model of workers' self-management and has,

---

[1] A wide listing of many possible social and economic deviations which came closest to such a negative model will be found in an early essay by A. Veselinović: '*Stranoputnice*' (Deviations) in *Zbornik O Radničkom Samoupravljanju*, Belgrade, 1957 (ed. by A. Deleon and N. Balog, 456 pp.). This volume contains one of the most representative cross-sections of views and opinions on the early period of workers' management in Yugoslav enterprises.

as such, acquired a considerable measure of popularity in 'liberal' Western, particularly American, economics where private profit is seen as the sum of all values. It thus provides a useful introduction to two more realistic and consequently more complex models of behaviour developed in the early sixties by Yugoslav theorists, both based on Marxist economic theory, which seem to correspond to two successive stages of Yugoslav practice. One is centred around the concept of *surplus value* as appropriated by the emancipated worker-producers; the other introduces a new concept of the total net *income* (where labour costs and profit or surplus value form a single indistinguishable whole. Entirely new concepts of 'income rate' and 'income price' are consequently introduced as the key motivation and criterion of the economic rationality of the Yugoslav firm, seen as an autonomous collectivity of commodity producers. A fourth, infinitely more pragmatic and less formal model has developed from, and appears to be applied in, most Yugoslav enterprises as a result of various attempts to find a formula for an equitable distribution of income (and hence allocation of resources).

The 'Illyrian Firm' of Professor Ward, or a Simplified Econometric Model of Private Enterprise applied to the Worker-managed Firm
Professor Ward first publicly stated his model of the Illyrian (Yugoslav) Enterprise or, as he defines it, of 'Market Syndicalism', in 1958[1] and, in a 'slightly revised' but considerably expanded version, included it as one of three major 'models' discussed in his more recent volume on *Socialist Economy*.[2] It has attracted considerable attention and is the most widespread representation of the Yugoslav system among Western liberal and particularly American economists.

Professor Ward's economic model is extremely simple. It is operated by the workers, whose only motivation is the 'material self-interest of the individual, similar to that of *laissez-faire* capitalists'. Production and exchange of goods and services is governed exclusively by market considerations which, against the background of the workers' self-interest, also determine the allocation of resources. Decisions are taken by an elected manager, accountable to the workers, but with sovereign powers over them when at work, and endowed with infallible capacity to discern their best interest and to act accordingly. Actually, the workers are interested (exclusively) in current money incomes (wages and profits). They may leave and be laid off at any time. The State merely has the tax collecting and 'usual watchdog' function of a capitalist

---

[1] *American Economic Review*, No. 48, 1958, pp. 566–89.

[2] New York, 1967, 272 pp.: a 'study of organizational alternatives', this volume deals, in addition to 'Illyria', with the Soviet model of central planning and a 'command model' alternative based on Professor Ward's own definitions (partly related to examples drawn from the People's Republic of China). A distinct but clearly parallel 'model of a producer-managed firm' has been developed in an article by Professor E. D. Domar on 'The Soviet Collective Farm', *American Economic Review*, No. 4, 1966, which is often used along with Professor Ward's writings. Both 'models' have been closely reviewed (but only as regards the firm's behaviour in a competitive situation) by B. Horvat in *Ekonomska Analysa*, Belgrade, No. 5, 1–2, 1967.

State. In fact, there is only one tax, corresponding to an interest charge on the capital advanced to the firm by the State.

In order to relate this simple and most unrealistic model to the extremely limited tool of econometric analysis, further simplifications are introduced. The firm makes only one product and has only one variable input (abstract labour, i.e. with no differentiation in skill or rate of income); implicitly, a single technology is assumed.

Furthermore, the firm reacts to only one type of outside change: marginal increase or falls of market prices. (Changes in costs and in the interest rate are also covered in the 1967 version but only as outside given data, comparable to market prices.) This it does by seeking the highest rate of profit per worker on its 'production function'; this is assumed to be known to the manager, who acts accordingly, in adapting both the firm's output and labour force to attain the required maximum profit per worker (including himself and the members of the workers' council). Expressed in terms of marginal behaviour, this condition is satisfied in a competitive firm when marginal revenue per (additional) worker equals marginal cost per worker. As all workers' shares in profit are equal, and all profits are distributed to individuals, the firm cannot increase output, nor employment, unless the profit derived from any marginal increase in output is higher than the average profit per worker at the same point of time. A limit is thus set both on output and on employment, which are necessarily lower than that of a capitalist firm wherever the latter makes a profit. (Where capitalist profits are zero, the Illyrian firm would achieve the same level of performance; where the capitalist firm makes losses, it would produce and employ more.)

There seems to be little need to use mathematical formulae to understand that a firm so curiously and arbitrarily defined would display quite unexpected patterns of behaviour in respect to changes in prices (or outside determined costs, interest, etc.). As demonstrated by Professor Ward, to act rationally, it would indeed have to reduce output and employment when faced with higher prices (or lower costs or interest) and expand them as prices fall. It would therefore perform less efficiently than a capitalist firm in similar conditions, this being true not only of firms facing competitive markets but also of monopolies or oligopolies.

While not considered by Professor Ward, the extreme (but under his assumption rational) behaviour of certain types of monopolistic enterprises would be for the 'manager of the workers' council'(!) to lay off all workers but one (himself), and achieve the highest income by charging an infinite price for one single unit of production. Thus, the General Director of a Post Office enterprise could satisfy the maximization rule by dismissing all the other employees and delivering one single letter at an infinite charge. Similarly, if the firm was making losses, in Professor Ward's own words, 'output would continue to increase as the worker-managers strove to minimize losses'. The fallacy of geometric rationality applied to economics has never been so clearly demonstrated.

When assumptions are somewhat relaxed, and the workers permitted to vary the amount of capital at their disposal (in a more long-term perspective as compared with the rule of instant hire and fire imposed on themselves), their behaviour is on the whole found consistent with the capitalist ideal. The worker-managers will borrow for investment (they are not permitted to generate capital themselves) only where the expected profit is greater than costs. Where investment is linked with additional employment, however, the earlier conclusions continue to apply. In other words, the Illyrian firm will 'have a tendency to invest in more capital-intensive processes than its capitalist counterpart, even to the point of occasionally investing under conditions in which profits (but not profit per worker) are expected to fall as a result, such behaviour not leading to Pareto optimality. It is only when fully automatic (i.e. if labour cost become irrelevant) that the Illyrian firm truly attains capitalist efficiency.

We should add that all the conclusions are flawlessly demonstrated in economic terms and verbal argument and, in the 1967 version, presented as neat theorems, to which both a normative and an empirical meaning seems to be attached by the author. This second version also contains two chapters containing the author's own speculations on the Illyrian environment and the conditions of stability of such an economy which we cannot examine here in any detail. Obviously, most extraordinary phenomena make the whole economy shatter with utter violence, the workers' councils selling their plant in boom conditions to retire on the profits and workers leaving firms *en masse* where earnings are low. The latter tend to increase employment in order to 'spread their losses', while the more profitable enterprises are laying off their workers and reducing output.

To conjure up this Apocalyptic Vision of Terrible Disorders which, in the author's cautiously academic language, 'suggest that Illyria may be both economically and institutionally unstable', no better alternative is seen but the State, its planners and enterprise managers endowed with full authority, their Infinite Wisdom bringing about the Required Solutions. However, as Soviet central planning has already been shown by the author to perform rather poorly, and his own ideal 'command economy' only fractionally better, the path seems open back to private enterprise, which naturally finds the optimum spot on its 'production function', has higher levels of output and employment, and generally tends to 'Pareto optimality'. Indeed, as the author suggests, 'private promoters' could play a major role in getting Illyria out of its Procrustean bed.

Actually, Professor Ward does not see the full extent of the disorders to which his Illyrian economy would be exposed and which would make its instant death an absolute certainty. He admits to the possibility of a more stable equilibrium if all enterprises operate at a level corresponding to zero profits of a capitalist firm (not realizing that this would require the presence at every works of a State inspector constantly adapting taxation to make the workers achieve zero results, with all their 'materialistic' motivation being lost in the process). He also recognizes a positive feature of the Illyrian experiment, i.e. the 'strong measure of industrial democracy' (!) it provides and the corresponding likelihood of less intra-enterprise conflict.

We would not feel justified in paying so much attention to this 'model',

142

much of which looks like a practical joke, merely because of its wide acceptance as a true image of the Yugoslav economy among liberal Western economists and particularly American econometricians, harmful as it is to international understanding and economic progress throughout the world. However, although rejected by most serious Yugoslav commentators, this 'model' has received some attention within the country by genuine students of the system, particularly those most prone to use their newly acquired skills in higher mathematics and geometric representation of economic phenomena, while largely unfamiliar with enterprise practice generally and that of workers' management in particular.[1] In a somewhat adulterated form, this 'model' also seems to have shaped the image of the latest (1965) Economic Reform as interpreted by some Yugoslav economists who, until spring 1968, saw a kind of absolute good in mass lay-offs of workers and closure of factories, and felt deeply frustrated when these goals (perhaps tantamount in their mind to a search for some form of 'Pareto optimality') proved unattainable.

The formal logic and mathematical demonstrations displayed by Professor Ward in his model are indeed unquestionably correct. Nor would it seem proper to question his subjective good faith. But the substance of his argument calls for the strongest rebuttal, as it is based entirely on false premises and inadequate tools of analysis. It is particularly hard to accept that since his 1958 article (which, although based on wrong premises, seemed a genuine enough initial contribution to the study of the system as it could then appear

---

[1] Cf. B. Horvat, *op. cit.*, being a part of a 'vast research programme financed by the Federal Economic Chamber'. Although rejecting the Ward-Domar model as inapplicable on essentially practical grounds (the objective necessity for the enterprises to invest and expand and the impossibility for the work collectivity, as for the self-employed peasant, to conceive of itself as being its own employer in the capitalist sense), he seems to accept most of the theoretical premises of the two authors despite his own quite different global view of the motivation and behaviour of the worker-managed firm, mainly geared to a stable growth of income in time.

For a most outstanding achievement in econometric analysis of the enterprise model, providing a generalized formula covering both the capitalist and the worker-managed enterprise, cf. D. Dubravčić in *Ekonomske Analyse*, Nos. 1–2, 1968. The author actually seems to believe his neatly symmetrical conclusion, according to which if the entrepreneurial function is vested in one factor (capital or labour) more than optimal use will be made of the other, 'neutral', factor. This delusion makes him conclude in favour of a system based on fixed remuneration of both capital and labour (through fixed interest and wages), thus unwittingly supporting the case for central planning backed by a team of infallible econometricians.

For a rather similar reaction by two Czechoslovak authors, who took Professor Ward's 'model' as a starting point for the examination of the 'socialist enterprise as a participant in a market economy' etc., see R. Kocanda and P. Pelikan in *Politicka Ekonomie*, Prague, 1967, pp. 93–103. In this case too the conclusions derived from the 'model' would have disastrous results at the level of practical policy for the actual development of a participative enterprise, in as much as a systematic intervention of the State and its planners would appear indispensable, as would other cumbersome devices aimed at overcoming the anti-employment bias of the enterprise (e.g. hire of new workers as pure wage earners, with profit participation reserved to existing incumbents, a principle totally incompatible with any system based on workers' management).

to a casual observer), Professor Ward has found it possible to disregard all subsequent development of Yugoslav theory and practical experience. It is hard to believe that a 'model' of this kind could be developed by anyone who has seen a single set of sectoral or enterprise accounts as shown in Tables VI and VII above, attended a single session of a workers' council or perused a few reports or articles on the subject.

The list below indicates the main fallacies underlying his basic assumptions and his methodology. The list will also provide a useful background for the examination of further more realistic models:

(i) Labour is conceived of by Professor Ward as existing in two different, quite unrelated forms: managerial labour (the worker-managers) and labour at work (the 'labourers'). While such a distinction can reasonably be made as between a capitalist entrepreneur and his capital, it is inadmissible when extended to 'labour' which does not exist (cannot be sold, etc.) independently from the person of the worker (a point well known to all classical economists and not worth elaborating).

(ii) The 'purely material motivation' ascribed to the worker-managers is too restrictively equated with the search for highest profit (or wages plus profit) per 'labourer', for even if exclusively so motivated, the latter has several other major avenues to increase his income:
(a) through greater efficiency on the job
(b) through advancement to a better paid job
(c) through a higher ratio of employment within his consumption unit (e.g. family).

No rational model can assume these possibilities as absent from the 'labourer's' mind when he acts as decision maker, even if they appear 'model wise' of no concern to the capitalist entrepeneur.

(iii) The position is similar where essential services are lacking or deemed grossly insufficient by the workers, even where of no direct concern to the capitalist entrepreneur. Their provision is then a 'must' from the workers' point of view, and hence an incentive to output and growth.

(iv) As a degree of solidarity among the workers is an explicit assumption of the system, however, it cannot legitimately be dismissed at this stage of model building. There is no evidence to prove that the worker manager would play no part in local and regional development, and have no stake in prosperity and progress at all levels. Actually, quite unlike the typical entrepreneur or owner, he is bound to live among the fellow workers he has laid off or refused to employ, and must provide for their support in some way or another. Even if he is purely materialistically motivated, they are a real and tangible cost, and not a distant menace which could be left to local police to handle.

(v) All this also goes to show that labour under workers' management cannot be reasonably regarded as a short-term variable input, hired and fired in automatic reaction to changes in outside conditions (prices, etc.). No human organization could achieve any degree of stability if it acted in this manner, which is typical of the 'inhuman' conditions of entrepreneurial capitalism. Such behaviour, particularly as regards whimsical instant lay-off, is ruled out in the case of the Yugoslav firm, both institutionally and in practice, and there is no logical justification for different rules of the game to be assumed.

Professor Ward would probably agree that few modern capitalist firms would openly profess the necessity of such a behaviour, which indeed is strictly limited by legislation of many countries. He sees the difficulty for the workers' councils acting in this manner, but suggests that where less than half of the work force are to be laid off, the majority would back such a decision, no doubt for the sake of economic rationality. As his model has no time dimension, all the work force but the last man could thus be disposed of in a few successive sessions of the workers' council.

(vi) The entire entrepreneurial activity of the Illyrian firm is represented as the 'manager's' search for the correct 'factor mix', the correct proportion of capital and labour to be used for the optimum output as found on the 'production function' of a comparable capitalist enterprise. All this is obviously inapplicable to the Yugoslav case. No such omniscient and omnipotent manager exists anywhere, least of all in Yugoslavia, nor has he anything in common with the 'model' director of the worker-managed enterprise. There are scores of ways and means by which greater efficiency can be pursued and attained other than adapting the 'factor mix' (the organic composition of capital). The latter has perhaps least importance in Yugoslav theory and has received least attention in enterprise practice. It is simply conceptually impossible for the workers or even their managers to see themselves as a 'factor', readily interchangeable with capital. Indeed, no free producer (such as a farmer, etc.) can think of himself (or be expected to think) in these terms. He has innumerable other possibilities of increasing his earnings (if he so wishes): by working more and harder, by using the available capital better or saving to invest more, by eliminating waste and reducing costs, etc.

The worker-producer will therefore be mainly concerned with these various other possibilities. Once this is granted, the 'production function' disappears altogether as an objective norm of rational behaviour. Any behaviour (or rather any mix of possible behaviours) appears rational in so far as it leads to the attainment of a corresponding set of objectives. No two-dimensional function can possibly help in tracing the optimum point. Even if the worker-managed enterprise were supposed to have a definite 'production function' (e.g. for the purposes of some abstract argument) the latter would be necessarily different from that of a similar capitalist enterprise. As Professor Ward could find out without leaving the US, even private firms which introduced no more than a simple profit-sharing scheme perform systematically at different levels of profitability to those

145

which have not and cannot therefore be supposed to have the same production function.[1] It is common sense that such identity of the 'production functions' could not be assumed for any two free producers, be they peasants, cobblers, or co-operatives, which must by definition be assumed to perform differently (for better or worse) as compared to similarly endowed capitalist firms, as well as if compared among themselves. Nor can such differential performance be assumed by definition less efficient than Professor Ward's ideal 'Pareto optimality' of capitalism. There is no theoretical reason for excluding the possibility of such producers' enterprises performing on the average at much higher levels, or showing faster rates of growth, than similarly endowed capitalist firms.

(vii) It is similarly unrealistic to base a model on a 'one output' (i.e. one product) firm, such a firm being most atypical if existing at all. Yet, even in Professor Ward's peculiar universe, once plurality or multiplicity of product is accepted, the firms will behave in a completely different manner. The transfer of output to the more profitable products becomes infinitely more rational than the search for the right factor mix.

(viii) The 'capital' available in unlimited amounts at fixed interest is another basic fallacy which hardly calls for comment. In fact, it is a task for more than one generation to develop an institutional system which would make it possible for the workers' enterprise to replace and to create new capital assets, for these to be rationally collected where in excess and redistributed where required. While no definite answer can presently be given as to how this can properly be done, nothing is more certain than that Professor Ward's miracle will not materialize, and that no one but the worker-labourers will have to produce the capital resources they need to operate and to expand their enterprises.

(ix) Most of the above difficulties of the 'model' relate to the fact that the workers, their enterprises, and even their capital, are deprived of all existence in time. Only the capitalist entrepreneur, or rather a stock exchange operator, can care exclusively for current business and be able to switch at any time to other operations, with different capital assets and different labour. No such assumption is valid for a direct producer in general and the worker-managed enterprise in particular. Stability (of work, employment, etc.) and future progress are foremost in any worker's or producer's mind, far ahead of current income, in Yugoslavia as everywhere. Similarly, an enterprise has a definite time period for its production, a year on average, sometimes more; a longer one to which are tied its current investment or development programmes; and a practically infinite future of institutional existence, particularly where forming a social organization, be it a co-operative or a Yugoslav firm. The capital, in its physical form,

[1] Cf. B. L. Metzger, *Profit Sharing in Perspective*, Evanston, 1966.

has a long-term existence as well, quite distinct from its financial counterpart at any given time, and cannot be as readily manipulated by the worker-managed firm as by the capitalist entrepreneur. A worker-managed firm obviously cannot expect to find a ready buyer on the market and buy itself into some other plant. If a Yugoslav steel-works decides to grow plums and make brandy (possibly a rational economic objective) it can do so but it will normally take a very long time, all the time required to write off the steel plant, grow the plum trees and retain the staff. For a private mill owner, it may require just the time of two signatures. The worker-managers just cannot sell themselves away, be party to a take-over, etc. They can transform themselves and their resources into something quite different but must all the time be present and work 'at it' themselves.

A rational economic model, even for a predominantly materialistically oriented working population, could therefore equally be based on maximizing long term 'profit' (net income) with appropriate discount. Indeed, it is only in this long-term perspective that worker-managers can hope to achieve a real increase in their earnings as 'labourers' (and so to achieve the satisfaction of their materialistic urges) while in Professor Ward's timeless universe, they only move around the starting point in a hectic search for the right factor mix.

(x) One of the causes of these and other basic inconsistencies of Professor Ward's model is clearly related to his methodology. Marginal analysis is basically ill-adapted to accounting for the time dimension involved in all economic decision making, and therefore unsuited as a guide for policy making and not used as such, even in the capitalist enterprise. There is simply no way of making the underlying reasoning understood by anyone responsible for decision making in a Yugoslav worker-managed firm. It is simply impossible to conceive that a marginal change within a worker-managed enterprise should affect anyone's personal existence. Nor could any 'manager' face a workers' council with such a proposal. Their agenda is sufficiently clogged up with matters of quite different magnitude. (This also applies to capitalist firms.) Even a more than marginal change in price levels is often a quite negligible development, as there are scores of ways to compensate for it within the enterprise. The existence and future development of effective demand (not its marginal changes) is quite another matter.[1]

In actual practice, even in the very short-term perspective, they are kept busy enough dealing with choices or problems of measurable dimensions, for which no infinitesimal calculus is required, but where the possible profits or losses may be shown by simple arithmetic and in so many figures. (A marginal change can always be

[1] The complete absence of 'marginal mentality' among Yugoslav managers is confirmed *inter alia* by T. A. Marschak in a recent article in the *Quarterly Journal of Economics*, 1968, p. 585, but is wrongly attributed to lack of intellectual understanding which—Marschak hopes—may be caught up with by the 'managerial elite of the future'.

worked into the current programme; actually it mostly works itself into it quite unnoticed.) Each of them involves quite a few non-quantifiable elements and the final decision is a question of weighing them all against the work collectivity's preferences and objectives. Whether to step up production so as to satisfy a prospective major customer or to avoid penalties for delay, whether to continue to produce as planned when demand is lagging (not marginally, but by a significant percentage): such questions simply cannot be answered by any outsider in the name of a self-employed producer (a peasant or a Yugoslav worker-manager), nor can he be expected to respond to any general laws of economics or geometry. (He can obviously be advised on the best course to follow but on his own terms, within his own system of references or, if put in geometrical terms, his own set of vectors; such advice can then, and only then, make use of the most sophisticated methods of analysis, mathematical or otherwise.)

(xi) Because of his close dependence on methods and models of behaviour derived from another system, Professor Ward leaves unnoticed some of the major characteristics of the Yugoslav firm, its specific qualities as well as problems; a few only will be listed here:

(a) The sharing out of each firm's net income among all who work must have an obvious effect on the *pattern of income distribution* within the nation (more or less egalitarian according to the point of comparison), it will thereby affect the entire demand side of the economic process, and this in turn must produce a specific allocation of resources; if all the economy is 'worker-managed' there cannot be any other final demand, nor any production other than that which aims to satisfy the needs of those who work, in proportion to the value of their work.

(b) The question of the firm's costs arises in an entirely novel manner, there being no common denominator as between the cost of material and the cost of labour. The pressure on reducing the former should in theory be infinitely greater than in any other type of enterprise, for any such saving adds to every worker's potential income. The institutional set-up is suited for such direct cost control at all levels of the firm.

(c) As in the case of any self-employed producer, there is a very considerable flexibility of labour's remuneration in the short term (as no one but the worker has to agree) so that the firm can, if it wishes, considerably increase its output and employment while reaping as it goes on the possible, but initially uncertain benefits of such a policy (economies of scale, fixed costs, entering new markets or launching new products, etc.), which then automatically accrue to the workers.[1]

---

[1] This potential quality of the worker-managed firm has been briefly demonstrated by Jaroslav Vanek, in *Weltwirtschaftliches Archiv*, Kiel, No. 2, 1965, pp. 206–14 (*Workers' Profit Participation, Unemployment and the Keynesian Equilibrium*).

The advantage of the worker-managed firm is more striking if union wages are considered, rather than the minimum competitive wages on which Professor Ward builds his entire comparison with capitalism. It is only because a minimum (non-union) wage is assumed throughout for the capitalist enterprise that the latter can appear more employment prone than the Yugoslav firm. This assumption is, however, not stated anywhere by the author (a minor omission, but which has its weight in the real world). This income flexibility offers a great advantage to the worker-managed firm in a smaller country with little or no industrial background and tradition, which has actually to force its way into the world markets. Indeed, a capitalist company could never ask its workers to accept short term sacrifice in order to achieve entry into foreign markets (or to back other similar projects), as they could soon be frustrated as a result of a merger, a take-over or a decision by the parent company to close operations.

The commercial or other responsible director of a Yugoslav firm cannot only reasonably make such a proposal (in which his own short-term income and long-term future are known to be at stake), but such a decision may actually be imposed on him by a more forward-looking work community (perhaps with a longer time dimension or more time to read the calls for tenders by foreign developers). Actually, such flexibility is essential for any decision making within the worker-managed firm, which would be entirely paralysed were Professor Ward's assumptions to be taken literally, as any decision involving expense means that the corresponding amount is withdrawn from the potential maximum short-term workers' income for the sake of future advantage. (Any new machine installed, canteen, or bus transport provided, housing or school paid for means less cash earning today.) This is less miraculous than it may appear at first sight, a type of decision taken each day by millions of craftsmen or farmers, each time they subscribe a co-op share or wait for settlement of a bill, add a new head of cattle to their herd, etc. In Professor Ward's world, they would have to go to the bank (the State) for each nail they intend to hammer in the wall.

(d) The work collectivities have a very specific inducement to save and invest, even where no 'profit' is involved (but not necessarily a 'humanistic' motivation either) to which thought may be given by a more thorough model builder. As 'labourers' they may even in pure theory be concerned with getting rid of heavy, unpleasant, unworthy or even useless tasks, and spending their working time in a more pleasant or even comfortable work environment. This may appear 'uneconomic' in traditional economics (except where special classes of 'labourers' are difficult to attract at a given wage); it may in fact be done as a sign of 'welfare' consciousness of an enlightened management. It is sound economics for the worker-managed firm.

(e) Similarly, the worker-manager does not maximize income per 'labourer' (as assumed by Professor Ward in analogy to maximization of profit per unit of capital), since for him the quantity of work to be done (measured in time, intensity, boredom, etc.) is a corresponding variable which he tends simultaneously to minimize. The alternative: 20 per cent more income or 17 per cent less work, is obviously not comparable to that of the private entrepreneur who would draw no advantage from withdrawing part of his capital from economic use. The workers seen by Professor Ward as laying off their comrades out of sheer prosperity may equally shorten their working hours or 'take it easy'. No 'humanism' is required here either; merely sound economics of workers' management.

(xii) The comparative method adopted by Professor Ward throughout his writings on Illyria is ill chosen on several counts. First of all, the Yugoslav enterprise has not evolved directly from the capitalist system, but essentially through the mediation of central planning, and is therefore two stages away from private enterprise. In the process, it has acquired quite new features which cannot be brushed away as secondary; nor can the background of Marxist economics be dismissed as a secondary or superficial adjunct. The concept of 'surplus value' and the underlying labour theory of value have become part of popular culture.

Second, the worker-managed firm operates on its own producers' market and not a capitalist market and, despite many similar (or rather homologous) features, there is no complete identity. No economic 'model' can therefore be built on this assumption.

Third, the workers' specific concern with stability in a perspective of regular growth (as opposed to the speculative short-term profit motivation of the private enterprise model) remains unnoticed. The specific value attaching to the absolute size of the firm and its rate of growth in terms of a strictly economic motivation of the worker (stability and security of employment and welfare services, advancements and benefits on seniority, etc.) is thereby eliminated from the model.

Finally, in the case of Yugoslavia, comparison with capitalism is quite unrealistic as it never really took shape, nor was it ever likely to develop for lack of domestic capital and entrepreneurship. Even if allowed to, it would in all probability have continued in the dominant form of extensive foreign-owned industries coupled with a rather large State sector. Thus, even if performing no better, or perhaps worse, the worker-managed firm would still provide a favourable alternative for the Yugoslav economy or workers as a whole, since they could retain all the benefits of industrialization, whether in terms of skill, profit, or capital resources. The experience of countries which in similar circumstances have chosen a development model based on foreign-sponsored private enterprise offers no ground for comparison on Professor Ward's terms.

So far Professor Ward's Illyrian model has only been considered on his terms of 'sound' economics, of workers who have only purely materialistic motivations, no other needs or preferences. The system cannot be fully apprehended on the basis of such limited premises alone. Its social or humanistic objectives are not mere appendages which could be dispensed with, even in a purely economic model. Principles such as solidarity, co-operation or mutual help, social and human development and equality of opportunity are not just a part of some ideological superstructure, but are directly built into the economic model, both as a part of the incentive system and as fundamental strictures to which it must respond. Nor is there any reason to suggest that such principles are not relevant or not operative in Yugoslav practice, even if they are frequently in very imperfect forms or as reactions to serious consequences resulting from major infringements. Failure to integrate the human or humanistic aspirations of the system based on workers' management at the stage at economic model building creates conditions of relative instability within such a purely rationalistic model, even if more stable and long-term maximization criteria were introduced, as suggested in the twelve points listed above. Actually, in its Yugoslav form, workers' management cannot be understood other than as an attempt to combine, on an equal footing, economic rationality and socialist humanism. Should it fail to be this, and it would obviously do so if it followed Professor Ward's school of thought, it would simply cease to exist.

Is there no positive lesson, then, to be drawn from this model? There are two major points worthy of attention. First, when stripped of its many incursions into the unreal worlds of imaginary numbers (such as the areas of negative profits shared out as negative remuneration to an ever-growing labour force), the model rightly stresses the intuitively perceived investment proneness and labour-saving bias of the Yugoslav firm when acting purely in the light of short-term economic rationality. This is particularly clear when comparison is made with central planning or a self-perpetuating Galbraithian corporation, but also evident when the traditional entrepreneur is taken as a point of comparison. Long-term economic rationality and the 'humanistic' principles which are directly built into the firm act, however, in the opposite direction. The resulting conflict of interest is thus mainly perceived—and must be solved—within the firm and not in its relations with outside agents.

Second, the model brings to light some of the causes of what we have called 'over-reactiveness' (Professor Ward's 'relative instability') of the firm and the system as a whole, which again can be intuitively perceived, it is common to all producers' markets (such as individual farmers') in their response to short-term economic market incentives (as distinct from the

151

traditional patterns of behaviour of an archaic society. In its modern form, typified by Yugoslav economy, as in the modern farmers' case, this peculiar quality of the producers' enterprise requires a higher level of producers' co-operation and must not be overlooked when shaping financial and fiscal policies. It makes for a special type of multiplier effect entailing particularly heavy penalties if unnoticed.

The principal lesson from Professor Ward's model is, however, one of general warning. Warning against applying in a dogmatic fashion laws or 'theorems' formulated for the use of other systems under different skies. The purely semantic identity, based on the existence of a 'market', is specially apt to lead to confusion, particularly in a system built out of, but in oppostion to, a non-market type of planned economy. This may lead to over-rating the purely financial aspects of business operations in assessing the behaviour of the firm, while it is actually only the real newly created goods and services, and the increase in such real product, which can provide a true gauge for the performance of an economy based on work only. In the humanistic perspective of the system, the laws and theorems of purely rational economics can find their proper place only as subsidiary tools of analysis which have ceased to rule over men but can help in finding ways to, and assessing the cost of, progress towards the destination they have themselves chosen.

Conversely, should such ultimate goals entirely dominate the short-term economic activity of the enterprises, in the shape perhaps of the various 'laws of socialism', there would be nothing left for the worker-managers to choose between, no free exercise of their powers and responsibilities. Although such principles as solidarity, equality, or harmonious (proportionate) planned development are obviously of a higher order than profit maximiza-tion, no one but the enterprise work collectivities, both separately and in their various combinations, can say at any point of time what degree of inequali-ties they are ready to tolerate as a price for economic efficiency, or what precisely are the proportions which they see as leading to harmoniously planned development. In other words, no abstract laws or theorems could possibly serve as the foundation of a faithful model, economic or otherwise, of the worker-managed enterprise and the self-management system. If applied in a normative sense, they are apt to lead to its destruction; if used for understanding practice, they inhibit all progress of such understanding.

Needless to say, there is no empirical evidence of Yugoslav firms displaying a behaviour consistent with Professor Ward's model. The most striking proof of this is that they continue to exist and operate in conditions of relative stability at points manifestly at variance with the required zero level of profitability. They do on the whole expand production and employment where prices are more favourable and costs declining, and reduce or phase out output where demand is slack. Nor is there any significant correlation of profitability and the 'capital-labour mix'; the distribution of the enterprise population in the real world appears quite incompatible with any definite pattern of behaviour derived from the 'model'. It is impossible to say whether this is due to their fundamentally subjective performance, or to the obvious inaccuracy of the tools of analysis presently available. By analogy points regularly spread on a Euclidian surface would appear quite differently spaced if projected on to a spherical one. The difference in complexity of the economic system based on workers' management would seem, in fact, of a much greater magnitude and the assumption of symmetry with capitalism appears as basically fallacious. The two hypotheses are not mutually exclusive, however, and may help in pushing further the analysis of the Yugoslav's firm behaviour.

CHAPTER VII

General Models of Economic Behaviour (2) Realistic Models in Yugoslav Theory and Practice

No *ex ante* theoretical model of economic behaviour of the self-management enterprise which could be compared or opposed to Professor Ward's has ever been proposed by a Yugoslav writer, even though there seems to be no theoretical obstacle to such an attempt.[1] Both their rather pragmatic basic outlook and the immense complexity of the practical tasks they are facing make them generally choose the real world. Even in the economic literature, most authors rely essentially on the legal-constitutional framework of the enterprise and of the system as a whole as a background for charting the behaviour patterns of the enterprise in the various areas of its economic activity. Such an approach could not, nor does it pretend to, present a full explanation of the self-governing enterprise in terms of economic theory or practice.

To our knowledge, there are only two major schools of thought in Yugoslavia which have the explicit ambition to provide a complete economic theory of the worker-managed firm. Both have been formulated as *post factum* representations of actual behaviour, drawing largely on past experience and, hence, having no normative pretensions. If these are present, they are addressed as advice to those responsible for general economic policy. There is also at least one major model, with many possible variations, which attempts to cover the various areas of economic decision making of the self-governing enterprises by means of a corresponding series of more or less co-ordinated formulae. Pragmatic as it is, and adaptable to most circumstances, this approach has a wide following in the enterprises and leads not infrequently to their own original model building. These various approaches will be briefly surveyed below in this chapter and the next.

---

[1] Polish economists are known to have given considerable attention to such abstract model building, partly no doubt because they had less opportunity to deal with urgent practical problems. Thus, M. Todorović (cf. infra *op. cit.*, p. 82) cites a formula proposed by B. Minc 'for analysis of prices and profitability' in a socialist system, which could possibly also be applied in the normative-ontological manner of Professor Ward's. Although possibly closer to the reality of things, this would represent a similarly unwarranted voluntaristic imposition of a purely personal view on the outside world.

(a) *The Emancipated Labour and Profit or Surplus Value Maximizing Enterprise*

This model broadly corresponds to the Yugoslav firm of the earlier period (the fifties). Couched strictly in Marx's terminology and, in line with the legal-institutional development of the time, it seems to unfold and desegregate Marx's basic tools of analysis of capitalist enterprise in a way which would turn them into tools of decision-making and action by the emancipated work collectivities. No symmetry or analogy of behaviour with the capitalist enterprise is assumed, but may appear to be in some more simplistic presentations of the model. (Here is a possible explanation for some of the basic errors of facts and interpretation in Professor Ward's model as his main contact with Yugoslavia appears to have taken place in the mid-fifties and must have been considerably limited by linguistic difficulties.)

A systematic and most explicit presentation of this model has been published in one volume by Mijalko Todorović under the heading 'Emancipating Labour'.[1] By the choice of this title, and in his Introduction, he resolutely sets his model in the humanistic strain of man's history. He also most resolutely rejects all 'capitulation in the face of the laws of commodity production' (the market), including the glorification of the Liberalism of the eighteenth and early nineteenth centuries supposed to re-live some sort of 'Indian summer' under the Yugoslav system, as well as the pseudo-realism of those who propound its adaptation to the 'positive experiences' of modern capitalist economy and society.

Yet Todorović's approach is purely economic. In a few closely argued chapters he draws a series of equations reflecting the general conditions of rational economic behaviour in a worker-managed firm where workers are entitled to a basic wage and share out the surplus or profit according to work. The basic categories of Marx's analysis are thus fully preserved in the worker-managed enterprise: the constant (fixed and circulating) capital (c), the variable capital (the 'wages') (v), and the surplus value (m). His workers are obviously interested in increasing their incomes over time through expansion and investment, financed both from current income and outside repayable borrowing. This makes for a major 'realistic' departure from Professor Ward's model, where a non-repayable capital seems to be forthcoming *ad libitum* from an unknown Centre.

They also have to provide, out of their profits or suplus value, for the replacement of the capital assets used up in the production process, for their own collective needs, and for those of the society as a whole. The specific destinations of the enterprise net product are listed as follows: replacement of the means of production; personal consumption of the workers; social

[1] *Oslobadanje Rada*, Belgrade, 1965, 287 pp. Economist and politician, the author was President of the first Yugoslav Federal Assembly under the 1965 Constitution and later Secretary of the Executive of the League of Communists of Yugoslavia (1965–9). It should be stressed, however, that the model discussed here has no official standing within the League nor does it exert any significant influence on State or public policies, which lean more heavily on the Income Maximization Model discussed below. Enterprises choose their own maximization or optimization criteria (if any) as they see fit.

reserves; social accumulation for expanded reproduction; social welfare and similar expenditure (pensions, health, culture, schools, etc.); costs of government and national defence. These various categories are seen as costs imputable to the profit or surplus, but, despite their quite differentiated impact on the enterprise behaviour, are not taken into consideration in the general flow of analysis.

The workers are humanized to the extent that for instance, they revolt against a preposterously high rate of interest which the business banks may consider 'economic'. The author is aware that his formulae have no normative value, but merely indicate a possible rational mode of behaviour of the worker-managed firm. Their proper understanding is however clearly perceived as an essential precondition of rational planning or economic policy making.

The model is perhaps best presented through the following general price formula:

$$P = (c+v)+(c+v)\frac{\dot{\Sigma} \ m}{\Sigma(c+v)}.$$

This formula is based on the production or cost price in any given industry (or for any given product). The first term $(c+v)$ is the actual costs of capital (or past labour) and of (living) labour, while the second relates the volume of the enterprise operations to the average rate of profit of the industry (or product). The normal or rational behaviour for any individual producer (firm) is to maximize the latter (its profit or surplus). The relationship is obviously complex, for though it is essential for the firm to keep capital and labour costs to a minimum, their volume at the same time determines the volume of production and thereby the absolute size of the profit or surplus. It also shows that no economy on labour is desirable if it results in a corresponding (or greater) increase in capital costs and vice versa.

The actual rate of profit of the individual firm, as distinct from the industry (or product) average, is then defined as $m/c+v$, where m is the difference between the price and the costs of production $[m = P-(c+v)]$. Considering that in this model (as indeed in Yugoslavia) 'the workers have the *obligation*, the *responsibility* and the *right* to provide for the expansion of their economic activity', it is indeed rightly assumed that they would maximize their profit against their total costs, both of capital and labour. As shown convincingly by the author, the maximizing formula M/V (profit per unit of labour) would apply only where capital costs were equal or tending to zero, i.e. in the most primitive type of production. In other words, Professor Ward's maximization formula is seen as a special and atypical case within a general economic model. Conversely, the more capital intensive its production, the more surplus would be required by the average firm to maintain its competitive position in a growing economy. The interest on capital is clearly an essential part of this model, ensuring an optimum use of capital resources.

There is no cause to worry about the rationality of behaviour of a firm acting on this basis. It has a very strong incentive to use its capital resources and the available labour as efficiently as possible, and minimize its unit costs in order to increase both the absolute volume and the margin of profit or surplus it generates. It also has every incentive to switch over to products, technologies, etc., offering higher returns in relation to its available labour and capital resources. If such moves require additional capital or labour, their profitability can easily be established as against current rates of interest and wages. In a competitive economy, such progress is a necessity if the firm is not to lose its relative position within the industry and on the market generally. Given a high rate of demand expansion and technological progress, the possibility of attaining higher rates of profit may reasonably be assumed for average firms at all levels of factor endowment. Through the market, the entire production and business activity of the enterprise, the results of both present and past work of the collectivity, is valued by all the other members of the community (and possibly foreign customers). The value so determined is again allocated by the work collectivity between remuneration of its own members and future expansion. Those who proved more efficient will have a greater opportunity to expand than those who fared less well. An automatic process of negative selection and expansion governed by demand and relative efficiency can thus be anticipated.

All this indeed seems too obvious—even tautological—to require a detailed demonstration at the level of general theory or Yugoslav practice. The more basic problem arising within this model in the Yugoslav context is that of the necessarily unequal conditions of operation of different enterprises or branches, and the concomitant risk of their being perpetuated or even increasing. Without being able to follow in any detail the various lines of argument on this point, the following three key propositions form part of this model.

(a) Differentiation and departure from abstract equality is a necessary corollary of any system based on (even if only in part) material incentive. To eliminate the latter would mean to 'deprive the worker, the direct producer, of his basic rights and status which make him aware that he is himself responsible for his own destiny, forging his own happiness'. In other words, it would mean the suppression of the system of workers' management. The profit or surplus value is not appropriated by individuals, but by the entire work force of each firm and only in proportion to the work actually performed. The possible differentiation in earnings is basically different from, and cannot reach an absolute size comparable to, the difference of income between workers and capitalist entrepreneurs.

(b) A process similar to Marx's 'law of the tendency of declining rates of profit' can be expected to operate in a worker-managed economy, probably with much greater vigour than under capitalism, as many obstacles to its operation have been removed or are disappearing (artificial monopolies, occupational immobility of the workers, etc.).

(c) Nevertheless, the process of income differentiation cannot be left to develop on its own, without an appropriate system of checks and balances. An adequate fiscal system, including both indirect and direct taxation, is a necessity of the system, the role of which is not limited to collecting funds for common social purposes. The planned foundation of new firms in areas where profits are highest must also form a part of the system.

157

As stated here, the model is obviously incomplete for it does not cover all the major areas of the firm's decision making which would make it tend to maximize either the absolute size of its profit or surplus, and hence its growth (as, for instance, the welfare services which to some extent are comparable to a lump sum self-imposed levy); or profit in proportion to its constant capital or labour costs. There is indeed a major ambiguity as to the nature of the capital (c) against which profits are maximized (the full capital, depreciated or not, or only capital costs?), nor does it cover the possible savings on direct material costs (which are quite distinct from savings on financial costs arising from the circulating capital). Thus it does not, and could not, provide guidance for specific action, as there is a limitless range of patterns of enterprise behaviour which satisfy its basic premises. The actual parameters of normal or average behaviour could only be derived from direct observation of the economy, The model is 'realistic' in this sense as well.

Once the enterprises are known (or supposed) to behave within the general limits of this model, the essential consideration within the context of the self-management system is to establish whether and if so at what rate, a decline in the relative rate of profit operates. Also, what are the possible reactions of the enterprises to measures necessary to keep the existing income differences within socially acceptable limits? Obviously, no norm can be set in advance and in the abstract for socially tolerable differentiation between profitability of different enterprises, or the rates of personal earnings of their workers. However, the hypothesis regarding the decline of relative rates of profit, or the trend towards equalization of earnings, is open to both theoretical analysis and empirical verification. The best approach would seem to be to examine separately the behaviour over a period of time of various groups of enterprises classified according to their level of profitability, particularly those in the more extreme situations, i.e. where profits are relatively high or relatively low. The questions may then be formulated in the following terms: what are the economic forces which would act on the worker-managed enterprises with significantly above or below average rate of profits (or surplus), to make them revert in the long run to a medium position; and can they be expected to counteract forces acting in the opposite direction? In any event, what are the economic or financial policy instruments which could stimulate such relative equalization of rates of profit whilst not substantially reducing the development of the system? A related practical question has often been asked in Yugoslavia: is there an optimum rate of investment which could be proposed to worker-managed firms at various levels of profitability? And the question may of course rightly be asked: what has Yugoslav experience to say about all this? These are the several basic questions which we will keep in mind when examining the various areas of the enterprise operations in the subsequent chapters.

As regards the profit or surplus maximizing model itself, a lot can clearly be said in its favour. It certainly corresponds to the dominant (although receding) mental framework of the Yugoslav population as a whole, at the practical level and given the wide familiarity with Marxist economics. Superficially, there is no problem in the concept of constant capital and variable capital (wages) and even the surplus value is a very concrete phenomenon in a rural setting of small-holding peasantry or craft workshops. Its 'sharing out' among the workers became the major manifestation of the workers' management system in the concrete life of the enterprises and in popular imagination and imagery. It also corresponds rather closely (but superficially) to the normal mental process and accounting evaluations which serve as a background to rational decision making in a Yugoslav firm. Most projects or proposed decisions can be evaluated in terms of their requirements of capital and in employment and the resulting profit or surplus (or deficit), either against the present average profitability of the enterprise or against alternative courses of action. Any 'humanistic' or 'welfare' based departure from this most general form of reasoning may perhaps be neglected at this first stage of evaluation. This pragmatic formula can thus be taken as forming the economic background of most decision making in the real world of the Yugoslav firms.

The profit or income maximization formula, or the mental process which it describes, can also be reversed and is often so expressed by those who participate in decision making within the Yugoslav firms, who 'form their prices according to the "cost plus" formula', i.e. taking their capital and labour costs and adding their own subjectively determined rate of profit or surplus value. The key questions here are: what capital costs? and what wages? for the former are partly and the latter for the most part subjectively determined by the enterprises. The norm may thus be valid for internal enterprise purposes until modified by a policy change, but has no objective value in the outside world.

There cannot be the slightest doubt that while this model had some standing up to the early sixties, it has by now been completely abandoned, both by economic theory and by what may be called official or institutional practice. It meets with fundamental difficulties regarding definition of its basic concepts, difficulties which appeared quite insuperable in the Yugoslav situation. Capital, wages, and profits or surplus value simply are not, in the worker-managed enterprise, the same logical categories as were defined by Marx or other classical economists for the purposes of economic analysis of the early (entrepreneurial) capitalist enterprise.

It is only proper to say that this fact did not escape the attention of the protagonists of the 'model'. Thus, Mijalko Todorović,[1] makes it clear that the notations (c), (v) and (m) do not refer to such specific categories of capitalist production as constant and variable capital and surplus value, but have a more general meaning: social means of production, means destined for personal consumption and for social accumulation. A similar warning is attached to his cost price formula cited earlier. Yet the implications of this shift in definition seem to be unaccounted for in the development of the model itself. In this connection it should be stressed again that Mr Todorović is not the author of the model (in the sense of arbitrary model building as epitomized by Professor Ward), but merely of the most recent and, in our

[1] *Op. cit.*, p. 46, footnote and *passim*.

159

view, most complete expositor of an existing conceptual framework enjoying wide social support including, no doubt, his own personal preference. One of the purposes of his book is obviously to defend the model, and to expound some of the fallacies, as he sees them, of the 'dominant' model based on income rate maximization which we shall examine next.

The most striking difference is of course the disappearance of 'wages', and hence of profit and surplus value, as an objective economic category in a worker-managed economy. The elimination of wages as part of the master and servant, or hired labour, relationship is postulated as one of the major sociological and legal-institutional objectives of the system. As an economic category, however, wages do not necessarily disappear with the introduction of self-management. They continue as they were set previously, be it under planning ordinances or private arrangements. Yet, the workers' council is institutionally unable to fix wages in the ordinary sense of the term: all they can do is to determine the earnings of members of the work collectivity in terms of their shares in the available net income.

Hence, as time goes on and economic relationships change drastically (inflation, major increases in, and redistribution of, real incomes resulting from absolute economic growth and relative differentiation between branches and enterprises), the old wage rates have become increasingly meaningless as an objective economic category and are phasing out of existence. No worker could negotiate his wage with a worker-managed enterprise, as his rate must be equal to that of all others on a similar job, and his actual earnings unknown until the accounts are closed and the enterprise income allocated. Nor is there a logical possibility of any kind of customary collective bargaining, as both trade unions and organizations of enterprises (Chambers, etc.) have an identical membership and differ only in the functional definition of their respective roles. (Similarly a Federation of master craftsmen and the (same) Craftsmen's Trade Association cannot 'negotiate' their 'wages'. They could perhaps advise usefully on good trade practices, introduce a price schedule and recommend standard working hours, but could not 'bargain' with each other.) No one but the State could endeavour to fix and revise wage rates, thereby interfering with the central prerogatives of the self-managing producers. Not only were such attempts growingly resented as intolerable interferences by the bureaucracy, but they were also seen as the cause of major deformation of the normal or rational behaviour of the enterprises in the whole area of remuneration and costing. Nothing but a general minimum, legally guaranteed income—not tied in any manner to the actual rates of earnings determined by the enterprises—were found compatible in the long term with the operation of the system of workers' management.

A guaranteed minimum wage or income would be similarly meaningless if it was understood as something similar to minimum wages imposed on a private enterprise system. In a worker-managed firm, the work collectivity can obviously be relied upon under normal conditions to maintain its members' earnings at levels compatible with the financial results of its operations. If a minimum wage or income is to be guaranteed in the system of workers' management, this cannot mean a mere legal obligation imposed on the enterprise as an employer, but requires that there be public or social funds available to supplement the enterprise income, should it fall below the level necessary to ensure effective earnings of the workers at least equal to the guaranteed minimum.

Yugoslav experience in this respect is perhaps not entirely conclusive. It is possible, indeed probable that, in other circumstances, 'wages' as an economic category could subsist for a much longer period following the introduction of a system based on worker-management, particularly in conditions of greater stability of the economy or where wage rates—negotiated or planned—have become an essential part of the traditional conceptual framework of the working population. As regards Yugoslavia, it should be borne in mind that a majority of the present working population have never been employed as wage earners and the others were mostly so employed only for a brief period. Little or no corresponding working-class tradition and living patterns had time to develop. For most of them, work prior to or outside the worker-managed firm meant working for a natural income from farming or handicraft, with its very real component of surplus or deficit. Nor can the possibility be entirely ruled out of devising an autonomous and objective system of determination of basic 'wages' or 'incomes', even though the Yugoslav experience seems to point to insuperable difficulties. On the whole, however, any economic model based on profit or surplus maximization seems to apply essentially to the period of transition from a system based on wage earning employment to workers' management, since it clearly requires the existence of wages as an objective economic category. It would obviously be inapplicable in the case of direct transition from a natural producers' economy and can certainly find no support in more recent Yugoslav practice.

(b) *The Producers' Income Maximizing Enterprise*

The phasing out of the profit or surplus maximizing model of self-managing enterprise was accomplished in the late fifties and early sixties at the level of official policy, particularly in view of the practical difficulties of finding an objective procedure for 'wage' determination, and the consequent impossibility of distinguishing between the basic 'wage' and the enterprise profit or surplus. It became more and more evident that there was no theoretical basis for such a distinction in what was increasingly perceived as a producers' economy, where only the net product or income of each firm could clearly be seen as an objective economic category reflecting the results of its operations.

In its simple form, this now dominant school of thought sees the maximization of the total net income (D), corresponding to Marx's ($v+m$), as the central objective of the economic activity of the worker-managed enterprise, in both the short and the long-term perspective. The work collectivity is seen as a 'true commodity producer' (and not a collection of infantile hirelings), conscious of its income being derived both from its own work and from past labour (or capital). It is correspondingly motivated to make the best use of both in their particular combination obtaining within the enterprise. This may seem overcomplicated or overambitious, but it corresponds to the natural frame of mind of any self-employed producer. Peasants or a

161

craftsman would never attribute the result of their economic activity to their work alone, but even without valuing them would see in the land and the tools the necessary complements. They may even reckon their income per unit of land, machine, etc. Similarly, to improve their lot, they will not see more or harder work as the only choice open to them. Expansion and progress are for them an objective necessity, as they must keep up with their competitors and want to improve their lot. There are specific reasons for the work collectivity to aim at rapid growth of total net income (to be referred to in more detail in Chapter X).

However, the maximization of the total net income, or its rate of growth, is merely indicative of a trend and could not by itself provide a sufficient definition of the expected or normal behaviour of the enterprise. The most complete model of this kind, backed by a considerable volume of literature and empirical research, has been presented by a group of Yugoslav economists and is often particularly associated with Professor M. Korać.[1]

The authors formally deny any normative intent or purpose in their 'model', nor do they recommend that their 'model' should serve as direct guidance for general economic policy. They are also well aware that it does not cover all major aspects of the economics of the worker-managed enterprise. They see it merely as the single best available tool by which the economic position and behaviour of the enterprise can be meaningfully expressed, but which certainly could not serve as the sole index of accounting rationality. They are indeed loathe to apply it to individual enterprises, as they feel that much more elaboration would be required, and have so far limited the empirical application of their formula to the study of the position and behaviour of different sectors of the economy and their sub-groups, as defined for statistical and social accounting purposes. In this latter area, we owe to Professor Korać the hitherto most detailed and comprehensive empirical investigation into this essential aspect of the self-management system.

In accordance with the basic logic of the self-management system, the worker-managed enterprise has to maximize its total net income (D) against both the total volume of means of production at its disposal (Sp), and the total volume of labour used in the process of production and transformed thereby into new or added value (NV). Neither the means of production nor the living labour are seen as commodities. This shift of meaning is also expressed by the introduction of a new set of specific notations, despite the authors' close adherence to Marx's method of economic analysis. We have preserved the original notation corresponding to the authors' nomenclature in Serbo-Croat.

---

[1] The signatories of the initial volume published in 1965 by the group include also the present President of the Executive Council of Croatia (Mrs) Dr S. Dabčević-Kučar and several other professors from Zagreb and Belgrade Universities (Dr M. Samardžija, Dr V. Sirotković, Dr R. Štajner and T. Vlaškalić); cf. *Problemi teorije i praksa socialisticke robue proizvodnje u Jugoslaviji*, Zagreb, 1965, 207 pp. Professor Korać published his first essays on the 'Income Rate Theory' in 1961 and 1962, and has produced a major empirical survey based thereon in 1968; cf. *Analisa ekonomskog položaja privrednih grupacija na basi zakona vrednosti*, 1962–66, Zagreb, 213 pp.

The economic rationality (profitability) in the worker-managed economy is thus expressed through the following 'income rate' formula:

$$d' \text{ (the income rate)} = \frac{D}{Sp+NV}$$

where D is the total net *Income*, and corresponds to the difference between the actual sales price or total receipts (P) and the material costs of production ($D = P - mtp$). It includes the two now indistinguishable categories of Marx analysis (v) and (m); the *means of production* (Sp) is the actual value of both fixed and circulating capital available during the period under consideration. *The living labour, or value added* (NV) *corresponds to the* labour input of the work collectivity expressed in terms of simple labour at its average value within the economy. Thus, for the whole (worker-managed) economy the value added (NV) will necessarily be equal to the total net income D, but these two values will normally differ in any one particular sector or enterprise.

A few technical comments on the three new basic concepts seem called for before proceeding with the analysis of the formula as a whole. The trend towards income maximization expressed in the denominator (D) may lead to misunderstanding unless it is constantly borne in mind that D is equal to ($P - mtp$), i.e. that its size is directly related to the volume of production and the level of prices (P) as well as to material costs (mtp). The special importance of the latter is particularly clear if the income (D) is considered alone and intuitively equated to a mere product of the volume of output and level of price (i.e. confused with gross income or total receipts). As net income (D), the authors take net income before tax. The income rate formula can, however, also be used for net income after tax which, although not an 'objective economic category', enables the effect of taxation on the relative position of the various sectors or enterprises to be evaluated.

The means of production (Sp), as defined for the purposes of the formula, raise a serious technical problem. The work collectivity maximizes its income against the total capital assets at its actual present value and not merely against those assets which have been used in the production process during the period under consideration. This, of course, is correct within a purely abstract non-quantifiable theory (as in formal logic) and may be directly applied in the case of a self-employed producer facing a natural production period (a year in the case of a peasant). It is obviously against their total assets that all direct producers must evaluate their income. If they wish to develop, as assumed in the case of the worker-managed firm, they do so, on the average, in direct proportion to their existing assets. The assets always appear to have been fully used up during the period selected, or else their full replacement is required for future expansion during a similar period. If a year is chosen as the basic period—as was done by the authors—this would correspond to 100 per cent yearly rate of utilization of assets (or interest on capital) which is obviously exaggerated, for if the circulating capital has been

163

used up it has also been entirely replaced, as material production costs (*mtp*) were deducted before the net income (*D*) was arrived at, and the fixed assets have been amortized and replaced where necessary under the same heading, but at widely varying rates for different categories of inventory items. As regards the requirements of future expansion, the total volume of assets would be required only where 100 per cent self-financing is practised or assumed in respect of the period under consideration. If however the means of production are financed entirely through borrowing, only the actual costs arising from such loans would seem to enter into consideration.

As commodity producer but not owner of the means of production, the work collectivity is not concerned with the total volume of assets, but only with the actual costs connected with the availability of the means of production, such as interest and amortization charges, the risk involved including insurance premiums, and possible losses, and where the necessary rate of self-financing or repayment of loans would also appear as additional charges in respect of each period. In any event, the 100 per cent rate of use of assets within a yearly period, as applied by the author, obviously gives excessive weight to the means of production in relation to the volume of living labour, which can be expressed as the value added (*NV*) for a year or any other period. Thus the formula suggested would tend to show relatively lower 'income rates' for more capital intensive production and vice versa. It would clearly become inapplicable if calculated for shorter periods, for the labour component (*NV*) would tend to zero as compared with the means of production (*Sp*). The opposite result would be obtained if longer periods were chosen.

This difficulty has not been left unnoticed by the Yugoslav authors of the model but seemed never to have been examined on its own with a view to a solution.[1] It would seem that the difficulty was more clearly perceived by Professor Korać in his later publications, where he assumes that 'the totality of the means of production is actually used up within one cycle of production', a period of time which he does not identify as a year or any other specific duration.[2] It seems worth recalling, however, that in the various arithmetic examples (tables) in Marx's *Capital*, the means of production are not assumed to be used up entirely (their total value transferred to the product) within the cycle of production under consideration, but their wear expressed in terms of *n* per cent, where (*n*) is distinctly lower than 100 per cent.

It is not the place here to suggest a definite solution of this technical difficulty. It seems clear however that the 'income rate' formula could equally be calculated on the basis of the actual costs of the means of production as perceived by the average work collectivity. The first element of the numerator (*Ps*) would be made commensurate with the second (*NV*), and the income rate formula could then be applied to any period found useful for an empirical investigation, be it a week, a month or a quinquennium. Provided its basic hypotheses are borne out in fact, the income rate formula in its present form

---

[1] Cf. for instance reply of Dr Dubčević-Kučar to Professor A. Bajt (*op. cit.*, p. 130).

[2] Cf. M. Korać-T. Vlaskalić, *Politicka Ekonomija*, Belgrade, 1966, p. 313.

(i.e. with the total volume of the means of production used in the nominator) could provide a means for determining the economy's own specific period or cycle as seen through the actual behaviour of the average enterprise at any given point of time.[1] It may be intuitively assumed that for present-day Yugoslav firms this average or medium cycle would probably correspond to a period of close to three years. Empirical studies now available, based on a one-year cycle, must, and indeed do, show systematic differences as between the capital and labour intensive sectors, for they tend to overvalue the means of production in comparison to the labour input.

In considering the means of production not in their total value but in terms of their 'cost' as defined above, certain anomalies of the present income rate formula would also disappear. For example, as noted by Professor Korać with respect to the commercial sector, a major proportion of the fixed capital assets may appear on the firm's balance sheets as current costs of leasing of premises, etc., from others (building enterprises, co-operatives or municipal housing enterprises, or other institutions). This situation causes a major upward deviation of their corresponding income rate under the present formula.

As regards the *labour or value added* component (*NV*), an ingenious solution is suggested by the authors. It is not reckoned in terms of 'heads of labourers', as proposed by Professor Ward and still sometimes encountered in journalistic presentations, often leading to quite senseless comparisons or criticisms. Nor is it expressed as hours worked, since an enterprise (under whatever system) may provide higher average earnings per worker although paying each one less than what he could earn in another enterprise with lower average earnings per head, due to a higher proportion of less qualified jobs, and other differences in the composition and rating of the labour force (its working hours, etc.). Where a worker-managed enterprise hires a technician whose earnings are rated as three times those of an unskilled labourer, he must obviously be given a higher relative weight in assessing the rationality of his employment, and vice versa. Any formula based on 'income per worker' is particularly unsuited for the worker-managed economy, and for the Yugoslav setting, where the advancement and rational distribution of skill is one of the primary objectives.

Instead, the total time spent at work by the various categories of manual and white-collar workers is expressed in terms of simple (i.e. unskilled) labour, the latter being valued at the national average value attaching to such simple labour (including both the formal wage and surplus).[2] Thus, the

[1] i.e. such period in respect of which the average enterprise considers the cost arising out of its means of production (including the cost of their expansion by means of self-financing or loan repayment) is equal to their absolute size at the beginning of the period; such a period could be defined as one in respect of which the relative differences in their respective 'income rates' for the various branches or enterprises would attain the lowest possible absolute value (showing a trend to increase both in respect of any shorter or longer period).

[2] A rather ambitious *ad hoc* methodology, based on Marx's definition of the average simple labour and the job evaluation techniques, has been developed for the purpose by Professor S. Han and R. Vuković, Cf. Dr M. Korać, *Analisa* etc. (*op. cit.*, appendix Z and table 4).

work collectivity is not seen as maximizing its own income against its own performance or value added (the three being by definition identical, and the corresponding fraction meaningless) but against the value of its performance or value added expressed in terms of the corresponding national average. An increase in income (D in the numerator), in other words an improved performance, in no way affects the value added (NV), as expressed in the denominator, if accomplished by the same work collectivity. The improvement is reflected in the corresponding increase of the 'income rate'. On the other hand, if the national average value attaching to simple or unskilled labour is increasing without a corresponding improvement of the work collectivity's actual performance as reflected by its income (D), the decline of the income rate would necessarily reflect the less favourable relative position of the enterprise.

The only objection is that in a country as diversified as Yugoslavia, individual enterprises tend to compare themselves not only to the national average but also to the more proximate and tangible local and regional environment, where the value attaching to average simple labour may differ considerably from the national average. This objection has less value for sectoral analysis, to which the authors of the model have so far confined their attention, except where an industry shows a markedly uneven regional distribution (particularly where grouped in the most or the least advanced regions). It might nevertheless be worth attempting to express the labour component of the denominator too in terms of natural units (e.g. hours worked reduced to simple labour). This would necessarily require a similar transformation of the means of production (or their cost, i.e. the past labour embodied therein) into corresponding units of simple living labour. The resulting index would no longer be expressed as a percentage, but in currency units (income) per unit of simple labour.

The *income rate formula* itself is essentially an expression of the specific form of the law of value as it operates within the self-management system. While enterprises and sectors are obviously interested in attaining as high an 'income rate' as possible both in the short and in the long run, they necessarily *tend* as a whole towards the national average, despite various forces which act in the opposite direction and may indeed prevail at any one period of time. As time goes on, and the means of production develop, their value increases, as does their importance relative to living labour (NV) and to the net income (D). The average income rate gradually falls towards zero. At this stage, when past labour embodied in the means of production becomes of infinitely greater value than living labour, the present system ceases to operate and a new economic system for the future takes over. The 'income rate' model thus corresponds to a transitional state of affairs, that of socialism based on producers' self-government.

The national average income rate for 1962, calculated according to the present formula, i.e. $d' = D/Sp + Nv$ (where D necessarily equals NV), was slightly in excess of 20 per cent. (It would probably be in the vicinity of 50 if calculated along our earlier suggestions.) As indicated by Professor Korać on the basis of a *summary* evaluation of present trends, it should take approximately 150 to 200 years to see it fall at one tenth of its present level due to a

166

corresponding increase of *Sp* (the means of production), when, as he implies, the contribution of living labour would cease to represent a major factor of economic activity.[1]

This points to a major problem of both the theory and the practice of such a transition, for enterprises and sectors would necessarily reach this final stage at various times and some would therefore have to live and operate side by side with others lagging considerably behind. According to Professor Korać's own calculations, there is at least one sector at present (hydro-electricity generation), the income rate of which has fallen below the 2 per cent level and which displays certain specific peculiarities of behaviour. The problem of those first reaching the target would seem closely related to the very kernel of present-day discussions in Yugoslavia and should certainly merit closer examination.

Although other suitable formulae could probably be suggested, and there is no lack of critical suggestions, the 'income rate' model is certainly the closest to the conceptual framework at the root of the economic system of present-day Yugoslavia based on workers' management.[2] Within the narrow limits as drawn by its authors, it would seem to provide both a general guide and a common yardstick for the evaluation of the tendency shown by the various sectors and enterprises, towards a rationality inherent in the self-managing enterprise.

The overall rationality of enterprise behaviour based on this model, properly understood, can hardly be questioned and would seem to require no further demonstration. A point worth stressing, suggested by Professor Korać himself, is the likelihood of firms with high rates of capital intensity

---

[1] *Op. cit.*, p. 149, footnote 6.

[2] Yugoslav authors and foreign critics often seem unhappy with the obvious departure from the well-trodden grounds of Marx's basic categories and notations, in a manner similar to the inability or unwillingness of Professor Ward to liberate himself from the basic premises and tenets of the private enterprise system and the methodology derived there-from. Yet it is significant that Marx's own *Capital* contains passages pointing to basically different behaviour and performance of types of enterprise other than those he has chosen to examine, and to which his categories and notation would hardly seem applicable if they were considered as general systems. Thus, in Vol. III, Chapter XIII, dealing with interest and profit, pp. 388–9 of the English version (Moscow, 1966), two such examples are very briefly referred to which seem pertinent to our general arguments. One refers to the 'co-operative factories in England' of the time, i.e. prior to 1865, 'the public accounts of (which show) that—after deducting the manager's wages which form a part of the invested variable capital much the same as wages of other labourers—*the profit was higher than the average profit*, although at times they paid *a much higher interest* than did other manufacturers. The source of greater profits in all these cases was *greater economy in the application of constant capi-tal* ...' (the one major deficiency of the two Yugoslav models so far examined) '... the average profit presents itself (here) actually and palpably as a magnitude fully independent of the wages of management ...' The other example foretells in a few mighty strokes Galbraith's model of industrial corporation, which would correspond to the fully degenerate model of a worker-managed firm: '... a new swindle develops in stock enterprises with respect to wages of management, in that boards of numerous managers or directors are placed above the actual director, for whom supervision and management serve only as a pretext to plunder the stockholders and amass wealth. Very curious details concerning this are to be found in the City of London ...'

and low 'income rate', as compared to the national average, to seek expansion into activities which provide a similar income in absolute terms at less capital cost, thereby providing for a higher ratio of employment. Conversely, for firms with a high employment content, and a low level of income, investment in their own area, or in others, is a condition of survival in a developing economy and an age of rapid technological progress. A rapid 'migration' into other areas or the introduction of new products (different quality, etc.) with respect to which the income rate is higher represents a quite specific feature of worker-management if seen as a form of producers' economy. The income rate formula could provide a useful tool for assessing the comparative advantage of any such move. This is the major distinguishing feature of a worker-managed firm or economy as compared to other self-employed producers, individuals or collectives, who may be tied by the forces of tradition and of the economic system to their trade or industry (traditional craftsmen or peasants, even producers' co-operatives, communes and other producers' collectivities).

The income rate formula also points to the fact that development of the means of production must be built into the price levels of the various sectors, normally in proportion to their capacity for such development. It thus represents an essential requirement of a developing economy. Hence the corresponding 'income price formula' requires quite different price levels to when prices are based on labour alone (value added) or on a 'cost plus profit' formula. This partly dispels the 'mystery' of the Yugoslav worker-managed firms' proneness to invest and to finance expansion out of current income, thereby renouncing on current consumption. Where the average producer, be it a farmer or the Yugoslav firm, decides to invest and modernize, this decision will be reflected in the average price level, although technically such expansion or modernization is not part of the current costs of production.

The tendency towards price levels based on (average) income has important practical consequences. The authors of the income rate model compared the value of the product of some selected sectors of Yugoslav industry in 1962 at current prices with recalculations according to these other formulae, including the 'income price', the other two being based on the 'value added' (or living labour only) and 'cost of production'.[1]

Table VIII

Comparative Value of Product of Selected Sectors According to Various Price Formulae

Sector		At Current Prices	Value Added	Cost Price	Income Price
		(1)	(2)	(3)	(4)
11420	Steelworks	43·1	30·7	70·2	85·1
11811	Sea shipyards	22·6	17·6	23·6	28·5
12010	Heavy chemical	16·4	9·6	18·9	24·2
12740	Sugar	19·3	5·4	13·6	19·9
12211	Sawmills	26·7	41·5	32·6	29·1
41221	Building	121·4	137·6	96·5	85·5

[1] *Op. cit.*, p. 59.

The actual title reads *Primary Distribution of the National Income*. As to the authors' methodology, we refer to their publication cited above. In each case the value quoted includes the material costs, to which the average (value added) is added in column (2), average profit or surplus value in column (3) and average income as resulting from the income rate formula in column (4). In other words these columns approximately reflect a (just distribution) of national income as seen through (i) the classical labour theory of value (which in a most awkward adaptation seems to inspire Professor Ward's model), (ii) the profit or surplus maximization model analysed earlier and (iii) the income rate model, which are compared to the real situation as reflected by the enterprise accounts.

The choice between the various models is by no means a purely academic question. If any one were taken strictly in a normative sense, as the basis for a systematic public policy for instance, the effect on the various sectors and enterprises would in most cases be of shattering magnitude. Thus, however scholastic they may seem to a practical economist, the choice among the various possible models is by no means irrelevant. The absolute size of the discrepancies is also impressive, although it may partly be accounted for by the effect of different fiscal instruments, since all figures relate to values or incomes inclusive of all taxes and levies. The model based on value added tends to produce changes in the opposite direction to the two others while the 'current prices' seem to represent a median solution. The particularly extreme deviations of the 'income rate' model in the first and last line can probably be accounted for by the inclusion of the total value of the means of production in the numerator of the income rate formula, a point already commented on. Such extreme deviations would no doubt be considerably reduced if the time factor were taken into consideration.

Yet the discrepancies are quite considerable. Indeed, whatever the problems the Yugoslav economy is facing in the area of prices and income distribution, they are clearly not of similar magnitude and the 'current prices' would appear to offer a reasonable compromise solution as between the three models. Clearly, no definite conclusions can be drawn from a purely illustrative table, though there is a considerable amount of evidence pointing in a common direction. It would seem that no single formula can be taken as sufficiently descriptive of the worker-managed firm or economy in a manner similar to the widely accepted concept of profit maximization as applied to early capitalist enterprise. We have already alluded on a number of occasions to a variety of specific objectives and particular strictures which are characteristic of the Yugoslav firm. Thus, although the various concepts underlying two realistic but formal models we have analysed so far are—unlike Professor Ward's model—commonly used by most Yugoslav firms in evaluating the rationality of decisions or alternative choices, the simple formulae through which they are expressed are probably not acceptable as such even as *indicative* norms towards which an *average* enterprise would *tend* to adapt its overall policy making. As the proponents of the income rate model are careful to stress, their formula may serve as a useful tool for a first approximation in looking from the outside at the world of the worker-managed enterprises.

For the latter, however, the *game* is infinitely more complex, a game first of all with themselves and, second, with the outside world, each with multiple objectives and strictures; hence with a practically infinite number of combinations. They are not throwing dice, nor engaged in a unidimensional search for a *maximum solution* but, like a chess player, must abide by multiple and complex rules, including both a short- and a long-term strategy, for which no single formula is available and, most difficult, where the ultimate aim is not a classic 'end of the party' but the attainment of all the objectives by all players. The corresponding game theory is not likely to find its seven authors in the near future.

CHAPTER VIII

General Models of Economic Behaviour (3) The Pragmatic Enterprise Centred Models

A game with (*n*) objectives and (*n*) strictures and no pre-determined outcome, other than the disappearance and transformation of the game itself, can obviously neither be defined nor solved by means of a single formula in the present state of theory. Yet such games present no insuperable problem in actual practice, at least where players are endowed with average intelligence. The earlier comparison with chess offers a partial analogy.

Such games are played continuously in the real world, and even our unusual 'no outcome' proviso is not without precedent. Various confederal arrangements, where minorities are respected, and of which Switzerland or perhaps even the United Nations may serve as examples in the political world, are largely based on similarly complex and multi-level covenants for which no abstract formula can properly account. Closer to the economic sphere, confederations of direct producers, of co-operatives or other collectivities, such as trade unions, are also examples of systems of which no true comparative account can be given proceeding from one abstract general model. Although there is no single gauge which could be applied in and resolve all cases, the constituents must always know how to deal with any problem as long as the organization continues to exist, and they may indeed perform better than if they had to conform to any one single rule. The Yugoslav economy based on the worker-managed enterprise, and indeed some of the confederal enterprises themselves, may be seen as systems of this kind. The ordinary enterprise will be facing a considerably simpler matrix, yet there will always be *n* possibilities and *n* strictures, at least at two levels, one covering internal relations and the other relations with the outside world. If viewed in this light, there will, by definition, be no general solution.

Even if one spent a lifetime wandering through Yugoslav firms, it would be hard to find a score of men able to conceive of, and actually interested in the search for, such a solution. Never have we met, at this level, anyone in Yugoslavia who—as may often be encountered elsewhere—could spell out in one word the object of his enterprise's pursuit, be it profit, plan or even income or bulk of earnings. Consciously or not, everyone sees the enterprise as pursuing a large number of objectives of all kinds, which most of the time form a given hierarchy or set of priorities, but which can be toppled instantly, either by an inside or an outside change, or perhaps through an imperceptible development, over a shorter or longer period. At any moment, perceptible differences of outlook may be present among individuals or groups. Even people grasping the full complexity of the problems facing the enterprise may differ as to relative priorities. A wait-and-see attitude or a compromise will then be the usual outcome of such a situation.

The multiplicity of objectives and strictures will be most clearly present in the minds of those called upon to prepare, discuss and decide on the enterprise plans, accounts and balance sheets (as presented in the preceding chapter). These include the professional management, the finance, accounting and planning Services, and members of the workers' management bodies with general competence, particularly the workers' council and the Management Board.

Among the former, the accountants and planners quite obviously need tools for project evaluation and have not failed to develop and use them in everyday life. Every project or account statement is meaningless unless supported by some comparative evaluation, and at this level practically every Yugoslav firm of some size can be taken as a school of its own. This pragmatic approach may be very simple, perhaps limited to a time series of past or planned accounts. It will usually be supported by comparative indices. Some enterprises have gone far in this direction, to the extent of actually creating their own accounting methodology, their own 'economic system'.

It would be impossible to come to grips with such an enterprise-centred pragmatism (which is clearly incompatible with any one single formula or model), did it not proceed *by and large* from a limited number of common sources. One such source is the 'enterprise economics' school, traditionally the most highly developed and often the only economic discipline common to the majority of universities and university-level business schools in Central Europe and Germany. Although not a key subject of research at any of the major institutes, enterprise economics certainly is the most essential and popular branch of economic studies in all Yugoslav universities and other more advanced economic schools. It is undoubtedly the most common subject for publications and manuals of all kinds, including many dealing with specific aspects of enterprise finance and management, and is covered by a number of major reviews or weeklies of practical interest for enterprise technical managements, and workers' management bodies. It is to this branch of economic studies that enterprises largely look for their technical staff and their expert guidance.

With the official gazette, one or other of the enterprise-oriented journals will be among the most regular reference material arriving on all managers' desks and read widely by the workers' representatives themselves. It is through these journals (rather than the more formally worded texts printed in the official gazette) that they not only take cognizance of most major changes in their institutional and business environment, but also find suggestions as to possible alternative reactions. These journals (which the reader should not equate to something like the London *Economist*) are in a way without parallel East or West, particularly as regards the close coverage of all aspects of enterprise policy and the comprehensive discussions and practical developments offered to readers with respect to all major changes. They are themselves (as indeed are some other major publishing enterprises) active organizers of encounters and seminars and direct initiators of informal innovation in enterprise practice. In turn, they rapidly reflect problems encountered in enterprise practice and are thus perhaps the most flexible instrument through which enterprises' views are brought to bear on general economic policy.

Where special training is provided for the workers' representatives (as it often is on a large scale), it is couched essentially in terms of 'enterprise economics' rather than as a 'general economic theory' and the corresponding literature and periodicals are widely disseminated among non-professionals. The activities of many of the economic institutes and societies established at local (communal) level, as well as the courses provided by the numerous workers' universities and similar institutions, are also essentially geared to problems of enterprise economics rather than to general economic theory.

It is obviously abhorrent to accounting mentality to think in terms of one single formula when the available analytical accounts offer long series of relevant indices which allow for closer analysis of past results and of alternatives for future action. In the concrete conditions of a given enterprise, such quantitative analysis need by no means stop at financial or cost accounting, and is often extended to real or physical data in so far as they affect the enterprise's interests. Not surprisingly, the enterprise personnel generally, and particularly those involved more closely with finance and accounting systems, are particularly mistrustful of all attemps at abstract model building, however realistic they may purport to be. Such mistrust is reciprocal.

It should be pointed out that such practical methodology, simple or complex, applied in a given enterprise at the stage of elaboration of planning and accounting documents, does not have any formally binding effect on the actual decision making of the workers' management bodies. While the choice of one or other set of indices informally influences the understanding of this past and future by any decision maker, the workers' council would not tie itself formally to any single model of predetermined behaviour. Similarly, although not theoretically impossible, no formal methods of establishing priorities or weighing various objectives seem to have been introduced by enterprises in order to help the work assemblies or collectivities in dealing with complex issues. Methods and techniques practised by individual enterprises, as well as standards, quality and rationality, differ considerably from case to case, as indeed do the volume and quality of information available. Yet there is at least one pragmatic model which received some official standing during the early sixties and which may provide a useful introduction; it is briefly presented below.

(a) *The General Productivity Model, or Uniform Indices of Business Success and Income Distribution*

The search for a suitable gauge for evaluating the performance of individual enterprises has always been a major issue for all those concerned with the practical development of the self-management system within the enterprises

173

and outside. It was a major consideration underlying much of the financial and fiscal legislation of the fifties and specific indices were frequently introduced. Policies aimed at limiting all forms of State interference in the economy led, in the early sixties, to the understanding that the criteria for such assessment should best be defined by the economy itself as a form of self-government and an expression of its self-regulating powers at national level.

The results were embodied in several successive National Agreements, agreed on by the Congress of Trade Unions and the Federal Economic Chamber, which were approved and promulgated by the then Federal Secretariat of Labour.

The latest of these agreements, signed in June 1963, is most illustrative. It rested on a series of nineteen 'uniform indices' which the enterprises were called upon to apply in their decision making, particularly where the allocation of income was concerned. They were expected to assess thereby their situation and performance as compared to others and act accordingly.

The Agreement was thus a purely pragmatic attempt to collate all the major common objectives of the worker-managed enterprises and, without attempting to synthesize them in one formula, to oblige the enterprises to act in conscience as 'good managers'. Many of the indices listed in the Agreement have become a permanent part of enterprise methodology of self-evaluation, and continue to be referred to in most business manuals. The Agreement itself remains formally in force and the Federal Productivity Institute is preparing a new, fully revised, set of performance indices.

This approach cannot be understood unless the full list of indices as set out in the 1963 Agreement is given. Only the briefest explanatory comments will be included. Original Serbo-Croatian notations are preserved.

The indices are divided in three groups: the first five are termed '*indices of business success*', the *first* of which is clearly the most complicated as it aims at a synthetic expression of the enterprise's progress:

1. *Growth index or comparison of the net product.* The term 'net product' is identical with net income (total receipts less costs). Net product of enterprise (NP) compared either with its own product during past period or with the product of another enterprise or sector, (NPu):

$$\frac{NP \times 100}{NPu}$$

The denominator NPu is calculated according to a rather complicated formula which accounts for changes in capital assets (S), in numbers employed (R) and in the volume of personal incomes (ULD); the subscript (o) denotes values pertaining to the previous period or to 'others' with which the enterprise is compared:

$$NPu = S \times \frac{NPo - ULDo}{So} + R \times \frac{ULDo}{Ro}$$

The whole index can also be seen as an 'equitable' income-sharing formula and could be adapted to any profit-sharing scheme in a public or private enterprise.

2. Net product per worker: (R): $\dfrac{NP}{R}$

3. Net product per capital assets (S): $\dfrac{NP}{S}$

4. Volume of sales (Q) per worker: $\dfrac{Q}{R}$

5. Gross income (RP) per total costs (US): $\dfrac{RP}{US}$

The *second group* of six indices express favourable or unfavourable economic conditions of operation of the enterprise:

6. Capital assets per worker: $\dfrac{S}{R}$

7. Instruments of work at purchase value (On) per worker: $\dfrac{On}{R}$

8. Rate of depreciation of means of production (present value $= Os$): $\dfrac{Os \times 100}{On}$

9. Relation between means of production and total capital assets (OSn): $\dfrac{On \times 100}{OSn}$

10. Relation between turnover tax (Pr) and net product: $\dfrac{Pp \times 100}{NP}$

11. Relation between net income after Tax (CP) and net income: $\dfrac{CP \times 100}{NP}$

The *third group* include the main behavioural indices, related to income distribution:

12. The part of net income after tax shared out as personal incomes (BLD) and collective consumption (ZP): $\dfrac{(BLD+ZP) \times 100}{CP}$

13. The part of net income after tax shared out as gross personal incomes: $\dfrac{BLD \times 100}{CP}$

14. Gross personal incomes per worker: $\dfrac{BLD}{R}$

15. Net personal incomes per worker: $\dfrac{NLD}{R}$

16. Net paid out incomes (*ILD*) per worker: $\dfrac{ILD}{R}$

17. Allocations to enterprise funds (*F*) compared to capital assets: $\dfrac{F}{S}$

18. Allocations to funds per worker: $\dfrac{F}{R}$

19. Collective consumption per worker: $\dfrac{ZP}{R}$.

When introduced, these indices were meant to help enterprises in evaluating their performance and making their decisions; they were also to be assembled and discussed by social and economic organizations at various levels in order to follow the development of the economy and possibly bring major discrepancies to the attention of the enterprises or sectors concerned. They were hardly ever fully used in this manner and the whole agreement, although formally in force, may be considered as lapsed. Yet, the indices themselves are indicative of the type of rationality criteria in common usage, usually in smaller numbers, within the real enterprises of today (with the exception of the first, synthetic index). They all relate to what we called the game within the enterprise as distinct from its relations with the outside world. They refer only to the strictly economic aspect of enterprise activity, leaving out some of the major but less tangible relationships which may be of special importance to the work collectivity, such as the changes in working time and work intensity, in skill levels or labour turnover, income differentials, etc.

The nineteen indices listed make it possible further to analyse the enterprise model. At first sight, they would all call for maximizing behaviour. The higher they are, the better they compare with past performance and with 'others', the 'better off' is the enterprise, the more its performance has improved. Yet no single one can be maximized above a certain point without pressing down one or several others. Neither can a parallel increase in all indices be considered as *the* optimum solution, for there is no reason to believe that all should grow at the same speed, nor that a negative result (decrease) should ever be aimed at for any one of them. A rapid improvement in one specific item with high priority can largely compensate for a temporary setback on other counts. Although it could not provide any specific solution in view of the great number of entries, the games theory with its *minimax* solution would seem to offer a convenient framework for decision making within the Yugoslav firm, particularly in view of the latter's special interest in stability (or rather stable growth) as compared with the speculative behaviour of a profit-maximizing entrepreneur. It actually is widely yet unconsciously used by enterprises when facing a definite major decision, in so far as they usually have recourse to several indices (of their choosing) to evaluate the expected outcome. A non-negative outcome in regard to levels of employment is usually postulated as a major constraint, at least where levels of income are not tending towards a (partly subjectively determined) minimum.

176

However, this is still too simple a view of things. A more or less comprehensive list of indices reflecting the enterprise's economic interests could possibly be drawn up and weighted according to its own interests and preferences at any point of time. A decision-making framework which could be seen in terms of the games theory, or a set of vectors, open to an approximately rational solution. But whenever a significant change (e.g. improvement) is obtained with respect to any one (or several) of the indices (e.g. welfare), its former weight (or co-efficient) may change radically, even falling to zero or becoming negative, all others being transformed in consequence. Subsequent alternate changes in other indices may bring the former to prominence again, to a high level of priority, but in completely changed circumstances, at different levels of satisfaction of the various objectives.

Few if any of the various objectives which may be pursued by the worker-managed enterprise are perfectly divisible and, even where they appear to be (e.g. money incomes or working time) their division into marginal units will not bring about meaningful satisfaction. Normally, satisfaction in a significant proportion (in bulk) of one or several priority objectives will be sought in real life, and when attained, the objective may disappear from the agenda for a period of time. The duration of such a cycle will necessarily be different for each specific objective, and quite unpredictable even from within the enterprise, for no one can tell in advance for how long a satisfaction attained with respect to a particular need will be considered as sufficient. Hence, no single cycle can be assumed which would bring all or even most of the indices, and their weights or co-efficients (or the set of vectors), in a relative position identical or similar to their initial position. Thus, any formal model constructed on this basis within an enterprise, and possibly helpful at some point of time, does not allow for wider generalization, or application to other worker-managed enterprises. Nor can it be used by the same enterprise for a prolonged period of time without modification. Changes of direction and negative values are particularly difficult to deal with under any formal scheme or model. In a way, to perform satisfactorily on all counts, the enterprise is bound to grow at steady or accelerating rates at all times, otherwise the choices it faces are bound to be difficult.

The argument presented in the last paragraph may appear too abstract; it may usefully be supplemented by a concrete simplified example. Suppose a worker-managed enterprise which at first (*A*) has five competing objectives to which it has allocated its resources (100) in the following proportions:

   (i) expansion (e.g. construction of a new wire drawing plant): 30;
   (ii) increase in cash incomes of workers: 30;
   (iii) reserve (e.g. for future reduction of working hours): 10;
   (iv) welfare (e.g. housing): 10;
   (v) residual objectives: 20.

A change occurs at point *B* (e.g. menace of losing present markets to competition) which makes the urgent completion of the wire drawing plant imperative; if no change is made at point (*B*), the total resources would fall to 60 at point (*C*) and would have to be allocated as follows:

177

investment: 30 (under construction, incompressible);
increase in cash incomes: 20;
reserve (-10);
welfare: 10 (housing under construction, incompressible);
residual: 10 (partly incompressible).

The enterprise can however, by doubling the means allocated to investment, speed up the construction of the wire drawing mill to be completed in time, at point (C). It can thus rearrange its policy at point (B) as follows:

investment: 60;
increase in cash incomes: 20;
reserve: 0;
welfare: 10;
residual: 10.

Thereby, at point (C) it may achieve an increase of its resources to 120 but, more important, will have satisfied some of its major objectives and could be *free* to reallocate its resources. It will have to act in accordance with the new set of weights or co-efficients attaching to the various objectives in the new situation.

Assuming that the opening of the new mill will cause some redundancy of workers, their redeployment, or pensioning off, etc., will require a further necessary allocation to investment (e.g. 10);

to compensate for past sacrifice the minimum increase in cash incomes will have to be doubled (40);

the minimum housing requirements of a reduced staff have been satisfied and the programme can be reduced to a symbolic figure (e.g. 1);

the residual programmes will have to be brought above the original level in view of earlier compressions and new needs (e.g. 29).

The enterprise will then be left with free resources amounting to 40. It may realize its programme of reduced working hours, offer additional increase in cash incomes, undertake some new investments, or engage in entirely new welfare activities. In its decisions, it will obviously be partly guided by its relative position with respect to the environment, in matters of hours, *real* cash incomes and the level of welfare and technology. It is likely, however, to concentrate its resources on one or two major areas where significant results can be achieved.

The enterprise will thus, up to a point, be able to use a way of reasoning similar to that offered by the games theory, although no one but itself could prescribe the rules of its game. At every stage new outside information will be forthcoming from the outside, the content of which will not be known at the start of the game, and which will thus require a complete rearrangement of the rules. It should also be noted that in the case of negative development in the enterprise's overall position, no symmetry of behaviour can be expected with respect to the various objectives, the set of priorities being necessarily quite different. It would vary considerably according to the relative severity of the setbacks. (A ship in difficulties or sinking—with several distinct stages and patterns of behaviour—may provide some analogy; the ship's behaviour will in no case be symmetrical to the order of fitting and loading.)

(b) *The Enterprises' Own Models, and Actual Patterns of Behaviour*

The various general models discussed so far are by no means unknown in the enterprises, particularly the last one, but none of them can provide a single and concrete criterion of rationality of every decision similar to that of 'profit' or of the central 'Plan' under other systems. Whilst it is possible to subordinate all behaviour to a single objective, or one commandment, it seems beyond possibility to encompass in one single formula the pursuit of n objectives or the practice of seven virtues, under as many strictures. In fact, this is hardly ever necessary. In practically all enterprises visited, the situation was dominated by one, or a small number of major projects or problems, and the relative priorities were arranged accordingly. Often, in a few years, they may have changed completely, swinging the full range of possible values or even changing signs.

Moreover, the worker-managed enterprises each seemed to follow some sort of cyclical pattern of behaviour with respect to their various objectives, which in their case could be defined as the priority satisfaction of the highest priority objective(s), as commanded by both internal requirements and external changes, the other priorities being temporarily drawn in the background. In major enterprises, similar cyclical priority attention would seem to go to different specific projects within each set of major objectives or activities (investment, welfare, etc.). Only in very exceptional circumstances can such cycles be expected to meet at one point for different enterprises.

A most interesting case of such a 'meeting' was the claim made in 1968 by nearly all enterprises to have the pensionable age reduced by five years, under internal pressure for younger hands and minds (although comparatively young, the work collectivities were rapidly 'ageing' in an economy stagnant since 1965), and the external pressure of unemployment. There was a significant exception, i.e. that of Slovenia, where the level of unemployment was minimal (less than 2 per cent) and where the claim found least active support. Even more interesting is the conflict with the still unidimensional reasoning of the social security technicians and bureaucracy, who repeatedly advised the Federal Government and Assembly that such a move was impossible, supposedly on financial grounds (although no firm estimates were ever presented), despite the enterprises' stated readiness to bear the cost of such a change. (In view of the age composition of the population, the social security costs remained relatively low, at approximately 9 per cent of G.N.P., and the proposed change would only have increased the cost by one or two points at most.)

During the lengthy debates of the Federal Assembly on this point, one of its vice-presidents, a leading constitutional expert, aptly summed up the position: 'As these (i.e. the lower pensionable age) are indeed the workers' demands, the Assembly has only one choice: either we satisfy these demands, or change the system so as to eliminate (the possibility of making) such demands.'[1] What was a technical choice within an enterprise (but could not be solved at that level) thus became a major constitutional issue, due mainly

---

[1] Cf. *Borba*, 14 February 1969, p. 4.

179

to the difference in outlook between a central technocracy guided by a single objective rationality, and the complex system of multiple-cost-benefit compensations of the enterprises, combining both quantitative and qualitative objectives.

This circular or cyclical model of behaviour has never been formally spelled out, but it can clearly be identified in the enterprise's accounts for past periods and programmes or plans for the future, where the initiation of projects or measures to satisfy various specific objectives is seen to be tied to the timely fulfilment of programmes in other areas and where a delay in one, or advance attainment of it, is correspondingly reflected in the date of initiation of the other. At the same time, autonomous internal or external stimuli may bring one target area into the high priority zone or, on the contrary, make it disappear from sight. The various objectives of the enterprise, and its corresponding spheres of activity, could thus to some extent be seen as relatively autonomous elements of a cybernetic system, each of which is brought into action if and when the internal and external stimuli reach a given level.

This cybernetic view of the Yugoslav firm can again be of only limited help in so far as it explains the apparent cyclical priority attached to the various areas of activity or programmes. It cannot explain at all why the 'action signals' would be set at any particular level of achievement or danger in any one particular enterprise. Moreover, such signals would have to be constantly reset with respect to others, in the light of both internal and external developments. In other words, while pointing to the existence of an area of relative stability, within which each enterprise could advance without having to face any major strains, the model would be of no help in defining such an area of stability, the range between the minimum and maximum tolerable levels of satisfaction of the various objectives.

The picture will be quite different when seen from within the enterprise. There, hardly any model, cybernetic or otherwise, will be necessary to understand what is *the* objective at the time, what are the corresponding priorities and strictures. Everyone who cares, or has a responsibility, will know perfectly well what has been understood, what is aimed at, and what may be expected in various circumstances. An average director, or the chairman of a workers' council, management board or of one of their committees, will hardly ever have any doubts as to what can or cannot be proposed, what is or is not acceptable, hence rational, at a given stage, within a given set of circumstances. The same applies to those among the workers and their representatives who act as spokesmen or initiators. Much will, of course, depend on individuals. A competent and articulate technician, or accountant, a well read or active workers' spokesman can tilt the balance far into his direction, indeed create a specific climate, a 'model' of his own. Whether original or commonplace, the specific behaviour of any such enterprise will not normally be similar to its neighbour and will, in all probability, be reaching another stage of the 'cybernetic cycle'. It may perhaps be close to that of some other enterprises in other locations or other industries.

This wider perspective of a cyclical behaviour, with alternate attention to

180

specific objectives or projects, is hardly ever clearly preceived in the enterprises or indeed in Yugoslav theory; although a physiological cycle has been suggested by a well-known author.[1] Nor, as already mentioned, has the Yugoslav firm a common yardstick or model on which it could rest its plans and programmes for the various time spans or sections of the future, already referred to earlier and which—except for the accountant's year—correspond to its own specific periods. Despite this, and indeed possibly because of the absence of a single common yardstick or model, Yugoslav firms are actually showing exceptional interest in framing their own set of references, their own criteria of evaluation or even full scale economic 'models'. These can only partly be helpful for guidance on choices between major objectives, and are mostly applied only for guidance in specific areas or choices among specific projects. Backed by the very specific data pertaining to a given enterprise or type of enterprise, more comprehensive and even ambitiously complex enterprise-centred models may be envisaged and have been attempted. Models can obviously be devised—on the basis of the income maximization model discussed earlier—to guide within rather narrow limits the choice between current allocation to invest and personal incomes. However, either a sharp rise or a sharp decline in the enterprise's current income would render such a model inoperative and other more basic criteria would have to be resorted to. No economic model can be devised, or provide guidance, for most other choices (e.g. a housing scheme for members of the work collectivity as against a productive investment).

In an attempt to sum up the position as seen through a tremendous volume of mostly scattered documents, and a limited but significant number of direct interviews, the following tentative generalizations can be made, each with a different degree of probability attaching:

(i) Whatever its possible merit in abstract theory, there is no trace of considerations based on marginal theory influencing the enterprise behaviour, particularly in the short term and with respect to the relative use of capital and labour; greater than marginal changes in relative prices may, however, lead to the substitution of product even in the short term, where readily achievable without a major reshuffle of enterprise planning.

(ii) In the short term (within the yearly planning period) the main policy guideline will be the enterprise plan (in whatever form) setting the main priorities and the schedule of income distribution; the regular implementation of the plan will be seen as the best indicator of good performance and revisions will be undertaken only under extreme pressure; even where unexpectedly favourable results would seem to warrant, major programme revision will normally be reserved for the forthcoming planning exercise.

[1] Professor V. Gorupić. The author compares, rather incidentally however, the life of the enterprise to that of man, his youth, maturity, and decline. It is certain that this could provide a convenient basis for classification of most existing enterprises but these would certainly not be found to conform to the inexorable pattern of man's destiny.

(iii) During the short-term period, the interest of all units will be mainly centred on their own and the enterprise's general costs, these being closely detailed in the plan estimates and offering the best possibility of internal income increases, each unit and the enterprise as a whole being normally able to absorb in the short term considerable outside shocks, thanks to existing and planned reserves and informal changes (adaptations) in labour productivity.

(iv) The enterprise will be particularly loath to change its prices in this short-term period, displaying exceptional downwards inflexibility and only envisaging price increases where pressed by costs (including the non-attainment of planned income levels), market conditions permitting; such price changes would tend to be general for the same industry or product, mostly prompted by outside developments of a general character, e.g. increase in prices of imported supplies.

(v) Each enterprise will have its own, single or multiple, price formula, based on direct cost plus 'income margin', directly built in into its plans, including income distribution forecasts; possible departures from the formula will be one of the most closely regulated areas of decision making.

(vi) Thus, major policy changes based on short-term developments will mostly be reflected in the annual planning exercise (prices, levels of employment, output, costing, amortization, etc; new capital assets will be integrated as far as they are ready for production, but will not be normally seen as an annual planning variable).

(vii) In their long-term planning, the enterprise will tend to seek an objective formula for allocating its resources among the various major areas of its activity, while during shorter periods attaching special priority in turn to one or a limited number of objectives or projects; internal or external developments may, however, bring about sudden and considerable changes in such long- or medium-term strategy, such changes often marking a crucial moment in the existence of the enterprise.

(viii) The continued, harmonious and rapid growth of the enterprise in all its aspects (or its survival, where menaced) is normally seen as the central objective of the enterprise; considerations relative to wider social development as well as to local and regional development are rarely absent in enterprises of some size, particularly in smaller localities and within less numerous ethnic groups; as long as the relative prosperity of the enterprise permits, local employment problems will in most cases be borne constantly in mind in this context.

(ix) When evaluating their economic development programmes or projects, the most common first criterion is the existence of a secure and expanding market for any given type of product; complementary production may be preferred to completely new ventures where it offers a possibility of redeployment of the workers and/or of means of production in case of relative price changes; vertical expansion of activity will also be preferred in as much as it enhances the enterprise's security of supplies or sales outlet.

(x) Within and concurrently with this framework, most enterprises will use their own indices for their evaluation of future economic programmes or projects; among these, the so-called 'profitability' index, i.e. gross accumulation per unit of invested capital, seems to be used most frequently. In other words, this may be defined as the enterprise's subjective surplus after settling for all expected costs and deducting the future expected personal incomes of the workers. In another form, it may be expressed in terms of the time period necessary for the repayment of a project financed entirely by outside loan. A yearly rate of gross accumulation per unit of capital invested amounting to 40 per cent would thus correspond to a repayment period of two-and-a-half years. This used to be one of the key criteria for allocation of investment funds by the former Federal Investment Fund and remains one of major concern for the present banking system. All other things being equal, such an investment project offers greater security to the bank and is preferable, from the enterprise point of view, to one with a four-year repayment period. The difficulty is of course that 'other things' are in fact never equal.

Net product compared to total sales, or to the total cost of investment are also often applied as guidance, as is the impact on employment and skill composition of the work force. The income or surplus value (profit) per worker seem on the contrary never to have been used, the labour costs attaching to the projected investment being reckoned as one of the current costs of operation of the project. They will, however, be estimated at increased levels corresponding to the enterprise estimates and objectives. Thus, workers' incomes (or labour costs) arising out of investment projects maturing three or five years hence may be calculated as projected current costs, 50 or 100 per cent higher than the present levels of such incomes. Thus, while insuring the planned (or desired) rate of increase in its members' incomes (this being as if a 'stricture' in the sense of the earlier discussions), the enterprise's primary concern will be the speed with which it will be able to repay any outside loans connected with the project and to accumulate further capital to finance new investments or the pursuit of other objectives.

The following chapters aim to show, in greater detail and with due regard to major exceptions or 'deviations', both the underlying theory and the actual practice of the Yugoslav firms in dealing with major economic problems at hand in the various areas of their activity. It would seem appropriate, however, to show in a practical example the manner in which all the various objectives and criteria of evaluation can be brought together into one meaningful whole. The outline of an annual report of activity as suggested by one of the leading economic journals widely circulating in the enterprises, and typical of the approach followed in most enterprises, is reproduced below.[1] The outline, which merely provides a framework for more detailed suggestions as to the data and indices which could be included under each heading, indicates the global framework within which economic decision making is set, particularly in regard to a short-term period. The outline of a long-term plan or a report on past development would cover similar ground but with greater emphasis on investment and growth indices rather than current costs. In addition to an introduction and reference to general developments, the outline contains the following headings:

A. Report on the activity of the self-management bodies (workers' council, management board, assemblies of work collectivities).
B. Analysis of economic activity of the work organization:
    1. Principal activities—Production
    2. Subisidary activities
    3. Research activities[1]
    (Points 1 to 3 cover the volume of inputs and outputs in physical and/or financial terms.)
    4. Cost analysis—economy of operations
    4.1 The dynamics of operational costs (economy)
    4.2 Production accounting—analysis of cost increases or reductions according to different production and work units
    4.3 Analysis of general administrative costs
    4.3a Departmental costs of administration
    4.3b Administrative costs of sales
    4.4 Analysis of cost of production for the enterprise as a whole
    4.5 The work force and personal incomes
    6. Labour productivity
    7. Supplies of materials
    8. Sales (or marketing and all other forms of disposal of finished products)
    8.1 Dynamics of invoiced sales
    8.2 Sales on domestic markets
    8.3 Sales on foreign markets
    9. Analysis of assets of the work organization and their origin
    9.1 Basic assets (constant capital)
    9.2 Circulating assets
    10. Investment activity
    11. Collective consumption fund
    12. Gross income, net product, net income
    13. Distribution of net product and net income
    14. The effect of the enterprise operation per head of worker employed.

[1] Cf. *Informator*, Zagreb, 5 February 1969, p. 3: The enterprise has a legal obligation to establish annually a report on its economic activity which forms a part of its annual accounts and balance sheet; it determines itself the 'method and the coverage according to (its own) requirements'. In most enterprises, the reports are quite comprehensive and only extracts are normally presented to outside authorities along with the annual statement of accounts.

C. Conclusions and suggestions for future action.

This outline provides a fairly good insight into the general framework of a typical decision-making process, particularly with respect to a short-term period. Most of the different items cannot be correlated directly with others, and there is no way to find a common basis for direct comparisons in quantitative terms among different enterprises. Within the individual items, each enterprise can, of course, apply such methods of quantitative analysis, rudimentary or highly sophisticated, as it may see fit.

Although it reflects the situation of the enterprise or the work collectivity as a whole, the entire report on economic activity can also be read and interpreted in terms of a series of statements of the position, performance and reward (present as well as future) of each individual member of the work collectivity. Similarly, an underlying complex perspective model for each individual worker could be read into the yearly and perspective plans of the enterprise. In both cases, considerable, but in the abstract quite unpredictable, shifts in the patterns of satisfaction of each individual's objectives, as compared with the enterprise average, can be expected according to his position and prospects within the enterprise. A notable amount of differentiated pressure can thus be assumed to exist within most enterprises, even in such areas which at any given time correspond to apparently latent objectives, and which may rapidly come to the fore should circumstances change, for they are likely to have been viewed as priority areas by some at least of the members of the work collectivity. When circumstances become favourable, these cannot only be expected to press their point but may also be found ready to launch programmes and to see the implementation of the corresponding policies. Thus, the Yugoslav firm can also be seen as an iceberg where a number of latent models, more or less ready to enter into action, are poised under the visible strategy actually in operation. This, we believe, is another contributory element of the apparent instability or over-reactiveness of the worker-managed economy, at least in Yugoslav conditions.

The change from one model to another does not normally imply, but nor does it exclude, a major change in the management personnel and the workers' management set-up, It will usually bring to greater prominence the former spokesman of the latest 'submerged' set of objectives brought to the fore by a change of circumstances. Such model substitution or inversion may involve a switch of priorities between any two or more of the enterprise objectives or strictures; e.g. labour productivity—material costs; welfare—investment—welfare—cash incomes; local development—vertical expansion; job security—productivity; housing development—sales expansion; sales abroad—sales domestic; training—investment in technology; modernization—entry into new productions, etc. Our paired examples are only partly true alternatives and the choices in real life are nearly always much more complex, entailing a major or minor reshuffle in one or more other areas.

Within the very concrete knowledge it has of its own specific conditions, the enterprise may also attempt to correlate some or even all aspects of its activity into a partial or total model for evaluating and determining its behaviour. In this concrete situation, the model can indeed be normative without meeting insuperable technical difficulties or destroying the enterprise autonomy as it is set not from the outside, or by an 'invisible hand', but by the work collectivity itself. There are quite a number of enterprise schemes of this kind, sometimes backed by very articulate local 'brains trusts', while the existence of others, less prone to publicity, may be only suspected. The former indeed tend to provide, frequently with the help of local economic institutes or other research centres, the bulk of the 'real life' contributions to the various symposia and collations of essays. Often people who keep in touch with the enterprises will be able to recommend a visit to a particular enterprise which is operating a model of its own, often without being known even to the wider circle of specialists. Such enterprises would seem nevertheless to provide by trial and error the real leadership in the development of the theory and the practical progress of the system as a whole.

It seems proper to refer briefly to at least one such model. The example chosen refers to one of the most ambitious and particularly interesting systems, based on direct costing through a unit of concrete labour, referred to by its authors as 'System of work effect balances' or 'BREF'. This system is of exceptional interest as it attempts to develop properly autonomous economics of the worker-managed enterprise and has in this sense wider ambitions to general applicability. It proceeds from the individual, or rather his individual quantum of concrete work, and postulates the existence of a hierarchy of self-governing work collectivities within which his work is brought to fruition: the (small) work group, production unit, economic unit, community of economic units and the enterprise. The actual value of the unit of concrete work being assessed by the whole community through the process of equivalent exchanges. Hence, no fixed value of money is postulated or required.

As the authors themselves point out, Aristotle's basic equation—23 units of wheat = one ox—is a more appropriate foundation for a socialist market economy based on Marx's labour theory of value than a fixed monetary system based on gold such as was applied by Marx in his analysis of capitalism. They thus point to one of the more general problems of the present Yugoslav economy which, particularly since the 1965 Reform, strives to relate the value of national currency to a fixed gold exchange rate while, no more than in any other country of today, does this policy rest on any real gold reserves comparable to those of the central banks of Marx's times. This is actually perceived as creating one of most serious inbalances not only in foreign trade but in various major aspects of domestic economy due to the relative inflexibility of the monetary equivalents. Indeed, quite independently from the BREF system, the money circulation in Yugoslavia and particularly in the worker-managed and other direct producers' sector (farmers, crafts), should more properly be seen as the circulation of socially determined equivalents for a given total quantity of concrete labour.

The system aims at ensuring an automatic allocation of the value of the enterprise product to the various demand centres, including its distribution among the members of the work collectivity (the enterprise internal decision making being reduced to the minimum once it has determined its basic value or allocational coefficients, e.g. for various skills). The system implies its own methodology of production records and accounting. In 1968, it was reported in actual use within five medium size enterprises (4,000 workers) and performing satisfactorily.[1]

The fundamental proposition is quite original. It postulates that the value or effect of a producer's work (p) can be seen as the product of his concrete work (h), his unit income (n) and an exponential function of the natural number (e^x), the latter being sees as a convenient expression of the necessary growth requirement of a modern economy and of the corresponding natural progression of work efficiency. (The rate of such progression is expressed by (x), necessarily positive as distinct from the traditional stagnant economy where $x = 0$ and $e^o = 1$.) Thus:

$$P = h.e^x.n.$$

A natural progression of the rate of growth is thus seen as a built-in characteristic of the worker-managed enterprise and economy, while the rate of such progression (x) is one of their key dimensions, as is the unit value (n) of the concrete work. All other dimensions of work and production are gradually worked into the model's basic set of equations, particular attention being paid to the various elements of the value of labour (working time, job evaluation, production effect, personal assessment, etc.).

Although fully considered, the problem raised by material inputs (cost of production) seems less directly integrated into the model. As the authors themselves point out, the material inputs or costs are the only aspect of the enterprise operation which cannot be conveniently expressed in the form of both a coefficient and index. Contrary to all other elements, they cannot be seen as proportionate to other items in a worker-managed enterprise. Thus, the BREF system, similarly to the Yugoslav models discussed earlier, treats them merely as a cost to be subtracted from the gross income. It seems to safeguard their highly stimulative effect in that it implies that savings on such inputs or costs are proportionately incremental to the unit value of work. Or rather, in the optic of BREF, the work collectivity first fixes the desired value of its incomes and then treats the costs as a variable.

Fixed and administrative costs on the contrary are fully resolved into the various allocational formulae, as are the costs of welfare and of capital accumulation. The model can thus provide allocational norms for the various major activities of the enterprise, derived from the natural growth function e^x (transformed into appropriate coefficients) as applied to the enterprise or, for that matter, to any other levels of the worker-managed economy. In variously transformed shapes, the function e^x plays the key role of apportioning the reward for necessary labour and the surplus value allocated to self-financed development. Thus it also provides a measure of relative work

---

[1] The brief reference given here is based on a summary presentation of the BREF system contained in a collection of papers submitted to a Symposium on income accounting and distribution organized by the Zagreb University School of Economics (*Opatija*, March 1968), cf. *Obračum i raspodela*, Vol. II, pp. 361–88 (bibl.). The author of the model, I. Vlahović, is a staff member of the Zagreb Institute of Food Technology.

efficiency. It thereby also provides for the values realized by the enterprise, as an equivalent for its production, to be apportioned through the various levels of internal self-governing units among the individual workers. And once introduced by an enterprise, it certainly could provide a tool for a check at the planning stage on the feasibility, or conditions of attainment, of different hypothetical targets. It could perhaps throw new light on the actual behaviour of the enterprises as the mental process it presupposes is not unrelated to some aspects of enterprise practice.

Contrary to all the Yugoslav models discussed earlier, the BREF model does not relate surplus value to means of production (or past labour), but sees it only as a portion of the product of living labour; the excess over and above the latter's value, subjectively determined by the enterprise. While this certainly would not apply where major capital intensive investments are planned, it could apply to the planning of various elements of work efficiency (intensity, etc.), or where future development is based essentially on living labour.

Its principal advantage is to provide a stable but flexible criterion for the allocation of past results, in respect of which the work collectivities are less inclined to consider the contribution of past labour or capital assets, yet are at the same time in dire need of a rational norm of behaviour. The results obtained by the BREF model on the basis of the e^x function (where the surplus to reinvest is basically equated to (log $.x$) constant), seem to correspond to some of the basic requirements of such a norm, and to explain some features of the behaviour of the enterprises in this area.

A BREF version of the average cycle of the (exponential) growth of the Yugoslav economy and various sections (branches, regions, etc.) could perhaps also provide a useful tool of analysis and of development planning.

BREF is an outstanding example of the many models of systems through which the more articulate enterprises and work collectivities are attempting to pierce, and rationally to regulate, at least in part, the patterns of their own economic behaviour. Suffice it to say that while the models presented so far are to some degree representative of the prevailing trends of thought and of practice, Yugoslav theory and practice are considerably wider and richer than what has been included in these chapters.

CHAPTER IX

General Models of Economic Behaviour (4)
Elements for a Preliminary Synthesis

The search for a specific and autonomous model of rational economic behaviour which would suit the worker-managed enterprise and the system as a whole is a relatively new phenomenon in Yugoslavia. In the earlier period, during the fifties, such models were more or less strictly defined by way of legislative instruments but, discounting occasional interventions to check undesirable developments in specific areas, no such outside objective guidance has been available to the enterprise or the economy as a whole. The need to provide them not with a set of legal rules but with a deeper under-standing of the conditions and criteria of rationality in their economic policy and decision making is however increasingly recognized as a matter of the utmost urgency. It is seen as such by many of the work collectivities themselves and seems to be a prerequisite of the building up of a new system of sectoral and national planning which would be consistent with, and rest on, the self-governing enterprise.

In Marxist terms, the problem can be stated as one of defining the particular form of the law of value governing the worker-managed economy. This area has been repeatedly referred to as one of 'definite retardation of the (Yugo-slav) social sciences'; Dr V. Bakarić, a leading personality of the Republic and the League of Communists of Croatia, who pays particular attention to this problem, has frequently referred to it during recent years, *inter alia* in the following terms:[1]

'We have recognized for a long time that the law of value applies also to our economy (but) we have never clarified in what specific form. Granting that work was the foundation of that law, we have not yet determined *how*, through what processes, the prices of different commodities are formed, and the primary appropriation of the results of work and the primary distribution of the surplus value thereby accomplished.'

In face of the severe problems arising from the 1965 Reform, the urgency of tackling this basic issue is being recognized by a growing body of Yugo-slav economists; thus, the account of a 'Consultation on current problems

[1] Cf. Professor M. Korać, *et al.*, 'Problemi teorie i prakse' etc., *op cit.*, p. 12.

facing the economy and the possibilities of accelerating growth', organized by the Yugoslav Economic Research Institute (Belgrade, February 1968), contains the following significant paragraph: 'One of the conclusions which received the widest backing ... required the launching of a systematic research programme for the scientific study of the behaviour of the Yugoslav enterprise.'[1] In the previous number of the same review (1967) the Director of the Institute, H. Horvat, discussing the Ward-Domar model, remarks in a similar vein: 'Only an econometric investigation could determine whether an increase in the rate of interest leads to an increase of output, and if an increase of prices inhibits employment.' To our knowledge, no such programme has been launched so far, nor such a study completed, and this major lacuna of 'scientific knowledge' is not likely to be filled soon. Fortunately, the situation is less grim if publications of less scientific pretense are considered, such as those of the central banks, finance and labour authorities at various levels, which seem to generate a considerable volume of information on enterprise behaviour, adapted to their more practical purposes.

It can be maintained that no such definite solution or rational model can be provided for an economic system with multiple objectives. This is clearly so where 'pure economics' or formal econometric analysis are applied, once it is recognized that profit (even per head of labourer) is not acceptable as the sole criterion of rationality. The same claim has been made by some Yugoslav economists facing the bewildering complexity of real behaviour of the Yugoslav firms, which may partly explain their reluctance to approach the problem in global terms.

It would not seem that such a model can readily be constructed at the present stage of discussion. It obviously could not proceed from completely unrealistic premises such as that of a kind of Indian Summer of eighteenth-century capitalism in reverse, under whose features many foreign observers, from East and West, greet with joy or scorn the worker-managed experience of Yugoslavia. There simply is not such a thing, nor could it exist anywhere in the real world save as a reflection haloing the observer's own dreams.

Nor can the more realistic models or even the purely pragmatic representations satisfy those in search of a definite set of rules or principles governing the worker-managed economy. Despite their various merits and possible intellectual appeal, they lack one necessary major characteristic of such a model: its acceptance by the generality or at least a wide section of enterprises as a model of behaviour to which they should naturally strive to conform. Nor are they likely to be so accepted, in the sense at least that profit maximization came gradually to be accepted as the golden rule of rationality of private enterprise in Western Europe and North America.

It could be argued that, without formally acknowledging any such model, the enterprises could on the *average* act according to its premises and be unconsciously guided thereby. As indeed the capitalist *avant la lettre* maximized profits and France's Monsieur Jourdain unwittingly spoke in prose.

---

[1] *Ekonomska Analiza*, Nos. 1–2, 1968, p. 155.

190

This is more particularly a claim made in favour of the income maximizing model by its main protagonist Professor Korać. This on the whole seems unlikely, as all the policy and decision-making procedures in the worker-managed enterprises are handled by people who read and discuss rather too much theory to be regulating their behaviour according to a very specific set of patterns. Only systematic empirical verification on a large scale could, however, prove or disprove the predictive value of any one such model.

Despite the wealth of available data, such empirical studies are as yet scant and unsystematic and the evidence they offer utterly inconclusive. A few purely probabilistic findings of some of these studies may be briefly summed up as follows. There is no evidence of any significant correlation as between capital, labour, output, prices and incomes. On the contrary, in nearly all cases the enterprise population would appear scattered at random throughout the area of possible values. Indeed, such correlation coefficients as may be obtained, usually of very low levels of significance, are as likely to be negative where positive correlation is expected and vice versa. Several authors have found that the actual contribution of capital and labour as factors of production are of little significance or even negative (particularly labour).[1] In any event, clearly, the growth of output seems largely attributable to residual undefined or unknown factors which, according to the authors' preferences, may be seen as technology or technical factors, entrepreneurship, skill or others. Similarly, declining or rising prices may be seen as indifferently commanding increases or declines in relative output at varying rates. A major survey of a Slovenian Institute tends to show that there are no optimum size or factor proportions, the relation of size to output being on the average strictly linear (directly proportional). The author's tentative surveys of the effect of incremental changes in the use of labour and capital by individual enterprises of several major industries undertaken in co-operation with a member of another Slovenian Institute have not shown any significant correlation at that level, while a trend towards linearity seemed to emerge when the same question was approached at the subsectoral level.

Thus, Professor Ward's omniscient 'manager of the workers' council' could not find any rule of conduct in all his science for he would not be faced with the 'usual type of production function'; or else, a hypothesis not fully developed by Professor Ward, should he behave in a truly marginal fashion, he might be obliged to order drastic reduction or increase of the employment in the vain search of a marginal dime or penny of per capita profit. A more interesting general conclusion which may be derived from this empirical research finding is that, contrary to common belief, the worker-managed economy, at least at its present stage of development in Yugoslavia, faces no definite point corresponding to optimum volume of output (at lowest cost).

---

[1] Cf. for instance Professor A. Bajt in *Metode obračuna* etc.; Simposij, Opatija, April 1967 (Informator, Zagreb, 1967), p. 48; according to a study by S. K. Sharma, for the period 1948–67 the correlation between annual increases in global output is negligible for fixed investment (coeff. 0.11) and negative for labour (-0.29). Cf. *Ekonomist*, Belgrade, No. 2, 1968, pp. 381 ff.

There is, therefore, no definite theoretical limit to the expansion of the average firm to a level of full employment of available factors. Although this finding cannot be considered as proven in a convincing manner, restrictive policy recommendations based on the existence of and S-shaped production or cost function are not supported by any evidence whatsoever in the case of the worker-managed enterprise and should therefore be regarded with even greater caution. (In the author's view, the practice of the Yugoslav enterprises and of other highly participative firms points to the inexistence of a point of lowest unit costs in such enterprises and should in their case be regarded as a mere myth resting mainly on the fact that it is included in most elementary manuals of economics—usually as the very first table or diagram —as one of its basic laws not open to the slightest doubt.) There are of course cases where costs may rise after a point is reached on the output scale, but there is no evidence that they should not continue to decline indefinitely in many of most other enterprises.

The most empirical enquiry ever undertaken in this field in Yugoslavia, by Professor M. Korać, had the sole purpose of testing the premises of the income maximization model, rather than the actual behaviour of the enterprise, with regard to the main areas of economic policy.[1] On the whole the evidence supports the author's claim that, during the period covered (1962–6), the enterprises tended to move nearer to the national average income rate and, in so doing, proved a definitely rational behaviour. The tendency is not extremely strong, however, and there are many exceptions. They are shown only at the level of sectors and sub-sectors (the latter data remaining confidential), as the author has not attempted to analyse the behaviour of individual enterprises which could possibly contradict the above conclusion. The main difficulty, in our view, relates to the extreme differentiation of the income rates shown even at the level of the major sectors (not to speak of the narrower subdivisions or subsectors). The 'income rate bracket' for 1962 is as wide as 1:15 (30·4–475·7 in relation to 100 for the national average) for the two most deviant sectors (electricity and foreign trade respectively) and falls to 1:10 in 1966 (42·6:404·2) for the two industries which share the honour of marking the size of the bracket. The latter remains so immense, and the differences among other sectors so important that the predictive value of the model seems far from fully demonstrated at this stage and in its present form. The doubt seems particularly justified if it is considered that the two extreme deviants mentioned—and there are other similar cases—are both among the best performers in the whole of the Yugoslav economy. The one least endowed in capital (foreign trade) is also by far the best off in terms of income and a massive investor. The possible rationality underlying the income maximization model seems none the less to provide a working hypothesis well worth further elaboration.

As hinted at earlier, the relative incoherence of the results obtained in most empirical studies may partly be due to methodological problems. Moreover, all the data available being in financial or money terms, they are obviously

---

[1] Cf. Professor M. Korać, *Analisa ekononskog položaja*, etc., *op. cit.*

far from true reflections of the real position, and may thus obliterate certain correlations or regularities of behaviour.

Tenuous as it is, the empirical evidence so far available would seem to point in the direction of a tentative hypothesis formed in visiting a considerable number of Yugoslav firms at various times, and on the basis of a considerable amount of indirect evidence, but which certainly cannot be fully demonstrated at the present early stage of development and of empirical knowledge of the system. It would seem, indeed, that the behaviour and performance of the Yugoslav firm, its success or failure, is on the whole largely independent of its formal economic characteristics such as factor endowment (or the organic composition of capital), size or even level of technology, and that they cannot be directly related to any single outside factor such as changes in price levels or employment.

There are, of course, sectors or areas which display a common pattern of behaviour and perform on the whole better or worse than average, but in most of them striking exceptions can be found in the form of individual firms or groups and, more particularly, it does not seem possible to predict these or other results by any conventional means of economic analysis, even where looking back at past development. Indeed, the whole pattern may change within a relatively short period without any major, or at least observable, economic causation. The quite exceptional success of the foreign trade enterprises, for instance, can perhaps to some extent be understood, considering the general growth of the economy, but it could never have been predicted, nor could their particular behaviour have been assessed in advance. Innumerable other outcomes could have been envisaged at the start with at least a similar degree of probability. Nor is there a single purely economic explanation for the success of other sectors or individual enterprises, often achieved against tremendous odds, even as regards technology; or for the failure of others, which may be better endowed in terms of capital resources or enjoy a better position on the market. As in any comparison between regions or countries, and particularly for such self-employed producers' sectors as agriculture, there is no reason to expect that one which is less endowed with resources will necessarily perform or fare less well and vice versa. The opposite is very often the case, and this would seem to apply to the Yugoslav worker-managed economy as well.

This lack of determinism of the general economy does not imply, by any means, that no economic criteria are applicable. On the contrary, there are probably few countries where enterprise managements are as constantly on the watch for internal economies and external gains, and as fully convinced that their every move rests on their best interest and the most rational economic criteria. They may lag behind many others in the quality of information they gather, and the means of understanding and interpreting it, but even in these two key areas there are probably few countries which have accomplished similar progress in as little time; progress from a purely traditional, static view of the economy to a situation where most modern theories and rational methods of costing, market research, production control, remuneration, etc., are not only widely known and discussed, but also

193

where devices are adapted, experimented with and applied in enterprise practice. A system where any error or judgment, delay, or irrational behaviour may bring about severe penalities for all the active members of the enterprise, and where rewards are similarly considerable, necessarily offers a high premium for those who are best able to assess their position, their possibilities and their interest correctly, in the most rational manner, and with the greatest probability of securing favourable results.

A realistic approach to understanding this process can only proceed from the multiple interests of the enterprise. Only when these are known, and the possible reactions of the worker-managed enterprises to internal or external changes in the various zones of their interest spectrum brought to light, can there be any hope of attaining a more general understanding of their own rationality which commands their behaviour in various typical situations or circumstances. The principal spheres of interest, or objectives, of the worker-managed enterprise seem not too difficult to define in general terms. Although not limited to profit or income, they certainly are not infinite in numbers nor impossible to classify. Their actual dimension, the force with which they affect enterprise policies or decisions can to some extent be derived from actual practice, but it would also seem possible to approach the problem in a more formal manner in bringing to light the relative importance attached to such interests or objectives by the work collectivities and their individual members. The various types of behaviour which relate to the various zones of the interest spectrum can similarly be brought to light by rational deduction and checked against practice.

In this chapter, a skeleton of the theoretical side of this exercise will be presented. It will then be used in the following chapters as one possible tool for understanding the real behaviour of the Yugoslav firm. Obviously, even our abstract or theoretical reasoning will be heavily indebted to the Yugoslav setting, the only one where a worker-managed enterprise can be observed in action. It is possible that a rather different classification of interest or objectives, with different patterns of behaviour to match, would be required if a similar experience could be observed in other parts of the world.

(i) *Towards a Vectoral Model*
A convenient representation of the worker-managed enterprise is to see it as a producers' household, and the members of its work collectivities as members of such a household. An enterprise of some size is a complex hierarchy of interdependent but partly autonomous households, ranging from those of the individual workers or members, through the variously shaped economic units or autonomous departments, up to the full enterprise, which is itself more or less directly associated, formally or informally, into partial household communities with others. Each of these has a multiplicity of interests or objectives, some productive, some relating to consumption, some specifically 'workers'' or 'producers'' as are not commonly considered in conventional economics. The whole area of labour and industrial relations is inseparably integrated into the economics of each household. Each household is relatively permanent and seeks the maximum satisfaction of its various interests and

194

objectives according to its own possibilities and its own set of values or preferences; yet the individual or lower level households cannot achieve satisfaction on most major points unless corresponding objectives are adopted and attained at higher levels, particularly by the enterprise as a whole. They are thus obliged to co-operate in seeking optimum solutions and in implementing the corresponding policies.

Each can thus be seen as a householder, an 'economist' in the original sense of the term, allocating his resources or earnings (future or past, according to whether he is planning or closing his accounts) to his various major areas of concern, or objectives, connected with his productive activity, his consumption and his own personal welfare or status. If the resources do not match the requirements, whether insufficient or in excess, he will either change his behaviour as producer or revalue his objectives, or both, so as to find a satisfactory solution.

At this point, however, the analogy with the various types of collective household economics of the past or present comes to an end. The various households which form the worker-managed enterprise can only find a rationale of their economic decision making in the various objectives and interests, individual and collective, of the members of the work collectivity, including of course their own individual households. They cannot interpret them, nor evaluate their satisfaction or attainment, except against such norms or values as are proper to their particular work collectivities. Objectives which do not appear at the individual household's level, but are essential for the attainment of the collective ends of higher level households, are deemed a part of the individual's interest spectrum as well.

This structural model is, however, rather secondary. The essential point is to bring to light the main categories of possible interests or objectives which may be pursued by the enterprise (seen as a complex of different types of of households) and its work collectivity, and the various types of behaviour which they would seem, at least in theory, to command.

The concrete interest or objectives the various producers' households may wish to pursue are obviously countless and of widely differing intensity. It would seem possible, however, against the particular background of Yugoslav experience, to arrive at a fairly manageable and rational representation of these innumerable possible interests or objectives.

Besides grouping all such interests or objectives as are more or less intrinsically related, it seems possible to classify them for our purposes according to the type of economic behaviour they appear to command. Fundamentally, there seem two main types of economic behaviour open to the worker-managed enterprise, corresponding respectively to the denominators of the profit (or surplus value) and the income maximizing formulae analysed earlier, i.e. one tending towards the greatest efficacy of operations and the other towards maximum growth in absolute terms. Either can, with respect to some specific objective, also attain negative values (rather than maximizing such behaviour may be thought of as permitting, or allowing for, relative inefficiency or lack of growth).

If the enterprise or any other of the household levels is seen not merely as an average or typical one, but as a purely notional and timeless abstraction, it would lose its multi-dimensional character, and its various interests and objectives could then be seen as a set of vectors determining its behaviour, which could be graphically represented on a plane surface with the two axes corresponding to the two types of behaviour just mentioned; the orientation of the enterprise policy corresponding to the sum of the vectors. This is the basis of Table IX on page 209.

These absolute values attaching to the various vectors (i.e. interests or objectives) are of course not known and cannot be determined for our abstract enterprise or household, but may be expected to vary on the whole in the same direction according to different sets of particular circumstances. In any event, they may be assumed ascertainable in any concrete situation. A more serious difficulty is that, unlike natural forces, the interests or objectives corresponding to the various vectors are not homogeneous, so that any movement of the enterprise in the direction they command, i.e. towards their partial satisfaction or attainment, may result in a radical transformation of the original situation. Some of the vectors could be disproportionately reduced or disappear for a time, while others would attain commanding magnitudes. The predictive value of the model, if any, would be quite limited unless based on systematic study of past experience, and prediction would require individual analysis of the effect of the change on each vector separately. Moreover, such a formal model would be particularly inadequate to take care of another aspect of human time, i.e. that of learning both from one's own experience and that of others; nor can the propensity to imitate others be adequately represented.

The model could nevertheless describe quite adequately the main determinants of enterprise decision making at any one point of time (e.g. when sharing out past income and adopting plans for a future period), or for a short succession of decisions between which no major change is assumed to occur which would affect a given set of vectors. It could also help to analyse the impact of major outside changes on the behaviour of the enterprise (e.g. increase or fall in prices, fiscal measures, etc.); they could be seen as shifting the enterprise from the initial position (e.g. point 0) and affecting thereby all the vectors commanding its behaviour.

Before proceeding to examine more closely the different possible classes of interest or objectives, seen as the vectors of our simplified timeless model, the two axes or dimensions of the plane surface on which we have placed them, call for a brief comment. One, which may perhaps be seen as the *vertical* axes, has been so far rather arbitrarily related to the profit or surplus maximization, or efficiency of current business operation. It covers that dimension of the worker-managed enterprise which brings it closest to private enterprise, whereby it attempts to achieve, but only on its own specifications, the best economic results within a limited period of time. It includes the specific cost consciousness of the worker-managed firm. The other—call it the *horizontal*—axis, related to income maximization in absolute terms, or growth, must be seen as the more specific dimension of a producers' enterprise or economy, including not only the long-term growth motivation but also the relative or

196

desired permanent existence of the enterprise itself and of its members. Within the framework of our model or chart, the enterprise may be seen evolving, under the impact of a set of forces of uneven dimensions (i.e. its interests or objectives) along the vertical or the horizontal axis or at some definite angle corresponding to a combination of the two directions.

(ii) *The Vectors*

A brief survey of what would seem to constitute the main classes of vectors of the abstract and timeless worker-managed enterprise, the lines of its interest spectrum, would now seem in order. They are tentatively listed below, and given graphical form in Table IX (p. 209).

(a) *The increase in current or short-term cash income* is sometimes seen (as in the case of Professor Ward) as the only possible economic objective of the work collectivity. It can certainly be assumed as being sought by most if not all the members of the work collectivity, but not necessarily as their strongest motivation. In no event is it comparable to capitalist profit. Its possible size is necessarily limited due to the distribution of the enterprise's additional income among great numbers of recipients, while for the latters' family budgets a sizeable but limited addition to income will provide a more or less satisfactory achievement. Thus, a marginal addition to enterprise income will be meaningless when divided among great numbers. A massive increase of per capita income will not normally be sought, as this would be unrealistic in most cases and likely to produce only limited additional satisfaction.

Spelled out in more concrete terms, the argument may be stated as follows: assuming an average Yugoslav worker, with a net income of 1,000 dinars and family expense budget of 950 (corresponding approx. to December 1968 figures); a marginal increase of two or five dinars is from his point of view meaningless, perhaps even irritating; a ten per cent increase provides a considerable satisfaction as it trebles his saving capacity or offers the possibility of purchasing a sizeable volume of as yet inaccessible commodities; a hundred or three hundred per cent increase is not sought as it would be quite unrealistic and would not correspond to any strongly perceived and known consumption requirements. A possible reduction of his actual or expected income (other than marginal) would on the contrary have a drastic effect.

His situation is therefore not at all comparable to that of a hypothetical owner of an enterprise employing 1,000 workers operating a family budget at the level of 100,000 and able easily to absorb wide fluctuations of the short-term levels of profit, in terms of millions, or even falling occasionally to zero, without being affected in the least in his personal or family consumption budget. Similarly, the latter's decision making can rationally respond to marginal calculus (e.g. for the recruitment or lay-off of marginal workers) where no such rationality can be construed as a commanding factor by a self-governing work collectivity.

Increased cash income can thus be seen as a relatively strong motivation, which is however confined to a limited area of the enterprise's possible short-term achievement, within a definite minimum (possibly 3 to 5 per cent annually, or corresponding to a local, national, etc., average), and a less clearly defined maximum corresponding to the minimum level of full short-term satisfaction of the average member of the work collectivity (possibly ten to fifteen per cent per annum, perhaps thirty where existing incomes are substandard or a new level of consumption reached). The corresponding vector can be seen as parallel to our vertical axis, with definite minimum and maximum limits of absolute size. The lower limit forms a zone of considerable inflexibility downward, while beyond the upper limit the vector ceases to be operative, at least when in competition with others. This would seem to consitute one of the major technical characteristics of all the 'vectors' within our model.

(b) *The long-term security of income and prospect of regular increases* is at least as important for the average worker or work collectivity, although it may differ in comparison to a very considerable extent from case to case. Clearly, it has its importance even with regard to current consumption in a private household or any other budgetary unit which is interested in survival for an indefinite period of time, as it relieves it from the need to save on current income and facilitates planning. It also makes all past commitments (debts, etc.) easier to bear and new ones easier to accept. It would above all correspond to the inclination of most men to see their future securer and brighter than the present, a steady progress being probably favoured by the majority (but not all). For the existing members of the work collectivity, security corresponds essentially to absolute growth of their enterprise as it makes losing their job less likely in case of its declining activity; the corresponding vector $B(1)$ would thus be parallel to our horizontal axis. To guarantee a steady rise of future income, however, absolute growth is not sufficient; efficient business operation during each future period is also required; the resulting vector $B(2)$ can therefore be seen approximately at a middle distance from the two axes.

The size and direction of the two vectors are clearly dependent on the socio-economic environment: respectively infinite and zero in a traditional society and vice versa in the hypothetical case of a purely mercantile entrepreneurial mentality prevailing among the workers. A rational but widely varying mixture should be found in most development-minded communities. Both vectors would also have a minimum and a maximum size, since few would accept a job devoid of any security ($B1$) or any prospect of future progress ($B2$), nor would they require an absolute guarantee of lifetime employment (which would transform the enterprise into a purely budgetary institution), or extravagant rates of income increases. No wider consensus could indeed be reached on any one of these extreme terms, but such consensus can be reached at quite different levels even in nearby enterprises.

Where minimum levels of satisfaction for both $B(1)$ and $B(2)$ are approached, they could often cancel the A vector, and direct the enterprise's current operation into the zone of decreasing current money incomes (below the horizontal axis), to preserve its existence and long-term prospects of growth. Conversely, where the growth—and thereby security—motivation appears at least temporarily satisfied in the short term (e.g. by a windfall

198

gain), the two vectors would cease to be operative for a time. Vectors A and B being closely related, a combined vector AB could be drawn which would reflect their joint impact on the enterprise's economic behaviour; as neither A nor B is of even density at all points, and as their minima and maxima do not coincide, the precise shape of AB would be unpredictable except in a quite concrete situation. Whatever their respective density or strength, the vectors A and B have a dominant influence over all others, as long as their minimum levels are not attained.

(c) A very specific and important dimension of any producers' enterprise relates to the *reduction or economy of effort*, physical or mental, the liberation of man from the pains of labour which (as those of birth or death) are part of his destiny but which he is able rationally to regulate and minimize. This dimension is particularly stressed in the worker-managed model, since the latter is assumed to translate equally the desires and preferences of all workers. It is conspicuously absent from the model of private enterprise with its special form of profit-maximizing economics, which at best consider the workers' strain and effort as irrelevant (provided he attains the standard rates of productivity at minimum cost), leaving it to non-economic institutions, such as the State or the labour unions to provide for improved standards. Even today, most conventional manuals of economics will entirely neglect this aspect of production and a situation where no limit is placed on the entrepreneur's freedom will be considered as ideal.

In an economy based on workers' self-management, this dimension is directly built into the economics of the system; several major lines can be easily distinguished in this part of the worker-managed enterprise interest spectrum. One, say $C(1)$, would relate to the workers' interest in the reduction of working time. The worker-managers cannot claim, following Marx's analysis, the elimination of hours worked in excess of the necessary labour and which generate the surplus value or profit, for the latter, if present, is already part of their income and placed at their free disposal. A simple reduction of working time (at constant productivity) would thus entail a proportionate reduction of short-term business efficiency, and would be likely also to reduce progress on the long-term growth axis.

An objective aimed at reducing working time, as commonly present as objectives A and B, may thus be seen as in direct opposition to these two combined vectors of our model. It may thus be represented by a vector $C(1)a$, pressing the enterprise into the area of negative short- and long-term performance. Its dimension is determined partly by the socio-economic environment, and partly by the actual quantum of time worked during the week, month, etc., presumably approaching zero at some very low level. Only in exceptional circumstances could this vector be assumed to draw the enterprise into the area of negative performance, more particularly if the vectors A and B were rendered inoperative by outside circumstances (e.g. if improved business performance were imposible due to lack of demand, or growth inhibited by an absolute objective limit). A simple reduction of working time would correspond in part to rational adaptation to objective circumstances. In the normal course of events our vector $C(1)a$ would be operative

199

only at and beyond the point corresponding to satisfactory achievement of objectives A and B (the maxima of the corresponding vectors). From that point onwards, the work collectivity could be seen as exchanging its present and future surplus income against present (and also future) additional leisure.

The same objective can however also be pursued by other means, including additional effort to improve short-term performance (parallel to A) and long-term prospects of growth of income ($B2$), as well as in terms of output and employment ($B1$). A corresponding vector $C(1)b$ could be seen as operative at any level above the minimum point of AB and in a closely parallel direction. Where both $C(1)a$ and b were operative, i.e. in the region beyond the maximum point of AB, they would be likely to attain rapidly their common point of satisfaction (their maximum value) and cease to be operative for a time.

The *reduction of work intensity* within a given work timetable ($C2$) can be seen as another separate component of the reduction of effort, which is to some extent interchangeable with $C(1)$. Its immediate effect on short-term efficiency is obviously negative, corresponding to a downward-sloping vector, the work collectivity exchanging short-term business success for less physical or mental strain at work. If purely irrational (corresponding to the once widespread notion of the inborn laziness of the working classes), this tendency would similarly affect the long-term growth prospects of the enterprise. Yet, if rationalized within the worker-managed system, particularly in the light of the dominant character of vectors A and B, attainment of the objective actually requires the long-term growth of the enterprise, in terms of better equipment and/or more employment, which alone can alleviate the strain on the present members of the work collectivity. (If such strain is already minimal, the corresponding vector, as in the case of working time, would cease to be operative.) The vector $C(2)a$ can thus be represented as negative along the vertical and positive along the horizontal axes, with a starting point around the maximum value of AB.

The *suppression of non-work* can be seen as a quite specific, partly compensatory component of the C group. While it may aim at shorter working time and a slower pace than imposed by outside decision-makers, the work collectivity has every interest in imposing its own norms of effort or output on all its members. Closely related to the socio-cultural environment, this output-unifying and self-disciplining tendency of the work collectivity may be extremely strong in most circumstances (as in any other type of team work), and may indeed partly check or compensate $C(2)a$, although it can hardly be seen imposing on itself the pace of Chaplin's *Modern Times*. It will rapidly eliminate non-work practices or related privileges which workers and management are apt to tolerate or condone in other circumstances, or which result from technological change.

While trade union restrictive practices such as feather-bedding may first come to mind, in the Yugoslav context this tendency may also be seen as checking the trend to over-employment in the clerical grades of the traditional type of public enterprise, and the formation of excess manpower reserves and purely adminstrative employment creation as under central

200

planning. In the very early years of their existence, this was certainly one of the major areas of concern of the workers' councils. In view of the magnitude of the problem they were facing at the time, they did not hesitate to take radical measures, including major restrictions of employment and lay-offs, thus clearly marking their intention of introducing rational principles in work and management. No such radical measures would be required or resorted to in order to deal with similar problems of much smaller magnitude as may arise in the normal course of operations of a worker-managed enterprise.

Where excess or useless employment occurs, a strong pressure aimed at its suppression can be expected to operate generally not by way of laying off those involved but by the provision of more productive employment (even perhaps at levels well below existing average short-term output). A vector $C(2)b$ will thus press substandard individual performance up towards the enterprise general norms of output and discipline, thereby raising the corresponding average. It has a direct positive impact along the vertical axis, and as far as it generates effective (productive) employment, also along the horizontal axis (probably to a lesser degree on the average, although the provision of productive jobs for those whose productive employment opportunities are disappearing under the impact of rationalization may be a major stimulus to growth in a great number of enterprises, particularly as it is of concern to all or most members of the work collectivity). The vector changes its direction, from vertical to horizontal, in direct proportion to the results of current business operation. Where conditions of full satisfaction of A and B are attained, it too may cease to operate.

The improvement of the work environment, independently of working time and work intensity, is a relatively autonomous component of the C family of vectors $C(3)$. Quite obviously, more convenient lay-out of plant and machinery, less ambient noise or air pollution, better hygiene, modern buildings, transport to and from work as well as scores of other similar factors can have a direct economic value for the work collectivity, quite independently from their effect on the short-term results or long-term growth prospects of the firm. They are in *themselves* worth additional outlays of funds. Except for the bare essentials, this could only be undertaken well beyond the minimum level of satisfaction of vectors A and B. It could then be one of the more powerful positive motivations in the main direction of the horizontal axis, closely related to the general area of welfare (discussed under H below).

(d) *The local or sub-regional development objective* comprises two major components (independent from any solidarity or purely social motivation). One is related to local levels of employment $D(1)$, the other to the provision of local amenities or social development generally, $D(2)$. *Increased density in local employment*, or reduction of local levels of unemployment or underemployment is of direct interest to the work collectivity as it has to bear the corresponding costs, partly through the local rates or tax surcharges where levied against enterprise income, and partly as an additional charge on its members' private budgets. (Apart from intervention by a central fund, financed by a tax on all enterprises, there is no other possible source of financing in a producers' economy.) The higher the local level of unemployment, the less costly it is to provide additional employment, even at levels below the existing short-term output of those already employed. The corresponding vector $D(1)$a thus pushes the enterprise in the direction of absolute growth, along the horizontal axis, and admits a limited negative effect on short-term efficiency, corresponding to a downward slope.

The growing density of local employment can offer an even more direct advantage for workers' households with several dependants able to work. This integration into the work force may very radically increase their budgetary incomes, even at stable or falling rates of *per capita* earnings. The corresponding vector $D(1)$b is thus closely parallel to $D(1)$a, while allowing perhaps for even greater negative movement on the vertical axis. The operation of both $D(1)$ vectors can in practice be seen in the form of discriminatory local loans by enterprises which can afford to provide credit for others where additional employment can more rationally be created (or existing employment safeguarded), including the creation of entirely new enterprises or activities (e.g. the establishment of individual service craftsmen). This vector is one of the strongest motivations of entrepreneurial activity under the conditions prevailing in most regions of Yugoslavia.

The provison of local amenities, or social development at local or subregional level, can comprise innumerable specific objectives corresponding to local needs of all kinds. In Yugoslavia, this would include practically all public services, such as education, health, local transport and housing development, etc., including part of local or enterprise-centred national defence amenities. In a more restrictive sense, it may be seen as the provision of such additional amenities as cannot be provided under the regular communal budget and which may be undertaken on the initiative of, and with funds supplied by, the local enterprises, particularly in areas such as culture and sport. Again, except for the hypothetical intervention of a higher level budgetary collectivity, no one but the hierarchy of enterprise and workers' households can provide the necessary means for the attainment of such objectives in a worker-managed economy. In most cases, such amenities will entail a significant but not recurrent expenditure, and would thus, similarly to $C(3)$ above, correspond to a lump sum self-imposed single levy, not related to future expansion of output and employment, and hence pressing the enterprise mainly in the direction of absolute growth, i.e. along our horizontal axis $(D(2))$.

(e) *The acquisition of skills and career advancement* (promotion) can be seen as another set of built-in objectives of the worker-managed enterprise. They may not be shared by a majority of members, but represent a strong economic motivation, particularly for the younger ones and those in pursuit of promotion and thus particularly interested in the affairs of the enterprise, hence likely to carry particular weight within its decision-making bodies.

The economic interest of the enterprise in the improved skill—in the widest sense—of its members is as obvious as it is for the individual. The intrinsic value of both is increased even though skills cannot be directly marketed in the worker-managed economy. The provision and acquisition of skill normally represent a cost for both the enterprise and the individual, its employment at work multiplying as if it were the labour content of production and requiring additional assets. All these factors make the skill vector ($E(1)$) operate closely parallel to the horizontal axis of our model, with a slight rise along the vertical axis corresponding to an expectation of better performance in the future.

Professional advancement or promotion offer at least as much satisfaction in terms of job security and raising of income as any possible attainment along B above. The corresponding vector $E(2)$ is thus parallel to $E(1)$, both reinforcing vector B.

(f) *Innovation, technical progress and current savings on production costs* are a necessary part of the interest spectrum of any modern enterprise, but would seem to be placed in a very special context in the worker-managed firm. They also represent independent personal objectives of a limited but varying number of individuals in any society, the nature of the enterprise being a major determinant of their active integration into the development process.

Major innovations or inventions ($F(1)$) fare least well in our model of the worker-managed firm (as compared with the modern capitalist enterprise or centrally planned economy), since the enterprise does not accumulate profits or funds sizeable enough to finance original research or to offer adequate reward for major new inventions. Where considerable labour or capital savings follow, their implementation would involve very special costs, as existing labour cannot readily be laid off, nor capital assets sold or otherwise disposed of. Where entirely new industry or enterprise is necessary, a rather cumbersome and probably rusty procedure must be set in motion outside the existing worker-managed economy in the absence of ready-made entrepreneurs or special development services of the economic ministries. The only practical solution *within* the framework of the worker-managed system would seem to consist in higher level industrial or regional economic communities (not mere associations of existing enterprises but actual economic interest centres, i.e. higher level 'households' or 'husbandries' capable of autonomous economic motivation and action). The corresponding vector $F(1)$ is thus of relatively minor size and operates mainly along the horizontal axis with a significant downward bend, but only at levels well above the full (maximum) satisfaction of the firm's short-term objectives.

Adaptation to externally generated technical progress ($F(2)$) is a major interest of the worker-managed firm at least to the extent that a failure so to conform would most likely prejudice the attainment of the B set of objectives. Early adaptation may ensure considerable progress along both A and B. The enterprise neither has real (i.e. private) capital reserves to fall back on in case of loss of markets to competitors, nor commands the market itself in the manner of the central planners. Even though it entails comparatively high costs, similarly to $F(1)$, this partly enforced objective enjoys a quite high priority. The corresponding vector $F(2)$ is closely parallel to $F(1)$, possibly less downward sloping but of much greater absolute size.

Minor innovations leading to a reduction of current material costs ($F3$) may

203

partly seem a tautology as they correspond to one of the meanings of the vertical axis of our model. This is true in so far as this objective is shared equally by all members of the work collectivity within a fully centralized enterprise (corresponding to the early model of the Yugoslav firm). However, the present decentralized intra-enterprise planning and income sharing makes it appear as a separate objective of a variety of diversified self-governing units. It may thus exert an influence of its own, possibly a very strong one, in the same direction as vector A. In so far as this objective is shared by most or all such intermediary household units, the corresponding vector $F(3)$ may be seen as one of the strongest motivations for short-term efficiency of the enterprise operations and a very specific trait of a worker-managed firm. At high levels of achievement, it may turn into an additional motivation for long-term growth, while, along with others mentioned earlier, it corresponds to a major area of 'hidden reserves' on which the enterprise can fall back to protect its current incomes or its existence. Its size may thus be inversely proportionate to the achievement by the enterprise of its short-term objectives (as required by vector A).

(g) *Welfare and social benefits provided by the enterprise*, correspond to another major set of objectives which may be shared by all or nearly all households, individual and collective, within the firm, but with different emphasis on different amenities or benefits. For example, a social benefit proportionate to the workers' income or corresponding to a lump sum per capita payment to all members, particularly where in cash, may actually be seen as a special form of personal income; such as the customary annual leave bonuses served by most enterprises in Yugoslavia to cover the extra cost of annual holidays. But where the number of dependents is one of the criteria of distribution, such a holiday allowance can properly be seen as a welfare measure. Their impact on enterprise behaviour will thus vary considerably, not only with changes in the socio-economic environment, but also according to the nature of the various welfare measures and benefits. Some of these may constitute a legal obligation on the enterprise; others may be voluntarily added by the enterprise (e.g. extra paid leave or special holidays or days of justified absence from work, additional notice or separation allowance, etc.), or introduced entirely on its own initiative (particularly as regards cultural activities, sports and social life generally). Provision of housing to members of the work collectivity is obviously a matter of exceptional concern and economic impact.

All these welfare activities correspond to major consumption needs of a greater or lesser number of individual workers' households, which the latter could not provide for themselves, either at all (e.g. holidays or days off), or at disproportionate and mostly unattainable levels of cost (e.g. housing, maternity leave, etc.). In some circumstances, such as those prevailing in most parts of Yugoslavia, the interest of the workers in these various benefits may be seen as at least equal to their concern for their present and future cash incomes.

In one way or another, all these various activities represent a special category of costs for all the households forming the enterprise, and their interest is to keep them to a minimum for a given standard of performance e.g. minimum building costs per standard flat or minimum sickness compensation per worker employed. At the same time, while there is a 'hard core' of welfare practically assimilable to fixed costs, most of these activities are conditioned by the enterprise's capacity to finance them out of its current income. They may thus be seen as pressing for the maximum performance of the enterprise in the short term.

However, many of these schemes will not be proportional to employment but will comprise one lump payment, possibly chargeable to future incomes (repayment of a loan, etc.). Many will also offer considerable economies of scale (e.g. housing schemes, holiday or medical centres, etc.). For both these reasons, the corresponding commitments will constitute a lesser future burden for an enterprise committed to rapid growth.

The resulting vector G will thus be operative in the vicinity of AB, possibly with a similar magnitude. Its impact may often be seen as dominant (as compared to AB), not only because of its absolute size, but also since it would normally be most forceful in areas well above the minimum and maximum levels of AB. It nevertheless loses its dominant position when major welfare objects are satisfactorily met (e.g. through the completion of a housing scheme meeting the workers' needs).

(h) In addition to the seven classes of objectives or vectors listed above, which may be considered as part of the economics of the system, the economic behaviour of the worker-managed enterprise may be highly responsive to certain non-economic urges or objectives of its members, which on the whole would seem to press in the direction of absolute growth, this in addition to such economical growth objectives referred to under B and C. This *growth per se motivation* operates at several levels within the enterprise. (We are not concerning ourselves here with outside non-economic influences, as we have so far excluded the whole matrix of outside economic forces and their impact on enterprise behaviour.)

Rapid growth of the firm is of greatest attraction to those with positions of responsibility or with prospects of acceding thereto, as both an above average rate of growth, and considerable size of the firm, may bring about a qualitative change in their career, status or living patterns, be they managers, technicians, or workers' representatives. The very reputation of their firm will make them a focus of interest for the general public as well as for more specialized groups or organizations of an economic or technical character. It may obviously provide a start for a political career but, more significantly perhaps, may lift them into higher levels of responsibility within the economy either on elective posts or as full-time officers. Even without job changes it may entail considerable status satisfaction where the enterprise begins to attract numerous domestic and foreign customers or observers, and offers the possibility of frequent business travel, participation in congresses, etc. In acquiring national or even international status, a medium size enterprise can begin to offer highly interesting positions in the regional and foreign capitals, possibly reaching quasi-ambassadorial status. Even the lower ranks of personnel may share in these non-economic benefits (not necessarily devoid of economic advantage) where works are undertaken or contracts executed in distant locations or continents. Even the lowest paid member can share to some extent, perhaps through having his employment and income certificate immediately recognized by the salesman in a shop where he seeks instalment credit.

Absolute growth may also be prompted by ethnic national (or religious, etc.) background motivations among the members of the work collectivity which may sometimes be stronger among the rank and file or mid-level personnel (and particularly the self-management bodies) than among the top specialists and managers, perhaps otherwise motivated.

A rather diffuse consideration of prestige and pride of *belonging* to a rapidly growing and powerful firm—as typified in a most striking form by the Japanese worker—must also be assumed as a part of the motivational spectrum of an 'abstract' worker-managed enterprise.

Rapid growth also offers a remedy to most human and personnel problems arising in an enterprise, particularly through the transfer to less exacting posts of the ageing members. Where family employment is at least partly practised (as it must be in a smaller community), such growth provides in many cases the most convenient and secure bridging of the generations in active employment (in addition to greater security of the household's income). It is thus possibly of some interest even for the older or less active member of the work collectivity.

An independent vector H—of sociological rather than economic nature—thus operates within the worker-managed firm in the direction of long-term growth. Once this growth motivation is made operative, it may require short-term sacrifices, but would normally aim at more distant efficiency objectives as well.

(i) To complete the list and make it applicable to any (or an abstract) firm, room should be reserved for a hypothetical, unknown or unforeseen objective, which may be regarded as related mainly to the anthropological or ethnic-cultural background or dominant ideology (if any). It should also cover major outside events which may completely transform the basic outlook of the various households and work collectivity (war or menace of same, major destruction due to natural causes, total disappearance of a major market or source of supply; and of course the corresponding positive events, although perhaps less frequent and less striking, such as the appearance of a so far unknown major source of supply, natural deposit, etc.). The corresponding motivational background may not be noticeable within any one stable society but becomes clearly apparent when the observer travels from one to another or such major event actually occurs.

Thus for instance, in a recent survey of the economy of Slovenia by a Belgrade economic weekly, the 'Slovenian mentality' has been shown—by the Slovenian spokesmen themselves—as the one major factor determining the specific behaviour of the Slovenian economy and enterprises, of their relative success, their limitations and characteristic features (e.g. prevalence of small firms showing exceptional degree of entrepreneurship, absence of inter-firm co-operation, etc.). Such 'mentality' could of course not be perceived within Slovenia (where it would appear as natural to human behaviour generally) but only in comparison with other parts of the Yugoslav Federation.[1]

The corresponding vector I is of unknown direction and size. It may be purely negative along the two axes of our model ($I(1)$), to the point perhaps of cancelling all other positive vectors, as is typical of most traditional societies; or even prove stronger than all as where self-destructive motivations prevail. It is not however proposed to deal with such cases in this study, nor are they seen as of major relevance in the Yugoslav case.

Other groups may be exclusively motivated by the prospect of earning a lump sum in cash, as in the case of task workers or temporary migrants from rural areas to industry. Their particular objective would point in the direction of short-term efficiency but with a pronounced negative bent as to long-term growth. While they may be more relevant in the Yugoslav case, they seem most unlikely as a social group to exert major influence on decision making within the self-management bodies, where the informal criteria of selection necessarily include permanent employment and some seniority, not to speak of the general bias in favour of industrialization and urbanization of society as a whole.

A similarly backward-sloping vector ($I(2)$) would correspond to the behaviour of a 'purely materialistically motivated' work collectivity as postulated by Professor Ward's model, but where the improperly defined 'materialism' is equated to short-term cash income motivation; it *may* correspond to the equally improperly defined tendency to 'capitalist mentality' which is occasionally referred to in Yugoslavia as an explanation of the negative performance of some enterprises, usually well-off and endowed with sufficient resources. Lack of entrepreneurship or even 'trade unionism' would seem to provide a better definition of this possible deviant behaviour, which also corresponds to a possible reaction to an outside event or disaster as defined above.

Even the so-called 'vulgar' or popular interpretation of materialism (in the sense of greed, covetousness or the hoarding instinct) would not seem incompatible with long-term development projects or self-financing, as witnessed by the works of the captains of early capitalist industry. Professor Ward identifies the workers with the schoolbook behaviour of their organizations in a capitalist environment where, for lack of other avenues of progress, they mainly concentrate on short-term wage claims, while paying little or no regard to their long-term impact on the enterprise, industry or economy, and on the future prospects of their own membership. While this view of the workers and their union may be held tolerably true to reality in the United States and perhaps in Britain, it would certainly not come to mind to anyone familiar with the workers' movements in 'capitalist' Western Europe or Japan. Our own economic model is traced within the limits of such rational materialism but it does not equate human natural needs to the greed of a hungry animal.

[1] Cf. *Ekonomska Politika*, 7 July 1969, pp. 8–12.

A purely ideological motivation for growth may be more frequently en-countered, at least in conditions similar to those of Yugoslavia, particularly among successful revolutionary or military leaderships, where industrial management is apt to be likened to the partisan or guerilla strategy of disre-garding short-term costs and results. The corresponding vector $I(3)$ would thus point in more or less the opposite direction to $I(2)$. This would be per-fectly rational in conditions of absolute penury or non-development (or indeed following complete destruction of material resources), as indeed $I(2)$ would not be devoid of rationality in conditions of relative plenty. It may however be prejudicial to the attainment of its own ends at the intermediary levels of the development process, where a rational balance must be struck as between short-term and long-term objectives.

In the light of the widely differentiated levels of development, the discus-sions in Yugoslavia on the orientation of economic policy may be interpreted as a search for such a rational balance, or of an equilibrium solution as between our vectors $I(2)$ and $I(3)$. It is a specific quality of the worker-managed economy that this debate can be and is also pursued within each enterprise and each of its 'households'. Any one of these decisions—or lack of decisions—can thus be interpreted as an explicit or implicit vote of the enterprise in one or other direction. Indeed this is often done, particularly by politicians and political sociologists. Such interpretations, however, are devoid of any accuracy or predictive value as far as they leave out of sight all the other possible economic motivations of the enterprise behaviour as repre-sented by our vectors A to H, which may cause the enterprise to move in one or other direction under the pressure of major economic interests inde-pendently of any ideological commitment to growth or to 'vulgar materialism'.

The presence of purely positive motivations ($I(4)$) in the combined direction of long-term growth and short-term efficiency—independently from those covered so far under A to C—should not be ruled out as a matter of prin-ciple. Indeed the existence of a reasonable man, the 'good householder' of Yugoslav legal theory or the *oikonomos* of antiquity, is one of the basic assumptions of the system and may prove decisive for its yet insecure exis-tence. A man who, unwittingly perhaps, accepts the law of balanced (planned and proportionate or harmonious) development of his various households, his commune and the country as a whole, who indeed can discuss and weigh on his own scales of economic and human values the pronouncements of any authority, be it sacred, profane, fashionable or forgotten. It is our main contention that such men actually can be found in the Yugoslav enterprises and that they have largely been formed by practice of the system of workers' management.

The behaviour of the worker-managed enterprise must clearly be ap-proached and interpreted in terms of conflict, more so indeed than any other form of enterprise, for it lacks the father figure of the sole arbiter and contains no supreme principle regulating conduct. This conflict, which may be seen through our set of vectors—and indeed on many other levels—is however integrated into the enterprise and is thus permanently present everywhere to such an extent that it simply must partly cancel itself out, lest the enterprise

Table IX

A Graphical Representation of the Vectoral Model Reflecting the Interest Spectrum of the Enterprise Work Collectivity

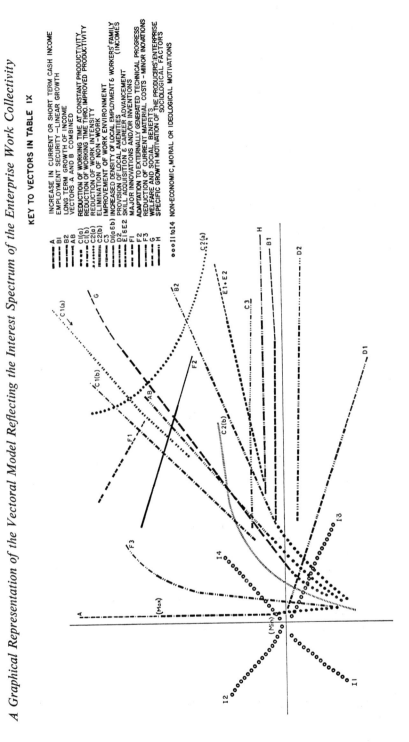

KEY TO VECTORS IN TABLE IX

A	INCREASE IN CURRENT OR SHORT TERM CASH INCOME
B1	EMPLOYMENT SECURITY —LINEAR GROWTH
B2	LONG TERM GROWTH OF INCOME
AB	VECTORS A AND B COMBINED
C1(a)	REDUCTION OF WORKING TIME AT CONSTANT PRODUCTIVITY
C1(b)	REDUCTION OF WORKING TIME THRO. IMPROVED PRODUCTIVITY
C2(a)	REDUCTION OF WORK INTENSITY
C2(b)	ELIMINATION OF NON –WORK
C3	IMPROVEMENT OF WORK ENVIRONMENT
D1(a & b)	INCREASED DENSITY OF LOCAL EMPLOYMENT & WORKERS' FAMILY (INCOMES
D2	PROVISION OF LOCAL AMENITIES
E1 & E2	SKILL ACQUISITION & CAREER ADVANCEMENT
F1	MAJOR INNOVATIONS AND/OR INVENTIONS
F2	ADAPTATION TO EXTERNALLY GENERATED TECHNICAL PROGRESS
F3	REDUCTION OF CURRENT MATERIAL COSTS – MINOR INOVATIONS
G	WELFARE AND SOCIAL BENEFITS
H	SPECIFIC GROWTH MOTIVATION OF THE PRODUCERS'ENTERPRISE SOCIOLOGICAL FACTORS
oo o I1 to I4	NON–ECONOMIC, MORAL OR IDEOLOGICAL MOTIVATIONS

complex should blow up altogether. Occasionally, this may happen, but for those who survive, it provides a permanent lesson not of abstract compromise but of learning to weigh all things on their concrete scale of values. No Utopian idyll of stable equilibrium or chanting masses should be read into this contention; the weighing is and will remain quite noisy at times, but it is quite likely to train a growing number of attendants to such scales.

Although by definition unknown, hence indeterminate, where an 'abstract' enterprise is considered, the vector I must take a broadly positive value along the two axes in any community which has introduced, or intends to introduce, any form of workers' or producers' self-management within its enterprises. It may assume partly or temporarily negative values in individual cases to the extent that other positive economic motivations remain predominant. Where negative motivations predominate in a limited number of cases (enterprises, households, etc.), such deviants are (as in any other system) ejected or reformed through the process of natural selection. If too numerous to be coped with in this manner, they would result in a regression or mutation into another economic system. As hinted at earlier, this is also seen by the Yugoslav theorists as the natural end of an essentially transient form of development of the economy; for when all the short-term and long-term goals have been attained, the principles underlying the worker-managed economy cease to operate.

(iii) *Potential Uses and Limitations*
Needless to say, this is not model nor a basis for an exercise in economic calculus or formal geometry. Neither the direction nor the size of most of the sets of vectors are known, nor could they be established with the degree of precision necessary for an abstract exercise of this kind. In a way, all we have done is to propose a complex game which could not be played by automats or calculating devices but only by rational and conscious players aware of the consequences of each of their moves, and weighing them.

All that is intended is to demonstrate that the worker-managed enterprise has a plural but finite set of major objectives, which for the most part can be rationally apprehended and which thus provide one single set of guide posts to rational conduct of business for any one particular work collectivity. Such guideposts should then provide a single optimum solution for any set of non-equivalent alternatives.

A subsidiary finding, or criterion, which we have not attempted consistently to demonstrate, is that our vectors, or at least most of them, present a point of minimum required satisfaction below which a considerable degree of downward inflexibilities prevail, and a maximum point of minimum satisfactory attainment beyond which they gradually cease to operate. In this regard various vectors were shown as predictably relaying each other, or acting as a reserve force thanks to which the last defences of others (i.e. the minimum points) can be held for a time, or as a supply of additional motivation at levels where other vectors tend to lose their operative significance. This in our view may also partly explain or strengthen the tendency to cyclical attendance to major objectives referred to earlier, the main cause of which is simply the inability of the human mind to attend at the same time to a variety of diverse objects, or to find adequate satisfaction in parallel but marginal advances on a variety of fronts.

Some confirmation of the existence of such a mini-max zone, as defined by the corresponding points on the various vectors, could be seen in the peculiar regularity of statistical distribution of the existing Yugoslav enterprises, not in the sense of the so far untraceable correlation coefficients, but merely as regards their numerical distribution according to incomes, including personal incomes of the workers, investment levels and self-financing assets, net product and other similar indices of their position or behaviour. Although the available evidence is limited,[1] there seems to be a consistent tendency for most enterprises to aggregate in the vicinity of the average values, while only a limited section (approximately the first and last decile) tend to drop to extravagantly low, or rise to correspondingly high, values. A well-marked reverse S-shaped line with very sharp bends downward and upwards at the two extremities is thus obtained, although there seems to be no compelling reason for the distribution of enterprises not to be linear or indeed to be concentrated at the two extremities of possible behaviour or performance indices. Table IIIB above provides an illustration of this phenomenon.

A plausible explanation, which direct observation and other evidence would seem to support, is to think of the enterprises which are under the menace of a catastrophic, or at least very sizeable, fall in short-term performance as being able to muster considerable reserves or savings, material and immaterial, real or hypothetical, corresponding to our various growth-oriented vectors; while those reaching the point of upward swing into the area of plenty (i.e. extremely favourable short-term performance) are likely to tend to satisfy first such other manifold long-term development objectives as may be on their books. Thus all appear to remain closer to a median position than would be warranted by their true, more diversified, performance. In any event, if this hypothesis and the underlying tendency of the enterprises to remain in the mini-max area were able to stand up to enquiry, it would certainly tend to show that the behaviour and performance of the worker-managed economy, at least at its present stage of development, is basically dependent on the vast majority of such median enterprises rather than on those showing extremely low or high levels of performance, which often tend to monopolize the attention of both the public and the specialized observer. It could perhaps also justify the search for special solutions for these two extreme but not numerous categories of enterprises.

The proposed model may perhaps offer some other more practical insights into the operation of the worker-managed economy. While again excluding any direct calculus, it could help in assessing the impact on enterprise behaviour of autonomous or induced changes in the economic environment,

---

[1] The only systematic investigation on these lines has been undertaken and published by the Federal Statistical Office for the years 1961 and 1962 (fortunately a rather average period): cf. Vera Krstić and M. Nikolić *Survey of Size and Condition of Yugoslav Manufacturing Enterprises*, Belgrade, 1964, 83 pp. There is however a considerable amount of other evidence which seems to point in the same direction.

i.e. in the market conditions or instruments of economic policy. It would show that there are no such unidimensional correlations, as are often assumed by analogy to private enterprise, be they in the mode which still predominates in Yugoslavia, equating greater income (higher prices, etc.) to greater inducement and better performance, or indeed the opposite view as taken by Professor Ward and which also has its Yugoslav protagonists. The effect of any such change would have to be analysed separately for any set of vectors and major category of enterprises, the 'model' providing a comprehensive analytical framework for such iterative evaluation.

The model helps to avoid the trap of unidimensional lines of reasoning, where a high level of investment or of personal income is either praised or despised, interpreted indiscriminately as the sign of good or bad behaviour of the enterprise; where employment is seen by some as extensive, hence bad, or is approved by others as an act of solidarity, etc. It would seem indeed more fruitful to attempt to bring to light the complex internal causes and external circumstances which appear conducive to a given type of behaviour or performance. While it is obviously impossible to recall them all on each point, such an understanding would seem difficult or impossible unless the complex set of the firm's possible objectives is kept constantly in mind.

A limitation of our model is that it has no direct support in enterprise practice, except in so far as it corresponds to the major allocational choices at the planning and income distribution stages. All the same, some of its other major features are demonstrably present in the enterprise behaviour, as, for instance, the exchange of additional income for reduced working time, or the stiffening of discipline under the pressure of development programmes, etc. Although not formalized in a manner directly corresponding to our model, it is a contention—and indeed a tentative empirical finding—that a system of complex weighing of objectives or interests, related satisfactions, and their minimum required and minimum satisfactory (or maximum) levels, actually underlies most, if not all, major decisions within the worker-managed enterprise as it exists presently in Yugoslavia, and could be expected to operate in other environments as well. No definite rationality need be postulated; indeed it must be assumed that most decisions or general orientation taken by a collectivity will appear irrational to most outside observers if their own rationality is their sole gauge or criterion of valuation. No common or single optimum, nor a general equilibrium, either can or should be as-assumed as a condition, a norm or a goal. Such an assumption is actually destructive of the system in most circumstances, since it deprives it of all its major incentives (except where a fully homogenous population of individuals and households is postulated, a sadly boring and fully unrealistic hypothesis).

As time goes on, the practice of planning and accounting (financial and otherwise) tends to formalize the decision-making process along these lines. Possibly it could be deepened, both at the level of the definition of priorities (or coefficients and directions of our vectors) by the various levels of households, both individual and collective, and by the introduction of corresponding voting procedures in the self-management assemblies. This could obviously never be achieved by the Gallup Poll techniques of irrelevant questioning (irrelevant to real decisions, not necessarily by its substance) but rather by allowing the individuals and collectivities concerned to rank and express the strength of their policy preferences in full awareness of their responsibility and of the implication of their choice.

There is in our view a fundamental difference between expression of opinion (whether anonymous or not) which is *ex hypothesi* irrelevant to the future course of events, and one which has a direct bearing on a future decision, particularly where the latter directly affects the situation of those who are called upon to answer, and which would normally take care of all relevant contingencies (i.e. be determined by our set of vectors). On the one hand, a 'representative' sample of workers is asked by an outsider, usually an unknown and irrelevant interviewer, the usual type of question (whether they like their superiors, are satisfied with their earnings, etc.). On the other hand, they have to indicate what is to be done (their particular superior removed or retained, hours reduced or cash incomes increased, etc.) with the full awareness that their views will set the guidelines for actual decisions directly affecting their existence. A few workers' collectivities have actually set up special services of their own with this end in view.

Clearly, except on very specific issues or within an agreed formula, or within a numerically small group, even such surveys could not possibly be substituted for decision making, but only provide an overall guidance to be interpreted by the worker management bodies. Within the latter, a voting system allowing for the selection and ranking of priorities as between major areas of interest and policy, and as between major projects within the latter, would also seem to provide a more rational solution than the usual Yes–No division which is increasingly recognized as ill-adapted to a complex set of choices, economic or otherwise. Within such a context, the abstract model could perhaps help in rationalizing the selection among the various alternatives as well as its necessarily cyclical patterns.

Only after the actual choices, including their ranking and timing, are arrived at by the enterprise in a rational manner, so that they can be known with some degree of certainty and be accorded some stability in time, can the behaviour of the worker-managed enterprise be considered as predictable and open to rational evaluation. While such formal rationality is by no means a necessary condition of efficiency and success (it may indeed impede either or both in numerous circumstances), it would seem to constitute a prerequisite of rational planning and policy making at higher levels of the economy. This in itself may in turn appear as a condition of satisfactory performance of the enterprise in some circumstances, and is indeed increasingly recognized as such at the present stage of development of the Yugoslav economy. In this sense, our 'model' provides a response to a basic requirement of rational consumers' preferences, their demand elasticity and its prospective changes.

While not claiming any normative or predictive value, the rational model suggested here could thus provide a useful tool of analysis and of rational decision making by the various work collectivities and particularly the worker-managed enterprise. It is a tool compatible with the use of other more

213

strictly economic models or methods, provided they do not postulate a single determinant objective, and it can assist in interpreting some of the more concrete aspects of enterprise behaviour and performance.

CHAPTER X

The Medium- and Long-term Policy of the Enterprise (1) Capital, Investment and Growth

The interest of the worker-managed enterprise and its corresponding internal motivation for medium and long-term growth have been spelled out in general terms. More particularly, in the last chapter an attempt was made to list, and briefly to define, the main categories of objectives or interests which may cause the worker-managed enterprise to give priority to medium or long-term growth over short-term maximization of income or profits. These abstractly defined internal growth motivations must now be viewed in the actual economic environment of the enterprise, which may activate or inhibit the corresponding objectives of the enterprise, in order to study its resulting behaviour and performance of the enterprise and, as far as possible, to bring to light the underlying relationships. In the present chapter we shall consider more particularly the financial and physical components of the enterprise environment, i.e. the world of capital and of the means of production, their reproduction and expansion, including the effects of changing technology and demand patterns; the work and employment aspects of the enterprise behaviour will have to be examined separately in a second volume.

Within the overall performance of worker-managed industry since 1952 or 1956, the medium- and long-term growth motivations clearly appear as the dominant component throughout the whole period, with the possible exception of the 1966–8 triennium. A five-fold or three-fold increase in industrial production (according to the year taken as reference), and similarly high levels of growth in other sectors, with average annual rates consistently close to or above 10 per cent, are in a sense part of the economic environment of the Yugoslav firm as they made it impossible for any enterprise in normal circumstances to rest satisfied and refuse to develop. Indeed, a major enterprise, reasonably prosperous in 1956, had it made such a choice, would appear shrunk to dwarf-size today. The quest for understanding thus partly faces a self-perpetuating set of circumstances, at least within the purely economic context, where growth explains growth and appears to an extent independent of any specifically economic motivation.

However, the concrete experience of Yugoslav worker-managed enterprises is sufficiently diversified, in time, sectorally and regionally, and indeed in hundreds of individual enterprise destinies, to dispel this overall impression

215

of some extraneous historical force or set of circumstances beyond human control which leads the Yugoslav people and their economy inexorably towards growth in a manner akin to that of Greek divinities or the modern myth of the Plan. At the global level, major contributory forces were no doubt present. Prior to 1952, high growth motivation and discipline inspired by the Soviet Five Year Plans, combined with the overwhelming requirements of political, military and economic defence, had pushed to the utmost limits the country's capacity to save on current consumption. Any subsequent easing of tension necessarily liberated formidable material and human resources, able to (but by no means bound to) serve for purposes of economic development and growth. Since then, however, a global interpretation of the country's single destiny is rapidly losing its early justification. From 1957 onwards, no truly predictive or normative value can be attached to the planning documents while, in the absence of practical experience and coherent economic theory, the behaviour of the economy remains unpredictable in terms of economic or statistical projections.

In other words, the rapid overall growth from the mid-fifties onwards can no longer be interpreted as an outside given necessity. There is no lack of examples of collective or individual setbacks or total failures, as unexpected as certain spectacular recoveries or growth performances, to prove that no one could have foreseen with any certainty the results attained by any one sector, region or enterprise. The strong negative correlation between most plan forecasts and actual performance in the sixties[1] is indicative of the difficulty or indeed impossibility of such a task, at least within the conventional framework of economic analysis. Yet, despite the growing diversity and unpredictability of performance, very high overall growth rate remained a dominant feature of the worker-managed economy, at least until 1965-6. Hence they require a more specific explanation. They dominate enterprise behaviour to such an extent that they form a necessary background for the understanding of current business management in regard to matters considered as the very kernel of conventional economics, particularly prices and short-term outputs.

The perhaps unusual priority attaching to the growth aspect of the Yugoslav system corresponds to the importance which naturally attaches to growth at the earlier stages of economic development (short-term considerations becoming practically meaningless in the initial stages) and to the usual perspective in which things economic are seen in Yugoslavia. Growth performance is also the system's main claim (along with the 'direct democracy' component) to the wider practical interest of the international community. It corresponds to what a Yugoslav author, hardly suspect of mysticism, referred to as the central 'mystery' of workers' management which has not so far been fully explained in rational terms.

In undertaking this survey of the growth oriented behaviour of the Yugoslav firm, against the background of its own complex interests and outside stimuli, it will also be necessary to take a closer look at the institutional and

[1] Shown, *inter alia* by B. Horvat in *Ekonomska Analiza*, 1968.

quantitative aspect of the various tools which it may put to use in furtherance of its development policy. These also seem best suited to order the main steps of our enquiry, which covers physical assets and financial capital in their chapter, and amortization, interest and loan-financing in Chapter XI. First of all, however, it would seem proper to review in general terms the nature and the main classes of possible growth-oriented activities of a worker-managed enterprise.

(i) *General Survey of Growth-oriented Activities of a Worker-managed Firm*

In most traditional economic thinking, economic growth is closely related to a particular form of management of capital, i.e. the activity of a limited number of economic agents, private persons or public bodies, who dispose of productive assets and are motivated to accumulate more by saving from current income in order to expand the volume of their operations. They were endowed with a particular virtue, usually referred to as entrepreneurship and believed not to be shared by other members of mankind, which enabled them to allocate rationally the accumulated new resources in a manner generating an optimum or maximum rate of growth. By present-day standards the volume and role of financial or physical capital as such was extremely limited in early Western capitalist manufacture, or in the first phase of Soviet planning. Its growth function depended essentially on the underlying social relationship bestowing on the entrepreneurial agents the right to extract an unprecedented volume of new capital accumulation through their own productive activity and from the surrounding traditional economy.

Accumulation of assets is not a monopoly of entrepreneurial capitalism or of a centrally planned economy. In its physical form, it may and indeed constantly does, happen in the still widespread pre-capitalist forms of natural non-monetary economy, and also their modern equivalents, particularly in farming and crafts sectors based on self-employed producers' or co-operative organization of production. Correspondingly, entrepreneurship can be and is derived from such accumulation of assets. In the capitalist or planned economy, where social development and welfare, including growth of remuneration for labour, appear as part of general costs to be minimized or at least to be kept within strict limits. In a producers' economy, however, they are an integral part of total accumulation and entrepreneurial motivation generally.

As a producers' enterprise, placed within a modern or modernizing market economy, the Yugoslav worker-managed firm combines the various types of growth-oriented behaviour found in other systems into a new synthesis. As part of a market structure, it is able and indeed bound to accumulate financial capital, not from or against a third party but exclusively through the work of its members. These may also accumulate directly, in their natural form, the results of their work for future productive or other purposes. As an enterprise collectivity, they have full entrepreneurial responsibilities for allocation of the new accumulated resources, but may also form all kinds of sub-collectivities with varying degrees of entrepreneurial autonomy. Their accumulation and entrepreneurship extend not only to the physical assets (including such forms of intellectual property as are usually included among such assets), but cover all aspects of their work, production and business activity as well as their own welfare and wider social envirnment, which all combine into a single set of interconnected, growth-oriented and often quite indistinguishable motivations.

Investment in productive assets and its financial equivalent, however important, cannot thus be seen as the sole form of growth-motivated activity of the worker-managed enterprise, particularly where measured by financial accounting data relating to fixed or even total assets. Their actual value can be fundamentally altered by any number of financially unaccountable changes enhancing the firm's economic efficiency, or improving the workers' welfare at work or in the wider social context.

Technology, understood in its widest sense as corresponding to any change contributing to the firm's economic efficiency, other than where reflected by an increase in the financial accounting value of productive assets, must thus be seen as a second major component of the growth-motivated activity of the worker-managed enterprise. It is particularly important where new capital is scarce or lacking and where considerable progress can be achieved through major or minor improvements in efficiency not reflected in the accounting value of the assets. Growth through unaccounted changes corresponding to this wide definition of technology may be of great importance at all levels of development up to but excluding that of full automation. It is particularly noteworthy where savings on material costs are concerned, the impact of which may be quite independent from, and of considerably greater magnitude than, that of the corresponding volume of circulating capital. However, it may cover scores of other items such as more efficient layout of machinery, better product mix, closer co-operation or a merger with suppliers, new marketing policy or better packing, elimination of all kinds of losses due to negligence, etc. None of these will appear as such on the enterprise balance sheet, yet if they should lead, for instance, to doubling the enterprise net product, at constant level of capital and labour, both would appear correspondingly appreciated but, in the worker-managed world, the latter alone would reap all the benefit. Similarly the worker-managers would alone bear any corresponding losses, whether real or due to lack of adaptability or unproductive work.

The important point to bear in mind here is that all these invisible components of the enterprise growth are essentially controlled not by 'labour' but by the actual workers, members of the work collectivity including everyone in the enterprise from the night watchman to the top experts and managers. Hence, if there is a real benefit to reap, or loss to avoid, those who first come to notice it have no third party to convince (e.g. an owner, a ministry, etc.) nor need they go against anyone's major interest (e.g. the workers, or their unions). If necessary, internal reorganization or revision of rules can always provide for an accommodation or compensation of conflicting interests. (We remain here at the level of the rational 'model' of the Yugoslav firm where, if a change is in the real interest of the work collectivity, the existence of a solution of concomitant problems or hardships is definitional. There is, of course, no guarantee that it will actually be found or accepted in any one concrete situation.) Given the necessary time, and particularly in conditions of rapid overall growth, there is a fair chance that an adequate solution will be found and accepted.

We have included under this heading changes which elsewhere, and in most business theories, are considered mostly as involving instant decisions or short-term programmes. Actually, they are hardly ever introduced by a mere stroke of the pen or a staff circular, as it may appear in a manual. In the worker-managed enterprise, the corresponding period will nevertheless in most cases be considerably longer, given the time necessary to find an agreed solution within extremely complex machinery. This search for an agreed solution will, however, coincide more or less with the period of implementation, as all those concerned will be made aware of and accept the change. Of course, if urgency is widely recognized, decision and implementation may be achieved with extraordinary rapidity in a worker-managed firm, due to the spatial and personal unity of the decision makers and those implementing the decisions. (Similarly, a self-employed producer, e.g. a farmer, may deliberate at length with himself whether to acquire a piece of machinery, e.g. a tractor but, once he so decides, the decision is practically implemented and the machine ready to use. In case of urgency, the deliberation and implementation may be completed instantly.) A somewhat similar argument, and corresponding findings, may be found in a recent volume dealing with the economics of the co-determination system as practised in the coal and steel industries of the Federal Republic of Germany.[1]

A third sphere of growth motivated activity, at first sight incidental to the economic object of the enterprises, corresponds to its *welfare and socio-cultural development* functions. Surprising as it may seem, this is the only ultimate finality of the worker-managed enterprise (wherein it rejoins in such concrete terms that of the centrally planned economy or, less strikingly, of the modern Welfare State). For to provide for higher incomes, more leisure and comfort, better services and a more civilized or humanized environment is, in the final analysis, in no one else's interest but the workers'. Only they themselves can provide the necessary finance and entrepreneurship, as there are no private profits to squeeze nor an all-powerful State to command them out of nowhere. Welfare oriented growth partly escapes the direct control of the enterprise, but partly remains embodied in non-productive physical assets which form a part of enterprise capital and may indeed serve as special reserve in case of emergency. Even the apparently lost, non-recuperable welfare spendings may be seen as enhancing the value of the workers' collective and individual existence, and thereby the growth of their enterprise.

None of these three major areas (investment, technology, and welfare) of the growth-oriented economic activity of the enterprise exists in isolation. Most projects will imply choices among combinations of all three of them. The important characteristic of the worker-managed enterprise is precisely their existence as if on an equal footing, presenting the work collectivity

---

[1] Cf. Nemitz and Becker, *op. cit.*, pp. 261–7.

with equivalent, not predetermined choices, or possibilities to devise their own growth mix formulae. Should any one single rule be spelled out which may define or be seen as guiding the enterprise's conduct in the three main areas of growth oriented policy, its overall aim could perhaps be stated as being the global valorization of the workers' collective and individual work and existence within their own time horizon. Any rational decision on policy affecting capital, technology and welfare, as defined above, would have to originate from, and conform to, this basic principle of the worker-managed enterprise.

(ii) *The Capital Resources of the Yugoslav Firm: Physical and Financial Assets, their Origin and their Management*

The capital resources originally entrusted to the work collectivity of each enterprise were in the shape of physical assets and it is the growth of the latter that can alone be *seen* by the collectivity as development of its productive capital resources. Their financial equivalent, as put down in the enterprise balance sheet, has on the whole a mere notional significance, since it never had, nor could it assume, a real autonomous existence comparable to that of the financial value of assets of a private capitalist enterprise, or even of a self-employed producers' firm in the modern sector of a private enterprise economy. No real market value can, save in very exceptional circumstances, be attached or ascribed to such assets, except during the short transitory period of their purchase and insertion into the productive process. Thereafter, their real value, if any, is essentially subjective, derived from the income the work collectivity can thereby obtain, and may indeed depart radically from their book value as shown on the balance sheet.

This is manifestly obvious in the case of the enterprise's fixed assets, such as buildings, machinery and other equipment. If they contribute little or not at all to the creation of income, their real value for the collectivity is manifestly nil, whatever their valuation on the enterprise accounts. Conversely, the real value of assets yielding high returns may attain considerably higher levels than their balance sheet valuation. This also applies to the capital necessary to finance current production, including advances on personal incomes, which may be vastly depreciated or appreciated according to the effective valuation by consumers of the results of the enterprise operations. Should such valuation be negative or zero, this part of the enterprise capital would in real terms disappear from existence, while any improvement would entail its corresponding appreciation.

The danger often referred to in Yugoslavia of the work collectivities 'eating up their factories' can therefore be seen not merely in its crude form of lack of maintenance and of replacement of physical assets, excess distribution and pilfering of resources forming the enterprise's circulating capital, but also in the more subtle form of greater or lesser depreciation of all assets in real terms through improper or inadequate operation of the enterprise. Within our reference framework, such a development could be seen as a purely negative orientation of the enterprise in regard to the 'technology' of its operations. Conversely, a sound attitude in this area of 'technology' (which in a sense can be seen as invisible natural investment, opposite to invisible disinvestment through lack of maintenance, pilfering, etc.) offers the work collectivity practically limitless possibilities for appreciating, in real terms, their existing assets.

Reflecting the original value of the enterprise assets, the balance sheet of the enterprise, of a sector or of the whole economy, merely indicates an abstract or notional value of productive resources which may vastly differ from their actual contribution to the productive process. The balance sheet capital values of the worker-managed enterprises would have become utterly meaningless in the course of time, were it not for several general revaluations of fixed assets of enterprises, imposed on the economy by Government Orders or (later) special legislative enactments (amounting to approximately 17 per cent for each two year period, while a 60 per cent revalorization of assets was a part of the 1965 Reform). The circulating capital is, of course, more or less automatically revalued in line with the corresponding inflationary price increases.

It is not surprising, therefore, that capital as such, i.e. the financial equivalent of the enterprise assets, is found to play only a very minor role in the growth performance of the worker-managed economy as a whole. Empirical analysis tends systematically to show the relative irrelevance of abstract capital, be it in terms of growth performance or of net income (which may be seen as indicative of enterprise growth potential). Analysing the sectoral data for 1965, for instance, the Federal Productivity Institute found that an additional unit of productive assets per worker (measured in financial terms) corresponds to 0·0067 units increase of net product per worker: for all practical purposes, no correlation whatsoever. The product or income per worker appeared for the most part as independent from the financial value of the corresponding assets. A somewhat closer correlation was obtained for 1963 and, more significantly, for 1964, but these rather arbitrary variations suggest that negative correlation could be established for some other period of time.[1] Nor does any definite correlation appear as between the volume, or increase in time, of the enterprise assets and the increase in value added (for certain selected industries such as leather, textiles or the metal trades).

This of course is essentially a paradox attributable to the abstract nature of the capital considered, and undue generality of the reference framework. It may nevertheless help to formulate two more specific hypotheses concerning the role of financial capital in the present-day Yugoslav economy. First, the uneven distribution of capital among sectors and enterprises, as perceived in financial terms through their accounts and balance sheets, would not seem to warrant the contention that fundamental inequality of opportunity results. In positive terms, it would appear that growth opportunities are on the whole evenly distributed among the various sectors and enterprises whatever the apparent size of their financial capital or its intensity (the capital coefficient). Second, no generally applicable behavioural rule can therefore be derived from the apparent size or intensity of the enterprise capital assets, expressed

[1] Cf. *Productivnost*, No. 1, 1968, pp. 41–2.

in financial terms. In other words, no significant results could be expected if additional financial assets were distributed at random throughout the economy, and no major growth incentive appears to attach to accumulation of financial capital.

Table x

Capital Intensity, Accumulation and Yields in the Principal Sectors of the Yugoslav Economy

Branch of Activity	Capital-Labour Ratio (1966)	Workers' Personal Incomes as percentage of total net income	Number of years required to double productive capacity through own accumulation (self-financing)			Workers' yearly income (reduced to simple unskilled labour)
			1962	1964	1966	
	(1)	(2)		(3)		(4)
National average (entire economy)	2·72:1	67·9	45·5	20·5	13	3,400
Electricity generating	19·58:1	42·8	226·5	106·5	27·5	5,269
Coal and coke	2·62:1	79·0	369·5	132	60·5	3,219
Heavy metallurgy	7·43:1	64·4	246	40·5	30·5	4,411
Non-ferrous metals	5·97:1	62·9	134	40	13	4,697
Metal industries	2·93:1	65·4	33·5	13	9·5	3,541
Electrical equipment	3·43:1	62·8	23·5	6·5	6·5	3,582
Chemical industries	6·29:1	48·2	30·5	11·5	8	4,414
Building materials	3·04:1	68·6	82·5	23·5	14	4,105
Timber and woodwork	2·31:1	72·4	32·5	12	12	3,405
Textiles	2·99:1	61·0	36·5	11·5	6	3,595
Food industry	7·39:1	57·0	37	14	7	4,415
Printing	2·11:1	65·3	19·5	8·5	4	5,349
Agriculture	3·31:1	66·3	92·5	33	13·5	4,527
Forestry	1·78:1	61·6	42·5	30	18·5	4,440
Construction	1·93:1	74·3	55·5	19·5	7	4,923
Railways	5·27:1	77·1	575·5	—	315	3,121
Road transport	2·77:1	75·3	88·5	18	14·5	4,595
Retail trade	0·94:1	63·2	6	3	2·5	4,066
Wholesale trade	2·04:1	57·1	13·5	4	3	4,713
Foreign trade	2·27:1	41·0	3	1·5	1	6,351
Hotels and catering	2·98:1	78·7	44·5	34·5	19	4,203
Private sector (commodity production)	0·63:1	86·1	14·5	10·5	8	2,014

The uneven distribution of such assets, their uneven rate of growth and uneven yields in terms of workers' incomes nevertheless form a useful set of background facts which may be helpful in considering the behaviour of enterprises within any particular sector. The table above, drawn from Professor Korać's survey already mentioned,[1] provides such an elementary background, particularly regarding the size of the differences and their uneven changes in time.

As shown in this table, the paradox of the non-meaningful contribution

[1] *Op. cit.*, pp. 40 and 46.

of financial capital appears to be not only notional but real, for the enterprises are visibly prone to invest out of their current financial income, no doubt at varying rates[1] but according to definitely regular patterns, (e.g. marked growth in the period covered in Column 3). Several lines of reasoning may be pursued in the search for an explanation.

First, the paradox obviously collapses when investment in real assets is considered, i.e. abstract financial capital coupled with 'technology'. No real enterprise can be so up to date and perfectly designed that those who work there could perceive no minor or major change which could lead to a significant improvement of overall performance. This quite obviously is not the case of the average Yugoslav firm, which offers practically limitless possibilities for such improvements.

Some of these may be neutral with regard to financial capital, or even capital saving. This may often be the case for simple savings on costs of materials, in certain mergers, or in specializing production. Thus, a recent merger of several Bosnian enterprises was claimed, according to the documentation distributed to the work-collectivities concerned on the occasion of the referendum, to lead to a 90 per cent or more increase in yield per unit of capital, mainly through specialization of production. Similar results were achieved in other circumstances but through co-operative arrangements (e.g. transfer by firm A of a particular line of production (Z) to firm B, the latter reserving further procession of its total Z product to A.

Most however will probably require a corresponding and sometimes considerable expansion of capital assets promising nevertheless well above average yields. When, in the mid-fifties, distribution of capital was effected by sectoral auctions, enterprises were known to tender up to and even above 100 per cent yearly interest, and the actual return on certain investments was believed to reach up to 300 per cent in certain cases (in the building industry particularly). Similar phenomena were also observed at the parallel hard currency auctions. Although this thirst for capital has considerably abated, returns of corresponding magnitude should not be uncommon even today, particularly where specific inefficiencies can be eliminated within an established enterprise, or quality changes introduced. The informal rate of interest of 25 per cent per annum (for extra-legal borrowing) was referred to as not altogether uncommon in 1968 by a contributor to one of the major economic weeklies.

The institutional set-up of the worker-managed enterprise, with its innumerable committees and elective management, most geared to some specific medium or long term growth target, can be seen as a contributory element providing autonomous pressure towards growth, due to continuous project formulation and periodic accountability. Most enterprises will at any time have numerous projects ready or under way, waiting for means to implement them. The absence of such independent pressure on investment is

[1] The average rate of investment from current income corresponds to the difference between the percentage shown in column 2 and the total net income (i.e. 100 per cent). It could be transformed into a hypothetical rate of investment per unit of capital if divided by the corresponding figure in column 1 (see also Table XI, p. 230).

quite exceptional, particularly in larger firms. This pressure may on the contrary often be excessive, particularly in an inflationary situation. All outside sources of financing (public funds, banks, etc.) are known to be constantly clogged with demands for investment credit which, if impossible to satisfy, press the enterprise to make use of its own only source of finance, the current income of its members. Since they have been permitted direct recourse to foreign capital resources, Yugoslav enterprises are also known to wage a hard struggle for such supplementary means of development financing. According to a highly qualified Western source, the volume of projects ready for implementation, and the aptitude of the Yugoslav enterprises to implement them as promptly as finance is forthcoming, represents a very distinctive feature of the Yugoslav economy among countries at less advanced stages of development. The relationship between this institutional factor and technology is apparent in enterprises formed by or from former technical institutes, which mostly show an extreme propensity to growth, no doubt attributable to the special composition and background of their staff. The opposite behaviour is usually related to the absence of technical project elaboration rather than to lack of means.

Table XI also brings to light a definite but not entirely conclusive correlation between the levels of current income and investment, i.e. the greater proneness of the high income sectors to plough back a higher proportion of current income. Professor Korać sees in this a partial confirmation of the income rate model of enterprise behaviour. Others, particularly Professor Županov, have maintained that the particular proneness to self-financing shown by the high income enterprises is due mainly to social and administrative pressure against excessive increases of personal income. Such pressure is certainly present but could not alone explain the investment proneness of such enterprises. This appears normal if one accepts that, from the point of view of the individual member of the work collectivity, the subjective value attaching to cash incomes (or the subjective rate of discount applied to deferred income) declines in direct relation to its absolute size. What is striking, however, is the countervailing tendency of the low income sectors not to reduce their investment activity to an absolute minimum. Indeed some of the least well off maintain a rate of investment well above the national average (e.g. textiles 39 per cent as against 32·1 per cent national average in 1966). The same tendency may indeed be observed at local or regional level, or for individual enterprises.

An additional consideration relating to 'technology' as defined above seems to offer at least a partial explanation. Clearly, an innovation or change able to cause a major increase (e.g. to double) in the income of a relatively depressed enterprise or community (sector, etc.) may have a comparatively smaller effect, or none at all, for those having already attained much higher levels of income. Hence, if a uniform inflow of domestic or foreign technology is assumed, its introduction may provide a greater economic stimulus to innovate, to save and to invest as necessary (including possibly a greater security of corresponding loans) in low income industries or areas.

In a penetrating essay on producers' behaviour in combining factors of

224

production, two psychological arguments are advanced by a Yugoslav economist: (a) the known tendency of the poor rural classes to forego minor, marginal improvements in their original environment and to migrate into the suburbs of big cities, ready to wait for years at a very low level of existence (i.e. saving and investing in their own transformation) in the hope of substantial future improvement; (b) the revolutionary changes in society opening the way to a collective development of entrepreneurship which reflects the readiness of entire generations to sacrifice themselves for the society's future welfare.[1]

Both these forms of collective and individual entrepreneurship were manifestly present in Yugoslavia throughout the period under consideration. As to (a), the country offers a rather unique example of decentralized development with limited internal migration, where the readiness to 'sacrifice' within the original setting of a natural rural economy may be assumed even stronger than that of possible migrants, in view of their having even less need for cash income as they have not left their original environment of natural economy. A glance at the last line of Table XI (private sector, i.e. mostly natural rural economy, the modern private craft and service sector being one of highest cash earners) will make it clear that there is no question of real sacrifice, the passage from a poor rural existence to unskilled industrial employment implying necessarily a substantial improvement, even where low current incomes are paid out in view of low productivity or a high level of investment.

Of course, a strong motivation to growth, including investment in terms of 'notional' financial capital, must be assumed present throughout the Yugoslav economy in order to understand its overall performance since 1952 or 1956. Little can usefully be added at this stage to the analysis contained in Chapter IX, of the major motivational forces which must all be drawn on in order to understand the underlying behaviour of the average enterprise. With varying intensity, but generally with a positive sign, all the growth vectors of our model may be assumed operative throughout the country during the whole period.

The key *institutional arrangements* concerning the management of enterprise capital should be briefly recalled here, as they are directly relevant to enterprise behaviour. In the early period, enterprise fixed assets, when first handed over to the worker-managers, formed a separate Basic Fund of the enterprise, alongside the circulating capital which was gradually remodelled, from a right to a bank credit into a separate Circulating Capital Fund of the enterprise (financing the cost of material, production in progress, including workers' incomes, and the stock of finished product). A separate Collective Consumption (or Welfare) Fund was also set up including the existing welfare assets of the enterprise and financed by voluntary contribution out of current income, as well as a legal Reserve Fund to which contributions were obligatory, but which could be drawn on only in legally defined emergencies. Most enterprises also tended to create their own additional (voluntary) reserves, or kept them in the form of so-called non-allocated incomes.

---

[1] Cf. Dr D. Dubravčić, *Ponašanje samoupravnog poduzeća etc.*, Zagreb, 1967.

Moreover, payments due in respect of depreciation of fixed assets—at legally determined single rates—had to be paid into a special Amortization Fund at regular intervals and be used exclusively for replacement of fixed assets.

This initial rather complex set-up of funds with strictly defined destinations was considerably simplified in the early sixties when the two main funds (the Fixed Asset and Circulating Capital Funds) were merged into one single Business Fund, including both the long- or medium-term investments and the funds necessary to finance current operation. Thus since 1961, the enterprise can freely transform its operational capital into fixed assets and, as far as this is possible, vice versa within the limits of its single Business Fund; if it so wishes, it may draw on the resources of its Welfare and Voluntary Reserve Fund, whilst only the Legal Reserve and Amortization Funds preserve a strictly limited destination. The initial value of the assets, as originally established and agreed by the workers' council, can at any time be increased by allocations from current income. The accounting value of the funds is periodically (or continuously) checked against their real position, and a full inventory must be established at the end of the year under the supervision of a special commission appointed by the workers' council. If deficits are noted, they must be replaced by drawing on current income.

Despite the relative permeability of the Funds, the actual destinations of the various types of expenditure can be followed in great detail and at all levels, as has been shown earlier in Table VII. Actually, where proper financial planning exists, the enterprise may be thought of as having as many separate 'funds' as there are analytical accounts. The position of each, in terms of cash deposits, fixed assets and all possible intermediary items (stock, customers, etc.) can at any time be identified. (See Chapter V *in fine*.) The cash assets of each Fund (actually deposits on call), if not required immediately, can be used for short- or medium-term loans or invested in any other manner compatible with their original destination and the principles of good management. This was discussed in Chapter IV in relation to the object of the enterprise. It should however be made very clear again that, for instance, in amortizing its installations or expanding its Business Fund, the enterprise is not obliged to maintain, renew or modernize its existing productive or welfare assets, but may divert the corresponding monies to other economic or welfare pursuits. Table X, p. 222 (particularly Column 3), shows the wide range of possibilities of increasing returns on investment offered by inter-sectoral changes of object (the extreme case being that of the railway enterprises orienting their growth into foreign trade); the specific possibilities of inter- or intra-sectoral transfers are practically limitless.

The means available to the Business and Welfare Funds can of course be increased by means of outside borrowing from banks, other enterprises or public funds. With the exception of the initial funds vested in workers' management in the early fifties, the importance of which has declined very considerably in the course of time, capital resources advanced to the enterprises are normally repayable at agreed rates and bear normal interest. Non-repayable advances by public authorities are ruled out in principle, although they may still be encountered, particularly where some form of public service is performed by a particular enterprise. It is however possible for the enterprise itself, instead of financing its own development, to advance funds to others in the shape of credit or outright subsidy, and several enterprises may establish joint funds for any lawful purpose whatsoever.

In the final analysis, however, within the self-management system, only the enterprise and its work collectivity can be seen as creating, through the income resulting out of their work and through their own decisions regarding its allocation, the new resources which are added to the funds of the enterprise for various development purposes. This applies not only to self-financing out of current income, but also to borrowing, which is simply an advance on future self-financing. While direct public subsidies are of little economic importance, they can equally be seen in most cases as a compensation for past or future losses in income due to the performance of a public service. In any event, they must be financed by fiscal or voluntary contributions of other productive enterprises. Hence, the formation of capital assets within the worker-managed economy is derived exclusively from work and determined by the conscious decisions of the workers. The Marx (or Marx-Ricardo) vocabulary and mode of reasoning—based on the labour theory of value—in the everyday context carry-on of the Yugoslav firm cannot therefore be interpreted as a mere ideological import. Even the worker least oriented towards theory cannot fail to see that if half or a third of the enterprise income (including *his* income) is allocated to financing growth, this corresponds to the equivalent part of his working time. In other words, capital formation is visibly financed out of and transformable into extra income or leisure. An indirect confirmation of this can be found in centrally planned economies where no similar penetration of the labour theory of value into the everyday life of an enterprise can be observed, despite a common ideological background. The Plan—both as reality and myth—is interposed between the process of creation of value through work and its distribution according to plan instruments.

An even more specific theoretical conclusion can be drawn at this point regarding the nature of capital assets. As they are added to the enterprise balance sheet (i.e. in their financial equivalent), they manifestly take their origin from the financial means accruing to the enterprise through its current marketing operation (sales), and appear transitorily as financial capital. Yet once they are transformed into real assets, they lose the essential quality of any capital, i.e. their objective value as would be determined by the market. Indeed, there is no real market for capital assets (plant, machinery, etc., taken as a whole).

The fact that the work collectivity can occasionally dispose, through the market, of some individual mobile pieces of equipment (an automobile, lorry, etc.) does not alter this basic characteristic of the worker-managed economy. Even if this were not contrary to existing legislation, the collectivity simply cannot sell all its assets as it would deprive itself (or that group of its workers affected) of all means of existence. It can possibly, for the sake of greater efficiency, specialization, etc., transfer part of its assets to others (including a new enterprise), but along with the workers concerned. It may possibly obtain a limited financial compensation but it is as likely that it may transfer a portion of its cash resources along with such fixed assets as part of the workers' endowment. There is no one within the system who could desire to 'buy himself into' an existing enterprise, save perhaps a group of unemployed workers, but they are by definition devoid of means to do so.

Thus no real value can be attached to the fixed assets. Their book value becomes a purely accounting, notional quality which has no equivalent in financial terms. The real value of fixed assets must also be seen as a purely notional, hypothetical amount, independent of their purchasing price or book value. The only remaining link, at present, between the book value of assets and the reality of economic life is the depreciation system and the rate of interest, which will be examined in the next chapter, with respect to which the book value serves to determine the corresponding current obligations of the enterprise. The Yugoslav firm obviously has no interest in systematically boosting the value of its assets (or indeed its income), as this would entail increasing the fiscal and related costs attaching thereto, but may be expected rather to understate the corresponding book amounts. (Expressed more bluntly: any self-financed investment or income which could escape the accounts would represent a very considerable saving for the enterprise.)

The notional or hypothetical 'real value' of assets would thus essentially be determined by the efficiency shown by the work collectivity in putting them to use, and the valuation placed on their product by the consumers. Assets which result in little or no income for the workers are manifestly worthless or of small value, whatever their initial cost or present book value; others, which may be entirely or partly written off, may present a considerable real value for the work collectivity if they are operated at a high level of current income. In so far as the capital assets are actually divorced from any real market values, as shown in these two extreme examples, they lose all characteristics normally attaching to capital and are transformed into mere material support of the workers' productive activity. This again is not a mere paradox or entirely unprecedented. Any vast agricultural or forestry holding, private or State, or indeed any other large productive unit (co-op, etc.), the 'marketing' of which is ruled out in given circumstances, cannot be properly valued in terms of financial capital (its book value being thus devoid of any reality). Its real value is exclusively determined by the efficiency of its management and the present and future market for its products. It thus serves as a mere support for production and business activity, with no 'intrinsic' value.

This comes even more clearly to light when the possibility of investment in natural terms is considered. Any enterprise can and does produce fixed assets for its own use; these would normally be valued at their 'market price' and passed through the accounts into the balance sheet (as 'sales to self'). Yet the work collectivity of the Yugoslav firm has innumerable other possibilities for increasing the real value of its assets, without the resulting improvement ever being reflected in the balance sheet, or even in the current account statements. This includes not only voluntary work not paid for (rather exceptional but not to be ruled out in present-day Yugoslavia), and improvements covered by a token reward (as under a suggestion scheme), but also all changes resulting in increased productivity of the assets.

These would normally but not necessarily be reflected in the volume of the enterprise capital funds. At the same level of per capita income, work intensity and book value of assets, a plant would obviously be of greater value to the work collectively if the same output were achieved in a forty, as against a fifty hour weekly shift, a result which may be attained by purely intangible changes (e.g. greater technological discipline). In other systems similar improvements would normally be capitalized through an increase in (share, etc.) value of a private company, or absorbed through the centralized Funds of the Exchequer or Planning system with no direct benefit nor interest to those personally involved. In the Yugoslav firm, the work collectivity is the primary beneficiary of such changes (although the wider collectivities may receive their share through increased volume of fiscal receipts or lower prices).

Any work for less than the maximum possible income can be seen (and actually is increasingly so viewed by the workers) as a form of natural investment, particularly where they accept to forego current incomes in order to maintain current levels of production. Such a decision is nothing but an invisible or natural investment into the enterprise Business Fund (its circulating capital section). This, of course, is an everyday phenomena in any producers' enterprise, and offers one of the possible explanations of the relative stability of the Yugoslav economy in terms of real output, including its capacity for continued operation, even in conditions of most severe deflationary pressures. Individual enterprises when facing severely adverse market conditions display a similar capacity.

Once average efficiency is considered as given at any point of time, the value of the enterprise assets can be seen as being directly related to the effective demand facing the enterprise, which in turn depends on the volume of money and credit available to final consumers. If demand is lagging, the real value of all capital assets tends to fall rapidly. Changes in the circulating capital are, however, perceived much more directly through the accumulation of unsold stocks or a fall in prices. A radical squeeze of effective demand could thus reduce the real value of the enterprise capital assets rapidly to very low levels, as well as its investment activity and output considered in purely financial terms. However, invisible investment through reduced workers' incomes could preserve the economy in operation in 'natural' terms at relatively higher levels of output and investment. In other words, the downward—or deflationary—changes in money circulation and credit grossly destabilize the current and long term growth orientation of the worker-managed enterprise, as they directly affect the real value of its capital assets, the accounting value of which must be maintained at its nominal level. Even a deflationary pressure of limited magnitude can absorb the entire financial results of the enterprise. In foregoing their current incomes in financial terms, partly or wholly, the work collectivities are, however, able to maintain their enterprise in operation in a natural form by creating assets without an equivalent financial counterpart.

In the extreme case, by the total withdrawal of money and credit, the entire economy could thus be expected to continue to function at a new natural level of output. This actually did happen in many instances during the radical money and credit squeeze following the 1965 Reform. Some enterprises began to issue their own certificates in respect of work performed for which no equivalent finance was forthcoming. Had the experience been pursued (and it obviously could not, in view of its disastrous effects on the current performance of the economy), such certificates could have led to the enterprises or communes creating their own new means of exchange based entirely on work (and would thus give meaning to the Utopian possibility of non-monetary exchange between producers' enterprises, envisaged by early socialist economic theory). In the real world of present-day Yugoslavia, this experience has led to growing recognition of the need for direct control by the worker-managed economy over the central monetary institutions.

A partial illustration of this phenomenon may be found in the chart below (Table XI).

Table XI
Production, Money and Credit, 1964–8*
Yearly Rates of Growth Based on Twelve-Monthly Revolving Periods**

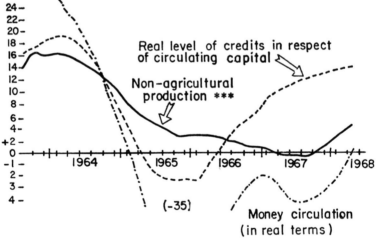

* From an article by Professor A. Bajt in *Economska Politika*, Belgrade, 10 February 1969, p. 22.
** The difference between the monthly indices of output and the value of money and credit can be taken as indicative of the volume of production 'financed' in natural terms by the work collectivities; this was obviously much greater in particular sectors, regions or enterprises than what is brought to light in terms of national averages.
*** The years 1966 and 1967 being particularly favourable as regards the volume of agricultural output (increase of 20 and additional 2 per cent respectively in the worker-managed sector, 15 and −2 in private sector); the supply of money and credit was further limited by the correspondingly increasing requirements of agriculture.

The behaviour of the enterprise during the 1965 Reform period has thus largely thwarted the hopes of those who expected to achieve the closure of less efficient factories, lay-offs of 'surplus manpower', increased productivity and accelerated technical progress. The enterprises—particularly in the less developed regions more severely hit by the credit and money squeeze—clearly demonstrated both their will and their ability to preserve their existence in the perspective of more long term growth—at almost any cost. Neither did employment prove compressible under such conditions, nor did the rate of increase of productivity rise. Indeed, 'technology' became in many cases the major victim of the operation since, unable to save sufficiently on 'labour', the enterprises were often reduced, particularly in the leading mechnical and other investment-oriented industries where demand deficiency attained greatest severity, to impose radical restrictions on expenditure on technological developments. Facing increasingly idle productive capacity, even the cost-free 'technological' improvements were obviously losing economic justification.

A more long-term view of the relative instability of the rate of growth of the worker-managed economy, in terms of investment expenditure in fixed assets and the rate of activity of two major investment goods industries (mechanical and construction), is presented in Table XII, p. 232. The strikingly cyclical movement of investment, as brought to light in this chart, is often obscured by the fact that the cycles are actually situated at very high average levels of growth and would hardly be apparent if shown on a usual chart of absolute growth. As with the two similar charts reproduced earlier, this novel presentation is due to the Yugoslav Economic Research Institute; it has the advantage of abstracting from the extremely high rates of growth of all the indices (which would result in vertically sloping lines with limited angular changes, even if logarithmical scales were introduced), and to concentrate attention on changes in the prevalent growth orientation of the economy. The reader will note that the average yearly growth rates of practically all the indices are at or above the 10 per cent level.

Several general comments can be made on the basis of Table XII. The overall rate of growth is obviously very high throughout the whole period, in excess of 10 per cent, but with a slight tendency to decline. The growth of current production (which may be interpreted here as growth of circulating capital), is closely parallel to that of investment spending and investment goods production. No time-lag—as implied in the common theory of investment cycles—is noticeable; on the contrary, the two sets of indices follow a closely parallel movement suggesting a common cause, as indeed they reflect one common source of financing, i.e. the current income of the enterprise. Hence, as suggested earlier, there can be no other cause but effective final demand, which is simultaneously reflected both in growth of short-term capital (or output) and of investment activity. This conclusion also rests firmly on findings within enterprises and seems largely confirmed by the various enterprise monographs and reports on activity.

The bulk of the variations brought to light in the above chart can thus be attributed to monetary and credit policy, including their fiscal components,

Table XII

Industrial Production, Investment Goods, Industry and Investment in Fixed Assets* (*Rates of Growth 1954–67*)

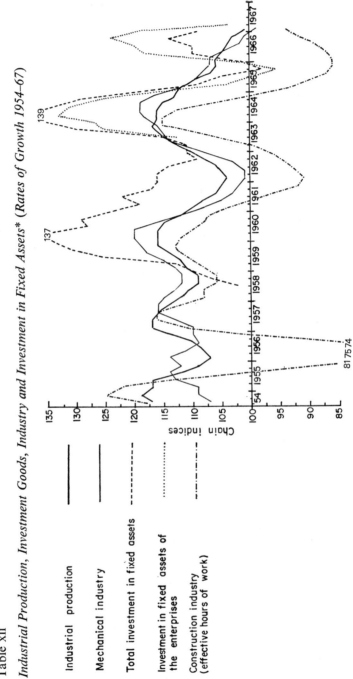

Industrial production

Mechanical industry

Total investment in fixed assets

Investment in fixed assets of the enterprises

Construction industry (effective hours of work)

*Yugoslav Economic Research Institute, *Sumarna Analiza* etc., op. cit., p.6

which could be traced as being the main operative cause of the periodic fluctuations in the short- and long-term growth of the worker-managed economy, often interpreted as so many 'crises' of the entire system. The Yugoslav economy clearly cannot respond to the classical instruments of money and budget management (as derived from the experience of early private enterprise economy) or even to abstract anti-cyclical measures inspired by Keynesian theory. Expansion of credit or tax reductions may merely result, if not geared to effective demand, in mere accumulation of additional stocks of final product (in excess of those formed in 'natural' terms), locked up in the inflexible accounting capital structure of the enterprise, with little or no ensuing increase in effective demand.

The two major downward movements of the economy (1956 and 1965–7) were undoubtedly the result of widespread official anti-investment campaigns, based on the concept of 'investment inflation', and belief in growth potential based on personal consumption generated by increased personal incomes. In the second case the workers' councils are known to have opposed for a considerable time any major cuts in their investment programmes, and these were finally induced only by the severe restrictions of credit and money circulation accompanying the 1965 Reform. The results seem to prove that no basic distinction can be made, in a worker-managed economy, between demand for investment and for consumer goods, the two being financed from one single source. Expressed in terms of Marx's analysis, as there are no capitalists nor any hired labour, there is no reason for distinguishing between demand for investment assets and demand for consumer goods, since both emanate from a single source, i.e. the worker-producers. The reduction in demand for investment goods resulted merely in a sharp drop in the overall rates of growth, with a short-term gain for the consumer but a global decline in the total volume of the workers' incomes and of private consumption in a medium term perspective.

One of the most striking features of the Yugoslav experience is the fact that despite the very high rate of investment activity throughout the period under consideration, prices of investment goods increased imperceptibly in nominal terms (1·58 per cent per annum for 1956–66, as against 11·50 per cent average annual increase in output). This was a strong relative decline compared to the average increase of producers' prices (3·78 per cent per annum for the same period), and their movement can indeed be interpreted as absolute decline if the effects of the 1965 Reform are discounted. Prices of consumer goods were rising rapidly in comparison (3·71 per cent per annum in nominal terms for the same period against a 12·75 average increase in output). The transfer of final demand in the direction of consumer goods could not but reinforce the price disparity between the two sectors and thus increase inflationary pressures.[1]

The Capital Assets of the Enterprise
Some indications should be given of the growth of the enterprise capital resources over the years, and the prevailing patterns of transformation of its

[1] Cf. M. Korošić, *Dinamika općego nivoa cena 1956–66*, Zagreb, 1967, p. 21.

Table XIII

Value of Fixed Assets in Yugoslav Economy 1952–60[1]
(At Constant Prices (1956) in 000 million new dinars[2]*)*

Position at end of Year	All Sectors[3]		Industry and Mining	
	000 millions of New Dinars	Index (1946=100)	000 millions of New Dinars	Index (1946=100)
1952	93·7 (55·2)	126 (130)	14·5 (9·6)	238 (395)
1954	100·6 (59·4)	135 (139)	18·0 (12·4)	296 (509)
1956	107·9 (63·8)	145 (150)	21·2 (14·6)	347 (599)
1958	117·4 (70·0)	158 (165)	23·8 (16·0)	390 (660)
1960	130·4 (79·2)	175 (186)	27·6 (18·5)	452 (759)

[1] According to I. Vinski, *Procena Rasta Fixnih Fondova*, etc., pp. 285–6.
[2] Purchase value (figures in bracket: actual value. i.e. after depreciation, etc.).
[3] Including private sector in agriculture, crafts, etc., as well as assets not in active use (investment in progress etc.) and all non-productive assets (housing, public services).

Table XIV

Value of Active Assets of Enterprises 1958–67
(Current Balance Sheet Figures at End of Year in 000 million new dinars)

Position at end of Year	Fixed[1] Assets	Circulating Assets[2]	Welfare Fund	Fixed[1] Assets	Circulating Assets[2]	Welfare Fund
I.		ALL SECTORS		INDUSTRY AND MINING		
1958	—	—	—	17·9(14·1)	10·1	1·1
1961	54·7(34·4)	20·8	3·6	26·9(17·2)	11·0	2·5
1965	97·8(59·3)	40·4	7·5	48·8(30·9)	20·8	4·6
1967	186·9(118·0)	67·9	4·1	82·9(52·6)	35·8	2·3

II. SELECTED SECTORS/INDUSTRIES (1967)

	Fixed Assets	Circulating Assets	Welfare Fund
Agriculture and fisheries	18·5(13·0)	8·6	0·50
Forestry	11·0(10·2)	0·5	0·04
Electricity	18·8(13·1)	1·5	0·13
Coal mining	4·7(2·5)	0·8	0·24
Transport and communications	52·7(26·8)	2·2	0·34
Trade and catering	10·8(81·0)	16·1	0·28
Crafts (production)	1·7 (1·2)	1·5	0·06
Crafts (personal services)	0·08(0·05)	0·03	0·00
Communal services (productive)	3·5(2·7)	0·32	0·03
Metallurgy (ferrous)	5·8(3·5)	1·9	0·18
Metallurgy (non-ferrous)	5·2(2·9)	2·0	0·24
Metal trades	9·0(5·1)	7·2	0·40
Textiles	6·1(3·6)	4·6	0·19
Wood processing	5·8(4·6)	1·8	0·11

[1] Purchase Value (figures in bracket: actual value).
[2] Annual average circulating capital.

Table xv

Total Yearly Expenditure for Investment in Fixed Assets 1957–67[1]
(At Current Prices [2] *in 000 million new dinars)*

Year	Total	Economy[3]	Industry and Mining	Agriculture and Fishery	Transport	Trade and Catering	Enterprises Own Funds (Self-Financed) Investment Expenditure)
1957	5·4	4·2	1·9	0·5	1·2	0·2	2·0
1959	7·0	5·4	2·2	1·1	1·3	0·4	1·9
1961	10·8	7·9	4·1	1·1	1·7	0·5	3·2
1963	14·6	9·8	1·4	1·4	1·6	0·8	4·1
1965	19·2	12·5	7·0	1·6	2·2	1·0	5·5
1966	21·2	14·8	8·3	1·8	2·7	1·3	8·3
1967	19·9	14·8	8·0	1·7	2·4	2·1	6·5

[1] Social Accounting Service (SDK) *Statistički Bilten*, May 1968; cf. also The Investment Bank of Yugoslavia, *Vesnik*, April 1968.

[2] For the corresponding movement of prices of investment goods, cf. data on p. 232 above.

[3] Excluding investment in housing and communal services; corresponds *grosso modo* to the worker-managed sector.

income into capital assets. Due to lack of fully comparable data for the entire period under consideration, some of the key indicators have been assembled in several separate tables below. They bring to light the radical qualitative changes which have occurred during the years in the volume of assets available, and of the growth oriented expenditure of worker-managed enterprise, at least in their financial equivalents. (No statistics can express this growth in natural terms.)

Whatever the possible effect of inflation or past revaluations, the growth in absolute terms of the 'actual' value (i.e. accounting or book value, after depreciation and write-offs) of the fixed and total assets of the worker-managed economy is most impressive. The value of the initial assets of 1952 (or 1946), particularly in the productive sectors such as industry and mining, would appear insignificant in comparison to the 1967 figures. The high level of current investment seems to maintain the 'actual' value of fixed assets near to the level of their purchase value, bringing to light the comparatively recent origin of such assets available to most enterprises. Their mean age (in value terms) could probably be estimated at three to four years only. In a region of comparatively old development (Croatia), it was estimated in 1968 that well over 40 per cent of available fixed assets of the enterprises had been installed since the 1965 Reform, while only some 10 per cent dated back more than twenty years.

The 'actual' volume of fixed assets in the hands of the workers' councils represented by 1967 well over half of the country's total assets and practically all its productive assets (outside agriculture). Their volume is also quite considerable in terms of the yearly net product of the worker-managed enterprises

Table XVI

Net Income of Enterprises and its Allocation to their Various Funds 1962–6[1]
(In Current Prices and Per Cent)

Branch[2]	Year[3]	Total Allocation to Enterprise Funds out of Net Income[4] (in 000 million new dinars)	Percentage allocated to various Funds				
			Legal Reserve	Voluntary Reserve	Business Fund[5]	Welfare Fund	Other and Sundry Contributions
All branches[6]	1962	2·8	13·2	11·7	38·8	22·3	14·1
	1964	7·0	8·0	7·3	48·8	21·2	14·7
	1966	13·5	7·7	7·3	56·5	25·5	2·9
Industry and mining	1962	1·4	12·9	11·9	40·4	26·0	8·9
	1964	3·7	7·2	7·8	51·2	23·6	10·2
	1966	6·9	7·0	6·5	59·5	23·2	1·8
Coal mining	1962	0·05	9·9	8·2	11·1	47·0	23·8
	1964	0·11	5·4	2·3	18·0	53·7	20·7
	1966	0·15	5·7	4·5	31·8	45·9	12·0
Metal industry	1962	0·25	18·2	10·5	38·0	28·8	4·6
	1964	0·6	9·3	6·7	53·5	26·3	4·2
	1966	1·1	9·2	8·8	52·3	28·9	0·1
Textiles	1962	0·11	15·4	15·5	47·9	20·2	1·0
	1964	0·38	8·0	9·2	65·0	17·5	0·4
	1966	0·9	6·8	4·8	66·6	21·4	0·4
Agriculture and fisheries	1962	0·16	38·7	10·6	29·5	16·9	4·1
	1964	0·4	23·6	4·6	47·9	18·7	5·1
	1966	1·2	19·4	3·0	52·5	20·0	3·1
Hunting[7]	1962	0·000	1·9	98·1	—	(98·7)[8]	—
	1964	0·001	3·6	—	95·0	1·4	—
	1966	0·01	1·5	3·2	59·9	14·4	21·1
Transport	1962	0·2	5·3	20·1	39·2	28·1	7·1
	1964	0·5	2·9	6·5	37·7	24·7	28·1
	1966	1·0	2·6	22·1	39·5	34·0	1·8
Railways	1962	0·07	8·0	26·0	26·5	38·9	0·7
	1964	0·08	4·9	1·7	—	30·3	64·2
	1966	0·33	2·5	45·0	13·1	35·0	4·4
Trade and catering	1962	0·5	19·0	7·4	51·5	16·6	5·3
	1964	1·3	12·1	6·3	61·6	17·1	4·5
	1966	2·4	9·4	5·6	63·3	20·9	0·9

[1] According to Dr M. Korać, *Analiza* etc., *op. cit.*, Table 6, pp. 206–13.

[2] Branches selected at random merely as an example of the size and the variations in behaviour of the various sectors; incomparably greater variations would appear if corresponding figures were given for groups (sub-sectors) or individual enterprises.

[3] It should be noted that the intermediary year 1963 and 1965, omitted for lack of space, frequently present considerable variations from the 1962–6 trend as reflected in the Table.

[4] i.e. the net income of the enterprises less workers' personal incomes; the proportion of the latter in the total net income has already been given in Table X, p. 222.

[5] Former Fixed and Circulating Capital Funds.

[6] Excluding private sector.

[7] An entirely new 'sub-sector' comprising only a few enterprises, which may be seen as indicative of the behaviour of an individual enterprise.

[8] In 1963.

Table XVII

Financial Reserves and Liabilities of Enterprises, 1957–67[1]
(*In 000 million new dinars*)

I. TOTAL FINANCIAL RESOURCES

Year	Total[2]	Deposits on Call[3]			Restricted Accounts[4]	Time Deposits	Foreign Exchange Accounts
		Total	Amortisa-tion Fund	Welfare Fund			
1957	4·8	2·5	0·36	—	2·0	—	0·4
1961	6·6	3·4	0·8	0·16	1·9	—	0·6
1964	12·9	6·6	1·5	0·27	3·8	1·2	0·4
1966	20·0	7·5	0·1	0·5	7·1	3·1	1·3
1967	23·1	5·4	—	0·5	7·2	7·0	2·8

II. TOTAL FINANCIAL LIABILITIES

Year	Total	Short Term Bank Credit[5]	Investment Credit by Banks		Special Housing Credits Total[7]	Credits from Social Investment Funds[8]	
			Fixed Assets[6]	Circulating Capital		Fixed Assets	Circulating Capital
1957	17·1	8·3	—	—	0·2	8·3	0·1
1961	37·9	14·9	—	—	1·4	17·7	4·3
1964	65·1	21·5	29·9	6·2	4·3	10·8	1·2
1966	88·1	26·7	49·2	10·9	5·0	6·8	0·3
1967	100·6	30·9	58·3	12·4	5·2	6·0	0·1

[1] Social Accounting Service (SDK), *Statistički Bilten*, May 1968.

[2] This total does not correspond to the sum of all the other columns as two minor items have been omitted.

[3] Current account, amortization, current account of the welfare fund and sundry.

[4] Legal Reserve, guarantee deposits for investment, accreditives, etc.

[5] Nearly exclusively for current production (circulating capital); the part of fixed assets is insignificant.

[6] Not including limited amounts for 'non-economic' investments, (i.e. the Welfare Fund, etc.) amounting to 1·1 and 0·7 billion new dinars respectively for 1965 and 1967.

[7] Including up to 50 per cent credit for 'commercial' house-building by construction enterprises.

[8] The Federal Investment Fund and other similar funds which represented the main source of investment financing up to 1963 and were mostly discontinued thereafter, save for the Special Fund for underdeveloped regions.

(in 1967, approximately 150 per cent) and in terms of workers' personal incomes (approximately 400–450 per cent). If the circulating capital is added, there can be little doubt that the worker-managed enterprises actually administer and handle by far the most massive and economic determining portion of the national resources. Nor can there be any reasonable doubt that, since 1952, not only have the enterprise collectivities created an overwhelming part of the nation's productive assets, but that they have also seen themselves as sole agents of this capital formation function. Not all new assets were created by and within existing enterprises; a significant but rapidly declining portion was channelled through the Investment Funds to new enterprises. The bulk of such funds were, however, collected for that purpose from existing enterprises,

237

in the shape of interest on their assets and repayment of earlier loans. Along with their banks, enterprises also appear as the sole major investors within the economy.

It should be recalled that the amounts given as 'purchase' or 'actual' value of capital assets are net of possible losses or complete write-offs of capital assets (fixed or inventories) which, as already indicated, must always be replaced from current net income before the latter is allocated by the workers' council. In other words, a loss of any given item of fixed assets or inventories represents a special type of cost of operations during that corresponding accounting period, as is any corresponding cost of insurance against the risk involved. Both can thus directly affect the amount of funds available for workers' remuneration and enterprise development. The voluntary reserves of enterprises (or special funds created to that effect) can partly be seen as a form of self-insurance against possible capital losses. The only case where loss on capital can actually appear on the balance sheet is where the current income is not sufficient to replace the lost assets, in which case the enterprise may draw on its reserve fund (thereby reducing its financial capital) or actually reduce the accounting value of its assets. The amount of such accounting losses was quite insignificant and, although it had grown substantially in recent years, it remained of negligible proportion as compared with the new funds allocated to investment.

All this is only true within the particular sphere of reference of the economic financial-accounting order. The real value of enterprise assets for the work collectivities, and thereby for the whole nation, is essentially a reflection of the current operational results and future prospects of the enterprise. Whatever their book value, and even if maintained in best physical conditions, assets which are not utilized for productive purposes have lost all real value, and those used in part only should be written off accordingly. Conversely, if assets which were written off entirely or in part are used to their original capacity (or more), they should be correspondingly appreciated in their real value through their productive performance. There is no doubt that both types of situation are encountered in the real world of the Yugoslav firms. The former is better known, as it imposes a special financial strain on the enterprises concerned, which are likely to claim special relief from the burden of interest and amortization payable in respect of assets which have become obsolete or were put out of use due to other factors. Thus, in Bosnia and Herzegovina alone, fixed assets with accounting (book) value of several hundred million new dinars (and in respect of which interest and provision for depreciation were due) were claimed in 1968 by several enterprises as having lost all real value for productive purposes due to various outside circumstances. This may also apply to inventories, particularly of finished products where demand has changed or is lagging.

Both these situations were typical of the post-1965 Reform period of radical deflation. Obviously, if all money and credit were withdrawn from the economy, both the fixed assets and the inventories (circulating capital) would lose all their value in financial terms and would only preserve their real value, if any, to the extent that the economy reverted to a natural form of non-monetary exchange (or created its own means of payment as suggested earlier). A partial withdrawal of money and credit would of necessity entail a corresponding loss of real value of enterprise assets, a loss not directly reflected in the enterprise accounts, but which may nevertheless create severe problems for its current operations and business management. More particularly, they cannot be written off (if fixed assets) or their accounting price reduced (if finished products), for this would normally entail severe cuts in, or complete disappearance of, the current net income available for work remuneration and development financing.

As this was actually happening during the post-1965 period, a certain flexibility had to be introduced in the area of capital management. The most important among such measures was the facility granted to enterprises of disposing of non-current inventories at radically reduced prices, without having to replace entirely the corresponding loss of circulating capital within the current annual period, but in up to five yearly instalments. This very curious arrangement could technically be called 'loan to oneself', somewhat similar to where a householder keeps his monies in a set of envelopes and takes a 'loan' for instance from one called 'provision for maintenance' to 'current expenses'. Enterprises in difficulty, particularly the coal-mining industry, have moreover been authorized to reduce or suspend amortization of their fixed assets, and were relieved from the payment of corresponding interest.

The impact of deflation is also clear from Table XV which reflects the sharp decline in investment in fixed assets in 1967 (continued into 1968); and, less directly, from Table XVII as regards short-term financial reserves and short-term debt of enterprises.

The causes of these radical policy changes are not difficult to understand. In the absence of effective demand, the real value of fixed assets dropped sharply and the inducement to expand diminished correspondingly. To continue to produce, as they were obliged to do to meet fixed costs and ensure at least minimum earnings for themselves, the work collectivities had to accumulate stocks of finished products to be financed by short-term loans. As such loans were forthcoming only in limited amounts, in view of administrative restrictions, further accumulation of stock was made possible by deferment of current payments to workers and by the unprecedented growth of formal or informal mutual credit among enterprises (agreed delays of payment of deliveries or accumulation of unpaid bills). Neither of these phenomena can be directly measured in financial terms as they both amount to financing current production through unpaid labour, i.e. in natural terms, either of the enterprise's own production or of its customers'. As this phenomenon assumed considerable proportions in 1967 and early 1968, the Yugoslav economy reverted to a significant degree to a special form of operation based partly on natural financing, both within the enterprises and in the economy as a whole. In other words, had they operated according to the rules of a private enterprise market economy, the Yugoslav enterprises would have faced extremely severe losses in the real value of their assets, both fixed and current inventories; for many among them their value would indeed have fallen close to nought.

239

Yet, the work collectivities proved willing and able to maintain their enterprises in operation, and thereby to preserve their assets, thanks to their readiness to sacrifice their present individual interests for the sake of the lasting existence of their enterprises and of their consumers even when facing no certain prospect of prompt economic recovery.

The amounts due by enterprises to their suppliers reached truly astronomic figures; some estimates being as high as 40 billion new dinars, or the approximate value of workers' yearly earnings. (The increase due directly to the current deflationary policy is difficult to estimate but would seem to represent at least half that figure.) In other words, in this form alone the work collectivities have financed, through their work, at least six months of their current production. It should be noted that the astronomic growth of mutual indebtedness of enterprises was seen by nearly all Yugoslav observers as the manifestation of a sudden (!) laxness in current settlement of suppliers' accounts due to bad will or bad administration, and not as necessary behaviour of a producers' economy. By insisting on full and timely settlement the creditor enterprises could have put out of business a great number, possibly the majority, of existing enterprises, yet would not recover their due, but merely physical assets devoid of practically all market value. Hence, their only chance to recover their dues in financial terms was to allow the customers' enterprises and their work collectivities to remain in operation until a general recovery of the economy. Delays in settlement of bills were caused not only by the worker-managed enterprises but also to a significant extent by public bodies, whose budgetary credits were severely curtailed and which could not therefore ensure timely settlement of bills to their suppliers.

By the end of 1967, the mutual indebtedness of enterprises, resulting in growing incapacity to pay, reached such proportions that a nationwide scheme of debt compensation was launched, under which enterprises were invited to register their financial claims against others, to be compensated through a specially devised clearing system. The latter, if generalized, would have amounted to a new parallel system of payment within the worker-managed economy. This move largely failed in its purpose since the enterprises were not obliged to participate and a major class of defaulting payees, i.e. the public authorities, were not included; creditor enterprises may thus have found themselves in the red at the end of the exercise and vice versa.

The general finding which may be drawn from this recent experience is that under severe deflationary conditions, the worker-managed economy as set up in Yugoslavia has shown a type of behaviour closer to that of a producers' than a pure market economy. Maintenance in existence and in production of the enterprise's own assets, and those of the wider circle of its customers and suppliers, is an overriding consideration. The objective of employment stability (vector B, in our scheme) can thus be seen as absolutely dominant under such conditions, even if sacrifices of unprecedented magnitude are required in the short term. The marked fall in value of assets of the Welfare Fund in 1967 as shown in Table XVI would seem directly relevant in this context.

The bare existence or survival of the enterprise in the worker-managed economy is thus more safely ensured than under other systems. This is obvious for the capitalist private enterprise economy, where closure of plant and withdrawal of capital from productive use would be the normal reaction to similar policies. It may be questioned in the case of central planning, which is understood as implying full employment of capital resources. However, a centrally directed planned economy has no autonomous stability against the planners' preferences which (possibly for efficiency motivations similar to those underlying the Yugoslav 1965 Reform) may include restrictive policies, particularly with respect to non-priority sectors, and may thus lead to massive liquidation of certain categories of enterprises which, in the Yugoslav case, would have a better chance to survive. The corresponding behaviour of the enterprise (the dominance of vector B), has of necessity a severely disturbing impact on all its other objectives, on all the other vectors which determine its behaviour under normal conditions.

The behaviour of the Yugoslav economy in an opposite set of circumstances, i.e. severe inflation, may be closely followed in the period prior to the 1965 reform (1963–4). Under inflationary pressure (leading to high demand levels and excellent financial results for most enterprises), the real value of fixed assets increases considerably. Even most of those written off are able to attain significant results. Similarly, circulating capital appreciates owing to increased prices and, more significantly, as a result of the fulfilment or overfulfilment of all the enterprise planned targets including the accumulation of massive cash reserves at various stages of production. Most if not all enterprise objectives, as represented by the various vectors, thus receive at least the minimum required satisfaction, resulting in very high rates of growth in both short-term expansion of output and medium- and long-term investments.

An extremely strong multiplier effect can thus be observed in the upswings of the economy. Little if any of the additional cash incomes of enterprises (and indeed of individuals) is saved in a manner which would withdraw it from productive use. The acceleration of movement of stock and inventories creates additional circulating capital. The full or overfull satisfaction of all objectives is perceived as an extremely positive performance by the enterprises concerned. Once attained, however, this level of satisfaction, leading to a sort of euphoria, gradually deprives the work collectivity of rational criteria for their policy choices. In the light of the extremely satisfactory financial results, and corresponding future expectations, *all* their projects or plans, both in the economic and social sphere, tend to appear equally feasible or attainable, even where, in real or physical terms, they actually are not. Moreover, some aspects of short-term efficiency of the enterprise itself, such as economy in current material costs, or possible increases in work efficiency, tend to be obscured by the prospect of future outside gains. Although conducive to very rapid expansion of productive assets, an extreme inflationary situation is thus also fraught with particularly disturbing forces in the worker-managed economy, as the guidelines to rational choices can be lost sight of significantly earlier than in other economic systems.

Although there is no fully objective gauge for evaluating the relative efficiency of the use of productive assets, there is little doubt that the Yugoslav worker-managed economy performed much better in conditions of severe inflation, in terms both of utilization of fixed assets (capacity utilization) and of circulating capital. In this latter regard, the index of inventories of finished products in individual enterprises for the period 1962–8 are particularly revealing (figures in brackets—1964=100): 1962 (107), 1963 (96), 1964 (100), 1965 (126), 1966 (157), 1967 (195), 1968 (204).[1] Similar trends can be observed with regard to the utilization of fixed assets (increasing capacity utilization from 1962 to 1964 decreasing thereafter).

The extreme variations in monetary policy have largely blurred the overall picture in recent years. Yet this recent period has demonstrated the capacity of the worker-managed enterprise to cope in a quite unexpected manner with extremely severe conditions imposed by the financial policy environment. They certainly proved their relative aptitude for at least partial survival, in conditions of absolute scarcity of money and credit, and possibly developed their system of non-monetary exchanges. They have shown clearly that they do not consider their assets in terms of purely financial or economic accounting values, but most of all as a necessary support of their work and existence, which must be maintained and operated at all cost. Nor did they show any tendency, in conditions of severe inflation, to sit back and use up the apparent surplus accruing from their capital assets. They used it for the most part for future development.

The conclusions arrived at can be applied to any other situation of insufficient or excess demand which may affect the economy as a whole, a sector or an individual enterprise, for a variety of reasons (closure of or restriction of entry to foreign markets, drastic changes in demand patterns, etc.). Thus, at any point of time, and whatever the general state of the economy, there will be enterprises and sectors which experience a deflationary or inflationary situation and will present patterns of behaviour similar to those described above.

Capital assets, in no way owned by the work collectivity, appeared nevertheless as perhaps the major disturbance of the normal operation of the worker-managed economy. The fluctuation of their real, as compared to their book or accounting value, can become very considerable—much greater than current income for any one accounting period in cases of extreme changes of monetary policy.

Two solutions have been proposed in this regard: one would be to do away altogether with capital in its financial form, considering the assets as a mere physical support of human activity. Although certainly most painful in the transitional period, such a transition to a modern type of natural economy would not seem altogether impossible in the light of recent Yugoslav experience. It could provide a practical means (and perhaps the only one) by which the worker-managed enterprises would be able to develop their own system of values and exchanges, as well as of planning, based essentially on living labour, and of which they would be the sole masters.

---

[1] Position at end of the year; from *Privreda u Godinama Reforme*, Federal Office of Statistics (Belgrade, 1968), p. 29.

The other, more realistic solution, based on the present system, would consist of determining an overall rate of growth corresponding to the desires and possibilities of the enterprises, and to define and strictly implement a corresponding monetary *and fiscal* policy, so as to stabilize the average real values of enterprise assets at levels not too distant from their book or accounting valuations. While the 1962–4 inflationary experience has shown that a growth rate of 16 per cent per annum is excessive, earlier experience would seem to indicate that very high rates of growth would be not only possible, but actually necessary in order to ensure such relative stabilization of the value of capital assets, and thereby of the economy as a whole. A rate of overall annual growth of well over 10 and perhaps up to 12 per cent would seem necessary in order to stabilize the value of existing assets, while ensuring the minimum required satisfaction of most if not all major objectives of the average enterprise at the present level of development of the Yugoslav economy.

This solution would require a quite unprecedented policy in the monetary, fiscal and planning areas—for which there is no parallel elsewhere—which would make it possible to react promptly and with great flexibility to those changes in enterprise behaviour which are exclusive to the worker-managed enterprise. A fuller knowledge of the actual values attaching to the various categories of objectives as defined in Chapter IX (or to any others a closer enquiry may elicit) would seem to constitute a necessary starting point of such a policy. A permanent survey of possible changes would be a necessary condition of its continued implementation. In other words, only a complex policy combining an active use of various monetary, fiscal and planning instruments based on a high overall rate of growth, a policy closely reflecting the various and specific objectives of the worker-managed enterprise, drawn up and implemented in close association with the latter, can in our view eliminate the severe disturbances to which the Yugoslav economy has been subjected during the sixties as a result, to a large extent, of the peculiar status of capital assets in the worker-managed economy. In view of its high propensity to expand and to invest, only such a high rate of growth, based on a corresponding rate of growth of effective demand and backed by a growing supply of money and credit, can ensure the best possible use of available fixed assets (productive capacity), and rapid circulation of short-term capital, as long at least as the worker-managed economy preserves the characteristics of a monetary exchange or market economy in respect of current business transaction.

The second point covered in this chapter, i.e. the behaviour of enterprises as regards current allocations out of their net income to their various funds, a point which has been at the very centre of all discussion in Yugoslavia and elsewhere, does not present such awkward conceptual difficulties as do capital assets. The position regarding value equivalence is much more straightforward. A portion of current income is not distributed as remuneration for work but allocated to one or other of the enterprise funds, and for all practical purposes, transformed immediately into capital assets. Thus if an additional machine-tool, a plant, an item of material inventory, a block of flats or any

243

other asset is added to the enterprise fixed assets, it may be deemed of equivalent value to the corresponding amount not distributed as remuneration for work. The accounting data may thus truly reflect reality. They are the most tangible expression of the enterprise economic policy and behaviour. Precise figures appear on paper and provide material for comment and study. This may partly explain the considerably greater attention paid in Yugoslav enterprises to the current account statement rather than to the balance sheet. The latter is obviously devoid of real meaning where old or obsolete non-marketable assets are concerned (railways, forestry plantations and their road systems, etc.). A major discrepancy will be found in nearly all cases. The current account statement, on the contrary, reports on real movements of funds and equivalent physical assets in terms of the true values of the enterprise's own time and space environment.

The dangers involved in such a purely econometric analysis have already been spelled out. It is clear that the choices made by the enterprises, even at this stage, are not merely between quantifiable financial equivalents—such as one million dinars remuneration as against the same amount of new machinery—but also in a great variety of non-measurable factors, or factors which do not enter the accounting documentation of the enterprise. Working time (shorter hours, additional leave, etc.) is the most obvious example of the latter type; invisible investment in 'technology and skills' of the former. Work intensity, discipline, entrepreneurship and non-quantifiable social benefits are similarly a part of the invisible choices which contribute to the growth or decline of the visible net income available for investment financing, and which may in themselves be partly considered as invisible investments.

For the Yugoslav firm investment in welfare (social consumption in Yugoslav terminology), whether visible (i.e. expressed in financial terms and passed through the accounts) or invisible, does not basically differ from other productive investments, if seen in the true perspective of the self-governing enterprise and its work collectivity. If additional machinery is to bring in additional income to workers, a housing estate may attain the same result in enabling them to save an equivalent portion of their living expenses. In view of the structure of rentals in enterprise—or other—housing schemes, housing constitutes one of the major elements of the 'invisible' income of the enterprises and their workers. In other words, if 'free market' rentals were charged, their apparent income, and the national income as a whole, would be considerably inflated in money terms without there being any change in the total housing space available.[1] This is also true of education and training, mostly classified

---

[1] The 'invisible' part of the housing expenses may be estimated as at least 70 per cent of the total, probably more in enterprise housing. According to a 1966 enquiry into the standard of living, the *average* monthly rental per square metre in 1965 and 1966 was 0·8 and 1·3 new dinars respectively, while the corresponding 'free market' charges (for unprotected sub-lettings) were 4·2 and 5·3 new dinars. (Cf. Federal Office of Statistics, *Bilten* No. 472, p. 25. Hence, housing expenditure also represents only a very small percentage of workers' family budgets (4·1 to 4·8 per cent throughout the 1965-7 period), cf. *Statistical Yearbook*, 1968, p. 284.

under social consumption, and which, if any credit is to be given to econometric analysis, is the major factor behind the efficiency of the Yugoslav
enterprise.

This does not diminish the fundamental significance of the behaviour of
enterprises as expressed through the allocation of part of their current income
to their various funds. The actual volume of such allocations has already been
partly covered in several earlier tables. It represents a quite significant share
of workers' income and a significant contribution to their existing assets.
Tables XV and XVI, pp. 235, 236, show that, in 1966, allocations by the enterprises to their own funds represented 11·4 per cent of the value of their total
assets (fixed and circulating capital): 11·9 per cent in industry and mining, 9·0
in agriculture, 30·0 in the building industry, 4·9 in transport and 13·9 in commerce and catering. In terms of total net income available for distribution, the
allocations to enterprise funds represented 27·8 per cent for the entire economy
30·2 in industry, 26·9 in agriculture, 21·5 in the building industry, 20·3 in
transport and 32·8 in commerce and catering.

Expressed in yet another form, as a percentage of national income generated
in the worker-managed sector, allocations by the enterprises to their own
funds were as follows during the 1961–7 period (figures in brackets indicate
the corresponding percentage of total income of the enterprises paid out in
cash to workers as net personal incomes): 1961—12·9 (31·6); 1962—11·2
(31·7); 1963—11·0 (31·43); 1964—15·6 (33·0); 1965—20·3 (35·0); 1966—
21·2 (38·2); 1967—17·0 (39·9).[1]

Thus, the average allocation to the enterprise funds can be seen as varying
between a minimum of approximately 35 per cent (in 1963) to over 55 per
cent maximum (in 1965) of the net cash remuneration of the workers. The
branch or sectoral averages, and the allocations by individual enterprises,
naturally show much greater variations, from zero per cent (or occasionally
a negative percentage), to sixty or more for individual sectors (e.g. foreign
trade), and considerably more for individual enterprises.

The above comparison is not entirely satisfactory as the workers' incomes
comprise an incompressible minimum required to maintain their existence,
while the allocations to enterprise funds represent a net addition to its
assets, since the maintenance and amortization of the existing assets has
already been covered by depreciation allowances (charged to costs). Assuming
that the workers' existential minimum corresponds to between one-third and
one-half of their cash income (which would thus be assumed to constitute an
incompressible part of hypothetical 'labour costs'), the work collectivities
appear to allocate considerably more to their enterprise funds than they pay
out in terms of additional cash incomes to their members. In terms of our
'vectoral model', the growth vectors as a whole may be seen as distinctly
stronger than those relating to short-term efficiency in terms of cash incomes.

It should be stressed that not one dinar of the net income can be allocated
to the enterprise funds without the matter being duly processed through the

[1] Cf. Federal Statistics Office, *The Economy in the Years of the Reform* (text in Serbian),
Belgrade, 1968, p. 83.

workers' council including, in major enterprises, a wide discussion throughout the work collectivity (departmental meetings or councils, etc.). In principle, therefore, should the works councils decide to distribute all the enterprise net incomes to workers in cash, the latters' earnings could be increased considerably, probably doubled or more in terms of extra disposable income.

Hardly any enterprise could, of course, afford to stop investing altogether, but significant reductions would be within the reach of most if the work collectivity should press for such a policy. Individual or collective examples of such behaviour are not altogether uncommon, as may be clearly seen from the various series of average or summary data cited earlier. In the later fifties and early sixties various review procedures were in existence at various times, aimed at ensuring that the enterprise followed a reasonable investment policy in accordance with its possibilities, under which, more particularly, the worker in accordance with its possibilities, under which, more particularly, the workers' council could be made to reconsider its income distribution policy. (These procedures were for the most part exhortatory, and in no case did they devolve on others the right to determine the workers' share in income.) Since 1963–4, however, the work collectivities were exposed to strong pressure in the opposite direction, to make them reduce the level of self-financing and increase cash earnings. As our figures show, they have however acted quite independently from such outside pressure, stepping up investment at least up to 1966. Allocations to the enterprise funds were always distinctly above the expected or planned minimum levels, and represented a voluntary response of work collectivities to their truly perceived economic interests.

The 1961–7 data also show that the yearly variations in the allocations to funds are greater than those of workers' personal incomes. They clearly show the tendency to step up investment more than proportionately when 'business is good' (1964–6) and vice versa, in a rather similar manner as indicated in Table XII, p. 232, in relation to output. In most respects, the amplitude of investment (or allocation thereto) appears greater than that of other changes. In terms of our model, the short-term vectors (A axis) are stronger at lower levels of performance, while those oriented towards long-term growth take over the lead when a high rate of performance is attained. This is true also—as shown by Tables XV and XVI, pp. 235, 236—for individual branches and sectors of the economy, and for individual enterprises. (Although not shown graphically, the upward swing of the investment 'cycle' appears parallel to that of business performance and not delayed, as is usually expected. The reason is that, for all practical purposes, the net income is shared out as and when achieved due *inter alia* to the pressure of a volume of projects and of needs much greater than can be dealt with, even at very high levels of performance.) The enterprises thus seem to follow their own rational economic criteria, largely disregarding the changing fancies of the economists and the resulting mood of the political world and public media.

The rapidly changing minds of the economists and the public in the investment versus consumption debate only epitomize one of the several major swings of policy which, were they actually followed with due diligence by the enterprises, would bring the economy to the verge of ruin. While often sound in their basic principles, such changing 'fancies' of opinion are mostly contra-dictory and neglect the time element (e.g. where size of the enterprise is dis-covered as a major element of economic efficiency, and Yugoslav firms found small compared to others, amalgamation is decreed the universal remedy and great disappointment shown when enterprises are not massively merging within a year or two). As indicated earlier, the irrelevance of the concept of 'investment inflation' to a worker-managed economy (in the absence of private reserves of financial capital) is only beginning to be understood.

The overall operation of the Yugoslav economy thus favours the expansion of those firms (sectors, etc.) which proved successful in carrying out their business and the latter undoubtedly avail themselves of this. As pointed our earlier, however, this is by no means a 'law' and there is considerable scope for the less profitable firms to invest and to progress at higher rates than the average of their group or of the economy as a whole, obviously at the cost of greater short-term sacrifice but also with the prospect of more considerable gains. In other words, the actual values attaching to the various 'vectors' of our model must vary widely from sector to sector, from region to region, and from enterprise to enterprise.

The underlying motivations for the overall prevalence of growth-motivated behaviour have been briefly spelled out, in abstract terms, in Chapter IX when defining the corresponding vectors. The way in which current income is allocated to the various funds of the enterprise makes it possible to take a closer look at the specific motivations of the worker-managed firm as presently in existence in Yugoslavia. Tables XIV, XV and, in particular, XVI are rele-vant in this context.

During the 1962–6 period of fast growth and inflation covered in Table XVI,[1] the allocations to enterprise funds show an extremely rapid increase both in absolute terms (close to 300 per cent), and as a proportion of the workers' net income (from 35 to 55 per cent). Enterprise behaviour during this period must be seen within the framework of rapid overall growth and the even faster growth of their investment activity. The fourfold increase in allocations to funds within a four-year period is partly due to the considerable reduction of taxation aimed at enabling the enterprises to finance the major part of their development themselves (as compared with the earlier predomin-ance of public credit), as well as to increase workers' cash incomes. While the enterprises responded positively to both these intentions of the 1965 Reform, up to 1966 they gave priority to the former. Deflationary processes made them adopt the opposite attitude in the subsequent years (1967–8).

The allocations to the *Legal Reserve Funds*, being obligatory by their very nature, constitute a special category. Their rapid fall throughout the whole period (1962–6) would seem in the main to reflect the growing number of enterprises reaching the statutory minimum volume of reserves, and thereby being relieved of the corresponding obligations. However, as in the case of the rail transport industry, contributions to legal reserves may also be low or nil

---

[1] Limited amounts of corresponding data for 1953–60 may be found in: ILO, *Workers' Management in Yugoslavia*, Geneva, 1962.

in sectors or enterprises experiencing financial difficulties. The very high percentage allocated to legal reserves in agriculture corresponds to special provision for the industry's special risk in terms of uneven yearly returns.

The *Voluntary Reserve Fund* (often referred to as non-allocated reserves of the enterprise) is of particular interest. It does not correspond to any specific legal provision but is a creation of the enterprises themselves in response to practical needs. It may be regarded as a special purse of the workers' councils for urgent intervention in unforeseen circumstances. (If all funds were actually allocated at the end of any accounting period, as required by the formal model of income distribution, such intervention could become impossible for lack of means, particularly in the early part of the following period.) Its main object is to regulate short-term output and, thereby, employment, but it may be used in any emergency. If funds accumulated are not required, they may be allocated in the normal course of business to any other purpose, including welfare or incomes. The formation of such voluntary reserves thus mainly reflects the need for short and medium-term employment and income security (vector B). As may be expected, the corresponding allocations rapidly decline, at least in percentage terms, in a period of high level activity and growth (Table XVI), where the requirements of employment security are largely satisfied. The opposite trend is to be expected in periods of scarce money and credit, when cash reserves may be essential for survival, although the actual reserves may be more heavily called upon due to lack of operating funds (as partly illustrated in Tables XIV and XVII, pp. 234, 235). While the sectoral variations show no particular deviation, the formation of non-allocated funds seems to represent one of the major distinctive features of individual enterprises pointing out their business habits and their security preferences.

The largest portion of the allocations goes, as may be expected, to investment proper. Yet it is by no means necessarily the greatest part of the total allocations. In our 1962–6 sample (Table XVI), the allocations to the *Business Fund* reach an average of over 50 per cent only in 1966 for the entire economy, and two years earlier for industry and mining. Most of the 'better off' industries perform better on this count as well (metal trades, trade and catering), while those in poor shape mostly invest well below the average (coal, railways), although textiles is again an exception, particularly striking in this context. The improved overall performance of most industries during the period boosted the average allocations to the Business Fund by 40 per cent, considerably more than all others, making for a total increase of over 550 per cent in absolute terms within four years. The real trend towards growth during a period of rapid expansion of demand is thus further accentuated in comparison with the overall allocations to enterprise funds. In other words, all the various interests making for a strong growth motivation of the average enterprise, and particularly those less tangible than our B set of vectors, appear dominant in such circumstances

However, the figures concerning the allocations to the Business Fund are particularly hard to interpret as they cover not only investment into fixed assets and the necessary circulating capital, but also all increases (or reductions) in stocks of finished products due to lagging (or growing) demand. The switch from the former to the second type of expansion had probably already begun in 1966, and became the major feature of enterprise behaviour in 1967 and early 1968, when accumulation of stock dominated in most branches of economic activity. The strength of the motivations relating to medium- or long-term growth can thus be considered in the last analysis as dependent on, and highly variable in direct proportion to, upward and downward movements in effective demand.

According to preliminary figures in the first quarter of 1969, following the various new incentives to effective demand late in 1968, the Yugoslav economy was able to operate an upward swing of 12 per cent in output and 23 in investment (compared to the first three months of 1968) without any major change in price or employment levels. In a very short time, the excess stocks (or excess circulating capital) were absorbed by the market and, it would seem, transformed into fixed assets and increased workers' incomes, the expansion of both having been delayed by lack of effective demand. In other words, excess stock (or circulating capital) in the Yugoslav firm (or economy) can actually be seen as deferred investment and deferred incomes. More significantly, they are actually thus seen by the workers *present* in the enterprise (in a manner in which a craftsman or peasant would see *his* stock of temporarily unsellable products).

The allocations to the *Welfare* (or Social Consumption) Fund appear as the most stable element of the distribution process, representing on average one quarter of the yearly totals. They are an important part of the enterprise policy, particularly as they relate mostly to areas where a lot can often be achieved with little funds (with the major exception of housing). Their size would seem to confirm that welfare motivations are far from insignificant within the interest framework of most work collectivities. The needs to be satisfied are numerous and urgent; yet it is only as a result of very rapid overall growth of the enterprise income that these social objectives of the enterprise can be attained. This seems to be the major cause of the relative priority given to the allocations to the Business Fund in a period of rapid expansion. The share of the Welfare Fund varies most markedly from sector to sector (and could be shown to vary even more in individual enterprises), this time in reverse proportion to their relative prosperity. The less well-off sectors or enterprises, where interest in self-financed expansion in terms of fixed assets may be minimal, have still to meet certain incompressible social or collective needs of the workers, while if money is relatively plentiful such needs are increasingly satisfied and the corresponding motivation weakened. A relative downward inflexibility—as compared to investment proper—in deflationary conditions may thus be assumed.

It would be most interesting to pursue the investigation into the many quite distinct fields covered by the general concept of welfare (or collective consumption) such as housing, catering and holiday facilities, training schemes, etc., which have all been the subject of major policy changes by the enterprises in recent years. These changes too seem to evince the capacity of the worker-managed enterprise to react swiftly in this area to changing economic circumstances and workers' needs.

One example concerns holiday camps (workers' hostels, etc.) which were one of the major early developments in the area of workers' welfare under central planning, and considerably expanded in the fifties. Due to the deflationary pressure of 1966 onwards, the earlier noted trend towards reduced investment in this area, correlative to the general improvement of workers' incomes, was markedly strengthened, and the enterprises began to opt out of this field of activity (transforming the holiday installation into independent enterprises, 'selling' them to others or opening them to the public on a commercial basis). Although this development met with significant opposition from the low income section of the working population (who could not as yet afford holidays on a commercial basis), it clearly was made possible by the relative lack of interest of the bulk of the workers and prompted by urgent financial needs of the enterprises. This example also shows the role of 'special reserve' which may be played by the assets of the Welfare Fund.

As shown in the various tables, the Welfare Fund of the Yugoslav firm (and indeed in other European countries where such activities of enterprise are managed by the workers' representative bodies, as is the case *inter alia* of France) is a very peculiar economic phenomenon. It comprises its own fixed assets and circulating capital, including cash deposits, may even generate a limited amount of its own income, and can thus be seen, particularly in the major firms and where it has its own personnel, as a specialized welfare enterprise within the firms. Its 'behaviour' would thus seem to warrant a special enquiry. The Yugoslav literature in this area—with the exception of excellent statistical surveys—is comparatively underdeveloped and the importance of the Welfare Fund from the point of view of enterprise economics is generally not acknowledged by most authors. It is one of the major commanding factors of enterprise behaviour and performance, as shown *inter alia* by the recent findings concerning the paramount role of investment in training and skills. Similarly, housing can have a decisive impact on various aspects of employment economics, and other social facilities and benefits may often acquire much greater weight than the cash earnings in determining the behaviour of the work collectivities and of individual workers.

*   *   *

The motivation to growth as brought to light by the actual behaviour of the worker-managed enterprises—as at present constituted in Yugoslavia—seems on the whole very strong—at least equal to and probably stronger than their motivation for short-term efficiency and cash incomes—if considered against the background both of the expansion of their total assets, productive or otherwise, and of the share allocated out of their current income to their expansion. In both these respects, the forces commanding enterprise behaviour, i.e. the dimension of the corresponding growth vectors) appear to be subject to considerable variations—certainly greater than those commanding short-term behaviour, or those which may be found in other market economies—in direct relation to the state of effective demand. A relative stability, corresponding to a minimum satisfaction of the corresponding growth objectives of the average enterprise, could be achieved, but would require a very high rate of growth of effective demand, probably in the region of 12 per cent annually. While the overall motivation for growth seems rather evenly spread throughout the various sectors and regions of the country, these specific objectives and levels of satisfaction are likely to vary considerably, and would require a much closer study if overall steady growth is aimed at. Similarly special attention would be required by enterprises or sectors at the two extremes of the 'performance spectrum', which are likely to show strongly deviant patterns of behaviour, leading possibly to less than optimum performance as compared with the average enterprise.

CHAPTER XI

The Medium- and Long term-Policy of the Enterprise (2) Amortization, Interest and Loan Financing

In the preceding chapter, an attempt has been made to show that capital in the usual sense of the term does not and cannot exist in the worker-managed economy. Enterprise assets cannot be marketed and transformed into financial capital, nor is there any financial capital which could take the form of an enterprise independently from the existence of actual workers endowed with management powers over the corresponding assets. This finding may seem surprising, and is indeed in contradiction with some popular beliefs (including Professor Ward's model and of course much of the criticism of the Yugoslav model from the point of view of central planning or radical State socialist doctrines which, like Professor Ward, see the Yugoslav workers' enterprise as a revival, or a degenerate form, of capitalism), and with the common Yugoslav vocabulary. It seems good logic nevertheless, for in as much as labour is not a commodity, neither can productive assets as such be marketable. This again is a feature common to all producers' economies, but particularly stressed in the worker-managed system where a sale (take-over, etc.) of the assets is both practically impossible and institutionally ruled out.

There will be no capital market in a self-employed peasant economy (as opposed to capitalist agriculture), but an occasional synallagmatic transfer of ownership may occur as a result of a change in personal or family circumstances, bad management, etc. The work collectivity of the Yugoslav enterprise is not likely to be affected by similar personal circumstances, as it is a self-recruiting, relatively permanent organization and, not being the owner of the assets, has neither an interest in, nor the possibility of, transferring them to others against financial capital equivalent. Like the farmers', its very existence is tied to the productive assets, but with the considerable difference that it could not make use of the financial equivalent of its assets for personal consumption.

There is of course the theoretical possibility that the work collectivity would sell itself *with* the assets in a manner akin to the emphyteutical leases of the end of the Roman Empire, by which the free peasantry were entering the feudal bondage. Although obviously contrary to positive law, and hardly of interest to any domestic 'buyer', this possibility is not entirely irrelevant in considering their relationship with foreign sources of financial capital. Clearly perceived by the Yugoslav legislators, this danger is particularly real, in conditions of extreme scarcity of financial resources, when any price may be paid in order to safeguard sheer existence. As shown in the preceding chapter, the Yugoslav enterprises have demonstrated in such conditions a considerable capacity for self-defence in having recourse to natural financing and creating their own credit system. The danger was nevertheless present, particularly since they negotiate their financial arrangements abroad directly, and these to an extent remain hidden from the authorities and to the public.

There are nevertheless two very specific real links between the assets of the worker-managed enterprise, or their financial equivalents, and its current operation, which are at present built into the system. One is depreciation (or amortization) of fixed assets; the other is the interest due with regard to all assets of the enterprise. The interest and repayment of principal due in respect of loans will also be briefly referred to in this connection.

Table XVIII

Extracts from the 1967 and 1968 Annual Accounts of the Worker-managed Enterprises (16,843 firms)[1]
(in 000 millions new dinars)

	1967	1968	1968 1967
Amortization	8·25	9·45	116
Net product	65·04	74·13	114[4]
Interest on loans	3·26	4·04	123
Interest on business fund	2·07	2·26	109
Insurance premiums	1·14	1·31	116
Membership fees[2]	0·29	0·35	122
Federal turnover tax	6·43	7·38	115
Republican and communal T.O. tax	1·82	2·09	115
Allocated to personal incomes	35·21	40·48	115
Personal incomes charged to costs[3]	1·33	1·46	110
Personal incomes charged to investment and to welfare fund	0·32	0·37	104
Contributions to Skopje[5]	0·90	0·97	109
Workers' personal incomes and other receipts (net)	29·59	32·47	110
Workers' incomes (gross of taxes, etc.)	44·69	49·03	110

[1] Cf. *Ekonomska Politika*, 7 April 1969: data supplied by the Social Accounting Service. The reader will note the rapidity with which the accounts were established, decisions on income distribution made, data collected and processed by the central auditing agency and made available to the public. Not all accounts (particularly those regarding allocations to enterprise funds) were, however, available at the above date.

[2] To the Economic Chambers and other organizations of the enterprises.

[3] Daily allowances and similar payments to workers which are not directly related to the work performed.

[4] The considerable increase of the 1968 net product of the worker-managed enterprises already reflects the economic recovery in the second half of the year which, as mentioned earlier, continued into 1969 at levels of output and investment well above those of the early months of 1968.

[5] Sum of three different contributions, paid by the enterprise from monies (i) allocated to workers' incomes; (ii) for investment; and (iii) by the workers out of their income.

To set these various items in some general perspective—for they can be approached from a variety of angles—it seemed best to reproduce a few key items of the 1967 and 1968 summary accounts of the worker-managed sector (16,843 enterprises in 1968). These have the advantage of updating some of the data given earlier, while also bringing in a few key data concerning other fiscal instruments.

Being a part of the current costs, *amortization*—compared to other items of the accounts—is less likely to attract the attention of the general public, or even specialists. Yet the above figures show that the amortization process generates very considerable financial resources corresponding, for instance, to nearly 30 per cent of the workers' net incomes. Moreover, despite their specific destination these resources are, as it were, added to the disposable current financial resources of the enterprise. Although they can be used only for the replacement of existing assets or the purchase of new ones, the work collectivity actually enjoys much greater freedom in using the resources of the amortization fund (as indeed, any other item of its costs) than in contracting outside loans or even than in investing out of its own current income. Not surprisingly, therefore, since the system of fixed obligatory rates of amortization has been abandoned, the work collectivities tend to fix their own rates above the legal minimum levels.

In 1967, the volume of amortization funds corresponded to approximately 8 per cent of the book value of the fixed assets of the worker-managed sector, and 70 per cent of the actual allocations out of the net income of the enterprises to their various other funds. The minimum legal rates vary from 1 or $1\frac{1}{2}$ per cent for such items as land, roads, forests, hydro-electric generating stations (sometimes reduced to half that level, as in the case of air-strips of airport enterprises), up to 33 per cent for most classes of cattle and 100 per cent for short-term forestry plantations (nurseries). Up to the early sixties, amortization rates were actively used as an instrument of planned economic policy, but the present minimum rates may be considered fully stabilized. They can only be changed by special legislation (as in the case of recent measures regarding coal mining). The 1965 Reform has resulted in a significant increase in the real rates of amortization (from approximately 5·5 to over 8 per cent on the average).

In fact, the rapid growth of the Yugoslav economy could not be understood without taking into account both the volume and the very specific nature of depreciation by the Yugoslav firm. As to the volume, little needs to be added. Amortization generated throughout the years approximately one-third of the capital available for investment, and probably a much greater proportion with respect to fixed assets. Without it, little or no development of productive capacity would have been achieved.

Contrary to a commonly held opinion, amortization as practised in Yugo-slavia was probably one of the major factors behind such development within the worker-managed economy. Since they were endowed mostly with new capacity, the work collectivities did not actually require, during the first years of their operation, the resources generated through amortization to replace worn-out plant and equipment, but were able to invest them into further

254

expansion of modernization of their enterprises. As they continue to invest part of their income into additional new capacity, this multiplier effect of amortization continues to operate within the Yugoslav economy. Actually, the amortization funds are one of the fastest growing elements of Yugoslav social accounting. Since 1961 they grew as follows (figures in brackets are for industry and mining), in 000 million new dinars: 1961—2·2 (1·2); 1962—2·4 (1·3); 1963—3·3 (1·8); 1964—4·3 (2·2); 1965—5·0 (2·5); 1966—6·8 (3·3); 1967—8·9 (4·6).[1] In any event, the depreciation system as practised in Yugoslavia cannot be seen as providing for the mere replacement of the fixed assets (as assumed generally by economic theory), but as a major factor of growth.

This peculiar effect of amortization, which mostly remains unnoticed by economists, has been convincingly presented in an early work by B. Horvat.[2] In concrete terms, new enterprises with an initial capital of 1,000 practising, from the start, a policy of linear depreciation at realistic annual rates (i.e. corresponding to the actual life-span of the corresponding assets), will increase the book value of its assets in a significant proportion quite independently of any additional self-financed investment. The 'multiplier' effect is shown by Horvat to increase with the depreciation period (i.e. rate of depreciation decreasing) to stabilize finally at levels such as 60 per cent above that of the original capital if assets are depreciated within a four-year period; 75 per cent if within seven years; and 82 per cent if in ten years. Even higher multipliers (practically doubling the volume of fixed assets) are observed within the first period of amortization. The same applies to any investment in new assets which is added to the enterprise funds. This little known (or at least little publicized) effect of accounting practice in respect of depreciation has recently been 'discovered' in a different context by the French fiscal authorities and gave rise to a wide debate.[3]

The quite considerable funds collected by the enterprises in terms of depreciation allowances add significantly to their flexibility as regards modernization or changing the object of the enterprise. Even where the net income is too low to allow for a significant additional investment by way of self-financing, the funds generated through depreciation may still allow for significant reorganization or reshaping of the orientation of the enterprise development programmes. Thus, for instance, the Yugoslav railway enterprises, which were not able to allocate any, or only token, funds to self-financed growth in the 1962–6 period, have nonetheless some funds at their disposal to proceed—at a slow rate—with the implementation of their modernization programmes.

The amortization funds also have the advantage of being available for use as and when generated, normally on a monthly basis, without having to wait for the approval of the periodic accounts and the formal decision on income allocation. Each enterprise is bound to adopt at the beginning of the year its

---

[1] See also *Utvrdivanje, obračun i korišćenje amortisacije* (Privredni Pregled), Belgrade, 1967.

[2] *Ekonomska teorija planske privrede*, Belgrade, 1961.

[3] Cf. *Le Monde*, 23 March 1968, p. 22.

amortization plan for existing assets, and the bank then automatically transfers the corresponding monthly instalment from the current account to that of its Amortization Fund. Newly added fixed assets are inserted into the amortization process as and when brought into operation during the year.

Their existence also increases the loan-worthiness of the enterprises, particularly those with a low level of income, for they offer a strong guarantee of regular loan repayment. Where productive assets are acquired on the basis of a loan, the corresponding amortization funds can (and indeed must in the absence of other resources) be used for the repayment of such loans. The amortization 'tariff' in force contains a special provision regarding such assets, which must be amortized at the (minimum) rate of 10 per cent or at least at such lower rates as would correspond to the repayment schedule of the corresponding loan. In other words, provided it at least covers its costs, the enterprise must have sufficient funds available to pay its creditors. Considerable additional appreciation of fixed assets may result in consequence (e.g. where buildings are amortized at the rate of 10 per cent corresponding to a ten-year repayment period of an investment loan).

In the case of the most unfavourable results ever attained at the level of a whole industry (i.e. the paper industry in 1967) where negative net investment actually appeared for the first time in the annual accounts of a sector ($-61\cdot4$ million new dinars), accompanied by a fall in workers' incomes, the operation of the amortization system nevertheless placed fresh funds of considerably greater magnitude at the disposal of the industry ($166\cdot3$ millions). Significantly, the balance sheet of this sector shows a very high level of new assets, and the allocations to amortization represent an unusually high proportion of net income (approximately one-third) and of the workers' net incomes (approximately two-thirds), in comparison with other industries. A very high level of investment (or relative over-investment) in recent years thus seems to be at the root of the industry's exceptionally severe difficulties (particularly in the then prevailing conditions of radical demand squeeze). Thus a slight alteration of the amortization rules (e.g. progressive instead of linear) would have considerably transformed the whole picture by bringing to light the industry's basically sound position.

If it can propose an investment project offering the prospect of a given level of returns, the low income enterprise is in no less favourable position than its more efficient competitor as it can guarantee the repayment of loans at equal conditions. (As noted earlier, it may actually make a better showing in view of the presumably lower levels of workers' personal incomes.) The binding minimum levels of amortization also offer a guarantee to enterprises that the total costs (and hence price levels) of competitiors with similar productive assets must include a corresponding item of current cost of 'capital'.

Despite its striking economic importance, the amortization system gives rise to relatively little public debate or criticism, incomparably less indeed than various other fiscal or financial instruments. It would appear widely accepted by the enterprises, since the obligations it entails in the short term are largely matched by corresponding benefits in the perspective of development and growth. The only major criticism of the present amortization system voiced by some enterprises is that they have to amortize assets which are actually out of active use.

Amortization may thus be seen as a technical-accounting modality allowing for the transformation of short-term business results into medium- and long-term growth performance. The amortization system and enterprise practice has very little in common with the corresponding phenomenon in traditional private enterprise economy. It differs basically in its objectives, its rules of implementation, and the nature of the assets to which it applies, the differences being too numerous to be examined in any detail. Nor is it a mere accounting device as in the planned economies, for it entails transfers of real financial resources from current consumption to investment, and is controlled directly by the work collectivity using the assets in question.

The present system under which the work collectivity itself determines, subject to a statutory minimum, the rates of depreciation of its various assets, has gone a long way towards severing the link between the latter and their financial accounting value. In so far as the work collectivities significantly increase their rates of depreciation—as indeed they seem inclined to do—they are becoming free to vary, both upwards and downwards, the volume of funds generated in this manner. The latter thus appear increasingly independent of the book value of their assets seen as a form of 'capital'. The depreciation policy of an enterprise is thus entirely separated from the book-keeping value of its assets, and merely translates the work collectivity's desire and aptitude to develop its operations. Along with workers' incomes and allocations for self-financement, it is becoming one of the variable elements of the enterprise's current financial policy and decision making, forming a necessary part of the industry's costs (and thereby prices), yet allowing them to operate at uneven levels of short-term efficiency and income.

The interest on capital assets (the Business Fund of the enterprise) arouses traditionally much more interest both in Yugoslavia and abroad, although, when seen in proper perspective, as in Table XVIII, p. 253, it clearly appears of much lesser significance than amortization or various other fiscal instruments. A slight change in the rates of amortization, or in the tax on turnover, can have an impact on enterprise behaviour and performance at least equal to that of the total value of interest paid by enterprises in respect of their business funds. Indeed, the volume of this interest hardly represents twice the special contributions paid by enterprises and their workers for the reconstruction of Skopje, the capital of Macedonia, a town of 260,000 inhabitants severely damaged (but far from totally destroyed) by an earthquake.

The actual share of interest in the gross income or in the material costs of the enterprises is similarly insignificant, at 1·2 and 2·4 per cent respectively in 1967. Nor does interest on capital play a positive role within the enterprise comparable to amortization, which not only subtracts a considerably greater volume of funds from gross income, but puts these funds at the enterprise's disposal for new developments.

The basic rate of this special class of interest was fixed for many years at 6 per cent per annum, with considerably lower rates applying to most branches of the economy and industrial sectors. Thus, in the years 1959–63, the actual rates of interest paid by average enterprises varied from less than 2 to close to 3 per cent.[1] The 1965 Reform measures reduced the maximum interest to 4·5 per cent (with a preferential rate of 1·7 per cent for some industries), while the average rate of actual payments by the enterprises remained at less than half that level (although the actual burden it represented for enterprise income has increased somewhat due to the revaluation of the book value of fixed assets.

All this goes to show, along with a considerable volume of additional evidence, that only limited importance can be attached to this category of interest among the various outside factors which determine the real behaviour of the enterprise. In evaluating the economics of a given project (investment, launching a new product, etc.) the interest on capital will hardly ever appear as of primary importance, even within the specific category of financial and fiscal policy instruments. Depreciation allowances and the tax on turnover and on income will in practically all cases appear as of considerably greater magnitude, not to speak of a variety of other minor items which are of decisive importance (e.g. communal taxation or inducements offered by the local authorities). Any economic model, such as Professor Ward's, which considers the interest (or tax) on enterprise capital as the single, determining outside factor of its economic behaviour, appears totally unrealistic and in any event inapplicable to Yugoslav conditions, even if the need for considerable simplification in economic model building is fully recognized.

In the early years of the system, the rate of interest was expected to play a much more ambitious role within the economy, particularly with respect to distribution of investment credit, but experiments proved impracticable and had been abandoned by the mid-fifties. This does not mean that the impact of the interest paid by the enterprises on their Business Fund can be considered as nil or completely negligible. Expressed as a percentage of the net income of enterprises, the volume of interest paid in respect of the Business Fund was as follows in some selected branches of the economy.

	1964	1966	1967
Industry and mining	5·7	4·1	5·5
Electricity generation	5·2	6·7	10·8
Petroleum industry	16·5	9·0	12·4
Agriculture	0·4	1·6	2·5
Building industry	2·8	2·2	2·3
Transport	5·7	3·2	4·0
Commerce	2·8	2·6	3·5
Crafts	1·7	1·7	1·9
Economy (total)	4·3	3·4	4·4

In the more capital-intensive sectors (such as electricity generation or the petrol industry), interest on capital assets may reach a more significant proportion of net income (up to and over 10 per cent). This correspondingly increases the industry's costs (hence its price levels), thereby protecting to some extent their more labour-intensive competitors. It also marks—as was intended—the minimum level of utilization of existing capacities (or the minimum level of output) which the work collectivities must attain in order to

[1] Cf. *inter alia* Dr M. Trklja, *Kamata na investicione kredite* (etc). Belgrade, 1966, pp. 73–4.

preserve their autonomous existence (particularly since they are not obliged by any plan or other administrative instrument to attain any given level of output).

Yet in the light of these figures, it is hardly creditable that even a significant change in the rate of interest (or in the capital content of an industry) could have a major effect on the behaviour of an enterprise or of an industrial sector, with the exception of electricity generation, the petrol industry or any similarly highly capital-intensive enterprise.[1]

The existence of interest charges also brings clearly to light the fact that any assets which are kept idle, or are insufficiently used, actually generate net losses for the work collectivity. The effects of interest on capital can certainly be considered present in most cases but, in view of the prevailing low rates of interest, they appear more symbolic than real. In order to equalize conditions of operation of enterprises, or to impose a meaningful level of output, a considerably higher rate of interest, close to the average rate of profitability, would have to be introduced, a measure which would face insuperable practical difficulties, and which would appear impracticable in the light of the basic principles of a worker-managed economy. A high uniform rate of interest, close to the average rate of profit, would obviously result in the closure of most existing capital-intensive industries, which are the actual leaders of the economy in the field of technical progress, while by no means releasing the corresponding capital for other sectors. (A closed electricity or steel works is indeed of little use to the expansion of craft-type hand-weaving or reopening of surface mines and quarries.) A rate of interest confiscating the average profit or surplus generated by the enterprise would similarly mean the end of workers' management as presently understood (i.e. precisely as the right to dispose of such surplus), and would confer to others (the State or the banks) the key decision-making powers in the management of the economy. Moreover, while a fixed and relatively low rate of interest is morally acceptable, possibly as a token return to society for assets made available to the enterprises (as accepted, for instance, in most Rochdale-inspired co-operatives), the practice of necessarily extravagant 'economic' rates of interest would soon appear (and indeed did appear in Yugoslavia) intolerable in the conditions of a socialist society, even where such interest was not appropriated by a private person or group, but reverted to social development objectives. Indeed, in so far as they cannot be attained at the present low rates, the major objectives ascribed to interest on the Business Fund can be effectively achieved by other less cumbersome instruments of fiscal or financial policy.

Yugoslav public opinion is increasingly accepting the point of view of those economists who, for these and other reasons, claim that interest on capital assets serves no useful purpose, and should be abolished.[2] A resolution providing for its suppression by the end of 1970 has actually been adopted by

---

[1] According to Social Accountancy Service; cf. Professor M. Samardžija, '*Kamata na osnovni fond, etc.*' in *Socializam*, April 1968, p. 438 and M. Ilich in *Ekonomika Preduzeča*, 8 September 1968, p. 535.

[2] Cf. *inter alia* articles by Professor Samardžija and M. Ilich cited above. We have referred earlier to similar views of Professor Korać.

the Federal Assembly and seems likely to be implemented in due course. Despite the more or less 'symbolic' nature of interest as presently applied to enterprise basic capital, the change would be of considerable importance. It would actually do away with the 'economics' of worker-management as devised in the early years and practised throughout the fifties. It would do away more particularly with many of the difficulties arising from the specific nature of 'capital' in a worker-managed economy (as discussed in the preceding section) in that it would break the last link between abstract financial capital and the concrete means of production of the enterprise. At the same time, it would place a considerable new responsibility on the work collectivities, as it would free them from the last objective norm tied to the past and regulating their present and future economic behaviour, making the efficient use of assets essentially a matter of conscience and of conscious interpretation of their present and future interests. As this change seems to receive a wide measure of support in the enterprises (even in those which would benefit relatively little) it can hardly be doubted that the work collectivities would do their best to face their new responsibilities, and are actually ready to face them.

Interpreted in terms of the vectoral model, the main effect of interest on capital was, and still is, to reduce the apparent short-term income of the enterprise, thus strengthening the corresponding short-term efficiency motivations of the work collectivity. At the same time it permits the collection each year of considerable funds outside the worker-managed economy proper (in the central or territorial public investment funds), and their reallocation among possible investors (i.e. growth-motivated enterprises or other collectivities) in accordance with social and economic criteria adopted at various policy-making levels. If interest is abolished, the apparent efficiency of enterprises will consequently improve (even if often in a rather symbolic manner) and it will depend entirely on each enterprise collectivity whether and in what manner it will use the resulting gains for growth-oriented investments or transform them into short-term benefits. As in the case of similar measures taken in the past, such as the abolition of the progressive income tax in 1961, considerably differentiated behaviour may be expected to result for different categories of enterprises, particularly in the first period of readjustment.

The interest paid on the basic capital assets of the enterprise is a very specific institution of the worker-managed system, since it is paid independently of any loan or comparable contractual relationship. It has thus very little in common with what is usually understood under this term. The closest parallel is the specific tax levied in certain countries on the assets of perpetual foundations (particularly ecclesiastical), in lieu of the death duties which they avoid, which also has the purpose of establishing relative equality among the various categories of taxpayers, and a minimum level of utilization of such assets. In this regard, it is noteworthy that, similar to such foundations, the Yugoslav enterprise (being unable to use up its basic assets but only to expand them) has the theoretical capacity for indefinite growth.

The Yugoslav firm is however not restricted to its endowment assets (as received at the start of its operations or created during the years), but has the capacity to contract loans for which it normally pays interest at an agreed rate.

The *interest on contractual loans* is obviously much closer to the usual meaning of the term despite the basic difference in its object. The loan contracted by a Yugoslav firm cannot be seen as the usual form of borrowing private or public capital, which would (or could if invested elsewhere) give the owner a right to be associated in the management of the corresponding assets, or to share in the results of the enterprise operations. Both these rights are exclusively reserved to the work collectivity. The loans were traditionally obtained from funds, collected for that purpose only from the whole economy through various fiscal instruments (including the 'interest' on the basic capital assets). They entail no obligation other than repayment of the sum involved, with interest at the agreed yearly rates. The new banking system similarly does not handle true financial capital, but operates rather as a mutual credit society, where fixed-interest savings are used for fixed-interest loans. (Additional inflows of money and credit from the central monetary institutions are of course necessary to finance growth and maintain the required level of effective demand.) The main income of the banks consists at present in the repayment of loans and interest which they have inherited from the former public investment funds, and which form the major single item on the credit side of their balance sheets.

A system of free interest rates, determined by bidding at open auctions, had been experimented with in the early fifties and rapidly abandoned. Bidding for public funds in terms of future interest and repayment periods proved impracticable for a number of reasons. Extreme scarcity of essential productive assets brought the profitability of certain investments up to astronomic levels (over 300 per cent per annum in certain cases), correspondingly high but unrealistic rates of interest being 'bid' by the enterprise. Widely differing levels of interest were reached at different auctions, resulting in considerable inequalities between enterprises regarding their obligations in respect of loans, particularly intolerable where long-term investment loans were accepted at strikingly different rates of interest. The equalization of the latter became one of the major tasks of financial policy during the mid- and later fifties.

Even today, most enterprises have a number of projects with respect to which the subjectively assessed returns may reach extremely high levels, and for which they are sometimes ready to 'bid' (in the 'unofficial' money market) intolerably high levels of interest. Paradoxically, a fixed ceiling on the rate of interest had to be imposed, and remains necessary, in order to protect the enterprises against their own excessive entrepreneurial motivation. Maximum levels have been between 6 and 10 per cent.

The actual rates levied on investment credits by the public investment funds were kept at most times well below half this maximum, e.g. between 3 and 4 per cent on average during the 1959–61 period (with a maximum of 6 per cent for some industries, such as shipbuilding and tobacco manufacture).[1] Bank credit for circulating capital was significantly 'dearer' at most times. The real interest rate on loans was and remains comparatively higher (possibly twice as

[1] Cf. Dr M. Trklja, *op. cit.*, p. 63 and *passim*.

costly) than that levied on the enterprise's own capital assets. Thus, as shown in Table XVIII, p. 253, while 'loans' represented, in the 1967–8 period, just over 40 per cent of the 'capital' of Yugoslav enterprises, the volume of interest paid in respect of such loans was significantly greater than that of the interest on the Business Funds of the enterprises.

The real cost of such loans for the enterprise is of course much greater, as it includes the repayment of the principal, i.e. the so-called 'annuities', which obviously must be reckoned with when planning any given loan-financed investment. The combined interest and annuities can thus be seen as a major factor affecting enterprise decision-making with regard to loan-financed investment projects.

The repayment of loans in the worker-managed economy has hardly any-thing in common with similar processes in a private enterprise or even publicly-owned economy. In repaying its debts (out of its net income or amortization fund), the work collectivity merely adds to the assets held by the enterprise Business Fund but of which no one, least of all the work collectivity, can claim actual ownership. In saving on their income, the work collectivity has merely added to the concrete productive resources which form the support for the work of its present and future members, thereby expanding the overall productive assets of the economy, without making anyone richer in terms of capital holdings. The system of loans can thus be seen as a powerful instrument of expansion of the nation's productive assets out of, as it were, the future output of its economy.

This may more clearly be visualized in a practical example. An enterprise with a basic capital of 1,000, having contracted a loan for modernization and expansion of an equal amount, at say 5 per cent average interest and a ten-year repayment period, will find itself at the end of the period with twice the amount of its initial assets held by its 'Business Fund'. At the same time it has contri-buted the sum of 500 to the resources of the public (or the bank's) investment funds which, along with the principal (1,000) can be used for the financing of other productive ventures. The work collectivity will be creating these addi-tional social resources, amounting to 1,500, through its work during the ten-year period, but without any real sacrifice on its part in so far as it has invested the initially borrowed capital in a project yielding at least 15 per cent annual returns on average (which presumably was the very minimum yield considered at the planning stage and can easily be attained by an average investment project).

More bluntly stated, this means that under the worker-managed system the additional resources generated by work are lost neither in the private pockets of domestic or foreign entrepreneurs, nor in the unfathomable reserves of the Exchequer or central planning agencies. In this latter regard, it is interesting to note the considerable interest paid by the Yugoslav firms to the final destination of that part of the additional resources they have seen formed in their enterprises but had to pay back in terms of interest and of amenities. The present banking system actually gives them the possibility of keeping their eye on them, and playing a part in their redeployment throughout the economy.

This very peculiar status, and very high cost of loans in the Yugoslav economy, partly compensates for the often excessive entrepreneurial drive of most enterprises and other likely investors (such as the communes). This is prompted partly by the fact that they are not investing their own 'capital' and, in this regard at least, not bearing the full risk of the capitalist investor (as distinct from that of the free entrepreneur whose risks they share in more fully). The considerable costs attaching to these loans limited to some extent the corresponding demands of the enterprises. In several instances, work collectivities have preferred to finance the full reconstruction or a massive expansion of their enterprises on their own, rather than touch a 'single penny' of outside borrowed resources. In many other cases, the self-financed share of the enterprise has been increased in the same spirit of independence, for which the real cost of the loan provides an economic justification.

This is the key to understanding the massive release of entrepreneurial initiative in an underdeveloped and largely traditional rural society (such as that of most parts of Yugoslavia) where private investment in productive and more long-term ventures is inhibited by prohibitive rates of subjective interest (often of 100 per cent and over) which are required to release privately held capital reserves for productive purposes. (The hoarding of gold is still customary in many of the more remote areas of Yugoslavia.) Pure but collective entrepreneurship, based either on direct work input or on social resources generated through fiscal or financial instruments, seems in such conditions to provide a practical alternative to central planning, able to generate development out of domestic resources and under local management. The worker-managed enterprise would thus seem to offer a solution of one of the basic problems of underdevelopment, particularly in a non-stratified rural society.

The demand for investment (and other) loans was nevertheless at all times much greater than the funds available. It is extremely difficult to evaluate the real volume of demand for credit, but it can safely be said that at any time the social investment funds or, later, the banks, could allocate, at current rates of interest, the volume of funds available several times over (in other words, a sum probably equal to or greater than the national income of the corresponding period). It should be noted that only projects elaborated in great detail, backed by full technical and economic documentation, can be entertained by the lending agencies. There is in such conditions a great advantage for whoever is in charge of granting such loans, as there is a wide possibility of choice among projects and stiff criteria for selection of projects may be imposed.

At the same time, such choices involve a considerable political responsibility, even if entrusted to an 'expert' body (as they were within the framework of the former investment funds). As recalled earlier, the administrative system of credit allocation actually proved unworkable for this very reason in a country with as widely differing socio-economic conditions and levels of development as are encountered in Yugoslavia. The allocation of credit was therefore vested into the new banks, conceived as a special type of association or credit union of the enterprises themselves. The latter thus can, and indeed must, determine their own criteria for the bank's credit policy and supervise its implementation. A loss on a credit operation by the bank thus reduces hope of future credit for its members and vice versa.

The enterprises are not the sole members of such banks, but may be joined by any other public body or social organization which is under similar obligation to operate through a bank. Thus, in the extreme case of the Belgrade communal bank, the enterprises represent only a minority of the total membership, the majority being composed of the various other self-governing social organizations (health, education, etc.) and other organizations or administrations the number of which is obviously disproportionately high in a capital city. If dissatisfied with the bank's policy, the enterprises could change their affiliation or set up their own bank. Significantly, the Belgrade Bank engages—along with others—in an active promotional policy (through advertisements, etc.) stressing particularly the services it renders to the economy.

The criteria for allocation of loans developed by the former investment funds, or those applied since by the banks, cannot be readily summarized as they obviously were and are contingent on specific circumstances of time and place. They are public, issued in the form of rules, and adjusted from time to time (normally by the yearly plan of the bank); both demands received and credits granted are publicized. Thus, in each monthly Bulletin of the Federal investment banks, such lists of current demands and loans are regularly brought to the attention of the public. A similar practice is followed by other banks. This does not apply to short-term credits, but their volume and the names of the enterprises are not withheld from others concerned, including the press, which often discusses and comments on the details of any such decision. In other words credit policy is known to all who may be interested or concerned. This publicity naturally often gives rise to most heated debates, for instance on competing investment projects.

Such debates may become the foundation stone of more systematic planning through the formulation of socially acceptable norms of behaviour of enterprises, banks and other investors, and the rejection of deviant, socially unacceptable patterns of behaviour. The wide coverage by all public media, as well as the specialized publications, of investment decisions at various stages of elaboration appear at present as the strongest element of development planning in Yugoslavia, in so far as the latter is understood as conscious regulation by society of its economic and social future (and not a set of mathematical formulae, be they capital coefficients, commodity balances, or multi-sectoral linear programming tabulations, all of which are not really meaningful unless used by, and commanding the acceptance of, the real decision makers within the economy).

Two generally applied criteria of project selection are however particularly relevant. First, participation by the investor in directly financing the project is almost always required, particularly from existing enterprises. Minimum levels of such self-financing were usually prescribed for the various branches or sectors of the economy under the former social investment funds. These rules, governing the allocation of credit, constituted a principal planning instrument. Such participation was, and still is, seen as a necessary token of commitment to and confidence in the project for which a loan is sought. It also

264

makes it possible to defer some of the investment projects, i.e. those for which the investor has not yet accumulated the necessary funds, or has done so to a lesser degree than others. On the whole, it clearly favours the efficient and the thrifty, though those who cannot participate in the initial financing of their investment project are not entirely lost sight of. Provision is always made for the needs of the less developed regions (as at present by the special Fund financed by the interest on basic assets of existing enterprises) and self-financed participation can always be supplied by others (the commune, the republic, a local bank, a customer enterprise, etc.).

Security of the loan itself is of course a second major criterion, which is likely to be particularly stressed within the new banking system. The more efficient, better off enterprise seems at first glance a better choice and is usually so regarded in Yugoslavia by most economists and public media. Yet, as already hinted at, where the less favourable results of an enterprise are due to less advanced technology, such an enterprise is actually more attractive for loan-financing, not only from the overall social point of view, but also from that of a relatively restricted interest group such as the present Yugoslav bank. The low income enterprise can often invest with considerable benefit, and at little cost, in some intermediary technology which would be of little or no benefit for its more advanced competitor. It can thus, thanks to a greater income differential, offer a greater security to the bank, provided of course that it shows adequate standards of entrepreneurship and of management generally. Although rarely mentioned, this point is not unknown to Yugoslav authors.[1] It is implicitly considered in any comparison of relative profitability of investment projects, as used both by the former social investment funds and by the banks (comparison of results obtained before and expected after new investment). Thus, in the light of this criterion, the less well-equipped—hence normally less well-off—but efficient enterprise does not appear as a bad risk from the lender's point of view. The full use of this criterion of relative efficiency and security of investment by the present banking system is a condition for it to play the role it is expected to, i.e. to ensure a free flow of financial resources throughout the country, to be used to the best general advantage.

These and all other possible efficiency criteria (e.g. comparative unit cost of future output, export content, etc.) used by the loan allocating agency are of course meant to penalize lack of entrepreneurship and general inefficiency. Undoubtedly, as in any other country, there exist in Yugoslavia a number of key enterprises whose closure is out of the question in the public interest. The number of such enterprises may indeed be greater than elsewhere, particularly at the regional and local levels, in view of the wide economic responsibilities of the territorial self-government bodies (republics and communes in particular). If they perform poorly, however, such enterprises have no right to unlimited credit as is mostly the case elsewhere. The work collectivity will be the first to feel the consequences, by seeing its income dwindle, often in very

---

[1] Cf. for instance Dr M. Trklja, *op. cit.*, pp. 105–6, showing that a less technologically developed enterprise can offer a higher rate of interest for loans.

significant proportions. In most instances, this danger signal is sufficient to bring about such changes of policy as are required. The absence of such a reaction nearly always seems due to personal conflicts within the work collectivity. Increasingly, solutions seem to have been found by the workers' councils bringing in, from outside or within the enterprise, a new management team likely to restore the morale and the credit-worthiness of the enterprise. This may largely explain, along with other points made earlier (e.g. the readiness of many supplying enterprises not to press their claims to the point of imposing bankruptcy proceedings on their customers), why only a limited number of mostly small enterprises are ever actually placed under a receiver's management.

This measure, barring the most exceptional case of judicial wind-up, implies a special form of public credit to cover not only the current incomes of the workers, but also the launching of such new projects as would be likely to bring the enterprise back to normal levels of efficiency. The communal and republican solidarity funds provide the main source of such credit, financed through a special contribution paid by all enterprises out of their investment spending, presently at the rate of 4 per cent, as well as by voluntary contributions and, of course, the repayment of past loans. Any other interested party may also contribute directly and, according to Yugoslav legislation, the majority of creditors may decide to reduce their claims against the enterprise, a decision which, if approved in court, is binding on all others. In the light of the earlier discussion concerning the enterprise's 'capital' assets, this latter solution would seem to meet the creditors' interest in most cases. The communal and republican solidarity funds are in themselves of special interest, for they provide an example of the 'self-raising' type of funds, like the former social investment funds, where current contributions are added to the repayment of past advances so that the funds financial resources are bound to grow in a semi-geometrical manner (barring of course a general collapse of the monetary system).

Naturally, since it involves the disposal of considerable financial resources by various agencies which did not visibly contribute to their creation, the system of loan distribution, in its various shapes and forms, attracts considerably more attention from the public, the specialists and the enterprises, than does the practice of self-financing and amortization. The strongest criticism of the former social investment funds, whereby the greater part of investment loans was allocated through expert committees attached to public agencies at various levels of government, was however essentially of a political nature. It was seen to operate a transfer of investment resources between the various regions of the country while granting considerable say in their use to the federal planning authorities, as well as to the local communes which appeared, formally or informally, as the main initiators of new investment projects. The suppression of these funds was at the same time advocated by most economists, in the hope of introducing a fully free flow of capital, satisfying general criteria of economic efficiency.

The present banking system can hardly be said to have satisfied such hopes. No miraculous crystal ball was found by the banks to make them conform to schoolbook theorems, and they are certainly subject to no less public criticism than were the former social investment funds. Indeed, no single set of policy guidelines can be defined or applied in this area, in view of the fundamentally pluralistic nature of the worker-managed economy.

Significantly, both the former investment funds and the present banking system have met with considerably less criticism from those directly concerned, i.e. the enterprises and their managements, although their demand for credit was hardly ever satisfied more than to a limited extent. There are two sets of reasons for this on the whole positive attitude, as compared with that of the public media. First, being in touch with the concrete reality of life and work, the managements—including the worker-managers—are well aware that their development projects cannot all be implemented at once. The allocation of loans cannot thus proceed from any abstract criteria, political or economic, but involves a largely imponderable mixture of factors which cannot be defined once and for all in a single formula. A wide public, as well as internal (e.g. through the various economic associations) discussion can however bring to light the conditions of an equitable policy which would suit existing circumstances.

The second, more down to earth reason was that practically all enterprises had some loan-financed project in progress, and others 'in the pipeline'. The non-granting of loans was not seen as a blunt refusal, but rather as a deferment which made it possible to pursue technical elaboration and possibly to come back with better or even more ambitious solutions. The follow-up of investment projects, including particularly their loan components, would seem in most cases to constitute the major single preoccupation of the top management personnel, both professional and elected representatives, of the Yugoslav firm of some size.

Thus, for instance, a major reconstruction and modernization project of an enterprise which was already in a fairly advanced stage of preparation in 1957, was actually brought to the full implementation stage only ten years later, under a different management and on an incomparably greater scale. Yet it was a part of a single historical process of the enterprise's development, with scores of major changes in outlook and thousands of personal histories, through which a basically peasant worker population will have turned into one commanding one of the most technologically advanced works of the country. The history of the loan could provide a possible leading thread to a writer attempting to make a meaningful story out of the innumerable collective and individual destinies which make up this Yugoslav version of the once popular biographies of the early captains of industry. The twenty large volumes of the works council minutes, and the appended investment documentation and progress reports, could provide him with an uncommonly solid documentation.

The system of loans, investment or otherwise, undoubtedly represents an essential element of the worker-managed economy. Contrary to an opinion widely held in Yugoslavia, if all financial resources generated by an enterprise were left exclusively to the latter to enable it to finance its own development, the economy as a whole would certainly show much less adaptability to

267

changing circumstances and offer less scope for entrepreneurial initiative. In this respect, several Yugoslav economists and other writers seemed greatly impressed by comparative data published by the Economic Commission for Europe, according to which, in advanced industrial countries, self-financing represents by far the largest and, in the case of the us, a nearly exclusive, source of development financing. A possible solution to a state of affairs where no outside lending agency existed could no doubt be provided by a system of joint projects financed by several enterprises. This special lending practice has received considerable official encouragement. The corresponding transfers of funds accounted for somewhat less than 1 per cent of the overall income of the enterprises in recent years (in addition to the self-financed investment referred to earlier).

Geared however as it is to the expansion of the enterprise's operation, the lending of financial resources, accumulated out of current income by means other than traditional private savings, is an important, and often the only, means through which development projects of enterprises can actually materialize. The worker-managed economy offers only limited scope for private savings, just as the normal workers' family budget is largely based on equilibrium of income and expenditure. In the light of Yugoslav financial practice, such transitory private savings as may occur (e.g. as reserves for future purchases or unforeseen expenditures) should accordingly be used to finance private borrowings (consumer credit), so as to respect the overall relations between allocations to investment and consumption as determined by public policy and the self-governing enterprises.

In other words, the system makes it possible to guide such resources also towards the enterprises (or other original investors such as the communes) where the growth motivation is particularly strong, even though little or no development is possible on the basis of strict self-financing. It thus avoids inhibiting frustrations by opening the possibility of at least partial satisfactions of the various growth vectors of the model, and confers a strikingly entrepreneurial character to the entire economy and society. The lending system plays a similar, but less apparent—and not fully acknowledged—role with regard to the short-term financial efficiency of enterprises, in so far as it makes it possible for them, through current borrowing, to cope with short-term financial difficulties arising out of insufficient demand or other unforeseen causes, e.g. sudden dumping of a foreign product, error in rules governing foreign trade, etc.). Considerable, and often irretrievable damage to the economy, which would ensue if the formal accounting model of the enterprise was strictly applied, can thus be at least partly avoided. It thereby actually ensures the overall survival of the economy, since the less than minimum satisfaction in respect of the short-term vectors of our model (particularly an intolerably severe reduction of the workers' incomes) would have a totally disruptive impact on the enterprises concerned.

A major recent example, which could be extended to other sectors, is the post-1965 free import and low tariff policy applied to the iron and steel industry in a well-meant effort to combat the complacency of domestic producers and encourage them to modernize and expand. This drastic

268

measure, coupled with a general fall of foreign prices, proved however catastrophic for most domestic producers who, in addition to a steep decline in workers' incomes, were heading for considerable financial deficits. According to the formal model, and in the absence of current borrowing, the closure of a number of major steelworks would have been unavoidable in 1968. Yet they survived, and were able to increase production considerably (by well over 20 per cent in most major articles) as domestic demand picked up in 1969 and foreign prices happened to rise significantly as well. Although considered as a major objective by many economists, the closure of these steelworks, or enterprises in similar conditions, would have caused irreparable damage to the Yugoslav economy as a whole, which would be deprived of its major—and in the long term—cheaper source of supply.

*   *   *

Considered as a whole, the system of development financing as practised in the Yugoslav economy has attained a considerable level of sophistication. It has brought into being a number of quite specific institutions, the shape and form of which tended to change rapidly over the years, but which basically appear to constitute an essential part of the system. Only a very faint picture could be offered here of these various aspects of development financing such as self-financing, amortization, interest and loans, or of the behaviour of the enterprises in regard to the corresponding areas of policy. Yet, against the background of rapid policy changes, it would seem that this key area of public policy and enterprise operation is reaching a stage of greater relative stability, both as regards the type of active financial instruments and institutions (with the possible exception of interest on the Business Fund, which is likely to disappear), and with respect to the patterns of behaviour of the enterprises themselves. Such greater stability, which could be achieved within a framework of very rapid overall growth, is however conditional on a financial and monetary policy geared to attaining sufficient and rapidly growing effective demand, corresponding to the available productive capacities.

The technical problems which remain open are numerous and important, probably more so than in any other aspect of the Yugoslav system. Yet the fundamental message of the Yugoslav experience is extremely positive in this area. The worker-managed enterprises proved not only able but also eager to generate capital resources for their development and expansions, mostly at levels higher than planned and expected. They also showed an ability to cope with a relatively complex and unprecedented system of amortization of capital assets, of interest and of loans for investment and other purposes, which would seem a necessary part of any producers' economy, including a worker-managed one. Closer analysis seems to show that, as in the case of 'capital', the traditional concepts of 'amortization', 'interest', 'loan', or 'credit' acquire a fundamentally different meaning in a worker-managed economy, the definition of which has not yet been offered by economic theory. The worker-managers of Yugoslav firms, including their professional managements, have however shown a great ability to deal with the financial aspects of development on a largely pragmatic basis, and to create in the process their own norms of behaviour. This can by no means be seen as a proof that similar systems would necessarily prove feasible elsewhere. Indeed, a quite different, much more cautious and lengthy learning process would probably be required in most other social environments.

The Yugoslav experience would nevertheless seem to demonstrate that the complexity of the financial aspects of management is not—as is often argued—an insuperable obstacle to the practical operation of a worker-managed economy. In fact, it is the worker-management component which renders the corresponding economic exercise truly meaningful within a system based on public enterprise, or even in a large semi-public corporation, for it inserts real economic interest into what is otherwise nothing but an empty intellectual exercise of a State bureaucracy or the so-called managerial élite.

CHAPTER XII

Further Aspects of Enterprise Behaviour

There is increasingly widespread understanding in Yugoslavia—which amounts to a certainty for any articulate person involved in management practice within a Yugoslav firm—that the worker-managed enterprise exhibits a behaviour of its own, which is not comparable, homologous or otherwise, to that of a private capitalist enterprise, and which therefore requires both a distinct model in its own right and correspondingly adapted socio-economic planning and practical policies.

Any economy which aims at respecting human values, as the Yugoslav worker-managed system claims to do, must respect and hence reflect all the major dimensions of man's work and economic existence. Complex as it may appear at first sight, the understanding of the behaviour of the Yugoslav enterprise is nevertheless by no means beyond the grasp, as we have had occasion to demonstrate, of its own more articulate members, or of some of the local research institutes. Attempts at its more generalized theoretical expression are in fact increasingly encountered.

The multiple human interests included in the vectoral tentative model all point to one major dimension neglected in classical economic theory: that of TIME. A workers' enterprise—any producers' firm, co-operative or commune —is not located in the timeless one-dimensional universe of classical capitalism, but is deeply embedded in a time continuum where the past and, above all, the future are determining factors. Although this seems not yet to have penetrated the fossilized shell of formal economics, this time dimension is increasingly a part of modern enterprise theory generally, and has a specifically human time connotation for the worker-management system. At the same time, there is not the slightest doubt that the time-oriented behaviour of the Yugoslav firm, however complex, is not haphazard, whimsical or purely situational, but exhibits its own specific regularities pointing to the existence of its own 'economic laws', albeit correspondingly complex ones. Study of these 'laws' should certainly not be attempted along the lines of present-day formal Western economics, since this would necessarily require incomparably more complex tools of multi-dimensional dynamic and manifold analysis.

In this regard, the only firm conclusion is that just as the sum of the angles of a triangle would not equal two right angles in a non-Euclidian space (e.g. on the surface of a globe), so no 'factor-mix' or 'production function' can be deemed constant in a worker-managed economy. Hence any model based on such a faulty, simplistic assumption—excluding the very men who both determine and perform work, in their own personal time—omits an essential postulate of the system and must be deemed wrong.

271

The main object here is, however, to sum up such preliminary hypotheses as can be formulated regarding the Yugoslav firm's behaviour on the basis of its actual behaviour and performance in its various fields of activity. It is definitional, of course, that such actual performance is largely determined by the specific circumstances of Yugoslavia in the fifties and sixties of this century, and that generalization could only be based thereupon, at a much higher level of abstraction. Special warning is indeed due to English and American readers since the 'Yugoslav time' considered here is for all practical purposes the opposite of their own, the total absence of Max Weber's Protestant entrepreneurial background and ethics being but one major signpost to the understanding of the difference.

A. The Actual Economic Behaviour of the Firm

The main characteristics of the actual behaviour of the Yugoslav firm are discussed below under corresponding headings, beginning with a summary of findings from the previous two chapters.

(a) Capital, Interest, Investment and Growth

Perhaps the most striking finding of this study—greatly surprising even for the author—is that, contrary to prevalent opinion, the worker-managed enterprise does not accumulate and use true capital in the form in which it evolved in the system based on private capitalist enterprise. This appears to be a necessary consequence of the new status of labour, which ceases to appear as a commodity or factor of production, thereby ruling out, in the general case of a producers' economy, any 'marketing' of fixed assets or even financial capital independently of the workers concerned. The Yugoslav firm does indeed generate assets and funds (reserves, etc.), but does so in the light, and for the satisfaction, of the real needs of its workers or the wider social collectivity. Such assets or funds are thus inseparably linked to the latter. Nor have such assets any value distinct from their use value for the workers or the wider social collectivity concerned, a value which again is nothing but a reflection of the present or expected concrete yields to be generated by means of such assets. Even though their physical form is in most cases that of a modern enterprise, the status of the 'capital' assets is thus closer to their equivalent in the various forms of pre-capitalist production, particularly a free-peasant-co-operative economy where assets and labour form a single and inseparable whole. In modern terms, they could more adequately be likened to those of a corporation set in Galbraith's 'New Industrial Society'.

There is, therefore, justification for the contention of some Yugoslav authors that interest levied on such assets should not be used, as at present, as one of the system's major policy instruments and that the disappearance of such interest would represent a perfectly rational measure in full conformity with the real requirements of a system based on workers' management. This of course does not dispel the need for some other instrument of fiscal policy which would help the enterprises in assessing the relative advantage of any given level of capital intensity under which they operate or expect to operate their investment projects. In actual fact, it is the relatively low current cost of

272

capital assets as compared with heavily taxed 'labour' that would appear to be one of the major causes of the imbalances experienced by the Yugoslav economy.

The worker-managed enterprises of Yugoslavia have proved over the years their capacity to generate new assets at levels which are among the highest in modern history. This is particularly noteworthy since Yugoslav society is one where private capital accumulation for productive investment is least likely to occur—this indeed proved impossible in the past—as it goes against the most fundamental ethics and behaviour patterns of that society. Although such social accumulation of assets was assisted, and at times prompted, by various policy instruments, the worker-managed enterprises continued to accumulate and to invest at levels of their own choosing, even during periods when official policy was strongly opposed to and actively discouraging such investment prone behaviour.

The fact that accumulation and investment are not in terms of abstract invisible capital which could change shape and location practically overnight, but in terms of concrete projects (or indeed visible stock accumulation to finance employment, etc.) under the direction, and for the immediate benefit, of the real-life worker-investors, has no doubt been the main operative cause of their investment-prone behaviour. The local employment situation played a major part in promoting most such investments, particularly where the communes appeared as investors. Within existing enterprises the role of the forward-looking technician, unhampered by the bureaucratic controls of a multinational company or a government department and in direct contact with his workers' management constituency, was undoubtedly another major contributing factor.

The possibility—visible to all—of transforming the work and life environment in a relatively short period of time, and the knowledge that the results of any sacrifice accepted to this end were inalienably theirs were, of course, the basic premises of the behaviour of all concerned.

The enterprises alone could not, of course, be credited with all that has been achieved so far. Up to the mid-sixties, the Social Investment Funds were able to provide—and to re-locate—a sizeable proportion of the available investment funds, and the communes played a major part in initiating new investment projects and sponsoring major expansions of existing enterprises. The fact that, since 1965, the full burden of these responsibilities has been thrust on the existing enterprises (functioning as the sole major investors), while certainly enhancing the businesslike performance of this entrepreneurial function, would appear to lead to certain new imbalances, particularly regarding less developed regions or districts, where the existing enterprises may be too few and too weak (technologically, financially, etc.) to keep abreast of others.

The workers' management system has also had a major impact on the actual choice of development projects on many counts. One point of considerable interest—rarely fully appreciated as yet even by Yugoslav theorists—is that social or welfare investments are placed by and large on an equal footing with productive investment, at least where current earnings are sufficient to cover workers' basic cash requirements. Non-cash welfare services (e.g. housing, holiday facilities, transport, education or training, as well as all that is usually referred to as 'environmental control') may then be just as attractive as, or even more attractive than, the additional future cash income expected to result from productive investment.

As regards the latter, a vast survey would be required to assess the real trends of the Yugoslav firms' behaviour. It is clear, however, that this bears little or no relation to the assumed behaviour of a classical capitalist entrepreneur, for such investment is closely related to the existing location, and to the welfare and employment needs of the existing and potential working population. Only in exceptional cases, such as the confederal multi-plant firms or the exhaustion of locally available manpower or other resources, can a relatively greater mobility be assumed. Empirical evidence suggests, moreover, a widespread use of multiple criteria in project selection, the first being the existence of a secure market in a long-term perspective. Speculative or distinctly short-term profit considerations are likely to be disregarded, at least by productive enterprises and for productive ventures.

This does not apply, of course, where current short-term profit is the main object of the enterprise, as in the wholesale or foreign trade sectors, and where extremely rapid transfers of assets are a major feature of the firm's operation, but such cases cannot be assimilated to actual investment. Even these firms, however, tend to channel their actual surplus funds into more long-term growth-oriented investment (hotels, transport, etc.). Similar behaviour with regard to current profit has also been observed in some of the major agricultural combined enterprises, where rapid investment and disinvestment in particular fields of activity was one of the major functions of management (aimed for instance at counteracting the cyclical movement of meat prices, particularly pork). It should be noted, however, that in accordance with the premises of the system, such changes had no direct impact on levels of employment (when reducing the pig-farms to the basic herd and placing the meat on a foreign market, the enterprise could not simply sack its pig-farm personnel, whose maintained income thus had to enter its profit and cost analysis).

The main subsidiary criterion in general use is the comparative profitability of the funds invested, their rate of return or repayment, where the cost of labour is taken as fixed at the future planned or desired level. In no case has the *per capita* future income—as postulated *inter alia* by Professor Ward's model—been used as a criterion for investment project selection or for other similar decisions, e.g. on amalgamation of firms. On the whole, and despite many particular examples to the contrary, the existing Yugoslav firm has shown a distinct proneness to higher capital intensity than the situation—and particularly the availability, in most areas and at most levels of skill, of a considerable number of unemployed—would seem to warrant. The additional interest parameter of the worker-managed enterprise, the negative preference for heavy, dangerous or otherwise obnoxious work, to which the capitalist enterprise is formally indifferent, has no doubt played its part, as indeed has the increasingly heavy rate of taxation of labour in comparison with that of capital assets. While that negative preference corresponds to an important, positive aspect of the system, the proportionately heavier taxation on labour is a policy matter which, if suitably altered, could provide the necessary compensation to ensure a greater, and ultimately full use of the available work force. There also seems to exist among the Yugoslav economic and political leadership an absolute preference for the 'most modern and up-to-date' technology. This is both a residue of the early spirit of the Soviet Five Year Plans, and a reaction against the country's pre-war ruling ideology of preservation of the rural patriarchal order (seen then as both an objective necessity and a good in itself).

The investment-cum-technology motivation of the Yugoslav firm is basically tied to the existence of a strong and growing effective demand for any given commodity or service. Where such demand is artificially curtailed, both —but particularly technology—face exceptionally severe setbacks, for the workers' enterprise must in any event first preserve its own and its members' existence, and will therefore have to unload its costs in that order. This is the very opposite course to that usually assumed for a private capitalist enterprise.

In investing and expanding, the existing enterprises (as indeed other investors) not only have the choice between the existing or a modernized and presumably more money-capital intensive technology. They can also choose either to continue their existing production lines, or to enter a related or completely new field of activity. In fact, such choices are often indistinguishable in actual practice and are continuously being made by every enterprise. In recent years, particularly in the non-industrial sectors, Yugoslav firms have shown considerable ingenuity and initiative in this latter area, the leading firms in foreign trade, building and agriculture, as well as some of the technical research based enterprises, having some quite remarkable and unexpected 'branching out' achievements to their credit. There is no lack either of individual examples in industry proper (including mining). Clearly, in a rapidly growing and modernizing economy, scores of new needs are constantly coming to light or undergoing changes of unforeseen magnitude (private transport, tourism, etc.). It is thus of incomparably greater advantage for a firm to fill such gaps rapidly than to presume linear expansion of its existing business. Here economic calculus is of course not enough. It is the admission of a wide circle of qualified members to the intra-enterprise discussions and decision-making process (as compared with the traditional paternalistic firm or a bureaucratic company, private or public) that may very well constitute a decisive factor in this comparatively greater versatility of many Yugoslav enterprises. The direct interest/reward relationship it postulates is of course a constituent part of such motivation. Where this is weak or absent, and there is no lack of examples, the Yugoslav firm may, on the contrary, show a very poor performance indeed, for it is deprived of the central guidance and control given by top-level State or Company planners and specialists. Contrary to the technological aspect of investment, such versatility is less likely to suffer from, and may indeed be enhanced by, deflationary pressure and other curbs on effective demand. A drastic withdrawal of money and credit is also likely to frustrate initiative in this area.

To sum up: in a strongly growth-motivated working population, such as that of post-war Yugoslavia, the worker-managed enterprise has proved able to attain very high and sustained levels of investment, including technological progress, the determining economic factor being the existence of corresponding rapid growth of effective and partly unsatisfied demand. When faced with insufficient demand, the enterprises tend to protect their own economic existence, and that of their members, by switching their funds to finance current production and the accumulating stocks thereof. Where necessary they even temporarily forego part of current cash reward for work done, and continue to operate in some nascent form of non-monetary economy.

(b) *Labour, Work, Employment and Skill*

That 'labour is not a commodity', not a factor of production, is, of course, at a very general level, a basic postulate of any man-oriented economic system such as Yugoslav workers' management. However, the review of various 'models' in Chapters VI to IX showed that labour may be considered as a factor of production with a role akin to that which it plays under capitalism— a view which some theorists did indeed hold—or at least as a semi-commodity.

This was not entirely unwarranted during the early years of the system. Indeed, the first striking—and least partly unexpected—impact of worker-management on the Yugoslav economy was the massive release in the years 1952–4 of excess manpower, which the enterprises had had to carry on their pay-roll under the centrally planned manpower policy. This was due not so much to the emancipation of the workers themselves, as to the enterprise's management being the first to become fully alive to their liberation from the central administrative planning controls.

It was only in the later fifties that, with their emancipation from wage-earner status, workers really came to be considered as full members of the enterprise, and that growing stress was laid on their tenure and right to their jobs as individuals. Gradual extension of the legal notice periods and severance payments, further reinforced by additional guarantees inserted into the enterprises' own by-laws, whittled away the possibility of short-term lay-offs and turned even permanent dismissal into a most cumbersome process. Nevertheless, right up to the mid-sixties, enterprises were supposed to, and at times did, lay off their members when warranted by long-term economic considerations. As a rule, however, where staff restrictions were agreed to, a temporary 'no-hire' policy provided adequate compliance.

Up to 1965 the rate of overall increase in levels of employment was sufficient to provide work for all new entrants to the labour force, and for a portion of the underemployed rural population. No severe hardship was therefore entailed for those forced to leave their enterprise, as provision of alternative employment was comparatively easy, and was increasingly seen to by the enterprise itself.

During all this period the worker-managed enterprises performed on the whole extremely well, and certainly beyond all planned targets with respect to provision and expansion of employment. They showed none of the restrictive tendencies usually ascribed to producers' co-operatives. If anything, their performance inhibited the efforts made at various times to set up a fully-fledged national employment service. The striving for greater employment density in the modern sector (in other words, greater income per head of the population, as opposed to greater income per worker) was no doubt the main operative cause in most areas, providing additional motivation for extensive investment and growth.

The post-1965 policy aimed at operating a radical departure from such extensive development by means of severe credit restrictions, increased cost of labour (by way of higher taxation), etc. The enterprises were on the whole expected to react, as in the 1952–4 period, by releasing all surplus manpower and intensifying production. Their actual reaction turned out to be quite different, however. While the credit and demand squeeze arrested employment expansion, and indeed practically all intake of new workers, no significant release of workers ensued. Practically all enterprises of any standing strongly resisted the corresponding pressures, and their workers' councils formally inserted a no-retrenchment rule in their by-laws. The impossibility of restricting employment for economic reasons—barring, of course, a case of complete insolvency when a firm is placed under a receiver's management—must now be taken as one of the fundamental features of the Yugoslav system, and a point to be reckoned with when constructing any economic 'model' aimed at delineating or revealing its patterns of behaviour. This important restriction is a result solely of the workers' own will: to attempt to circumvent it would be to make a sham of their self-management.

As for the formal characteristics of the 'Yugoslav labour market', it is abundantly clear that there is not—indeed there cannot be—any such market. No enterprise is in a position to offer any set wage; hence no such wage can be assumed in the economy as a whole. No individual can ask any set price for his work, or attach any set value to his occupation, skill, etc. Therefore any economic model based on the presumed existence of such a wage is in direct contradiction with the basic tenets of workers' management as operating in Yugoslavia.

What the Yugoslav firm offers in lieu of wages is a (known) part of, or share in, its future (hence unknown) income, as well as many other known and unknown benefits in terms of career prospects and employment security, training, welfare services, etc. It does not offer all this on an abstract labour market, but to a very real, normally local, population seeking employment, and it does so in terms of its actual material need to have certain work done, a job performed. The population to whom the offer is made and in particular each individual directly concerned will similarly consider it not in terms of an abstract yardstick (e.g. so much an hour) since none exists, but in terms of their own conditions and preferences. Equal levels of satisfaction may be attained at quite different rates of income or actual cash earnings and vice versa. Moreover, since the cash and, to an even greater extent, the non-cash benefits (e.g. promotion, training, housing) are largely linked to seniority, extreme differentials may be required to make an offer at all appealing to persons already in employment. In any case, recruitment—other than that of top specialists—by enticing away the workforce of other firms, is widely regarded as unethical. In one rare case where a firm's personnel department was doing this and the fact came to public notice, the workers' councils concerned investigated the matter in joint session and unanimously condemned and prohibited such practice.

The 'tangible' nature of the employment relationship, i.e. the worker's membership of the firm, of necessity results in practice in low mobility of the employed active population. When, as in recent years, practically no alternative employment is available, a stage of quasi-immobility is reached. This is often seen as a negative feature of the Yugoslav experience, particularly by economists accustomed to the idea of operating mass transfers of labour in accordance with abstract schemes. It does indeed result in a relative insulation of the Yugoslav firm (as compared with mass transfers of hands and brains elsewhere), although there is compensation in the individual's greater sense of security, and closer adaptation to his socio-cultural environment. In reality in Yugoslavia the newcomers to the labour force and the older persons in search of employment (who are by definition fairly mobile) seem sufficiently numerous in all occupations and levels of skill to meet requirements for many years to come. Nor is it implausible that, in a situation nearer to full employment, greater mobility would result from voluntary departures from the sub-marginal enterprises, these being at present inhibited by lack of more attractive alternative offers of employment.

Despite Yugoslav firms' notable employment proneness up to 1965, to which they might partly revert given rearranged fiscal-financial stimuli, it would seem excessive to expect them to bring about unaided a fully satisfactory level of employment, and in particular to integrate the mass of highly qualified workers being produced by a widely accessible training and education system up to and including university level. While the need for an active employment policy at all levels hardly needs stressing as a necessary outside complement to the system, an ingenious proposal by an early Austrian writer —recalled by Professor Ward—suggesting that in a worker-manager economy all unemployed could and should be given the right to join a firm of their own choosing, could provide a systematic solution of a basic difficulty. The proposal, while Utopian on the face of it, does not seem impracticable. It would solve the basic problem of the denial of the right and access to work facing employment-seekers. At first it could be limited to certain levels of qualification. It assumes that such unemployed would tend to choose the more successful firms, with higher earning prospects and also greater ability to provide them with productive employment. A limit on the numbers to be so engaged could be set according to a scale taking into account the firm's absolute size and relative profitability or level of income. (A scheme of this kind, so far limited to the highly trained newcomers to the work force, is already in operation.) In the Yugoslav situation such a scheme would present the advantage of obviating the need for a personal incomes ceiling in some sectors, as funds would have to be shared with new entrants, and provision made for their employment. It would also apply a brake to excessive capital-intensive investment by many of the 'richer' enterprises.

The actual work done in a Yugoslav firm has even less in common with abstract labour or employment as envisaged in economic manuals. No one in

278

his senses would expect either that the worker-managers would impose maximum output standards, as in an early capitalist mill or mine, or that output would be systematically kept to a minimum through worker or union solidarity. Both situations may, in particular cases or at certain times, occur in practice, as may any intermediary levels of output, but the deciding factor in every case will not be an outside agent, but the workers' own degree of interest in getting the work done. As in any producers' workshop or farm, a working hour or day may thus correspond to a varying volume of output or effective performance. Being themselves the performers, the worker-managers will tend to press their physical effort beyond reasonable measure, or insist on a steadily increasing pace, only in exceptional conditions. On the contrary the emphasis will normally be on work-saving investment, and training for higher skills.

The necessarily uneven physical performance of various enterprises makes it difficult to assess the real causes of unequal earnings and other benefits (ascribed by some mostly to monopoly conditions), for they may be partly due to conscious or unconscious choices by the work collectivities concerned regarding work intensity. The same indeed applies to discipline at work, which may similarly vary from enterprise to enterprise as well as in time. Again, a relative leniency in this respect, a reluctance to impose and a readiness to remit severe penalties, seems a widespread characteristic of Yugoslav firms. A price must no doubt be paid in economic terms, but there may be invisible returns in terms of the human climate within the enterprise. Similarly, many enterprises are known to carry on their pay-rolls considerable numbers of workers who are partially or totally unable to cope with the work by reason of ill-health, age, family responsibilities or lack of skill, and who under a narrowly 'rational' or profit-motivated management would receive short shrift.

It is characteristic that physical performance is not exalted or specially rewarded morally or materially (except in the the usual form of remuneration per unit of output). Limited publicity given to the more successful workshops or teams concentrates rather on their business performance based on skill, new production methods, organizational changes, etc. While the term 'emulation' is as good as extinct, a measure of inter-firm or inter-regional rivalry on these lines (as distinct from purely market competition) often seems to have acted as a stimulus to better performance.

In the area of training and skill, significant results are undeniable. In a country where thirty years ago there were, for all practical purposes (and outside the railway system), no industrial, managerial or scientific skills available, the deployment of over three million workers in a modern sector of the economy, under the sole responsibility of nationals, is in itself no mean achievement. While, typically enough, this development is mostly attributed to capital accumulation and investment, the contribution of training and skills promotion must obviously have been of substantial importance. In any case, it is of particular importance here as, in the absence of a systematic national policy (as distinct from general education at all levels, which was one of the keystones of national policy throughout the post-war period), it was the

279

worker-managed enterprises which bore the brunt of the responsibility in this field. They provided their own training, set up training schools and systems, awarded diplomas, financed technical and University studies, developed their own up-grading programmes and, generally speaking, prepared their own members for jobs to be done. In most firms the necessary funds were readily forthcoming for this most profitable form of investment. Wherever possible, training abroad was included, together with other special forms of collective and individual skill promotion. In times of recession, etc., training schemes may provide a constructive outlet for an enterprise's surplus work force, e.g. accelerated training programme for workers temporarily not required in production, special study programme for a former director replaced by one better qualified, etc.

No other form of enterprise could provide such a fully comprehensive and efficient framework for improving skills and putting them to practical use. Of course only in worker-managed enterprises is there basic identity between those who require skills for production, those who finance their acquisition, and those who benefit from such training and can repay its worth as members of the same work collectivity. The decision makers who assess needs, plan, carry out and supervise in the training field, and disseminate the acquired skill, share also this same basic identity of purpose. In many areas of applied technology, such as telecommunications, civil engineering, building, shipbuilding or agriculture, the results achieved, mostly *ex nihilo*, by the former worker-trainees are quite astounding. The relative surplus of higher skills in most sectors at present is partly the result of this success, but is also due to a severe and unexpected demand deficiency. Should the earlier rates of overall growth be achieved again—as seems likely—enterprise planned training will surely remain a most positive feature of the Yugoslav experience.

A major finding regarding the labour-employment-work-skill complex of the Yugoslav firm is that, contrary to the common understanding of economists, it is a subject of long-term policies and planning by the enterprise, in a situation where short-term arbitrary interferences are either prohibited by the system (e.g. lay-offs and dismissals) or would obviously prove grossly damaging if resorted to. Despite a mass of individual grievances, appalling as these may be in some instances, it appears that in ordinary situations the Yugoslav workers are treated as men and not as a commodity and that, particularly in the younger generation, they are truly beginning to emancipate themselves, psychologically as well as materially, from the condition of hired labour and the subjections attaching thereto.

(c) *Current Business Management, Production and Marketing*
As questions of assets or investment policy and the labour-employment-skill component are essentially of a long-term nature, the Yugoslav firm would appear both in theory and in practice to be predominantly preoccupied with the future. Long-term preparations for themselves and for their wider social environment engage the attention of the main management bodies and principal managers to a very considerable extent, while short-term considerations, however important, take second place.

This section first touches on the question of prices—their determination by the enterprise and its reaction to outside price fluctuations—and then turns to some of the short-term aspects of the worker-managed enterprise, in particular its costs, including the cost of workers' remuneration.

The actual ex-factory prices administered by Yugoslav firms show a quite remarkable stability over the years, this in conditions of rapidly increasing retail prices, cost of living and, above all, cash earnings of the workers. If the 1965 price adjustment (essentially administrative in origin) is disregarded, the producers' price index shows almost complete stability throughout the worker-managed period. Empirical evidence tends to confirm that for most enterprises their own prices are a long-term, planned parameter, not subject to change barring exceptional developments. Current adjustments are automatically made as required through the enterprise cost structure.

The fact remains, however, that Yugoslav enterprises have to calculate, fix and occasionally change their prices both at a general level and for particular products. On the evidence available, none of the formal price formulae (e.g. as referred to in Table VIII) are applied, or even known or conceived of. The enterprise policymakers see themselves as fixing their own prices on the basis of cost plus their customary margin (which may of course vary in time and between products). This price is then tested against the market and, if it appears acceptable, is set at that level. The ideal situation obtains, of course, where the market appears able to accept a price higher than the enterprise's own level, as this holds promise of easy marketing for a long time ahead. If the market information is less favourable, other products may be tried out but, should no alternative exist, the enterprise has practically infinite possibilities of reducing the calculated price levels in view of the absence of a definite cost structure (see below). Similarly, should the market show a trend of increasing demand and prices, the enterprise will as a rule prefer to expand production, since it has a practically infinite possibility of doing so, and thereby to increase notably its workers' incomes while strengthening their job security. On the contrary, if demand and prices tend to decline, alternative products will be sought, while in the short term considerable price concessions may be made to maintain normal levels of output.

As a rule, however, prices have shown a tendency to decline in the expanding sectors and to rise where demand is slack, both phenomena being in our view closely related to the specific cost structure of the worker-managed firm.

The firm's costs of production, undoubtedly the commanding factor of price determination, call for closer examination. Obviously prices at any given level (throughout an industry, for one particular product, etc.) will tend towards the average cost-plus-margin of the producers concerned. Worker-management gives rise to several notable peculiarities, however.

On the one hand, such costs will contain all the planned or desired elements of expenditure (workers' earnings, investment, training, comfort, welfare, as listed in the vectoral model (Table IX)). In other words, if a firm decides to double workers' cash incomes, or its rate of investment, provide study grants for half its personnel, or three years paid maternity leave, install a bath per

281

room in its holiday or apprentice hostels, etc., such a cost will, of necessity, be part of the particular industry's price structure. Wherever such a planned or desired cost structure appears unacceptable to the market, the average enterprise will have to renounce on some or all such elements, eliminating them in an order and a manner corresponding to its relative preferences as suggested in Chapter IX. This means that, side by side in the same industry, firms may and do exist which charge identical prices for the same products, while at the same time their cost structures differ considerably. Differences in cash earnings, rates of investment, welfare, etc. may not uncommonly reach 100 or 200 per cent levels, partly compensating each other, in firms of apparently comparable standing without striking difference in their apparent prosperity, viability or future prospects. The concept of the 'marginal firm' is thus, in the absence of a set cost structure, considerably blurred or even inapplicable in the Yugoslav economy.

Moreover, the growing tendency to relieve the sub-average firms of their fiscal and other obligations, amortization, etc., is very significantly extending the limits within which the enterprise may continue to operate and fight for survival. Such apparent privilege is indeed preferable to the complete disappearance of such firms, even though they cause additional downward pressure on prices in the sectors concerned. The lack of amortization and investment in such sectors should assist towards a gradual return to more realistic price levels, at the same time leaving room for additional expansion in sectors where 'better-off' firms predominate.

Price levels and price behaviour are, as a result, not as expected in traditional economics. The patterns of price behaviour are rather cyclical, cybernetic, or as a Yugoslav author puts it, 'gravitational'. A steady growth of effective demand is on the whole likely, as in the case of peasant production, to bring about a falling trend of overall price levels, while a deficiency of demand would normally result in disordered behaviour of most enterprises. Price reductions may prevail in the short term, but price increases are likely to follow.

The relevance of prices, and their impact on the short-term behaviour of the worker-managed enterprise, is thus only limited. There are, however, two closely related areas wherein the enterprise can adapt to short-term changes swiftly and efficiently: these are actual production (volume, quality, assortment, etc.) and production costs.

As regards production, the Yugoslav firm, as compared to others, has ample leverage to vary the volume of output and to change the type of product at short notice as required. Not being bound to any norm of per capita productivity, it does not have to engage in short-term hiring and firing, with all the institutional obstacles that this implies. Nor is there any 'built-in' difficulty of convincing its members to reduce output of a possibly worthless commodity (with a negative impact on their actual earnings), or to step up production to meet market requirements (and to collect the corresponding rewards). The enterprise can thus cope with seasonal, cyclical, fashion-based or other major demand changes without any apparent change in capital or labour costs. (Hence no definite 'production function' can be assumed.) Overtime or

282

additional shift work can be used to deal with changes of quite considerable magnitude within the limit of existing capacities. Similarly, alternative products (different quality, etc.) can mostly be introduced extremely quickly, as the worker-producers are not likely to insist on continuing worthless lines. Anyone familiar with industrial *mores* will easily grasp the value of, and the rewards attaching to, such versatility, both from the firm's and the workers' point of view. Practically all Yugoslav enterprises officially report considerable unused capacity (and most have even greater potential reserves) which may provide a further explanation of the long-term trend of falling prices in the face of growing demand.

It should also be borne in mind that the Yugoslav firm's work collectivity can at any time radically transform the internal climate of the enterprise, the attitude to work, to discipline, the methods and structure of management, etc. New regulations can be adopted and enforced, new emergency services set up and managers replaced in a matter of hours.

The costs referred to earlier were merely those attaching to the enterprise's own planned or desired expenditures. The enterprise's control extends to other categories of cost too, primarily those of production materials, but also such items as publicity and other outside services, business travel and various incidentals. With internal decentralization of enterprise management and costing, it is possible in most enterprises to plan and to follow up such costs at the level of the work group or shop, and to make their members participate in the result of their cost management. A considerable amount of technical study and publicity is devoted to this aspect of the system, and its potential value is largely recognized in most enterprises. So far, however, major breakthroughs have been rare and the enterprises' performance in this area does not come up to that in current production management. It is impossible to analyse here in detail the causes of the relative failure of the work groups, particularly in the field of cost reduction, as these are probably more socio-logical than economic in origin. This should be kept in mind nonetheless as an area where the Yugoslav firm has all the institutional prerequisites for a radical transformation of its business performance, and may indeed begin to show its potentialities in the fairly near future, political and economic circumstances permitting.

All in all, the current business performance of the Yugoslav firm may be deemed satisfactory. Responding to its own rules and standards, it is simply not comparable with a private capitalist firm. Despite considerable differences it bears more resemblance to an enterprise in a planned but decentralized economy. A measure of global planning would indeed be likely to enhance significantly its short-term performance.

(d) Remuneration for Work and Overall Distribution of Personal Incomes
No other aspect of the worker-managed enterprise is more complex or of greater importance than the actual remuneration for work and the overall income distribution process. It is a topic on which scores of volumes have been written in Yugoslavia and scores more would be needed for a full under-standing.

When one gets down to the specific case of an individual firm, however, all becomes perfectly clear, as simple as the earnings and income distribution of any individual producer or practitioner (such as a farmer, a cobbler or a doctor). The construction of a valid theory on incomes applicable to all firms would present as much difficulty as valid generalizations for all individuals, and has simply not been attempted.

The Yugoslav firms are undoubtedly heterogeneous, ranging from a basket-making workshop or a barber's shop in a remote mountain village, to communications networks or building companies operating on four continents. Some general statements can be hazarded regarding both the income rates in Yugoslav firms, since these must be formally established in advance and duly publicized; and also the actual earnings of the workers, since these, unlike the earnings of cobblers, farmers or doctors in other systems, are regularly reported. Clearly, however, general statements based on statistical averages cannot be taken as reflecting concrete reality.

Intra-enterprise and intra-industry differentials in rates of income appear on the whole significantly reduced under the impact of workers' management. The job/qualification based differential within an average firm is generally situated at the 1:3 level, but significantly wider differentials, particularly at the top, are known to exist in individual firms and in the more remote areas. While there is definite pressure towards greater equality from most workers, there are not many instances of firms losing—or failing to attract—highly qualified staff by offering insufficient rewards. At the same time, there are still plenty of worker-manager-founders of enterprises of the old school who make a point of keeping their cash income down close to that of the other workers. Financial and technical management posts usually carry the highest rate of income. As regards inter-industry differentials, referred to in Table X, it should merely be pointed out that while they reflect the relative average profitability of each industry, they have no direct impact as stimuli for the transfer of manpower. The income—be it average, minimum or whatever— paid to and earned by workers is not 'on offer' to others, as would be assumed under classical theory.

A much greater differentiation in real incomes is known to exist *between* individual firms within the economy. Inter-firm differentials, of the order of up to 1:7 in extreme cases, are indeed a major source of criticism and tensions, even though they are by no means representative of the mass of 'normal' firms in ordinary conditions. These extreme differences are often ascribed by Yugoslav writers to so-called monopolistic practices or conditions. This explanation does not seem generally valid, however, as this differentiation is basically an inter-firm or intra-industry phenomenon and must therefore be largely due to the actual performance of the firms concerned and not to the monopolistic or oligopolistic character of any given firm or industry. Indeed, there appears to be no truly significant relation between the number of firms in an industry and levels of actual incomes or workers' earnings. The income differentials could, in so far as they appear excessive, be held in check by properly devised progressive taxation of incomes or other fiscal measures—a solution which was deemed contrary to the spirit of the 1961 and 1965

Reforms, but towards which recent developments seem strongly to tend.

A perhaps more fruitful but often neglected area of interest is the impact of the system on the overall distribution of incomes throughout the nation. Obviously, the income sharing process is poles apart from the absolute uniformity and formal identity of earnings within a single unified system of wages and salaries, which characterizes a traditional centrally planned economy, and which to many minds still represents the very essence of socialism. To return to such a system would clearly spell the end of workers' management. On the other hand, the Yugoslav form of remuneration eliminates all possibility of such extreme differentiation of income as prevails under private enterprise, since income formed in any one productive unit must be shared out among all those who participated in its creation, according to a scale agreed in common and in advance. In other words, no incomes can be paid out which have not been agreed upon by the work collectivity or are unacceptable to the wider social community. The income levels achieved in an enterprise basically reflect the real performance of its workers as valued by the consumers, i.e. other individual members of the working population or other workers' enterprises, and are open to their scrutiny. (Nevertheless, in Yugoslav reality several factors unrelated to workers' management disturb the normal flow of incomes. These include foreign trade, the existence of foreign firms' agents and agencies, and the private trade and craft sector, which are the source of unearned or at least incommensurable incomes in particular instances.)

The differentiation that obtains thus corresponds to another form of equality, more fundamental perhaps than any formal nation-wide uniformity of wage-rates and scales, for it takes into account factors such as local productivity (in the firm concerned, in the region, etc.) and local cost of living, as well as other objective and subjective factors making up the true value of a real work performance.

One consequence of the inter-firm income differentiation which is sociologically important and indeed unique is the coincidence at the same income level of a very weird mixture of working population. In other words, it is no longer an immutable fact of life that a labourer or a woman attendant must earn less than a trained craftsman or manager elsewhere, and vice versa. An equally interesting consequence of the inter-regional and intra-regional income differences is that the peculiar spread of incomes results in effective demand being no longer concentrated in certain categories of the working population, in certain regions, or industries, but becoming open to all. Most unusual patterns of consumer behaviour obviously result.

The existing income distribution system has certainly contributed to the productivity/profitability consciousness of most Yugoslav firms, and provides the central motive force of the entire system of workers' management. In its present form it is, however, beset with technical difficulties which, unless attended to, may become, along with the access to work of the unemployed, a major stumbling block to future development. It contains nonetheless a number of techniques and experiences of great value which would merit close consideration by all those interested in a genuine transformation of the status

285

and condition of hired labour and, indeed, in economic and social development generally in societies where private entrepreneurial motivation is absent or insufficient, or has ceased to be operative or socially acceptable.

B. Other Relevant Aspects of the Economic Behaviour of the Worker-managed Enterprise

The main elements usually covered in formal economics have been dealt with briefly in the previous four sections. The Yugoslav firm has, of course, a number of other dimensions and requirements of basic importance for the operation of the system. These will now be listed briefly.

The *entry and exit* of firms, their division and amalgamation, co-operation and integration is one such dimension. If any existing population of firms were supposed stable in time, the system would clearly be deprived of much of its dynamic quality. Clearly, the rapid rates of growth attained by Yugoslavia were due to a significant extent at least until the 1965 Reform, to the entry of new firms, mostly on the initiative of factors other than the existing enterprises, i.e. communes, social investment funds, etc. Similarly, considerable benefit may accrue to the national economy from arrangements between firms to co-operate or amalgamate, as also from the disappearance of those firms which have exhausted their economic objective. Yet each existing firm of any size forms to a great extent a universe of its own, its own 'gravitational field', an intricate manifold of its interest spectrum, which cannot normally be opened or broken into by outside pressure of purely economic forces. Although the calculus based on considerations of social benefit has never been absent from the minds of the decision makers of the worker-managed firms in Yugoslavia, and co-operative arrangements of all kinds are thus accepted more readily than might be the case if they were governed by purely economic considerations, they certainly are inhibited by the very system—as compared for instance with the capitalist entrepreneur roving freely over the five continents as opportunity calls—and they would seem in most cases to remain loath to expand, as initiators of projects or otherwise, outside their own geographical area. The various local and regional authorities have so far proved able to perform this entrepreneurial function within their own sphere, but the absence in recent years of corresponding industrial and, above all, national co-ordinating and initiating centres, which would help in opening the more restricted spheres of enterprise interest, may be seen as a grave lacuna of the system in its present form.

Reference has already been made, on the other hand, to the largely positive performance of enterprises in making use of the system's possibilities of *internal decentralization* of management, costing and income distribution. While, institutionally, the build-up of such 'federal' structures is well advanced within most enterprises, and many management functions are increasingly performed on such a basis, the tremendous economic potential of the decentralized worker-managed firm remains largely untapped. It forms a major reserve for future advances, which could indeed attain truly revolutionary magnitude if the so far concealed social forces of the autonomous work units were fully released.

To the dismay of many foreign observers, and indeed many Yugoslav critics, workers' management has by no means abased or destroyed the firms' technical or general management. It actually had very much to offer to the latter to compensate for the newly introduced workers' control, since it released the managers' technical, business and administrative initiative from the often formal, uninspired or ignorant controls based on outside ownership, whether private, public or institutional. It thrust on them a tremendous new responsibility derived from such independence, which for many of them was more difficult to bear than the impact of the change introduced by the workers' councils.

In fact where little or no management skills were available two decades ago, Yugoslav firms have formed their own management personnel which, all things considered, can stand up to their counterparts anywhere. Though their relationship with the workers' management bodies is not always unambiguous, they remain subject to a continuous training in 'human relations', not with some abstractly conceived 'labour force' but with the flesh-and-blood workers of their particular firm with their own very definite social, historical and economic dimensions. That the great majority of managers (as distinct from some management theorists) have fully accepted the principle of workers' control and decision making is beyond doubt.

The institutional set-up of the worker-managed enterprise leaves open the question of the personal *responsibility* of the 'one single manager' endowed with all powers—a question which seems to worry many foreign and domestic management theorists. While undoubtedly a firm may effectively function even under a more diluted form of collective responsibility (as, for instance, under the West German Company Law), it is a fact that the full responsibility in the Yugoslav firm is borne by the work collectivity as a whole, through their current and future incomes, and that the attribution of direct personal responsibility may often be difficult or impossible if attempted by an outside observer. It should not be forgotten, however, that in most cases the workers and their representatives and managers live, work and meet under the same roof. Even if written records do not always tell the full story, those responsible for any area of operation or decision making are well known to most people within the enterprise—certainly much better known to them than to some distant ministerial or company controllers, shareholders' assembly, absentee owners or landlords. The possibility of basing a manager's contract on the firm's planned minimum performance constitutes an interesting attempt by some of the workers' councils to pin down the concrete responsibilities of their managements.

The *initiative and entrepreneurship* shown by most Yugoslav firms in matters pertaining to business management is an obvious if surprising fact. The measure of creative initiative in management model building and everyday practice which may be encountered when visiting enterprises or studying their reports would seem quite unparalleled elsewhere. It is, however, easy to understand if due account is taken of the almost complete autonomy of the Yugoslav firm from any outside model setter or decision maker. This situation offers the wider possibilities for internally agreed changes and experiments.

One question remains unresolved, however, in the specific area of *technical progress*, and particularly that of more costly research and major original inventions. Most Yugoslav firms opted to make full use of foreign technology, securing patents, licences, or the co-operation of foreign firms, in preference to accepting the risks, uncertainties and costs of original research. Given its worker-employment-training orientation, the Yugoslav firm is certainly not the most propitious ground for a costly research team, or the placement of an individual inventor's patents, the cost of which might require the saving of scores of hundreds of individual workers' incomes. (A choice to which a private firm would be largely indifferent, while the opposite would actually be favoured by central planning.) The worker-managed economy would also require special technology and research-oriented support at levels above that of the enterprise.

Lastly we should at least touch upon the fact that the existence of workers' management in the economy has proved over the years to be incompatible with a massive *State sector*, which continued to cover in the usual way all activities not organized in the form of enterprises, and areas where receipts from 'sales' of goods or services could not be expected to cover expenditure, e.g. education, health, social security, general administration, inspection services, judiciary, etc. The bodies carrying on these activites were gradually transformed into autonomous 'work organizations'. These are akin to self-management enterprises, but have specific status and rules. Their budgetary receipts (added to receipts from 'sales', if any) are deemed to be in payment for the planned service performance agreed upon with each such organization. They are endowed with wide autonomy in respect of internal management and income allocation, and have power to expand or alter their activity in response to outside demand, subject of course to the minimum performance imposed by law.

Semi-entrepreneurial school, hospital and other systems thus exist in Yugoslavia alongside the economic enterprises in the strict sense. Their actual performance, although meeting with serious difficulties, has certainly not produced such catastrophic results as were forecast by many gloomy protagonists of bureaucratic efficiency. They certainly encouraged the entrepreneurial spirit of the worker-managed sectors, for instance by enlarging the area of competitive demand, and breaking down former monopsonic relationships with State agencies. They also opened the way to a more rational cost/benefit calculus in the wide sector of public service and welfare usually veiled by the impenetrable screen of bureaucratic methods of administration and financing. Interestingly, although imposed on a sector with a long bureaucratic tradition—unparalleled in the economy proper except for the railways—this reform met with less than the expected amount of grumbling and opposition among the employees concerned. The appeal of greater decision making, and indeed work and existential-autonomy, seemed to compensate in large measure for the loss of the high status and income guarantee for life attaching to public service. In view of its recent origin, however, this part of the Yugoslav experience is not yet ripe for a performance assessment.

Little need be said at this stage of the requirements of the Yugoslav firm in terms of *financial and fiscal policy*: they have been kept in mind throughout this volume, but their full exposition would require a separate study. It is clear, however, that the system based on workers' management requires its own methods of management of public finance, of taxation, and of economic and social planning. Empirical evidence so far available tends to show that its macro-behaviour is closer to that of a producers' economy (as epitomized for instance by the characteristic cycles of agricultural production) and that financial or fiscal measures derived from capitalist economics are ill-adapted to its requirements. The maintenance of steadily growing effective demand at fixed or slowly declining price levels, progressive taxation of high incomes and tax reduction or subsidy in cases of temporary set-backs would seem to provide the main guide-lines for the establishment of a policy conducive to high rates of growth. Several specific areas have moreover been singled out where a measure of global planning, or specific planned assistance, would seem to be required: prospective plans for major sectors such as energy, agriculture, transport, building, etc.; a national employment policy and corresponding training and guidance services to insert all available skills into the productive process; opening prospects for fruitful co-operation among firms; and assistance in the advancement of domestic research and technological progress where costs involved cannot be borne by individual firms.

Indeed, the real needs in all areas, including both private and collective consumption, are so immense in Yugoslavia—as indeed anywhere else—that a measure of overall global planning would seem indispensable. The present-day Yugoslav planner has, however, an inestimable advantage, so far clearly perceived only in some enterprises. He faces practically unlimited needs, readily transformable into rapidly growing effective demand sufficient to ensure, through implementation of corresponding projects, full employment of the entire working population in harmony with existing capacities and resources. The untying of this Gordian knot of the Yugoslav economy is not only a question of techniques of economic calculus, which are making rapid strides there, but above all of integrating the voice and will of the enterprises into the making of those major policy and planning choices which must be made at higher levels—industrial, regional and, above all, national. They have proved able to make such choices at their own level, efficiently but on the basis of their own criteria unsuspected by any planner or economist. They could also insert into decisions at higher level their own man-oriented criteria for weighing costs and benefits, which may appear even more surprising to formal economists or Gallup Poll-type sociologists, but which are absolutely essential for the system's sound operation and, indeed, in the long run, its survival.

To establish conditions for regular and efficient operation of the worker-managed economy is thus a long, tedious task, and inevitably a continuous process. It certainly is not one which could ever be left to any Invisible Hand —abstract 'managing workers' or the 'spirit of the working classes'—any more than it could be left to some technocratic élite. No one but the actual workers of Yugoslavia could successfully shoulder such a task and it is they

289

and their managers alone who know what their real objectives are, and how they may best be attained,

It may prove impossible within the narrow limits of present-day Yugoslavia to achieve a full development—a 'grand Siècle'—of workers' management. Too many alien, competing, outside and domestic forces constantly threaten the system's difficult equilibrium, and the Yugoslav economy may prove too small to form a real centre of gravity able not only to hold together but also to ensure conditions of full efficiency for its tens of thousands of manifold enterprises and work organizations. In other words it may prove too small, hence too unstable a 'macro-economic' framework for too strong and too diversified a 'mezzoconomy'. Yet whatever its future, its past and present performance has demonstrated beyond reasonable doubt—and in a uniquely convincing fashion as compared with all similar experiments in history—that an economic system based not on ownership, of whatever description, but on work, on the management by, and in the interest of, those who are the active participants in the process of production, is no mere Utopia, but a practical, viable proposition, able to engender at least in certain historical conditions and circumstances, high rates of economic growth and social development.

*   *   *

To define such favourable conditions and circumstances is a task for another day. Some of the more significant favourable facets of the Yugoslav setting and history have been touched upon, particularly in Part I. The absence of a feudal-industrial past, of the Protestant entrepreneurial motivation and the corresponding debasement of actual work and the worker in social ethics and actual social practice would seem to be the main non-economic background factor. The will of the population to develop by their own effort and according to their own criteria of rationality, coupled with the emergence of an appropriate institutional framework, has been the operative cause of the success of the Yugoslav experiment. That such will was essentially that of a rural, free or freedom-seeking population can hardly be disputed—even if the direct inspirational and action-guiding influence of Western proletarian socialisms—particularly Marx and the Paris Commune—must be fully recognized. This also clearly shows that some dogmatic interpretations of the dialectics of history and their élitist equivalents in the dominant schools of Western economics and sociology are not necessarily borne out in fact and that—as is indeed recognized even by some of the leading Soviet theorists—two or more stages of history may be skipped if a population's resolve encounters a combination of favourable circumstances.

So the Yugoslav experience can by no means be taken as a universal recipe, let alone a 'model' suitable in all circumstances. Similar attempts might well founder on well-nigh insuperable obstacles in many countries and regions, particularly where the lasting impact of the feudal-industrial past has deprived the population of the will and confidence in their ability to master their own destiny. A resurgence of such will and confidence is nowhere precluded, however. Recent history abounds in swift leaps forward whether it be

290

through the sudden release of social forces pent up through the ages, from the Pryamid builders, through the Conquistadores to Victoria, or through the fresh upsurge of young newly liberated generations. There is no single 'model' for all the societies involved—their parameters of social and economic conditions and preferences are infinitely varied—yet the Yugoslav firm and the Yugoslav economy are at least pointers to the possibility of a single, humanistic, man-oriented economy of the future. Such a possibility can no longer be flatly ruled out by the sneer of any self-appointed theorist or dogmatic ruler, and that finally is the major lesson which the Yugoslav people of the mid-twentieth century have to offer to all the peoples of the world. No one, however, and least of all the Yugoslavs themselves, could venture to suggest what conclusions each of these peoples will wish or have to draw therefrom.

Bibliography

INTRODUCTORY NOTE
The volume of studies and other documents relevant to our subject is immense. The number of items published each year since the early fifties which should be included in a fully balanced bibliography on workers' management in Yugoslavia and its economics amounts to hundreds, and indeed to thousands for the more recent period. Well over 3,000 items were included in 1965 in the sole general bibliography on workers' management published so far in Yugoslavia and a listing of studies dealing with the income distribution process for the 1965–8 period is believed to contain no less than 9,000 items.

This interest in workers' management, and particularly in its economics, is largely the product of the system itself as it created an unlimited number of real or possible publishers, in the form of the self-governing enterprises, including several major specialized publishing firms. It also provided them with a very wide and eager class of not impecunious customers in the shape of the enterprise workers and professional managers. More so perhaps than in any other country, publications on the problems of the enterprise and its economics have become one of the most profitable and rapidly growing fields of activity.

The bibliography presented below is thus necessarily highly selective. It is also incomplete and unbalanced in several major regards.

Only such works as were actually used in full or in part in the preparation of the study were taken into consideration. Among these, works which appeared since 1965 in the form of printed or mimeographed volumes were alone extensively listed, while only a few articles of direct relevance are included. Practically none of the 3,000 items included in the Yugoslav bibliography mentioned above has thus been included in the present bibliography, nor was use made of specialized bibliographies contained in most of the other publications used in the preparation of the study.

As only the material actually available to the author is listed here, the bibliography is heavily slanted in favour of Belgrade and Zagreb editors who were more easily accessible for the initial selection of background literature. A particularly serious lacuna is the nearly total absence of publications by Macedonian authors, while the other southern republics of Yugoslavia as well as Slovenia are also unduly under-represented. The bulk of the documents included actually originate mainly from two major institutes and one publishing house, while several other major Belgrade publishers were largely omitted. The names of the publishers or originating institutes have not been

292

included in the bibliography except where no name of the author appeared on the cover. The Belgrade Federal Institute of Social Sciences, the Zagreb Economic Institute and the Publishing enterprise Informator each account for a considerable number of entries in the bibliography.

The lack of proper regional balance is particularly regrettable since the content of most economic publications is largely determined by its regional origin. Actually, with regard to the period under review, the Belgrade and, particularly, Zagreb editors had a largely dominant position in the shaping of public opinion. The limitations of time and space also made it impossible to cover publications of sub-regional or local scope which tend to play a growing role in the actual shaping of the system.

Most of the publications listed are by academic writers. To compensate for their possible, or indeed in some cases quite obvious, alienation from reality, considerable effort was made to make the fullest possible use of other information surveys and findings reported in the daily press and other periodic publications. A list of the latter is given in part of the bibliography. Documents and periodicals published by the enterprises themselves or by their various organizations are not included. Nor are the specialized reviews published under the sponsorship of various government agencies (labour, finance, etc.) nor the reports of their inspection services, both of which contain a wealth of useful information and comments based on practical experience.

A brief selection of documents in non-Yugoslav languages has been included in Part I of the bibliography. It covers both general studies on Yugoslavia and its worker-managed economy, as well as a selection of more general studies consulted and found relevant.

For the sake of simplicity, no 'representative' listing of the works dealing with workers' participation or industrial democracy generally was attempted. Nor are the works of Marx and Engels or of the Yugoslav leaders and theoreticians—particularly those of President Tito, Edvard Kardelj, Boris Kidrić and others—the relevance of which is obvious, included in the listing.

Despite its numerous and severe limitations, including its quite pragmatic and subjective nature, it is hoped that the present bibliography will be found helpful both in interpreting the author's views and in grasping the type of publishing activity which has developed in Yugoslavia as a response to the requirements of a system based on workers' management.

The bibliographical entries have been listed under seven major headings and further subdivisions which run parallel to the various chapters of the study. Clearly, there is a considerable measure of overlapping between most of the works listed and the content of the various chapters. Titles included under earlier chapter headings are not repeated again, even where relevant (perhaps more directly) for one or other of the subsequent chapters.

A table of contents of the bibliography is appended.

CONTENTS

1. GENERAL

1.1 Bibliographies

Ačimović, Miroslav R., *Bibliografska grada o radničkom samoupravljanju*, etc. (Bibliographical Materials on Workers' Self-management in Yugoslavia and Aspects of Producers' Participation in Enterprise Management in Other Countries), Belgrade, 1966, 858 pp.

Institut za sociologijo in Filosofio (Institute of Sociology and Philosophy, Ljubljana University), *Literatura o komuni u Jugoslaviji* (Publications on the communes in Yugoslavia, a bibliography), Ljubljana, 1964, 134 pp.

Mihailović Mihailo and Plazinić Milan, *Registar pravnih proprisa*, etc. (Register of Laws and Regulations, 1954–67; including subject index), Belgrade, 1968, 704 pp.

1.2 Statistical documentation

Indeks (Monthly review of economic statistics of Yugoslavia), Federal Office of Statistics, Belgrade, monthly.

Jugoslavija 1945–1964 (Survey of statistical data), Federal Office of Statistics, Belgrade, 1965, 373 pp.

Privreda u godinama Reforme (The Economy in the Years of the Reform, 1962–8), Federal Office of Statistics, Belgrade, 1968, 108 pp.

Statistički Bilten (Statistical Bulletin), Federal Office of Statistics, Belgrade, irreg.[1]

Statistički Bilten (Statistical Bulletin), Service of Social Accountancy, National Bank of Yugoslavia, Belgrade, monthly.[2]

Statistički Godišnjak Jugoslavie (Statistical Yearbook of Yugoslavia), particularly Vols. X, XIV and XV (1963, 1967 and 1968).[2]

1.3 General works in non-Yugoslav languages

1.31 Yugoslavia and the system of workers' management

Bilandžić Dušan, *Management of Yugoslav Economy (1945–1966)*, Belgrade, 1967, 138 pp.

Bogosavljević, M. and Pešaković, M., *La Gestion ouvrière d'une usine en Yougoslavie* (monograph on the Rade Končar Works), Belgrade, 1960, 108 pp. (exists also in English).

Bobrowski, C., *La Yougoslavie Socialiste*, Paris, 1956, 237 pp. (bibl.).

Caire, Guy, *L'Economie Yougoslave*, Paris, 1962, 188 pp.

Djonlagich, Ahmet *et al.*, *Yugoslavia vo vtoroy Mirovoy Voyne* (Yugoslavia in the Second World War), Belgrade, 1967, 232 pp.

Grossman, Gregory, *Economic Systems*, Englewood Cliffs, N.J., 1967, 120 pp.

International Labour Office, *Workers' Management in Yugoslavia*, Geneva, 1962, 320 pp. (bibl.).

Jovanović, Aleksander, *The Social and Political System of Yugoslavia*, Belgrade, 1966, 91 pp.

Lasserre, George, *L'entreprise socialiste en Yougoslavie*, Paris, 1964, 129 pp.

Moch, Jules, *Yougoslavie, Terre d'Experience*, Monaco, 1953, 340 pp.

Morača, Pero, *The League of Communists of Yugoslavia* (a brief historical survey), Belgrade, 1966, 74 pp.

Pejović, Svetozar, *The Market-Planned Economy of Yugoslavia*, Minneapolis, 1966, 160 pp.

Philip, André, *La Démocratie Industrielle*, Paris, 1956.

Riddell, S. David, 'Social Self-Government: the Background of Theory and Practice in Yugoslav Socialism', *The British Journal of Sociology*, March 1968, pp. 47–75.

Stojanović, Petar, *Industry-Workers' Management in Practice* (four enterprise examples), Belgrade, 1966, 146 pp.

Sturmthal, Adolf, *Workers' Councils*, Cambridge, 1964, 217 pp.

Vukmanović Tempo, S., *La Voie Yougoslave*, Belgrade, 1967, 142 pp.

Waterston, A., *Planning in Yugoslavia*, Baltimore, 1962, 109 pp.

[1] 555 separate issues up to March 1969; for certain specific references, see below.
[2] English translation of text and terms available separately.

1.32 Related Experiences of other countries

Anker-Ording Aake, *Betriebsdemokratie in Norwegen* (Industrial democracy in Norway, the way to socialism), Frankfurt/Main, 1966, 132 pp.

Bettelheim, Charles, *et al.*, *La Construction du Socialisme en Chine*, Paris, 1968, 207 pp.

Coates, K. and Topham, A., *Industrial Democracy in Great Britain* (a book of readings and witnesses for workers' control), London, 1968, 431 pp.

Dvoriginski, N. E., *et al.*, *Khoziaystvennaya Reforma* (The Economic Reform, Experience and Perspectives), Moscow, 1968, 262 pp.

Leber, Georg, *Accumulation of Assets by the Workers*, Berlin, 1967, 187 pp.

Metzger, B. L., *Profit Sharing in Perspective*, Evanston, Ill., 1966, 229 pp.

Nemitz, Kurt-Becker, Richard, *Mitbestimmung und Wirtschafts-politik*, 2 vols., Cologne, 1967.

1.33 Economic and Social Theory

Adler, Max, *Démocratie et conseils ouvriers* (translated from German and introduced by Y. Bourdet), Paris, 1967, 124 pp.

Argyle, Bendix, Flinn & Hagen, *Social Theory and Economic Change*, London, 1967, 101 pp.

Austruy, Jacques, *Le Scandale du Développement*, Paris, 1965, 535 pp.

Behrendt, Richard F., *Soziale Strategie fuer Entwicklungslaender* (Social Strategy for Developing Countries), Frankfurt/Main, 1965, 639 pp.

Bendix, R., *Work and Authority in Industry*, New York, 1956, 464 pp.

Bettelheim, Charles, *La Transition vers l'Économie Socialiste*, Paris, 1968, 263 pp.

Blumberg, P., *Industrial Democracy: The Sociology of Participation*, London, 1968, 278 pp.

Brus, W., *Problemes généraux du Fonctionnement de l'économie socialiste*, Paris, 1968 (translation from Polish).

Clegg, H. A., *A New Approach to Industrial Democracy*, Oxford, 1963, 140 pp.

Friedmann, Georges, *Industrial Society*, Glencoe, 1956, 436 pp.

Fogarty, Michael, *The Just Wage*, London, 1961, 309 pp.

Galbraith, J. K., *The New Industrial State*, London, 1967, 427 pp.

Gross, M. Bertram, *The State of the Nation* (*Social System Accounting*), London, 1966, 166 pp.

Hagen, E. Everett, *On the Theory of Social Change*, Homeswood, Ill., 1962, 557 pp.

Horvat, Dr B., *Towards a Theory of Planned Economy* (translation from Serbian), Belgrade, 1964, 244 pp.

Jaurès, Jean, '*Esquisse provisoire de l'organisation industrielle; La production socialiste*' in *Les Annales de l'Economie Collective* No. 555, 1959, pp. 341–95 (not included in English edition of the Annals).

Kosik, Karel, *Dialektika konkretniho* (Dialectics of the Concrete), Prague, 1966, 191 pp.; in Serbian, Belgrade, 1967, 251 pp.

Likert, Rensis, *New Patterns of Management*, New York, 1961, 279 pp.

McGuire, Joseph W., *Theories of Business Behaviour*, Englewood Cliffs, N. J., 1964, 268 pp. (bibl.).

Meek, R. C., *Studies in the Labour Theory of Value*, London, 1958, 310 pp.

O.E.C.D., *The Residual Factor and Economic Growth*, Paris, 1964, 279 pp.

Šik Ota, *K problematice socialistických zbožních vztahů* (Problems of Socialist Commodity Relations), Prague, 1965, 400 pp.

Tannenbaum, Arnold S., *Social Psychology of the Work Organization*, 2nd edn, London, 1967, 136 pp.

Weber, Max, *The Theory of Social and Economic Organization* (edited by Talcott Parsons), New York, 1966, 436 pp.

1.4 Other Documents not Classified Elsewhere

Bilandžić *et al.*, *Današni trenutak reforme i samoupravljanja* (Present Stage of the Reform and Self-Management: account of a discussion), in *Naše Teme*, No. 5, 1968, pp. 712–821.

Deleon, A. *et al.*, *Historički kongres radničkih saveta* (The Historic Congress of the Workers' Councils: an Account), Belgrade, 1957, 343 pp.

Društveno samoupravljanje u Jugoslaviji (Social Self-Government in Yugoslavia), First meeting of specialists, Yugoslav Association of Sociology, Split, 1965, 336 pp.

Institut za Društveno Upravljanje, *Istraživanje samoupravljanja u proizvodni, etc.* (Institute for Social Self-Government: Research on Self-government in Production within the Context of the Present Problems of Socio-economic Development of Yugoslavia; materials for a symposium), Zagreb, 1968, 19 pp.

Matić, S. *et al.*, *Aktivnost radnih ljudi*, etc. (The Activity of the Working People in Self-government within the Work Organization: a local monograph), Zagreb, 1962, 208 pp.

Pregled podataka iz završnih računa etc. (Survey of data from the annual accounts of industrial and mining enterprises, 1958 and 1959; published jointly by the Federal Secretariats for the Economy and for Industry, the Federal Chamber of Industry and the Confederation of Yugoslav Trade Unions), Belgrade, 1960, 571 pp. (subsequent volumes only for 'internal use').

Prva Decenija Radničkog Samoupravljanja 1950–1960 (First Decade of Workers' Self-management), Essays and Reports, Belgrade, 1960.

Rašković, Dr Vladimir, '*Izučavanje sadržinskih društvenih odnosa*' etc. (The Study of Substantive Social Relationships in the Light of Priority Problems of the System of Workers' Self-management) in *Zbornik Radova I* (Collected Essays of the Institute of Sociology), Belgrade, 1967, pp. 9–29.

Vidaković Zoran, '*O Nekim problemime odnosa*', etc. (Some Problems of Relationship between the Theoretical and Empirical Components of Research in the field of Workers' Self-management), *Sociologija*, No. 2, 1965 (offprint).

1.5 Periodicals

1.51 In Yugoslav Languages

Arhiv za pravne i društvene nauke (Archives of Law and Social Sciences), Federation of the Unions of Jurists of Yugoslavia, Belgrade, quarterly.

Borba, Socialist Alliance of the Working People of Yugoslavia, Belgrade and Zagreb, daily.

Ekonomika Preduzeča (Enterprise Economics), Union of Economists of Serbia, Belgrade, monthly.

Ekonomist, Yugoslav Association of Economists, Zagreb, quarterly.

Ekonomska Analiza (Economic Analysis), Yugoslav Institute for Economic Research, Belgrade, semestrially.

Ekonomska Misao (Economic Thought), Union of Economists of Serbia, Belgrade.

Ekonomska Politika (Economic Policy), Publishing enterprise Borba, Belgrade, weekly.

Ekonomski Pregled (Economic Survey), Union of Economists of Croatia, Zagreb, monthly.

Gledišta (Point of View), Belgrade University and Youth Federation of Serbia, Belgrade, monthly.

Informator (Yugoslav Journal for information of cadres in the economy, administration and in institutions), Zagreb, weekly.

Komuna (Review of social and communal affairs), Permanent Conference of Yugoslav Towns, Belgrade, monthly.

Komunist, League of Communists of Yugoslavia, Belgrade, weekly.

Konjunkturne Informacije (Current Business Surveys), Institute for Market Research and Federal Economic Chamber, Belgrade, monthly.

Naše Teme, Youth Federation of Croatia, Zagreb, monthly.

Politika, Independent publishing enterprise, Belgrade, daily.

Praksa (Praxis: Review of Social Questions), Editorial-publishing enterprise Pobeda, Titograd, two-monthly.

Praksis (philosophical two-monthly), Croatian Philosophical Society, Zagreb, two-monthly.

Pregled (Survey: review of social questions), University of Sarajevo, Sarajevo, monthly.

297

Privredni Pregled (Economic Survey), Belgrade, weekly.
Produktivnost (Productivity), Yugoslav Institute for Labour Productivity, Belgrade, monthly.
Rad (Work), Confederation of Yugoslav Trade Unions, Belgrade, weekly.
Sindikati (Trade Unions), Central Council of the Confederation of Trade Unions of Yugoslavia, Belgrade, monthly.
Socijalisam (Socialism), League of Communists of Yugoslavia, Belgrade, monthly.
Statistička Revija (Statistical Review), Yugoslav Statistical Society, Belgrade, quarterly.
Vesnik (Bulletin), Yugoslav Investment Bank, Belgrade, monthly.
Vesnik u Sredu (News on Wednesday), Zagreb, weekly.
Other periodicals consulted occasionally include the regional daily papers of Bosnia (*Oslobodenje*, Sarajevo), Croatia (*Vesnik*, Zagreb,) and Slovenia (*Delo*, Ljubljana), as well as various subregional or local journals (usually weeklies), enterprise gazettes, and various other papers and reviews of a more general character (including the evening papers and cultural, religious or family journals).

1.52 In non-Yugoslav languages

Annals of Public and Co-operative Economy, International Centre of Research and Information on Public and Co-operative Economy, Liège (Geneva), quarterly.
Autogestion, Editions Anthropos, Paris, quarterly.
L'homme et la société (international review for research and sociological synthesis), Editions Anthropos, Paris, quarterly.
Socialist Thought and Practice (a theoretical, political and informative magazine), Belgrade, quarterly.
Questions actuelles du Socialisme (Paris), Belgrade, quarterly.
Yugoslav Law (Bulletin on Law and Legislation), Union of Jurists' Association of Yugoslavia, Belgrade, quarterly.
Yugoslav Survey (A Record of Facts and Information), Belgrade, quarterly.

PART I

2. YUGOSLAV SETTING AND THE INSTITUTIONAL BACKGROUND OF THE SYSTEM

2.1 The Yugoslav Setting: Geography, Population and Economic Background

Blašković, Dr Vladimir, *Ekonomska geografija Jugoslavije* (Economic Geography of Yugoslavia), 2nd edition, Zagreb, 1967, 326 pp.
Bazler, Marta, *Analiza stepena razvijenosti jugoslovenskih Područja* (Analysis of Levels of development of Yugoslav Regions), *Ekonomska Analiza*, Nos. 1–2, 1967, pp. 49–63.
Crvenkovski, Krste, *Makedonija danas* (Macedonia Today), Belgrade, 1968, 64 pp.
Ginić, Dr Ivanka, *Dinamika i struktura gradskog stanovništva Jugoslavije* (Dynamics and Structure of Urban Population of Yugoslavia), Belgrade, 1967, 239 pp.
Ilič, Dr Miloš, *et al.*, *Socijalna struktura i pokretlivost radničke klase Jugoslavije* (Social Composition and Mobility of the Working Class of Yugoslavia), Belgrade, 1963, 542 pp.
Institut Društvenih Nauka, *Šema stalnih rejona za demografksa istraživanja* (Permanent Territorial Divisions for Demographic Research), Belgrade, 1963, 132 pp.
Kardelj, Edvard, *Problemi socialističke politike na selu* (Problems of Socialist Policy in the Countryside), Belgrade, 1959, 409 pp. (also in French, Paris, 1960).
Macura, Dr Miloš, *Stanovništvo kao činilac privrednog razvoja Jugoslavije* (Population as Factor of Economic Development of Yugoslavia), Belgrade, 1958, 374 pp.
O.E.C.D., The Mediterranean Project (Education and Development), *Country Reports: Yugoslavia*, Paris, 1965, 143 pp.
Promena klasne strukture savremenog jugoslovenskog društva (Changes in the Class Structure of Contemporary Yugoslav Society; Second Scientific Meeting of Specialists, Yugoslav Sociological Society, February 1966), Belgrade, 1967, 614 pp.
Samardžija, Dr Miloš, *Privredni sistem Jugoslavije Vol. I* (Economic System of Yugoslavia: General Conditions and Characteristics of Economic Life), Belgrade, 1965, 336 pp.

Šefer, Dr Berislav, *Životni standard i privredni razvoj Jugoslavije* (Standard of Livin and Economic Development of Yugoslavia), Zagreb 1965, 205 pp.

Uvalić, Dr Radivoj *et al.*, *Problemi regionanog privrednog razvoja* (Zbornik Radova) (Problems of Regional Economic Development, collected essays), Belgrade, 1962.

Vogelnik, Dr Dolfe, *Urbanisacija kao odraz privrednog razvoja FNRJ* (Urbanization as a Result of Economic Development of Yugoslavia), Belgrade, 1961, 311 pp.

Žuljić Stanko, Zdunic S., *Redosled općina S. R. Hrvatske etc.* (The Ranking of Communes in Croatia According to their Level of Development, 1963), Zagreb, 1967 (offprint from *Ekononske Studije* No. 6, 1967).

2.2 Workers' Management; its Nature and Objectives

Centar za raziskivanje javnog mnenja: *Mnenja o actualnih političkih vprašanjih reforme* (Opinions on Current Political Problems of the (economic) Reform), Ljubljana, 1968, 62 pp.

Čulibrk Svetozar, *Želje i strahovanja Naroda Jugoslavije* (Hopes and Fears of the Peoples of Yugoslavia), Belgrade, 1965, 345 pp.

Damjanović, Mijat *et al.*, *Jugoslovensko javno mnenje o privrednoj reformi* (Yugoslav Public Opinion on the Economic Reform, 1965), Belgrade, 1965, 177 pp.

Dordević, Dr Jovan, *Demokratija i izbori* (Democracy and Elections), Zagreb, 1967 101 pp.

Dordević, Dr Jovan, *Socialisam i demokratija* (Socialism and Democracy), Belgrade, 1962, 536 pp.

Dragičević, Dr Adolf, *Reforma i revolucija* (Reform and Revolution), Zagreb, 1968, 206 pp.

Institut Društvenih Nauka, *Javno mnenje o prednacrtu novog Ustava* (Public Opinion on the Preliminary Draft of New Constitution), Belgrade, 1964, 542 pp.

Institut Društvenih Nauka, *Jugoslovensko javno mnenje 1965* (Public Opinion in Yugoslavia, 1965), Belgrade, 1965, 179 and 220 pp.; *idem* 1966, I vol., Belgrade, 1967, 220 pp.

Janjičević, Miloslav *et al.*, *Jugoslovenski studenti i socialisam* (Yugoslav Students and Socialism), Belgrade, 1966.

Jugoslovenski Institut za novinarstvo, Institut za društveno upravljanje (Yugoslav Institute of Journalism and Institute for Social Self-government), *Informacija i samoupravljanje* (Information and Self-government: a Symposium), Belgrade, 1965, 274 pp.

Kardelj E., Bakarić V., Vlahović V., Marković Lj., Rakočević Z., *Promena u biću radničke klase etc.* (Transformation of the Working Class and of its Ideological-political Avantgarde: a theoretical discussion), *Socializam*, Nos. 1–2, 1968, pp. 3–105.

Kostić, Dr Živko, *Osnovi teorije mezo-ekonomije* (Elements of Mezzo-Economic Theory), Zagreb, 1968, 280 pp.

Kozomara, Dr Olga, *Demokratisacija društvenopolitičkih odnosa* (Democratization of Socio-economic Relations), Sarajevo, 1965, 129 pp.

Marković, Mihailo, *Humanisam i dijalektika* (Humanism and Dialectics), Belgrade, 1967, 449 pp.

Pašić, Najdan, *Kritički osvrt etc.* (Critical Review of Different Concepts of Self-government) in *Socializam* No. 4, 1968, pp. 403–24.

Popović, Dr Mihajlo, *Predmet sociologie* (The Object of Sociology), Belgrade, 1966, 71 pp.

Programme of the League of Yugoslav Communists, Belgrade, 1958.

Pušić, Dr Eugen, *Samoupravljanje* (Self-Government), Zagreb, 1968, 295 pp.

Ustav S.F.R.J. (The Constitution of the Socialist Federative Republic of Yugoslavia), Belgrade, 1964, 152 pp.

2.3 Institutional Background and Economic Policy

Bicanić, Rudolf, *Ekonomska Politika Jugoslavije* (Yugoslav Economic Policy), Zagreb, 1962, 295 pp.

Centar za raziskovanje javnog mnenja, RS. ZSS (Centre for public opinion surveys of the Slovenian Trade Unions), *Delavci industrije in rudarstva o sinkikatu* (Miners and Industrial Workers on the Trade Unions), Ljubljana, 1967, 46 pp. (*idem* for agriculture, food and tobacco industries, 25 pp.).

Cvijetić Dragoljub *et al.*, *Bankarski i kreditni sistem Jugoslavije* (Banking and Credit in Yugoslavia: Legislation and Commentary), Belgrade, 1965, 484 pp.

Dolanc, Stane, *Demokratski centralizam u teoriji i praksi Saveza Komunista* (Democratic Centralism in Theory and Practice of the League of Communists), *Socializam*, No. 12, 1967, pp. 1509–20.

Džinić, Firdus, *Jugoslovensko javno mnenje i VIII Kongres SKJ* (Jugoslav Public Opinion and the Eighth Congress of the League of Communists), Belgrade, 1965, 102 pp.

The Economic Reform in Yugoslavia, Belgrade, 1965, 96 pp.

Fisher, Jack C., *Yugoslavia—A Multi-national State; Regional Differences and Administrative Response*, San Francisco, 1966, 244 pp.

Institut Društvenih nauka, *Izborni sistem u uslovima sampoupravljanja* (Electoral System in Conditions of Self-Government: a symposium), Belgrade, 1967, 359 pp.

Jelen, Olga, *Razvoj materijalne osnove radničkog samoupravljanja* (The Development of the Material Basis of Workers' Self-management 1950–60), Zagreb, 1962, 110 pp.

New Yugoslavia 1941–1965 (Secretariat of Information of the Federal Assembly), Belgrade, 1966, 275 pp.

Pešic, Nikola, *Science and Culture* (A Study of Self-management Practice in Three Yugoslav Scientific and Cultural Institutions), Belgrade, 1967, 71 pp.

Rat u savremenim uslovima etc. (War in Contemporary Conditions and the Forces of our National Defence), Belgrade, 1967, 116 pp.

Réorganisation de la Ligue des Communists de Yugoslavie (Documents), Belgrade, 1967, 149 pp.

Šesti Kongres Saveza Sindikata Jugoslavije (Sixth Congress of the Confederation of Trade Unions of Yugoslavia, Belgrade, June 1968: summary records and documents), Belgrade, 1968, 778 pp.

S.K.J. u uslovina samoupravljanja (The League of Communists within the Self-management System: a collection of documents), Belgrade, 1967, 794 pp.

The Socialist Alliance of the Working People of Yugoslavia (documents on), Yugoslav Survey No. 26, 1966, pp. 3729–80.

Vidaković, Zoran, *Sindikati i Komunistička avantgarda* (The Trade Unions and Communist Avant Garde) in *Socijalizam*, No. 5, 1968, pp. 557–68.

Vojnović, Dragomir, *Ekonomska nauka i privredni razvoj Jugoslavije* (Economic Science and Economic Development of Yugoslavia), *Ekonomska Pregled*, No. 10, 1966.

Zečević, Rajkz *et al.*, *Bankovni i Kreditni sistem* (Banking and Credit), Zagreb, 1965, 252 pp.

3. THE WORKER-MANAGED ENTERPRISE

3.1 The Enterprise and Workers' Management as an Institution

Braut Roko Ing. *et al.*, *Priručnik o organisaciji poduzeča* (Organization of the Enterprise: a manual), 2nd edition, Zagreb, 1966, 444 pp.

Dautović, Dr Mirko, *Osnovi ekonomike i organisacije preduzeća* (The Foundations of the Economics and of the Organization of the Enterprise), Belgrade, 1965, 360 pp.

Derganc Jože, Čukova Ana, *Delovna Skupina v sistemu delavskog samoupravljanja* (The Work Group in the System of Workers' Self-management), Ljubljana, 1966.

Fiamengo, Dr Ante, *Odnos članova kolektiva premi procesu samoupravljanja* (Attitude of Members of the Work Collectivity towards the Self-management process), Vol. I, Sarajevo, 1964, 279 pp.

Grozdanić Stanko, Poleti A., *Uvodenje nove organisacije samoupravljanja u preduzecu* '*Trepča*' (The Introduction of a New Organisation of Workers' Self-management in the Enterprise Trepča, 1961–2), Belgrade, 1962, 123 pp. and appendix.

Institute of Comparative Law,[1] *Laws of Enterprises and Institutions* (foreword by Dr N. Balog), Belgrade, 1966, 130 pp.

Kokoleča, Dr Stevan and Kostić, Dr Živko, *Organisacija kolektiva* (Organization of the Work Collectivity: Organization of a Producers' Enterprise), Zagreb, 1961, 323 pp.

Kavar-Vidmar, Andrea *et al.*, *Priručnik o normativnoj delatnosti u radnim organisacijama* (Normative Activity within the Work Organizations), Belgrade, 1967, 213 pp.

Lemân, Dr Gudrun, *Stellung und Aufgaben der oekonomischen Einheiten in den jugoslawischen Unternehmungen*, Berlin, 1967, 141 pp.

Samoupravljanje u privredi (Self-Management in the Economy: Election and Composition of the Self-management Bodies in 1968; statistical survey), *Statistički Bilten*, No. 559, 1969, 28 pp. (For previous years, cf. in particular *ibid.*, Nos 452, 389, 454, 77 and 35.)

Samoupravljanje u preduzečima sa 1000 i više članova radne zajednice u 1966 (Self-Management in Enterprises with over 1000 Members of the Work Collectivity in 1966: statistical survey), *Statisticki Bilten*, No. 492, 1967, 37 pp.

Statute of the Rubber Factory 'Sava', Kranj (translation from Slovenian), Kranj, 1966, 83 pp.

Vidaković, Zoran, *Uredjenje odnosa u preduzeču sampouravnim normama* (The Regulation of Relations within the Enterprise by Means of Self-governing Normative Activity: survey of opinion of workers and professional managers), Belgrade, 1961, 160 pp. and 53 tables.

Sbirka propisa o organisaciji i poslovanju etc. (Laws and Regulations Concerning the Organization and Activity of Economic and other Work Organizations, including Official Interpretations and Comments), Belgrade, 1967, 691 pp.

3.2 Enterprise Planning and Income Distribution

Albrecht, Roman, *Samoupravni društveni odnosi i ekstradohodak* (Social Relationship Based on Self-management and the Surplus Income) in *Socializam*, No. 4, 1967, pp. 439–70.

Butaš, Nenad, *Priručnik za primenu propisa o knigovodstvu* etc. (Reference Manual on the Regulations Governing the Accountancy of Enterprises), 3rd edition, Belgrade, 1968, 502 pp.

Drenjanin, Dr Milorad, *Sistem raspodele dohotka* (The System of Income Distribution), Zagreb, 1965, 166 pp.

Jugoslovenski Institut za produktivnost Rada (Yugoslav Institute of Labour Productivity), *Problemi organisacije ekonomskih jedinica i unutrašnje respodele u proizvodnim preduzečima* (Problems of Organization of Economic Units and of Internal Distribution within Productive Enterprises), Belgrade, 1964, 320 pp.

Kostić, Ž. K.-Kukoleča, S., *Raspodela dohotka u preduzeču* (Distribution of Income within the Enterprise), Zagreb, 1967, 256 pp.

Novak Mijo, Dr, and Franc Victor, Professor, *Planiranje u radnim organisacijáma* (Planning in Work Organizations), Zagreb, 1968, 244 pp.

Sredstva, Dohodak i Raspodela (Assets, Income and Distribution in Economic Organizations, Institutions and Administrations: Judicial Decisions and Interpretations), Zagreb, 1968, 364 pp.

Štajner, Dr Rikard, and Franc, V., *Ekonomski jedinice* (Economic Units: Organization, Management, Income Distribution; practical examples), Zagreb, 1962, 219 pp.

Tišma Toša and Vukobratović Petar, Dr, *Interna kontrola u radnim organisaciama* (Internal Supervision and Control in the Work Organizations), Zagreb, 1965, 323 pp.

Tomić, Teodor, *Unutrašnja raspodela u privednim organisacijama* (Internal Distribution in Economic Organizations), Zagreb, 1965, 157 pp.

Zbirka propisa o sredstvina i dohotku etc. (Laws and Regulations Governing Assets and

---

[1] English translation of several basic legislative and similar instruments, including that of the Constitution of Federal Yugoslavia and of the Republic of Serbia, the law on constitutional courts, the 'general usages of trade' etc., may be found in the same 'collection of Yugoslav Laws', published by the Belgrade Institute of Comparative Law.

Incomes of Economic Enterprises, Institutions and Administrations), Zagreb, 1967, 775 pp. (index).

4. ECONOMIC MODELS OF BEHAVIOUR AND DEVELOPMENT OF THE WORKER-MANAGED ENTERPRISE

4.1 Models of Behaviour

Černe, France, *Ekonomia iz novego zornego kota* (Economics Reconsidered), Ljubljana, 1966, 335 pp.

Čobelić, Dr Nikola and Stejanović, Dr Radmila, *Teorija investicionih ciklusa u socialis-tičeskoj privredi* (Theory of Investment Cycles in a Socialist Economy), Belgrade, 1966.

Dabčević-Kučar, Dr S. and Korać, Dr M. *et al.*, *Problemi teorije i prakse socialističke robne proizvodne* (Problems of Theory and Practice of Socialist Commodity Production in Yugoslavia), Belgrade, 1965, 207 pp.

Drolc, Ljuba, Peternel Vera, *Projekt revisije jedinstvenih pokazatela poslovanja* etc. (Proposed Revision of the System of Single Indices of Operation of Economic Organizations and the Method of their Application to Income Distribution), *Produktivnost*, No. 1, 1968, pp. 3–45.

Dubravčić, Dr Dinko, *Ponašanje poduzeča kod izbora kombinacije faktora* (Behaviour of the Enterprise with Regard to the Choice of Factors of Production), Zagreb, 1967, 58 pp.

Dubravčić, Dinko, *Prilog zasnivanju teorije Jugoslovenskog poduzeča* (Contribution to the Foundation of a Theory of the Yugoslav Firm), *Ekonomska Analiza*, Nos. 1–2, 1968, pp. 120–6.

Horvat, Branko, *Prilog zasnivanju teorije jugoslovenskog poduzeča* (Contribution to the Foundation of a Theory of the Yugoslav Firm), *Ekonomska Analiza*, Nos. 1–2, 1967, pp. 7–28.

Horvat, B., Bajt, A. *et al.*, *Nauka i ekonomska politika* (Science and Economic Policy: a collection of controversial articles), Belgrade, 1968, 168 pp.

Institut na Ekonomska Raziskivanja (Economic Research Institute), *Produkcijske funckije* (Production Functions: tables and comments), 3 vols, Ljubljana, 1967.

Jugoslovenski Zavod za Produktivnost Rada, *Metodologija korišcenja jedinstvenih pokazatela* etc. (Methodology for the Use of the Single Indices and for Comparison of Business Results of Economic Organizations), Belgrade, 1963, 148 pp.

Korać, Dr Miladin and Vlaškalić, Dr T., *Politička Ekonomija* (Political Economy), Belgrade, 1966, 456 pp.

Korać, Dr Miladin, '*Teorijska Analiza Društveno-Ekonomskih Osnova Jugoslovenskog Privrednog Sistema*' (Theoretical Analysis of the Socio-economic Foundations of the Yugoslav Economic System) in *Gledišta*, No. 10, 1968, pp. 1299–321.

Lassere, George, '*Profit, the Enterprise and General Interest*' in *The Annals of Public and Co-operative Economy*, No. 4, 1967, and No. 1, 1968.

Metode Obračuna u Privrednim Organisaciama etc. (Methods of Accounting in Economic Organisations in conditions of Direct Self-management by the Workers: documents of a symposium, Opatija, April 1967, 38 reports on economic and accounting theory and practical implementation), Zagreb, 1967, 620 pp.

Popović, Milentije, *Društveno-Ekonomski sistem* (Socio-economic System), Belgrade, 1964, 400 pp.

Rakočević, Živojin, *Načelo dohotka i desintegracija robne vrednosti* (The Income Principle and the Disintegration of Commodity Value) in *Socializam*, No. 4, 1962, pp. 29–92.

Sirotković, Dr Jakov, and Stipetić, Dr V., *Ekonomika Jugoslavije* (Yugoslav Economic System), Vol. I, Zagreb, 1967, 379 pp.

Todorović, Mijalko, *Oslobadžajne rada* (Emancipating Labour), Belgrade, 1965, 287 pp.

Ward, Benjamin N., *The Socialist Economy: A Study of Organizational Alternatives*, New York, 1967, 272 pp.

4.2 Capital, Interest, Investment and Growth

Blagojević, Dr Stevan, *Odnosi fiksnih fondova i proizvodnje u Jugoslovenskoj privredi* (Relation of Fixed Assets and Production in Yugoslav Economy), Zagreb, 1968, 125 pp.

Depolo, Boris, *Neki problemi u fazi realisanja investicija u S.F.R.J.* (Some Problems of the Implementation Stage of Investment Projects in Jugoslavia), Belgrade, 1964, 223 pp.

Economski Institut (Economic Institute, Zagreb), *Poduzeče u Reformi* (The Enterprise and the Reform; account of discussion of a symposium, Opatija, March 1968), Zagreb, 1968, 191 pp.

Gorupić, Dr *et al.*, *Investicije u poduzeču* (Investment within the Enterprise), Zagreb, 1963, 432 pp.

Horvat, B., *The Optimum Rate of Investment*, and *The Optimum Rate of Investment Reconsidered* (reprints), Belgrade, 1958 and 1965.

Horvat, B. *et al.*, *Sumarna analiza privrednik kretanja i predlozi za ekonomsku politiku* (Summary Analysis of Behaviour of the Economy, and Proposals for an Economic Policy), Belgrade, 1968, 108 pp.

Horvat, Dr Branko, *Uloga kamatne stope* etc. (The Role of the Interest Rate in the Yugoslav Economy), *Naša Stvarnost*, No. 6, 1960.

Institut za ekonomiku investicija (Institute for the Economics of Investment), *Investicije 1947–1962*, 3 vols, Belgrade, 1964.

Ivanović, Branislav, *Nov način odredivanja ostojanja* etc. (New Methodology for the determination of the Distances among Pluridimensional Statistical Groups with Application to the Problem of Classification of Districts of Yugoslavia according to the Level of Economic Development), and *Predvidanje Uticaja* etc. (The Forecasting of the Impact of Investment on the Future Economic Growth of Regional Units) in *Statisticka Revija*, No. 2, 1957, and Nos. 1–2, 1959.

Mesarić, Dr Milan, *Planiranje Privrednog Razvoja* (Planning of Economic Development), Zagreb, 1967, 256 pp.

Osnovni podaci o udelu novih preduzeča u industriji (Basic Data on the Share of New Enterprises in Industry, 1952–7), Federal Office of Statistics, March 1959, 20 pp.

Popović, Strašimir, *Izbor proizvodne strukture* (Choice of the Structure of Production), Belgrade, 1966, 91 pp.

Priručnik za primenu proprisa o popisu etc. (How to Apply Regulations Governing Inventories in Economic Organization), Belgrade, 1965, 90 pp.

Samardžija, M., *Kamata na Poslovni fond i socialistički ekonomski odnosi* (Interest on the Business Fund and the Socialist Economic Relations) in *Socijalizam*, No. 4, 1968, pp. 425–48.

Sovetovanje Jugoslovenskih Ekonomista, Ljubljana, March 1967 (Consultation of the Research Section of the Union of Economists of Yugoslavia: conditions of stabilization of the Yugoslav economy), Vol. III, Monetary and Credit Mechanisms, *Ekonomist* Nos. 1–2, 1967, pp. 1–274.

Tanasijević, Aleksandar, *Priručnik o amortisaciji osnovnih sredstava* (Amortization of Fixed Assets: a manual), 3rd edn, Belgrade, 1967, 238 pp.

Todorović, Mijalko, *Les problèmes actuels de la politique économique* (Report of the Vice-Chairman of the Federal Executive Council), Belgrade, November 1959, 80 pp.

Trklja, Dr M., *Kamata na investicione kredite u uslovima društvenog samoupravljanja* (Interest on Investment Credits in Conditions of Social Self-government), Belgrade, 1966, 148 pp.

Utvrdivanje, obračun i korišćenje amortisacije (Determination, Accounting and Utilization of Amortization), Belgrade, 1967, 233 pp.

Vasić, F., *Formiranje novčanih sredstava za investicije i njigov uticaj na privredna kretanja* (The Formation of Financial Resources for Investment and their Influence on Economic Activity), Belgrade, 1965.

Vinski, Ivo, *Procena rasta fiksnih fondova* etc. (Evaluation of the Growth of Fixed Funds in the Constituent Republics of Yugoslavia, 1946–60), Zagreb, 1965, 484 pp.

5. WORK, WORKERS' EARNINGS AND INCOME DISTRIBUTION

5.1 Work, Employment, Training and Skills

Anketa o ostvarinvanju prava radnika iz radnog odnosa u 1967 (Survey of the Implementation of the Rights of the Workers in the Area of Work Relations, 1967), Statistički Bilten, No. 556, 1969.

Brekić, Jovo, Kadrovska Politika u Privredi (Personnel Policy in the Economy: a survey), Zagreb, 1966, 125 pp.

Bricelj, Franc et al., Komentar k temelnemu zakonu o delovnih razmerjih (Commentary on the Basic Law on Work Relations), Ljubljana, 1967, 248 pp.

Čuk, Ana K., Psiho-socialni aspekti absentisma v industriji (Psycho-social Aspects of Absenteeism in Industry), Ljubljana, 1966, 212 pp.

Hadžiomerović, Dr Hasan, Ljudski faktor i stabilna ekonomija (The Human Factor and Economic Stability), Ekonomist, Nos 1–4, 1966, pp. 245–55.

Institut Društvenih Nauka, Demografski i ekonomski aspekti prostorne pokretlivosti stanovništva (Demographic and Economic Aspects of Spatial Mobility of the Population), Belgrade, 1968, 141 pp.

Institut za Društveno Upravljanje (Institute for Social Self-Government), Kadrovi u Rudarstvu (Personnel in the Mining Industry; a survey of nine non-ferrous ore mines), Zagreb, 1965, 141 pp.

Komisija za drušveno samoupravljanje RS. ZSS. (Committee on social self-government of the Slovenian Trade Unions), Delovna Razmera v statutih in Pravilnikih o Delovnih Razmerjih (Work Relations as Regulated by the Enterprises By-Laws and Rules on Work Relations), Ljubljana, 1967, 97 pp.

Laković, M. et al., Priručnik za primenu osnovnog zakona o radnim odnosima (Manual on the Implementation of the Basic Law on Work Relations),[1] 4th edn., Belgrade, 1966, 356 pp.

O Problemima zapošljavanja (Problems of Employment: reports and discussion), Ekonomska Misao No. 2, 1968, pp. 221–396.

Perić, Ivan, Razvoj sistema radničkog samoupravljanja u FNRJ na području odnosa Development of the System of Workers' Management in the Area of Work Relations), Zagreb, 1962, 187 pp.

Pešić, Dr Ratko, Radno Pravo (Labour Law), Belgrade, 1966, 396 pp.

Rašković, Dr Vladimir, Sociologija Rada (Sociology of Work), Belgrade, 1967, 208 pp.

Savezni Biro za Poslove Zapošlavanja (Federal Office of Employment), Savremena koncepcija zapošlavanja (A Modern Concept of Employment), Belgrade, 1968, 183 pp.

Šefer, Berislav, Kadrovi i naš dalji privredni razvoj (The Cadres and our Future Economic Development), Naša Stvarnost, No. 9, 1960.

Vidaković, Dr Zoran, Dva prilaza protestnim obustavama rada (Two Approaches to Protest Work Stoppages) in Gledišta, No. 1, 1968, pp. 29–46.

Zaposleno Osoblje (Persons Employed: census as of 31 March 1967 (i) in enterprises, according to levels of qualifications, value of fixed assets and of social product per worker; (ii) according to occupations), Statistički Bilten Nos. 533 and 536, 1968, 54 and 47 pp.

5.2 Remuneration for Work and Workers' Personal Incomes

Albrecht, Roman, Dohodak i raspodela prema radu (The Income and Distribution According to Work), Belgrade, 1966, 72 pp.

Anketa o porodičnim budžetima radničkih domaćinstva (Survey of Family Budgets of Workers' Households, 1st and 2nd trimesters, 1968), Statistički Bilten, No. 545, 1969.

Lični Dohoci (Personal Incomes, 1964, 1965, 1966), Statistički Bilten Nos. 392, 433 and 498.

Lični dohoci i iskoriščenje radnog vremena, 1967 (Personal Incomes and Utilization of

---

[1] For the English translation of this basic law, as well as other legislative instruments dealing with labour relations and workers' management, see International Labour Office (Geneva) Legislative Series.

the Working Time 1967; statistical survey), *Statistički Bilten*, No. 555, 111 pp. (for earlier surveys, *ibid.*, Nos. 548 and 460).

Visoka Privredna Skola (High School of Economics of the Zagreb University), *Obračun i Raspodela Osobnih Dohodaka u Radnim Organisacijama* (The Calculation and Distribution of Personal Income in the Work Organizations: a symposium), 2 vols, Opatija, 1968, 656 and 500 pp.

5.3 The Overall Income Distribution by the Enterprises

Baletić, Zvonimir, *et al.*, '*Politekomski aspekti dohotka*' (The Income: Politico-economic Aspects: a symposium), in *Naše Teme*, Nos 7–8, 1968, pp. 1053–190.

Džinić, Dr Firdus, *Samoupravljanje u oblasti zajedničke potrošnje u preduzećima* (Self-management in the Area of Collective Consumption in the Enterprises), Belgrade, 1964, 196 pp.

Hadjistević, Vojin, *et al.*, *Odnosi proizvodne i raspodele* etc. (Relations in Production and in Income Distribution and the Rules of the Enterprises), Belgrade, 1961, 181 pp.

Jovanović, Dr Vladimir, *Anketa o prisvanjanju i raspodeli dohotka u privrednim organisacijama* (Survey of the Appropriation and Distribution of income in Economic Organizations), Belgrade, 1962, 74 pp.

Korać, Miladin, '*Ekonomski položaj privrednih grupacija*' etc. (The Economic Position of Economic Sub-sectors in Primary and Secondary Distribution 1962–6) in *Ekonomist*, pp. 257–81.

Rašković, Dr Vladimir, *Društveno samoupravljenje i raspodela prema radu u Jugoslaviji* Social Self-government and Distribution According to Work; a sociological study), Belgrade, 1967, 308 pp.

Samoupravljanje, Formiranje i raspodela dohotka u preduzećima kojas, su organisovana po radnim jedinicama (Self-management, Formation and Distribution of Income in Enterprises which Comprise Autonomous Work Units), Belgrade, 1967, 490 pp.

Savez ekonomista Srbije (Union of Serbia economists), *Aktualna pitanja*, etc. (Current Problems of Management and Income sharing in the Self-governing Commodity Economy), documents for a symposium, Belgrade, 1968, 118 pp.

Sindić Miloš *et al.*, *Dohodak u radnim organisacijama* (Income in the Work Organizations), Belgrade, 1968, 375 pp.

6. CURRENT PRODUCTION, MARKETING AND RELATED ISSUES

6.1 Output and Costs

Branch Statistical Surveys 1967, Industry, Catering and Tourism, Internal trade, Transport and Communications, Forestry and Social Sector of Agriculture, Artisanal enterprises, *Statistički Bilten*, Nos 528, 532, 538, 543, 549, 551, 552, 553 and 557, 1969.

Dobrević, Slavko, *Linearno programiranje u privrednoj organisaciji* (Linear Programming in an Economic Organization), Zagreb, 1966, 204 pp.

Gorupić, Drago, *Poslovna politika preduzeča* (Business Policy of the Enterprise), Zabreb, 1963, 262 pp.

Kovačević, Dr Mihailo, *Industrijsko knigovodstvo* (Industrial Accountancy: cost accounting in producers' enterprises and in economic units), 3rd edn, Belgrade, 1967, 285 pp.

Mileusnić, Nenad, *Reserve u preduzećima* (Reserves in Enterprises), Belgrade, 1968, 373 pp.

Milosavljević, Dr Momčilo, *Troškovi kao faktor politike preduzeča* (Costs as Factor of Enterprise Policy), Belgrade, 1965, 218 pp.

Petrić, Jovan, *Matematičke Metode Planiranja i Upravljanja* (Mathematical Methods of Planning and Management), Zagreb, 1968, 268 pp.

Savezni Zavod za Statistiku, *Medusobni odnosi privrednih delatnosti u 1964* (Federal Office of Statistics, Inter-industry Relations in the Yugoslav Economy in 1964; input-output tables), Belgrade, 1967, 74 pp. and 38 tables.

6.2 Prices

Černe, Dr Franc, *Tržište i cene* (Market and Prices), Zagreb, 1966, 248 pp.

Drašković, M., *Trendovi cena* (Trends of Prices, 1952–61), Belgrade, 1962.

Gogala, Zdenka, *Utjecaj promena relativnih cena* etc. (The Influence of Changes in Relative Prices on the Position of Industrial Sectors 1956–66), Zagreb, 1967, 67 pp.

Marković, Žarko, *Zbirka propisa o cenama i tarifama* (Regulations Governing Prices and Tariffs), Belgrade, 1965, 195 pp.

Gorupić, Dr, Professor *et al.*, *Poduzeče u reformi* (The Enterprise in the Reform; contains in particular: Dutter I., 'System of Prices and Market Relations' and Fabinc I. *et al.*, 'Problems of Foreign Economic Relations', Zagreb, 1968, 220 pp.

Korošić, M., *Dinamika općeg nivoa cena 1956–66* etc. (The Dynamics of the General Price Level 1956–66, and factors which influenced the changes in the general price level), Zagreb, 1967, 98 pp. and tables.

Mesarić, Dr Milan, *Oblik gravitacione cene*, etc. (Gravitational Price Formula: in a worker-managed socialist economy), Zagreb, 1965, 72 pp.

Rakočević, Živojin, *Opšta regulativna cena proizvodnje i extradohodak* (The General Regulatory Production Price and Surplus Income), in *Socializam*, Nos 7–8, 1967, pp. 863–86.

Savezna Skupštna, Sekretarijat za Informationu Službu (Secretariat for Information of the Federal Assembly), *Sistem cena i Društvena Kontrola cena* (System of Prices and Social Supervision of Prices), Belgrade, 1966, 96 pp.

6.3 Marketing and Commercial Operations Generally

Fakultet Ekonomskih Nauka (Faculty of Economics, Zagreb University), *Vanjskotrgovinsko poslovanje radnih organizacija* (Foreign Trade Activity of the Work Organizations), Vols I and II; Documents for a symposium, Opatija Moj, 1969, 1,042 pp.

Goldštajn, Dr Aleksandar, *Privredno ugovorno pravo* (Law of Contract in the Economy), Zagreb, 1967, 422 pp.

Jauković, Dr Josif, *Uticaj tržišnog područja na razgoj privrede razvijenih i nerazvijenih rejona* (Influence of the Marketing Area on the Development of the Developed and Non-developed Regions), *Praksa*, Nos 3–4, 1968, pp. 33–46.

Mihailović, Predrag *et al.*, *Jugoslavia u svetskoj privredi* (Yugoslavia in the World Economy: a symposium on problems of foreign trade) in *Ekonomist*, No. 1, 1968, pp. 1–158.

Obradović, Dr Sava, *Odnosi razmene i privredni razvoj* (International Trade Relations and Economic Development), Belgrade, 1966, 130 pp.

Radunović, Dragutin, *Tržišna politika preduzeća* (Market Policy of the Enterprise), Belgrade, 1957, 208 pp.

Savezna Skupština, Sekretarijat za Informativnu Službu (Secretariat for Information of the Federal Assembly), *Devizni i spolnotrgovinski režim* (System of Foreign Exchange and International Trade), Belgrade, 1966, 77 pp.

6.4 Other Features of Current Business Operation

Horvat, Branko, *Privredni ciklusi, monetarni faktori i cijene* (Economic Cycles, Monetary Factor and Prices), in *Ekonomska Analiza*, Nos. 1–2, 1968, pp. 1–27.

Institute of Comparative Law, *Laws on Joint Investments of Enterprises*, Belgrade, 1967, 176 pp.

Juretić, Ivan *et al.*, *Analiza poslovanja industrijskih poduzeća* (Analysis of Operations of Industrial Enterprises, Vol. I; production, supplies, employment, fixed and circulating assets; Vol. II: sales, productivity, economy and profitability of operations, business results), Zagreb, 1964, 412 and 298 pp.

Medenica, Vuko *et al.*, *Suvremeni problemi jugoslovenske privrede i ekonomska politika* (Present Problems of the Yugoslav Economy and Economic Policy), Zagreb, 1965, 250 pp.

Županov, Dr J., *Proizvodač i riziko* etc. (The Producer and the Business Risk—some socio-psychological aspects of collective entrepreneurship) in *Ekonomist* (Zagreb), No. 3, 1967, pp. 389–408.

7. OTHER FACTORS AFFECTING THE ECONOMIC BEHAVIOUR OF THE ENTERPRISE

7.1 Entry, Exit and Formal Co-operative Arrangement Among Firms
7.2 Internal Decentralization and the Autonomous Work Units
7.3 Professional Management and Technical Progress: Initiative, Responsibility and Internal Supervision
7.4 The Non-Productive Sector: Self-Governing Administration and Institutions as economic Agents
7.5 Problems of National and Regional Planning and Development
7.6 Problems of Financial and Fiscal Policy
7.7 General Problems of a Socialist Market Economy (Private Sector; Inequality under Socialism, etc.)

Aktualni problemi integracije u privredi (Present Problems of Integration [of enterprises] in the Economy; reports and discussion of a symposium), Zagreb, 1963, 226 pp.

Cerić, Zoran, and Bačić, Hrvoje, *Propisi o udruživanju i poslovnoj saradniji* (Regulations Governing Association [of enterprises] and Business Co-operation), Zagreb, 1965, 164 pp.

Mrkša, Slobodan *et al.*, *Integracija u Privredi* (Integration of Enterprises within the Economy), Zagreb, 1963, 161 pp.

Poček-Matić, Mirjana *et al.*, *Samoupravljanje i integracija u privredi* (Self-government and Integration in the Economy), Zagreb.

Brozović, Zvonimir, *Kontni plan* (Accounting Plan with Practical Examples), 3rd edn, Zagreb, 1967, 253 pp.

Hadžistević, Vojin, Kratina, Husein, and Džinić, Firdus, *Tendencije i praksa neposrednog unpravljanja radnika* etc. (Trends and Practice of Direct Decision-making by the Workers in the Economic Units), Belgrade, 1963, 316 pp.

Gorupić, Drago, and Brekić, Jovo, *Direktor u samoupravnim odnosima* (The Director in Conditions of Self-management), Zagreb, 1967, 375 pp.

Kratina, Husein, *Položaj direktora preduzeća* (The Position of the Enterprise Director within the Self-management System; legal-political aspects), Belgrade, 1967, 179 pp.

Možina, Stane, *Angažiranost vodilnog kadra v sistemu samoupravljanja* (Participation of Management Personnel in the Self-management System), Ljubljana, 1966, 285 pp.

Vidaković, Zoran, *Socialno-ekonomiske determinante položaja i uloge direktora radnih organisacija* (Socio-economic Determinants of the Status and Role of the Director of the Work Organizations), Zagreb, 1967, 69 pp.

Višja Šola za organizacilo dela (High School for Organization of Work), *Simposij o strokovnih in vodstvenih delavcih v gospodartstvu* (Professional and Management Workers in the Economy: a symposium), Bled, April 1968.

Sirotković, Jakov, *Planiranje u sistemu samoupravljanja* (Planning in a System based on Self-management), Zagreb, 1966, 240 pp.

Mijović, Dr Branko, *Novčana i kreditna politika* (Monetary and Credit Policy), Belgrade, 1967, 129 pp.

Tišma, Toša, *Javne financije* (Public Finance), Zagreb, 1964, 352 pp.

Tkalec, Dragutin *et al.*, *Porez no promet* (Tax on Turnover: judicial decisions and interpretations), Zagreb, 1967, 152 pp.

Ranković, Dr Milan *et al.*, *Društvena nejedkost u socialismu* (Social Inequality under Socialism: account of a discussion), Belgrade, 1968, 72 pp.

Index

GEORGE ALLEN & UNWIN LTD

Head Office
40 Museum Street, London W.C.1
Telephone: 01-405 8577

Sales, Distribution and Accounts Departments
Park Lane, Hemel Hempstead, Herts.
Telephone: 0442 3244

Argentina: Roderiguez Pena 1653-11B, Buenos Aires
Australia: Cnr. Bridge Road and Jersey Street, Hornsby, N.S.W. 2077
Canada: 2330 Midland Avenue, Agincourt, Ontario
Greece: 7 Stadiou Street, Athens 125
India: 103/5 Fort Street, Bombay 1
285J Bepin Behari Ganguli Street, Calcutta 12
2/18 Mount Road, Madras 2
4/21–22B Asaf Ali Road, New Delhi 1
Japan: 29/13 Hongo 5 Chome, Bunkyo, Tokyo 113
Kenya: P.O. Box 30583, Nairobi
Lebanon: Deep Building, Jeanne d'Arc Street, Beirut
Mexico: Serapio Rendon 125, Mexico 4, D.F.
New Zealand: 46 Lake Road, Northcote, Auckland 9
Nigeria: P.O. Box 62, Ibadan
Pakistan: Karachi Chambers, McLeod Road, Karachi 2
22 Falettis' Hotel, Egerton Road, Lahore
Philippines: 3 Malaming Street, U.P. Village, Quezon City, D-505
Singapore: 248c/1 Orchard Road, Singapore 9
South Africa: P.O. Box 23134, Joubert Park, Johannesburg
West Indies: Rockley New Road, St Lawrence 4, Barbados